Rhetoric and Composition

A SOURCEBOOK FOR TEACHERS AND WRITERS

Rhetoric and Composition

A SOURCEBOOK FOR TEACHERS AND WRITERS

Richard L. Graves

Professor of English Education
Auburn University

BOYNTON/COOK PUBLISHERS, INC.
UPPER MONTCLAIR, NEW JERSEY 07043

Library of Congress Cataloging in Publication Data
Main entry under title:

Rhetoric and composition.
  Includes bibliographical references.
    1. English language—Rhetoric—Study and teaching—
Addresses, essays, lectures. I. Graves, Richard L. (Richard
Layton), 1931-
PE1404.R48 1984   808'.042   83-19099
ISBN 0-86709-029-4

For information address Boynton/Cook Publishers, Inc.
52 Upper Montclair Plaza, P.O. Box 860, Upper Montclair, NJ 07043

Printed in the United States of America

86 87 88   10 9 8 7 6 5 4 3

Preface

The purpose of the revised second edition of *Rhetoric and Composition* is to reflect a portion of the dynamic growth which has been occurring within our discipline and, at the same time, to consolidate the hard-earned advances already won. Since the mid-seventies when the first edition was originally conceived, the discipline has continued to grow and flourish. Each year seems to bring the best and last word on teaching writing, but then to our surprise the succeeding year brings even newer ideas, fresher insights, clearer perspectives. And although it is always gratifying to hear from the grizzled veterans among us, it is even more so to hear the voices of a younger generation of colleagues who hold so much promise for improving our work as teachers of writing. The second edition is not so much a balance as it is a blending of the old and the new.

The organization of the second edition is identical to the first, with one minor exception. The sections on pedagogy and classical rhetoric have been combined in order to make room for a section on new perspectives in the discipline. Otherwise, the general outline of the book remains the same. It begins with a general introduction, then emphasizes the role of motivation and personal commitment in the writing process, proceeds to describe the sentence as a rhetorical unit, moves on to the paragraph, looks at pedagogy from a variety of perspectives, and finally concludes with a look at some new horizons in the field. I believe the organizational pattern is sound, though a colleague criticized it as "moving from part to whole with the implicit suggestion that this is the way one would organize instruction." I believe most composition teachers organize their instruction holistically, with great emphasis on frequent writing. The education of writing teachers, however, must account, systematically, for all the components of the composition curriculum. Regardless of how the class itself is organized, the composition teacher must have command of the full range of rhetorical options. Thus the rationale for the organization.

One minor change worth noting is the addition of the word "writers" in the sub-title of the book. When working with my students, both undergraduate and graduate, and confronting a particular rhetorical problem, I often find myself thinking, "If only you knew what Professor so-and-so said about this." Even though there are hundreds of composition texts on the market, few if any contain the professional essays upon which so much of our teaching practice is based. Although *Rhetoric and Composition* is not intended for direct composition-class instruction, it would seem reasonable to assume that some of the philosophical and practical information here might also be helpful to young writers. Taking our students into our confidence by sharing with them the sources and limits of our knowledge might be a frightening experience for some teachers, for it takes away the false sense of authority we sometimes hide behind. The advantages, though, outweigh the drawbacks. Letting our students know the sources of our ideas firsthand allows us to stand with them on the frontier of knowledge. It's a kind of honesty that this generation has been asking for and in my opinion deserves.

The major change in this edition lies in the amount of new material that has been included. It is simply not possible to reflect the essence of current thinking about the discipline in an honest way without including much of the newer work. Unfortunately, limitations of space prevent some material which seemed current a decade ago (and which in some cases has become an integral part of our thinking) from appearing in this edition. Most teachers of writing are keenly aware that remarkable strides have been made in recent years in our understanding of the complex act of writing. Much of the credit for these gains must be attributed to the inspired editorship of the journal, *College Composition and Communication*—William Irmscher, Edward P. J. Corbett, and Richard L. Larson—and to the many contributors to that journal. In many ways *CCC* has been the vanguard of the renaissance in teaching written communication. Almost one-third of the essays reprinted here originally appeared in *CCC*. Three other NCTE journals are represented— *College English, English Journal,* and *Research in the Teaching of English*—as well as three NCTE monographs. It is especially gratifying to reprint quality material from those small journals and newsletters (*The Journal of Basic Writing* and *Freshman English News*, for example) which are making an impact on the profession.

Even though good material has been published in other countries, notably Great Britain, the essays here are limited to American sources, primarily because of the great wealth of material from which to draw.

I want to express my thanks to all those who have granted permission for their work to appear here. I also want to thank the many friends and colleagues who offered suggestions for changes in the second edition. These include Hugh Agee, Bob Bain, David Bartholomae, Tommy Boley, Lillian Bridwell, Ronnie Carter, Bill Coles, Frank Cronin, Harry Crosby, Don Daiker, Jim Davis, Ken Davis, Frank D'Angelo, Ed Farrell, Gene Garber, Don Gallehr, Patricia Gambrell, Constance Gefvert, Sylvia Holladay, Erika Lindemann, Andrew Kerek, Fred McDonald, Alan McLeod, Max Morenberg, Bill Pixton, Gayle Price, Lana Silverthorn, Isabelle Thompson, Tom Waldrep, Johnny Witcher, and Carol Whatley. I am deeply appreciative of the keen insights of Ann E. Berthoff, University of Massachusetts–Boston, and the frank, good-natured counsel of Bob Boynton. I am especially thankful for the constant support and understanding of my wife Eloise.

R.L.G.

Auburn, Alabama

Contents

PART ONE

Introduction

". . . Except he come to composition, a man remains un-put-together, more than usually troubled by the feuds within, and therefore a little more addicted to those without."

Robert B. Heilman

This section introduces the idea that writing is a worthy and personally satisfying activity in its own right, as well as an emerging scholarly discipline. In "Writing as a Way of Knowing," James McCrimmon convincingly explains the value of writing, not only for those who might benefit from the reading of it, but for the writer himself. (McCrimmon's work originally appeared in the NCTE Distinguished Lectures Series for 1970.) The next selection, the Foreward by Charles R. Cooper to Arthur Applebee's *Writing in the Secondary School: English and the Content Areas,* shows what the teaching of writing should *not* be. Maxine Hairston then looks at the discipline of rhetoric and composition in light of Thomas Kuhn's ideas about paradigm shifts in scholarly disciplines, and Ann E. Berthoff argues for a dynamic view of the composing process in which form arises organically from meaning.

A graduate student once remarked that he had "finished" his research and all that remained was to "write it up." Such a view, according to McCrimmon, is wrong, for in the writing process the researcher really discovers what he has found. It is not the raw data, the statistics, or even the research design which is most important, but the interpretation of one's findings, the determination of their meaning for human experience. Thus seen, the act of writing becomes a search to discover the precise language to convey one's meaning. As McCrimmon says so eloquently, it is a way of knowing as well as a way of telling.

In his discussion of prewriting, McCrimmon also reminds us that careful observation has long been a hallmark of great teachers, and that it is an equally necessary trait for becoming a skilled writer. If we could encourage students to examine their thinking and their early drafts in the same way, say, that Louis Agassiz required his students to examine zoological specimens, or that George Washington Carver meticulously studied common vegetables and nuts, then the quality of student writing would show a marked improvement. McCrimmon calls this kind of close observation "the best cure I know for the generality and incompleteness of student writing."

But new ideas are slow to be incorporated into the curriculum, as Charles R. Cooper suggests in the next selection. What is so discouraging is that Cooper's formula for failure is so often precisely what takes place in our nation's classrooms. Though the emphasis in this selection is largely negative, there is a broad hint of what the good writing program should be like—much emphasis on students' growing and gaining control of the written word, and in writing as a way of "thinking, learning, and personal development."

In the next essay, Maxine Hairston shows how Thomas Kuhn's ideas about the growth of academic disciplines apply to the teaching of writing. She aptly uses the phrase "The Winds of Change" to describe what is happening within our discipline. She provides a brief but thorough analysis of Kuhn's thesis, then shows in detail the inadequacy and breakdown of the current-traditional paradigm, and finally identifies certain key movements which offer promise in the emerging discipline.

Completing the picture, Ann E. Berthoff argues that form grows out of the early chaotic stages of composing. One can almost hear Berthoff say that the chaos itself is beautiful. Out of the void and darkness comes form, springing to life, growing, finally maturing. No "linear process." No "pedagogy of exhortation." Just unfolding. Berthoff's ideas hold the promise of breathing continuous new life into the dry bones of modern curriculum.

In a sense, many of the ensuing essays in this text are evidence of the emerging discipline, showing in greater detail the outline suggested in the introduction. Although no one can say with certainty what the future holds, most of us would agree that the infant is robust and healthy and shows signs of new growth almost daily. It is building on its successes and gaining more and more confidence in its ability. In spite of problems such as overcrowded classes, underemployment, and heavy paper loads, there is nevertheless a spirit of optimism and confidence that our work as teachers of writing is important, and that we really can make a difference in the lives of our students.

Writing as a Way of Knowing

JAMES M. McCRIMMON

I

Traditionally, the teaching of composition is slanted toward the needs of the reader. Students write for a reader, and the effectiveness of their work is usually judged by the ease and clarity with which the reader understands what is written.

This traditional concern with making the message clear to the reader emphasizes writing as a way of telling. The controlling assumption is that the writer has something to say to a reader and must choose the best way of saying it. In this assumption the writer knows and is willing to tell; the reader does not know but is willing, or can be induced, to learn. The study of composition in the schools, then, is largely concerned with mastering efficient techniques for telling. Thus, however much composition texts may vary, they have a common core of instruction dealing with the organization of material, the development of paragraphs, the construction of various types of sentences, the choice of appropriate diction, and the conventions of standard usage. When writing is considered as a way of telling, proficiency in these skills constitutes the goals of instruction.

These goals need no apology. If they are achieved, the young writer knows how to organize and present his material, and in a world that depends heavily on effective communication, this is a solid accomplishment. But . . . I am concerned with a different view of the writing process, with writing as a way of knowing, not of knowing in order to be able to tell others, but of knowing for self-understanding. I am concerned with the kind of insights a writer gets of his subject during the writing process, in which process I include both the planning and the writing of the paper.

The notion that a writer learns about his subject by writing about it doesn't quite make sense in the traditional view. It is likely to remind us of the student who complained to his instructor, "How can I tell what I mean until I see what I've written?" And that seems like a classic example of putting the cart before the horse, until we find distinguished writers saying the same thing in more sophisticated language. Listen to this comment by C. Day Lewis about his own writing:

> I do not sit down at my desk to put into verse something that is already clear in my mind. If it were clear in my mind, I should have no incentive or need to write about it, for I am an explorer, not a journalist, a propagandist, or a statistician. . . . The theme of a poem is the meaning

The Promise of English: NCTE 1970 Distinguished Lectures (Urbana, IL: NCTE, 1970), pp. 115-130. Copyright © 1970 by the National Council of Teachers of English. Reprinted by permission of the publisher.

of its subject matter for me. When I have discovered the meaning *to me* of the various fragments of experience which are constellating in my mind, I have begun to make sense of such experience and to realize a pattern in it; and often I have gone some way with the poem before I am able to grasp the theme which lies hidden in the material that has accumulated.[1]

Obviously there are great differences between a British poet laureate writing a poem and an average student writing a composition, but I suggest that the two situations have enough in common to make the Lewis quotation useful to us as teachers. The common element is the writer's need to understand his own private, and therefore original, view of the subject, to shape discrete impressions into a pattern which he can identify as his personal interpretation of the subject. The recognition of this pattern allows him to fit what Lewis calls the "constellating fragments" into a cognitive structure. By finding a unifying relation among the fragments the writer learns what they mean to him.

We use various names for this unifying relation. Lewis calls it a "theme," a painter or musician might call it a "motif," a journalist could call it an "angle." I prefer to consider it here as the *real* subject in contrast to the *nominal* subject. It is what the writing is really about, what it has to say. The nominal subject indicates no content. It is merely a topic to be explored, say, Chicago or Main Street. The real subject is what Sandburg sees in his "Chicago" or what Sinclair Lewis sees in his *Main Street*. What they see, and therefore what they say, is an interpretation of what the place means to them. This interpretation has to be discovered sometime during the writing process, and part of the function of the writing is to lead to that discovery.

We get a commoner illustration of the evolution of a real subject if we shift from writing to speaking. We all know that in any serious conversation on an important topic our view of the subject changes as we move through the conversation. Some lines of thought peter out; others open up and suggest ideas not previously thought of, and what we end with may be a considerably different view of the subject that we had at the beginning. In retrospect we seem to have been groping toward an understanding that was unknown or only dimly foreseen when the conversation started. Perhaps the noblest example of this process is the dialectic of a Platonic dialogue which transcends the limitations of the opening statements and discovers what Plato called the "truth."

A similar kind of inquiry goes on as we write. The process of writing is a process of making choices. Often the writer does not know at the beginning what choices he will make, or even what his choices are; but each fresh choice tends to dictate those that follow, and gradually a pattern begins to emerge and the constellating fragments fall into place just as they did in C. Day Lewis' poem. But, unlike speaking, the choices in writing are made in secret. Except on rare occasions when a reader can compare the first draft with the final version, he does not overhear the internal debate that went on in the writer's mind. All he sees is the finished product, and all the writer's conflicts have presumably been resolved before that product was submitted to the reader.

Usually, but not always. Recently I read a paper which gave me a kind of X-ray picture of the writer's thinking as he rejected what he was saying, reversed himself, and destroyed the unity of his essay by discovering his real position. I had asked each member of the class to play the role of final judge in an essay contest. Each student was given the same three essays and was told that a screening committee had chosen these as the three best essays out of all those written by freshmen during the term. My students were to choose the best and next best of the three essays as winner and runner-up in a freshman essay contest. They had two hours in which to study the essays and write their judgments.

This particular student began his paper by saying that although he felt that one essay had the most interesting and most mature content, he had to reject it because of a syntactic weakness. He then proceeded to explain the reasons for his first and second choices. But just as he had apparently finished his judgment he added another paragraph in which he reversed himself and awarded first place to the essay he had originally rejected. His explanation was that he found himself becoming increasingly dissatisfied with his decisions and that he now felt that he had overestimated the significance of what he thought was awkwardness in one long, involved sentence of the rejected essay and had consequently underrated the paper as a whole.

Perhaps we might think that he should have made up his mind before he began to write his judgment, but the fact is that he *had* made up his mind. He wrote what he intended to write and in writing discovered he was wrong. He had started with the assumption that syntactic correctness was a major criterion and that it must dominate his judgment, but in the process of trying to support his judgment he found it insupportable. If he had had time he would probably have rewritten his paper to conceal his change of mind. But in a situation that did not permit rewriting he had to choose between consistency and honesty. In my opinion he made the right choice.

I have chosen a very simple illustration of writing as a discovery process. Any editor could provide more complex examples of a writer who learned what he wanted to say through a series of rough drafts that groped toward his final view of the subject. This is especially true of fiction. The testimony of short story writers, novelists, and dramatists shows that during the writing a character will outgrow the author's original conception of him and begin to force changes in the plot, much as the characters in Pirandello's *Six Characters in Search of an Author* gradually took over the play from the manager. But it is also true of exposition. I have seen a memorandum by Wayne Booth, the author of *Rhetoric of Fiction,* showing the five-year evolution of that book, as he moved from the intent to write an essay refuting certain critical errors to a history of narration and finally to a rhetoric of fiction. Booth's concept of his subject grew with his writing about it, and it was only after he had written a 2500-page manuscript that he saw what he wanted to do in his 500-page book. At no time was Booth's problem one of trying to say clearly what he knew. Quite the opposite, he was trying to know clearly what to say. He was trying to find his real subject.

The tools that a writer uses to explore his subject are words. He is continually concerned with finding the words that most accurately record his impressions of the subject. But since the words he uses will help determine these impressions, he is in a constant process of trying to equate words with concepts and attitudes. Even at a time when he is not sure what precisely he wants to say he must understand the implications of the statements he makes so that he can see in what direction his writing is taking him. John Ciardi calls this procedure a groping for words that are intuitively recognized as right when they are discovered. In other words, the writer may not know precisely what he wants to say, but he recognizes an accurate statement of his meaning when he makes it.

In all this search for the right words young writers especially must be on guard against two kinds of corruption—vagueness and artificiality. At this point I am concerned with vagueness not as an offense against the reader, which it also is, but as an offense against the writer himself, or rather against the discipline of writing. Every instance of vagueness is a sign that the writer has settled for a superficial view of his subject by glossing over details that need to be investigated closely. Artificiality, which is often a major cause of vagueness, is a sign that the writer is more concerned with impressing readers with what he imagines to be stylistic virtuosity than in improving his knowledge of the subject. If writing is a way of learning, vagueness and artificiality are cardinal sins, perhaps the only cardinal sins in composition.

II

The practical difference between viewing writing as a way of knowing and viewing it as a way of telling is that the first view emphasizes the quality of what is presented and the second emphasizes the quality of the presentation. The classroom terms that come closest to naming this contrast are "content" and "style." These are not mutually exclusive terms, for content and style are so interrelated that it is often impossible to discuss either except in relation to the other. But they are pedagogically useful terms and, with a necessary expansion of the meaning of "content," they will serve to introduce a contrast of emphases in the practical conduct of a composition course.

We often use the word "content" to refer to the information provided about the subject, to what is sometimes called the "message." In this sense "content" refers to the writer's materials: the events he is relating, the objects he is describing, the contrasts and distinctions he is drawing, and the explanations and arguments he uses. But this sense is too limited for my purposes. As I am using "content" here it refers not only to the materials but also to the reason for using these materials—that is, the theme or controlling image that determines the kinds of things the author has to say about his subject. For example, the controlling image of Keats' "On First Looking into Chapman's Homer" is the theme of discovery, and that theme requires that everything that Keats has to say about his reactions to Chapman's Homer must develop that discovery image. In this larger sense "content" is a synonym for what classical rhetoric called "invention." It refers to the writer's unique conception of his subject, to what I earlier called his real subject.

I hope it will be clear that, in saying that writing as a way of telling is chiefly concerned with style and that writing as a way of knowing is chiefly concerned with content or invention, I am talking about two complementary ways of looking at writing. There is no possibility of accepting one view and rejecting the other, since both are necessary in the teaching of composition. But there is a practical question, since the emphasis defines the nature and conduct of the course, and therefore our professional image.

I think there is no doubt that the prevailing emphasis in a conventional composition course is on style, and often attention to style never rises above the level of usage. This is especially true in high schools. In *High School English Instruction Today*, which is a report of a study of more than a hundred schools conducted jointed by NCTE and the University of Illinois, James Squire and Roger Applebee report that

> The great bulk of comments and corrections found on student papers have to do with correcting faults in spelling, sentence structure, and mechanics—with proofreading rather than teaching. Moreover the majority of revisions by students are directed toward these matters to the exclusion of such elements as organization, logic, or even content.

And, as Albert Kitzhaber has pointed out, the situation is often only relatively better in colleges.

This emphasis on usage is a source of concern in the profession. Social pressures and college entrance requirements demand that high school graduates should have a reasonable mastery of the conventions of the standard English dialect; but linguistic habits are deeply rooted and often cannot be satisfactorily changed within the limited context of the school curriculum. This is especially true of underprivileged students, for whom the standard dialect is sometimes a foreign language. And this difficulty is increased by the fiction, maintained by many teachers and textbooks, that certain usages which are common in the speech of educated people, including English teachers, are not acceptable as "correct English." Students are literally expected to be more correct than the editors of Webster's Dictionary.

Under these conditions the teaching of usage is often a labor of Sisyphus: the time and effort expended by the teacher is out of proportion to the results obtained. Yet, by a curious kind of compensation, the greater the failure to change the student's native dialect, the more the failure is used to justify a still greater effort, until the teaching of composition is reduced to a series of proofreading exercises.

This overemphasis on usage has been condemned by linguists, rhetoricians, and teachers high in the councils of NCTE. For nearly half a century Mencken, Bloomfield, Fries, and I. A. Richards, to name only the best-known critics, have denounced the doctrine of "correctness" as unsound in theory and stultifying in practice, and some more recent critics have suggested that the only way to avoid excessive attention to usage is to stop teaching it altogether in the schools. More moderate critics, such as Robert Pooley, have urged that what is needed is a more realistic and selective approach to the teaching of usage. But there is little evidence that these criticisms have had much influence on classroom practice.

Of course, the decision about what usage to teach and how much time to spend on it will finally be made by individual teachers. Whether they follow the evidence and the weight of authoritative opinion or their own personal preferences is a decision only they can make. But I think it not unreasonable to suggest that usage is a very small part of the total composition process and that that fact should be taken into account in the composition classroom.

The study of style could be a valuable approach to improvement of student writing if style were considered in relation to the writer's attitudes toward his subject and his audience, as Walker Gibson believes; or better still, if we followed Richard E. Young and Alton L. Becker, who define style as follows:

> A writer's style, we believe, is the characteristic route he takes through all the choices presented in both the prewriting and writing stages. It is the manifestation of his conception of his topic, modified by his audience, situation, and intention—what we might call his "universe of discourse."

This is the most comprehensive concept of style I know. It subsumes everything under style, and so defines style as the whole art of discourse. Obviously if this were what we were teaching in the schools as style, there would be no reason for contrasting content and style, since the content of a paper would be part of its style. If we followed the Young-Becker definition we would be teaching style all the time, because there would be nothing else to teach.

With the possible exception of argument, composition teachers have tended to slight instruction in content. The Squire-Applebee report points out that the prevailing pattern of instruction in the schools visited was to say little or nothing about assignments until after the papers had been written and then to comment only on style. The inference to be made from this procedure is that these teachers believe that establishing the content of a paper is entirely the student's responsibility and that there is little the teacher can do about it.

There is, of course, something we can do about improving the content of student writing, and the best teachers have been doing it ever since Aristotle. We can, at the very least, show by our comments on student papers that we are concerned about the content and value it. Since students are always trying to guess what the teacher wants in a paper they will soon infer that he likes good content, and they may try to give it to him. At least they will have to give up the negative concept that good writing is writing which has no errors.

But we can do more than that. One of the most satisfying contributions of the new rhetorics is their reemphasis on invention through attention to prewriting—that is, to that part of the composition process that precedes the writing of the first draft. Let me briefly suggest three practical techniques for prewriting.

The simplest method, especially suited for junior and senior high school classes, is for the teacher and students to talk out the potential content of an assignment before any student begins to write. The students are given a subject and are asked to suggest pertinent materials. These suggestions are written on the board. If a suggestion is vague, it can be clarified by discussion. If it is too comprehensive, the class can be asked to break it down into more specific items. As the material accumulates it becomes more than any student could use, so the process of purposeful selection emerges, and with it an appropriate grouping or outlining of the selected content. When all this is done, each student takes whatever view of the subject he prefers and uses the appropriate content to develop that view.

Of course this method can be used only when the class is working on a common subject. When each student is writing on his own subject, he will have to do his own prewriting. But if he is familiar with this procedure through repeated experience with it in the classroom, he will have a way of getting started and can thus minimize the pencil-chewing stage when he is waiting for inspiration to strike. And the teacher can, if he wishes, consult with students on their prewriting plans, as he sometimes now does with outlines. The difference between the outline and the prewriting is that the outline shows only the structure of a projected paper; the prewriting shows both the structure and the content.

One advantage of such class exercises on prewriting is that not all prewriting has to be followed up with writing, since if the purpose of the exercise is to give the students experience in establishing the potential content of a paper, that object has been achieved once the prewriting is finished. Students can thus prewrite more papers than they have time to write, and teaching is not limited to what the teacher has time to grade. What the procedure does is to increase the amount of experience students have with thinking out the content of a composition without increasing the grading time. And for papers that are to be graded, it allows the teacher and the student to handle problems of content *before* the paper is written.

When, as in this procedure, learning takes the form of discussion rather than lecture or teacher-directed demonstration, both the attitude of the students and the quality of their writing improve. What students need, more than explicit instruction about writing, is the opportunity to explore a subject before and after it is developed into an essay. They need to do a lot of talking about writing and to make up their minds about how their work can be improved, and this talk is most profitable when it is removed from the pressure of grades. There is no good reason why everything a student writes should be graded, but there is a good reason why a student should have the opportunity of having his work read by others—preferably by more than one person—and hearing it discussed. James Moffett in his *Teaching the Universe of Discourse*, a book which in my opinion opens up a whole new view of what teaching could be like in a student-centered curriculum, makes a strong case for small group conferences in which students write for their peers and have their work evaluated by them. I have seen Moffett's suggestions worked out in college classrooms and I am impressed by the results.

A second kind of prewriting, one especially suited to college classes, stresses observation and inferences drawn from observation as the means of getting a detailed knowledge of the subject. It is surprising that, for all our talk about the importance of careful observation to a writer, so little time is given to it in the English curriculum. The only time I was ever asked to combine observation and writing in a composition was when, as a graduate student at Northwestern, I took a course in prosody from Lew Sarrett. Sarrett asked each member of the class to select some object, not too complex an object, and to spend not less than thirty minutes studying it with a view to writing about it. During the first ten minutes we were to examine the object carefully, noting everything we saw in it: its size, shape, contour, texture, color, function, anything that would give us a fuller knowledge of the object. Next we were to spend about ten minutes inviting in a relaxed way whatever associations the object suggested to us. Then we were to look at the object metaphorically. When all this was done we were to write a piece of verse or prose suggested by our total experience with the object. That was nearly forty years ago, but I remember the assignment as the best lesson on invention I ever received as a student.

Some modification of that assignment is the best cure I know for the generality and incompleteness of student writing. Most students start to write about a subject without any serious exploration of it, and because they have only a general knowledge of the subject they can give it only a shallow treatment. Usually we complain that their writing is vague and that they should choose more concrete diction. But often the diction is a symptom, not a cause. What they need is not a bigger vocabulary but more knowledge of how they see the subject. They are not likely to get that kind of knowledge in a dictionary or a thesaurus. Their best remedy is a closer look at the subject.

Close observation of details is a prerequisite for much of the expository writing a student does in high school and college. It is important in description, in definition, in classification, in reports of events and processes. It is especially important in any writing which requires the writer to infer a conclusion from his observations, as in contrasts, causal analyses, criticisms, and arguments. In view of its importance it would seem to merit a more prominent place in the curriculum than it usually gets.

The third kind of prewriting procedure I want to mention is one suggested by Kenneth Pike and his associates at the University of Michigan. Pike's theory is that any subject can be adequately defined or described only if it is approached from three points of view, which he calls "particle," "wave," and "field." From the particle view we get a knowledge of the elements of the subject, say, individual lines or sentences or metaphors or stanzas in a poem. From the wave view we get knowledge of the interrelation among the parts or particles—for example, the metrical pattern of a poem and the flow of the theme through that pattern. From the field view we get a knowledge of the poem as a whole in the various contexts in which it can occur.

The core of Pike's trimodal analysis is close oberservation of the subject, so that it could be described as a system for guiding observation. It gives the student a methodical procedure for studying his subject which emphasizes the personal nature of observation and so invites the student to define the subject by his personal insights of it. In its present state Pike's system would be a bit difficult for high school students, but at the college level it can be used effectively both for the interpretation of poetry and for the prewriting of an essay.

These three prewriting procedures are systems for helping a writer to explore his subject to see what can be said about it. Since each system will yield more knowledge than can be incorporated in a single paper, all of them impose on the writer the necessity of defining the subject in terms of his dominant interest in it. Of all the things that he could say he must choose the theme that identifies his own unique view. Thus the three roads all lead back to C. Day Lewis' problem of deciding what the subject means to him. In my judgment, this is the controlling decision in composition, out of which decisions about structure and style emerge. This, of course, is equivalent to saying that arrangement and style are consequences of invention, and that the way of telling is dependent on the way of knowing.

But whether we emphasize style or invention will make little difference unless the classroom provides an environment that encourages learning. The teacher-dominated, overly directed classroom does not provide such an environment. Students, especially modern students, cannot write effectively in a situation in which what they are to write and how they are to write it are prescribed by a teacher or a textbook. If they are going to mature as writers they must be free to make up their own minds about what they want to do and how they want to do it. This is not to say that their choices cannot be questioned. Young writers especially need the corrective influence of the feedback of an audience, whether that audience is a teacher or a peer group. But the criticism is most helpful when it consists of constructive suggestions of alternatives, and best of all when both the writer and his critics can engage in a free discussion of the consequences of making one choice rather than another in relation to the whole context of the paper. This kind of discussion requires a democratic attitude in the classroom. It cannot be maintained if all the wisdom and all the authority are presumed to be on one side of the desk.

Notes

[1] "The Making of a Poem," *Saturday Evening Post*, 234 (January 21, 1961), 19.

"A Writing Program Certain to Fail"

CHARLES R. COOPER

. . . As an example, let's propose a high school writing program certain to fail. Let's outline a program that not only thwarts students' writing development but also pointedly confuses them about how skilled writers compose and specifically precludes their gaining any insight into the ways writing can be useful to them.

How would we conduct such a perverse writing program—in all classes in the curriculum as well as in English?

We would very rarely ask students to produce original written texts of more than two or three sentences. Though students might have pencil in hand a good deal of the time, we would for the most part limit their writing to note-taking, filling in blanks in exercise books or lab manuals, writing very short responses of a phrase or at most a sentence or two to study questions or essay test questions, doing numerical calculations in math class, copying directions, or copying material from the chalkboard or from books. On the rare occasions when we did ask students to compose extended written text, we would tell them to keep it short, probably to less than a page of handwriting. We would usually request that it be finished on the spot, within just a few minutes or at most a class period. We would rarely set the due date more than two days from the time of the assignment. Students would nearly always write transactional (to convey information) discourse. We might occasionally in English class ask for fictional or personal-experience writing, but even there we would most of the time ask for informational writing. In no classes would we ask for persuasive writing. Students would write nearly always to the teacher as examiner, a reader who always knows more than they know. The purpose of the writing would be to display command of new facts or concepts or to offer proof of completion of a reading task or recollection of class lectures and discussions. Only rarely would students write to learn—to explore new insights or clarify information or examine personal experiences.

When we did ask for extended written discourse, we would limit our directions to a brief topic statement ususally stated quite generally. Sometimes, especially in social science and literature classes, we would give topics about which entire books had been written by scholars in the field. We would limit our comments about the writing task to matters of length and format, and we would expect students to begin writing within two or three minutes. We would provide no help with the writing task itself. Students would have to take one deep breath and dive in without the benefit of discussion or discovery procedures, planning and organizing, or hints about managing the drafting process itself.

When students gave us their writing, we would take it away to read, limiting our responses to matters of usage, spelling, and sentence structure. We would not talk to students personally about writing. We would not display it or publish it. We would not ask students to read each other's writing. On the few occasions when we asked students to revise their writing, we would be satisfied with small corrections and additions.

It will surprise and dismay many people to learn that the sober, cautious, sophisticated research study reported in this monograph demonstrates that the writing program I have just described is the standard program in American high schools. Even the bright and promising exceptions to the standard program—and they are documented as well in this report—do not alter this grim conclusion. . . .

Arthur Applebee's report, *Writing in the Secondary Schools: English and the Content Areas* is a model survey study. It is impressive in its comprehensiveness and thoroughness. It includes painstaking observational work in classrooms, interviews with students and teachers, and wide-scale surveying with a questionnaire. The report reminds us once again of the value of skillful surveys. So far all the evidence for a writing crisis has come from student writing or from various indirect measures like the verbal aptitude section of the Scholastic Aptitude Test. Now Applebee takes us inside the classrooms and shows us what is going on in writing instruction, not just in English classes, but in math, social science, science, foreign language, and business classes. Looking at his results, we can easily believe there must be a writing crisis, even if we had doubted it until now. We might conclude, too, that American high school graduates who have experienced only the standard program are writing better than we have a right to expect. Even as we point to the very real institutional constraints in American high schools—poor working conditions for teachers, crowded classes—we can still acknowledge the school-based causes of the writing crisis: lack of writing and poor instruction.

For the Research Report series Applebee's arresting report is unusual in the force of its implications for instruction, a forcefulness made possible by the widespread consensus on what a good high school writing program should look like. Knowing that consensus, Applebee confidently outlines the elements and practices of a good program, one that encourages all students' writing development by assuring that they all gain some control of the composing process and some knowledge of the many uses of writing for thinking, learning, and personal development. Because of the care and thoroughness of his study, his sound proposals are sure to command attention.

The Winds of Change:
Thomas Kuhn and the Revolution in the Teaching of Writing

MAXINE HAIRSTON

In 1963, the University of Chicago Press published a book titled *The Structure of Scientific Revolutions*, written by Thomas Kuhn, a University of California professor of the history of science. In the book Kuhn hypothesizes about the process by which major changes come about in scientific fields, and conjectures that they probably do not evolve gradually from patient and orderly inquiry by established investigators in the field. Rather, he suggests, revolutions in science come about as the result of breakdowns in intellectual systems, breakdowns that occur when old methods won't solve new problems. He calls the change in theory that underlies this kind of revolution a *paradigm shift*. I believe we are currently at the point of such a paradigm shift in the teaching of writing, and that it has been brought about by a variety of developments that have taken place in the last 25 years.

Briefly, Kuhn's thesis in *The Structure of Scientific Revolutions* is this. When a scientific field is going through a stable period, most of the practitioners in the discipline hold a common body of beliefs and assumptions; they agree on the problems that need to be solved, the rules that govern research, and on the standards by which performance is to be measured. They share a conceptual model that Kuhn calls a paradigm, and that paradigm governs activity in their profession. Students who enter the discipline prepare for membership in its intellectual community by studying that paradigm.

But paradigms are not necessarily immutable. When several people working in a field begin to encounter anomalies or phenomena that cannot be explained by the established model, the paradigm begins to show signs of instability. For a while, those who subscribe to the paradigm try to ignore

College Composition and Communication, 33(February 1982), pp. 76-88. Copyright © 1982 by the National Council of Teachers of English. Reprinted by permission of the publisher and the author.

the contradictions and inconsistencies that they find, or they make improvised, *ad hoc* changes to cope with immediate crises. Eventually, however, when enough anomalies accumulate to make a substantial number of scientists in the field question whether the traditional paradigm can solve many of the serious problems that face them, a few innovative thinkers will devise a new model. And if enough scientists become convinced that the new paradigm works better than the old one, they will accept it as the new norm.

This replacement of one conceptual model by another one is Kuhn's *paradigm shift*. He cites as classic examples the astronomers' substitution of the Copernican model of the solar system for the Ptolemaic model and the development of Newtonian physics. Such shifts are usually disorderly and often controversial, and the period in which they occur is apt to be marked by insecurity and conflict within the discipline.

Kuhn believes that because these shifts are so disruptive, they will occur only when the number of unsolved problems in a discipline reaches crisis proportions and some major figures in the field begin to focus on those unsolved problems. But even with mounting evidence that their conceptual model doesn't work, supporters of the traditional paradigm resist change because they have an intellectual and sometimes an emotional investment in the accepted view. They particularly resist abandoning the conventional textbooks that set forth the precepts of their discipline in clear and unqualified terms. Those texts, as Richard Young points out in his essay, "Paradigms and Problems: Needed Research in Rhetorical Theory," are usually so similar that one way to discover the traditional paradigm of a field is to examine its textbooks.[1]

Finally, however, most of the resistance to the new paradigm will dissipate when its advocates can demonstrate that it will solve problems that the traditional paradigm could not solve. Most of the new generation of scholars working in the field will adopt the new model, and the older practitioners will gradually come around to it. Those who cling to the old paradigm lose their influence in the field because the leaders in the profession simply ignore their work. When that happens, the paradigm shift is complete, and the theory that was revolutionary becomes conventional.

This summary of Kuhn's book is sketchy and too simple, but I think it accurately reflects the key points in his theory. When he developed the theory, he considered only the so-called hard sciences, particularly chemistry, astronomy, and physics. He did not claim or even suggest that his model for scientific revolution could or should apply to social sciences or the humanities, where research is not done in laboratories and usually does not involve measurements or formulas. Nevertheless, I believe that composition theorists and writing teachers can learn from Thomas Kuhn if they see his theory of scientific revolutions as an analogy that can illuminate developments that are taking place in our profession. Those developments, the most prominent of which is the move to a process-centered theory of teaching writing, indicate that our profession is probably in the first stages of a paradigm shift.

The Current-Traditional Paradigm and Its Proponents

In order to understand the nature of that shift, we need to look at the principal features of the paradigm that has been the basis of composition teaching for several decades. In "Paradigms and Patterns" Richard Young describes it this way:

> The overt features . . . are obvious enough: the emphasis on the composed product rather than the composing process; the analysis of discourse into description, narration, exposition, and argument; the strong concern with usage . . . and with style; the preoccupation with the informal essay and research paper; and so on.[2]

Young adds that underlying the traditional paradigm is what he calls the "vitalist" attitude toward composing: that is, the assumption that no one can really teach anyone else how to write because writing is a mysterious creative activity that cannot be categorized or analyzed.

In an article in the Winter, 1980, *Freshman English News* James Berlin and Robert Inkster ascribe other features to the conventional paradigm. Basing their conclusions on an analysis of repeated patterns in four well-known and commercially successful rhetoric texts, they add that the traditional paradigm stresses expository writing to the virtual exclusion of all other forms, that it posits an unchanging reality which is independent of the writer and which all writers are expected to describe in the same way regardless of the rhetorical situation, that it neglects invention almost entirely, and that it makes style the most important element in writing.[3]

I would make three other points about the traditional paradigm. First, its adherents believe that competent writers know what they are going to say before they begin to write; thus their most important task when they are preparing to write is finding a form into which to organize their content. They also believe that the composing process is linear, that it proceeds systematically from prewriting to writing to rewriting. Finally, they believe that teaching editing is teaching writing.

It is important to note that the traditional paradigm did not grow out of research or experimentation. It derives partly from the classical rhetorical model that organizes the production of discourse into invention, arrangement, and style, but mostly it seems to be based on some idealized and orderly vision of what literature scholars, whose professional focus is on the written product, seem to imagine is an efficient method of writing. It is a prescriptive and orderly view of the creative act, a view that defines the successful writer as one who can systematically produce a 500-word theme of five paragraphs, each with a topic sentence. Its proponents hold it *a priori;* they have not tested it against the composing processes of actual writers.

At this point some of my readers may want to protest that I am belaboring a dead issue—that the admonition to "teach process, not product" is now conventional wisdom. I disagree. Although those in the vanguard of the profession have by and large adopted the process model for teaching composition and are now attentively watching the research on the composing process in order to extract some pedagogical principles from it, the over-whelming majority of college writing teachers in the United States are not professional writing teachers. They do not do research or publish on rhetoric or composition, and they do not know the scholarship in the field; they do not read the professional journals and they do not attend professional meet-ings such as the annual Conference on College Composition and Communica-tion; they do not participate in faculty development workshops for writing teachers. They are trained as literary critics first and as teachers of literature second, yet out of necessity most of them are doing half or more of their teaching in composition. And they teach it by the traditional paradigm, just as they did when they were untrained teaching assistants ten or twenty or forty years ago. Often they use a newer edition of the same book they used as teaching assistants.

Out of necessity, apathy, and what I see as a benighted and patronizing view of the essential nature of composition courses, English department ad-ministrators encourage this unprofessional approach to the teaching of writ-ing. In the first place, they may believe that they have so many writing classes to staff that they could not possibly hire well-qualified professionals to teach them; only a comparatively few such specialists exist. Second, most departmental chairpersons don't believe that an English instructor needs special qualifications to teach writing. As one of my colleagues says, our de-partment wouldn't think of letting her teach Chaucer courses because she is not qualified; yet the chairman is delighted for her to teach advanced com-position, for which she is far more unqualified. The assumption is that any-one with a Ph.D. in English is an expert writing teacher.

I think, however, that the people who do most to promote a static and unexamined approach to teaching writing are those who define writing courses as service courses and skills courses; that group probably includes most administrators and teachers of writing. Such a view, which denies that writing requires intellectual activity and ignores the importance of writing as a basic method of learning, takes away any incentive for the writing teacher to grow professionally. People who teach skills and provide services are tradi-tionally less respected and rewarded than those who teach theory, and hiring hordes of adjuncts and temporary instructors and assigning them to composi-tion courses reinforces this value system. Consequently there is no external pressure to find a better way to teach writing.

In spite of this often discouraging situation, many teachers who cling to the traditional paradigm work very hard at teaching writing. They devote far more time than they can professionally afford to working with their stu-dents, but because they haven't read Elbow or Bruffee they have no way of knowing that their students might benefit far more from small group meetings with each other than from the exhausting one-to-one conferences that the teachers hold. They both complain and brag about how much time they spend meticulously marking each paper, but because they haven't read Diederich or Irmscher they don't know that an hour spent meticulously marking every error in a paper is probably doing more harm than good. They are exhausting themselves trying to teach writing from an outmoded model, and they come to despise the job more and more because many of their students improve so little despite their time and effort.

But the writing teacher's frustration and disenchantment may be less important than the fact that if they teach from the traditional paradigm, they are frequently emphasizing techniques that the research has largely discredited. As Kuhn points out, the paradigm that a group of professionals accepts will govern the kinds of problems they decide to work on, and that very paradigm keeps them from recognizing important problems that cannot be discussed in the terminology of their model. Thus teachers who concentrate their efforts on teaching style, organization, and correctness are not likely to recognize that their students need work in invention. And if they stress that proofreading and editing are the chief skills one uses to revise a paper, they won't realize that their students have no concept of what it means to make substantive revisions in a paper. The traditional paradigm hides these problems.

Textbooks complicate the problem further. As Kuhn repeatedly points out, the standard texts in any discipline constitute a major block to a paradigm shift because they represent accepted authority. Many, though certainly not all, of the standard textbooks in rhetoric and composition for the past two decades have been product-centered books that focus on style, usage, and argumentation; Sheridan Baker's *The Practical Stylist* and Brooks and Warren's *Modern Rhetoric* are typical examples. When Donald Stewart made an analysis of rhetoric texts three years ago, he found that only seven out of the thirty-four he examined showed any awareness of current research in rhetoric. The others were, as he put it, "strictly current-traditional in their discussions of invention, arrangement, and style."[4] And textbooks change slowly. Publishers want to keep what sells, and they tend to direct the appeals of their books to what they believe the average composition teacher wants, not to what those in the vanguard of the profession would like to have.

Signs of Change

Nevertheless, changes are under way, and I see in the current state of our profession enough evidence of insecurity and instability to suggest that the traditional prescriptive and product-centered paradigm that underlies writing instruction is beginning to crumble. I think that the forces contributing to its demise are both theoretical and concrete and come from both inside and outside of the profession. Changes in theory probably started, in the middle 1950's, from intellectual inquiry and speculation about language and language learning that was going on in several fields, notably linguistics, anthropology, and clinical and cognitive psychology. To identify and trace all these complex developments would go far beyond the scope of this article and beyond my current state of enlightenment. I can only touch on some of them here.

Probably one of the most important developments to affect writing theory was the publication of Noam Chomsky's *Syntactic Structures* in 1957. His theory of transformational grammar, with its insistent look at the rules by which language is generated, caused a new focus on the process by which language comes into being.* The publication of Francis Christensen's essays on the generative rhetoric of the sentence and the paragraph in the early 1960's also stimulated new interest in the processes by which writers produce texts. Certainly the tagmemicists also provoked a fresh look at the act of writing when they urged writers to generate ideas by thinking about subjects from a dynamic, three-faceted perspective. And when the humanistic psychologist Carl Rogers began to criticize behaviorist psychology just as Chomsky had criticized behaviorist theories of language, he probably hastened the shift away from the product-response evaluation of writing.

A major event that encouraged the shift of attention to the process of writing was the famous Anglo-American Seminar on the Teaching of English, held at Dartmouth College in the summer of 1966. In the final report of this gathering of eminent educators from Britain and the United States, the participants deëmphasized the formal teaching of grammar and usage in the classroom and emphasized having children engage directly in the writing process in a non-prescriptive atmosphere.

So the intellectual climate conducive to this change has been developing for more than two decades. Of course, if these shifts in theory and attitudes were the only forces that were putting pressure on the traditional approach to teaching writing, revolution in the profession would probably be long in coming. But other concrete and external forces have also been putting pressure on writing teachers. These teachers are plagued by embarrassing stories about college graduates who can't pass teacher competency tests, and by angry complaints about employees who can't write reports. And the professors agree. Their students come to them writing badly and they leave writing badly. Handbooks won't solve their problems, and having them revise papers does no good.

Worse, just at this time when they are most disheartened about teaching writing, large numbers of English professors are beginning to realize that most of them are going to be teaching a lot of writing to a lot of students from now on. The prospect is grim, so grim that the English departments at Harvard and the University of Michigan have given up and turned the bulk of their composition teaching over to specialists outside the departments. But most professors can't do that, and instead they feel insecure and angry because they know they are teaching badly. In Kuhn's terminology, their methods have become anomalous; the system that they have always depended on no longer seems to work.

But why should the paradigm begin to break down just now? After all, as Richard Young points out, thousands of people have learned to write by the trial-and-error method of producing a text and having it criticized. Why shouldn't that slow, but often effective, method continue to work most of

---

*I am indebted to my colleague Stephen Witte for bringing this development to my attention.

the time? Once more, I think, Kuhn has the answer. He says, "One need look no further than Copernicus and the calendar to discover that external conditions may help to transform a mere anomaly into a source of acute crisis."[5] I believe that the external conditions which have hastened the crisis in the teaching of writing are open admissions policies, the return to school of veterans and other groups of older students who are less docile and rule-bound than traditional freshmen, the national decline in conventional verbal skills, and the ever larger number of high school graduates going on to college as our society demands more and more credentials for economic citizenship. Any instructional system would come close to collapse under such a strain, and our system for teaching writing has been particularly vulnerable because it has been staffed largely by untrained teachers who have had little scholarly interest in this kind of teaching.

Following the pattern that Kuhn describes in his book, our first response to crisis has been to improvise *ad hoc* measures to try to patch the cracks and keep the system running. Among the first responses were the writing labs that sprang up about ten years ago to give first aid to students who seemed unable to function within the traditional paradigm. Those labs are still with us, but they're still giving only first aid and treating symptoms. They have not solved the problem. Another *ad hoc* remedy took the form of individualized instruction, but it has faded from the scene along with computer-assisted instruction. The first was too costly and too isolated, the second one proved too limited and impersonal. And the experiments with expressive writing also turned out to be *ad hoc* measures, although for a while they seemed to have enough strength to foreshadow a paradigm shift. Sentence combining, I predict, will prove to be another *ad hoc* measure that serves as only a temporary palliative for serious writing problems.

All these remedies have proved temporarily or partially useful; none, however, has answered the crucial question: what is the basic flaw in the traditional paradigm for teaching writing? Why doesn't it work?

The Transition Period

Someone who cares has to ask that question before the revolution can start because, as Kuhn points out, "novelty ordinarily emerges only for the man who, knowing *with precision* what he should expect, is able to recognize that something has gone wrong."[6] In the teaching of composition, the essential person who asked that question may not have been a man, but a woman, Mina Shaughnessy. In her book *Errors and Expectations*, Shaughnessy describes the educational experience that made her, a professor at a prestigious university, stop to ask, "What went wrong?"

> In the spring of 1970, the City University of New York adopted an admissions policy that guaranteed to every city resident with a high school diploma a place in one of its eighteen tuition-free colleges, thereby opening its doors not only to a larger population of students than it had ever had before . . . but to a wider range of students than any college had probably ever admitted or thought of admitting to its campus. . . .

One of the first tasks these students faced when they arrived at college was to write a placement essay. . . . Judged by the results of these tests, the young men and women who were to be known as open admissions students fell into one of three groups: 1. Those who met the traditional requirements for college work, who appeared from their tests . . . to be able to begin at the traditional starting points; 2. those who had survived their secondary schooling . . . and whose writing reflected a flat competence; 3. [those] who had been left so far behind the others in their formal education that they appeared to have little chance of catching up, students whose difficulties with the written language seemed of a different order from those of other groups, as if they had come, you might say, from a different country.

 . . . The third group contained true outsiders, . . . strangers in academia, unacquainted with the rules and rituals of college life, unprepared for the sorts of tasks their teachers were about to assign them. . . .

Not surprisingly, the essays these students wrote during their first weeks of class stunned the teachers who read them. Nothing, it seemed, short of a miracle was going to turn such students into writers. . . . To make matters worse, there were no studies nor guides, nor even suitable textbooks to turn to. Here were teachers trained to analyze the belletristic achievements of the ages marooned in basic writing classrooms with adult student writers who appeared by college standards to be illiterate.[7]

Relying on their previous experience with selectively-admitted students at the City University, Shaughnessy and her colleagues thought they knew what to expect from "college writers." The shock of facing a kind of writing that fit no familiar category, that met no traditional standards, forced Shaughnessy, at least, to recognize an anomaly. If these students had come through schools in which writing had been taught with standard textbooks and standard methods, then one had to conclude that the method and the textbooks did not work, at least not for a substantial and important group of students. The question was, "Why?"

To find the answer, Shaughnessy analyzed the placement essays of 4000 students and over a period of five years worked at trying to get at the roots of their problems and devise a way to overcome them. Eventually she became persuaded

 . . . that basic writers write the way they do, not because they are slow or non-verbal, indifferent to or incapable of academic excellence, but because they are beginners and must, like all beginners, learn by making mistakes. . . . And the keys to their development as writers often lie in the very features of their writing that English teachers have been trained to brush aside with a marginal code letter or a scribbled injunction to "Proofread!" Such strategies ram at the doors of their incompetence while the keys that would open them lie in view. . . . The work [of teaching these students to write] must be informed by an understanding not only of what is missing or awry, but of *why this is so.*[8] (italics added)

Shaughnessy's insight is utterly simple and vitally important: we cannot teach students to write by looking only at what they have written. We must also understand *how* that product came into being, and *why* it assumed the form that it did. We have to try to understand what goes on during the internal act of writing and we have to intervene during the act of writing if we want to affect its outcome. We have to do the hard thing, examine the intangible process, rather than the easy thing, evaluate the tangible product.

Although Shaugnessy was not the first investigator to try to move behind students' written products and find out how those products came into being—Janet Emig and Charles Stallard had both done limited studies at about the same time as Shaughnessy, and James Britton and his colleagues in Great Britain were working on a very ambitious study of the development of writing abilities—she was the first to undertake a large-scale research project whose goal was to teach the new students of the seventies to write. Her example, her book, and her repeated calls for new research in composition have undoubtedly been important stimuli in spurring the profession's search for a new paradigm.

Others in the profession have also given impetus to the search. In 1968 a journalist and professor named Donald Murray published a book called *A Writer Teaches Writing,* in which he suggests that if we want to teach students to write, we have to initiate them into the process that writers go through, not give them a set of rules. He insists that writers find their real topics only through the act of writing. In fact, Murray may have originated the admonition, "Teach Writing as a Process not Product" in a 1972 article by that title.[9] A resurgence of interest in classical rhetoric in the seventies also sparked interest in a new approach to the teaching of writing. The books by rhetoricians Richard Weaver and Edward P. J. Corbett provided the theoretical foundations for the view that writing can not be separated from its context, that audience and intention should affect every stage of the creative process. When this premise became widely accepted at major universities—for example, the University of Iowa and the University of Texas—it inevitably put strains on the old product-centered paradigm.

Another major influence on the teaching of writing across the nation has come from California's Bay Area Writing Project, initiated in 1975. A cardinal principle of that project has been the revolutionary thesis that all writing teachers should write in order to understand the writing process firsthand. When teachers began to do so, the traditional textbook model for writing inevitably came into question. And as spin-offs of the Bay Area Writing Project have proliferated across the country, largely funded by grant money donated by agencies and foundations alarmed about the writing crisis, a growing number of teachers are changing to process-centered writing instruction.

The Emerging Paradigm

But the most promising indication that we are poised for a paradigm shift is that for the first time in the history of teaching writing we have specialists who are doing controlled and directed research on writers' composing processes. Sondra Perl of Herbert Lehman College of the City University of New York and Linda Flower and John Hayes of Carnegie-Mellon University are tape recording students' oral reports of the thoughts that come to them as they write and of the choices they make. They call their investigative strategy "protocol analysis," and they supplement it with interviews and questionnaires to put together composite pictures of the processes followed by working writers. Sharon Pianko of Rutgers University has done a study in which she matched groups of traditonal and remedial writers, men and women writers, and 18-year-old and adult writers and compared their composing habits. Nancy Sommers of New York University has done a study comparing the revising practices of college freshmen and experienced professional writers, and Lester Faigley and Stephen Witte of the University of Texas now have a federal grant to do a more comprehensive study on revising. (An article based on this study appeared in the December, 1981, issue of *CCC*.) Lee Odell of Rensselaer Polytechnic Institute and Dixie Goswami are currently involved in a federally-funded study of the practices of writers in business.

From these and other studies we are beginning to find out something about how people's minds work as they write, to chart the rhythm of their writing, to find out what constraints they are aware of as they write, and to see what physical behaviors are involved in writing and how they vary among different groups of writers. So far only a small amount of data has been collected, and the inferences we can draw from the studies are necessarily tentative. As Linda Flower puts it, because we are trying to chart and analyze an activity that goes on largely out of sight, the process is rather like trying to trace the path of a dolphin by catching glimpses of it when it leaps out of the water. We are seeing only a tiny part of the whole process, but from it we can infer much about what is going on beneath the surface.[10]

What are we finding out? One point that is becoming clear is that writing is an act of discovery for both skilled and unskilled writers; most writers have only a partial notion of what they want to say when they begin to write, and their ideas develop in the process of writing. They develop their topics intuitively, not methodically. Another truth is that usually the writing process is not linear, moving smoothly in one direction from start to finish. It is messy, recursive, convoluted, and uneven. Writers write, plan, revise, anticipate, and review throughout the writing process, moving back and forth among the different operations involved in writing without any apparent plan. No practicing writer will be surprised at these findings: nevertheless, they seriously contradict the traditional paradigm that has dominated writing textbooks for years.

But for me the most interesting data emerging from these studies are those that show us profound differences between the writing behaviors of skilled and unskilled writers and the behaviors of student and professional writers. Those differences involve the amount of time spent on writing, the amount of time preparing to write, the number of drafts written, the concern for audience, the number of changes made and the stages at which they are made, the frequency and length of pauses during writing, the way in which those pauses are used, the amount of time spent rereading and reformulating, and the kind and number of constraints that the writers are aware of as they work. This kind of information enables us to construct a tentative profile of the writing behaviors of effective writers; I have sketched such a profile in another paper, not yet published.

From all this activity in the field, the new paradigm for teaching writing is emerging. Its principal features are these:

1. It focuses on the writing process; instructors intervene in students' writing during the process.
2. It teaches strategies for invention and discovery; instructors help students to generate content and discover purpose.
3. It is rhetorically based; audience, purpose, and occasion figure prominently in the assignment of writing tasks.
4. Instructors evaluate the written product by how well it fulfills the writer's intention and meets the audience's needs
5. It views writing as a recursive rather than linear process; pre-writing, writing, and revision are activities that overlap and intertwine.
6. It is holistic, viewing writing as an activity that involves the intuitive and non-rational as well as the rational faculties.
7. It emphasizes that writing is a way of learning and developing as well as a communication skill.
8. It includes a variety of writing modes, expressive as well as expository.
9. It is informed by other disciplines, especially cognitive psychology and linguistics.
10. It views writing as a disciplined creative activity that can be analyzed and described; its practitioners believe that writing can be taught.
11. It is based on linguistic research and research into the composing process.
12. It stresses the principle that writing teachers should be people who write.

Portents for the Future

I believe that important events of the recent past are going to speed the revolution and help to establish this new paradigm in the nation's classrooms.

First, the University of Iowa's Writing Institute, which received a $680,000 grant from the National Endowment for the Humanities to train freshman composition directors, has this year completed its work and sent out forty administrators for writing programs who will almost certainly base those programs on the new model. They are bound to have a profound influence on their institutions.

Second, graduate programs in rhetoric are rapidly increasing across the country. The last count in the Spring, 1980, *Freshman English News* showed that fifty-three institutions have added graduate rhetoric courses since 1974, and that was not a complete list. Enrollment in these programs is climbing because students realize that English departments now offer more jobs in rhetoric and composition than in any other specialization. Most of these programs are going to produce young professionals who have been taught by scholars who know recent research and are committed to the new paradigm: Richard Young, Ross Winterowd, Joseph Comprone, James Kinneavy, Andrea Lunsford, Elizabeth Cowan, Linda Flower, to name just a few. When these new graduates go into English departments where the traditional paradigm prevails, they are certain to start working for change.

Third, in many schools, even graduate assistants who are in traditional literary programs rather than rhetoric programs are getting their in-service training from the rhetoric and composition specialists in their departments. They are being trained in process-centered approaches to the teaching of composition, and when they enter the profession and begin teaching lower-division writing courses along with their literary specialities, they are most likely to follow the new paradigm. And, more and more, the methods courses for high-school teachers are also being taught by the rhetoric specialists; that change will have a profound effect on secondary school teaching.

Fourth, we now have process-based texts on the teaching of writing. Shaughnessy's *Errors and Expectations* is well known and widely used. It has been joined by Irmscher's *Teaching Expository Writing* and Neman's *Teaching Students to Write*. The authors of both these latter books incorporate research findings and recent developments in the profession into their philosophies of and methodologies for teaching writing.

Fifth, college composition textbooks are changing. Along with their traditional books, most publishers are now publishing at least one process-oriented, rhetorically-based writing text. Several are now on the market and more are forthcoming, most of them written by scholars and teachers who are leaders in the profession. Moreover, many major publishing houses now retain well-known composition specialists to advise them on manuscripts. The publishers sense change in the wind and realize that the new crop of well-informed and committed writing program directors who will be taking over are going to insist on up-to-date textbooks. The change will even reach into some high schools because one large company has hired one of the country's leading rhetoricians to supervise and edit their high school composition series. Many others will probably follow their example.

But no revolution brings the millenium nor a guarantee of salvation, and we must remember that the new paradigm is sketchy and leaves many problems about the teaching or writing unresolved. As Kuhn points out, new paradigms are apt to be crude, and they seldom possess all the capabilities of their predecessors. So it is important for us to preserve the best parts of earlier methods for teaching writing: the concern for style and the preservation of high standards for the written product. I believe we also need to continue giving students models of excellence to imitate.

Kuhn contends that "the transition between competing paradigms cannot be made a step at a time, forced by logic. . . . Like the gestalt switch, it must occur all at once (though not necessarily in an instant) or not at all."[11] He says, however, that, "if its supporters are competent, they will improve it [the paradigm], explore its possibilities, and show what it would be like to belong to the community guided by it."[12] I see this last opportunity as the challenge to today's community of composition and rhetoric scholars: to refine the new paradigm for teaching composition so that it provides a rewarding, productive, and feasible way of teaching writing for the non-specialists who do most of the composition teaching in our colleges and universities.

Notes

[1] Richard Young, "Paradigms and Problems: Needed Research in Rhetorical Invention," *Research in Composing*, ed. Charles Cooper and Lee Odell (Urbana, IL: National Council of Teachers of English, 1978), p. 31.

[2] Young, p. 31.

[3] James A. Berlin and Robert P. Inkster, "Current-Traditional Rhetoric: Paradigm and Practice," *Freshman English News*, 8 (Winter, 1980), 1-4, 13-14.

[4] Donald Stewart, "Composition Textbooks and the Assault on Tradition," *College Composition and Communication*, 29 (May, 1978), 174.

[5] Thomas Kuhn, *The Structure of Scientific Revolutions*, Second Edition (Chicago: University of Chicago Press, 1970), p. x.

[6] Kuhn, p. 65.

[7] Mina Shaughnessy, *Errors and Expectations* (New York and London: Oxford University Press, 1977), pp. 1-3.

[8] Shaughnessy, p. 5.

[9] Donald Murray, "Teach Writing as a Process not Product," *The Leaflet*, November 1972, pp. 11-14 (the New England Association of Teachers of English).

[10] Linda Flower and John Hayes, "Identifying the Organization of the Writing Processes," *Cognitive Processes in Writing*, ed., Lee W. Gregg and Erwin R. Steinberg (Hillsdale, NJ: Lawrence Erlbaum Associates, 1980), pp. 9-10.

[11] Kuhn, p. 150.

[12] Kuhn, p. 159.

Recognition, Representation
and Revision

ANN E. BERTHOFF

We should not be surprised that our students so often consider revision as a chance to get "it" right the second time around.[1] Despite recent attempts to differentiate editing and rewriting, most English teachers probably continue to instill the idea that revision is like taking another swing at the ball or shooting again for the basket. The idea of revision as correction is, like readability formulas and sentence combining, consonant with a view of language as merely a medium for the communication of our views of a reality *out there:* we have ideas and we put them into language. (Sometimes we might get the wrong slot: try again.) Language is often seen as a window which keeps us from enjoying an immediate vision. The pedagogical corollary is that the best we can do is to teach window washing, trying to keep the view of what's "really there" unobstructed by keeping the prose clean and clear. Revision, in this view, is polishing. I argue in the following that we can learn to teach revision as itself a way of composing if we consider it analogous to acts of mind whereby we make sense of the world.

One rainy afternoon last fall I stopped by to browse among some miscellaneous journals in the gaudy reading room of a graduate school library where, as it turned out, I witnessed a Basic Writer at work. He sat in a low-slung, purple velour settee, a pad of lined paper on his knee, a nice new yellow pencil and a pack of cigarrettes at the ready, and a Dixie Cup of coffee to hand. He seemed prepared for the labors of composition. He would write a sentence or two, light a cigarette, read what he'd written, sip his coffee, extinguish the cigarette—and the two sentences. He'd pretty much worn out the eraser by the time I'd left. (That would be an interesting research index: how long does the eraser last, if it's not bitten off in momentary despair?) My eyes glazed more quickly than usual as I leafed through *Research in the Teaching of English* because my mind was otherwise engaged in formulating what I would have said to this earnest graduate student, if I had had the nerve. Something like this:

> You need to get some writing down on paper and to keep it there long enough so that you can give yourself the treat of rewriting. What you need is a ball point pen so you can't erase and some cheap paper so you can deliberately use a lot of it—and one very expensive sheet of creamy foolscap for your inventory of glosses; it's a sensuous pleasure to write

The Journal of Basic Writing, 3 (Fall-Winter 1981). Copyright © 1981 by the English Department, City College of New York. Reprinted by permission of the editor.

27

on a beautiful surface after you've been scratching away on canary pads. But wait a minute! Where are your notes to yourself? Where are your lists? Where are your points of departure? Where are your leads? Where is your lexicon? Where are your quoted passages? Where is your chaos? Nothing comes of nothing! Here you are in this spaceship pod of a chair, this womb, with essentials like coffee and cigarettes, but without the essential essential—language! How can you know what you think until you hear what you say? see what you've written?

I think it's instructive to consider how the "writing behaviors" of this graduate student resemble those of our Basic Writers. There is, of course, a difference: whereas the graduate can't get beyond the compulsive readjustment of the (doubtless) insubstantial and formless generalization he has begun with, our students hate even to start—for a dozen reasons which have been carefully formulated and studied in recent years—and once they do have something down, they're loath to touch it: those few words are hard-won and therefore precious, not to be tampered with. The graduate destroys by re-statement because he doesn't know how to get the dialectic going; the undergraduate can't conceive of adjustment or development because his fragile construct might collapse. But insofar as neither knows how to make language serve the active mind, they both are Basic Writers: they do not understand rewriting because they do not understand how writing gets written in the first place.

My tendentious claim is that that is often true also of their teachers: revision is poorly taught, or is not taught at all, because composition teachers (and composition textbook authors) often do not know how writing gets written. Without a substantial understanding of composing as a dialectical process in which the *what* and the *how* continually inform one another—a non-linear process motivated by both feedback and what I.A. Richards calls "feedforward"—there will be no way to differentiate revision from editing, no way to teach revision not as a definite phase, a penultimate stage, but as a dimension of composing. Revision is, indeed, re-seeing and it goes on continually in the composing process.

There is, of course, a great deal of talk currently about "the composing process," but there are very few pedagogies which are consonant with the kind of process composing actually is. I have elsewhere discussed the reason for this state of affairs: current rhetorical theory has provided little guidance for our classroom practice because it has no philosophically sound way of accounting for how words work.[2] There is no understanding in current rhetorical theory that in composing everything has to happen at once or it doesn't happen at all: if there isn't something to think about, if there aren't ideas to think *with*, if language is not in action, if the mind is not actively engaged, no meanings can be made. The pedagogical challenge is to help students take advantage of *atonceness*, to see it as a resource, not the mother of dilemmas.

The linear sequence by which "the composing process" is commonly represented—Prewriting, Writing, Rewriting—is antithetical to the "audit of meaning," I.A. Richards' term for dialectic. Instead of atonceness, it suggests that there is a non-reversible order, a sequence of activities which unfold in a predetermined manner. The inter-relationships of the triad are obscure; the notion, for instance, that Pre and Re have anything to do with one another, logically or psychologically, seems unheard of. If Prewriting is in many instances presented as a matter of amassing the slottables, Rewriting is considered a matter of checking out what's been slotted. "Think of what you want to say" in Prewriting is matched by such instructions as these for Rewriting: "Go back over what you've written. Are there any unnecessary words? Does everything you say refer to your thesis? Is your main point at the end of the paragraph? Are there any mechanical errors?" These questions are only transformations of old imperatives: "Don't use unnecessary words. Assure that all statements support your thesis. Avoid mechanical errors." Get law and order. Plant a tree. Love your mother. People who have done a lot of writing themselves frequently consider it a self-evidently sensible thing to teach the use of this kind of checklist to inexperienced writers. What is left out of account is that the experienced writer has criteria which are brought into play by asking such questions: that's what it means to have "experience."

I think it is fair to say that the linear model of composing as Prewriting, Writing, Rewriting fosters a pedagogy of exhortation. Now, if we are to undertake to teach composing as a dialectical process of which revision is not a stage but a dimension, how can we prevent what was earlier described, the write—erase—write again—erase it all syndrome? The short answer is, as I have noted, to teach students to take advantage of the atonceness of composing, to assure that they continually rediscover how forming, thinking, and writing can be simultaneous and correlative activities. Beginning writers need the experience of seeing how it is that consciousness of the *what* leads to understanding the *how*. This is what Paulo Freire means by "conscientization," the chief principle of his "pedagogy of knowing."[3] If a pedagogy of knowing is to be the successor to the pedagogy of exhortation, we will need as models of knowing those acts of mind which are logically and psychologically analogous to writing, namely, perception and concept formation.

Taking perception as a model for writing lets us exploit the ancient wisdom that seeing and knowing are radically alike. (Our word *idea* derives from the Greek *oida* which meant both *I have seen* and *I know*.) The eye is not a passive recorder; Ruskin's notion of "the innocent eye" has been superseded by that of "the intelligent eye."[4] When we see, we compose. Rudolf Arnheim lists as the operations involved in visual perception the following: "Active exploration, selection, grasping of essentials, simplification, abstraction, analysis and synthesis, completion, correction, comparison, problem-solving, as well as combining, separating, putting in context."[5] Is there any aspect of the composing process not represented in that list?

From Arnheim, E. H. Gombrich, R. L. Gregory and other philosophers and scientists, we can learn that perception involves matching and re-ordering, from the molecular level on up: *vision* is through and through a matter of *revision*. Indeed, seeing is actually contingent on re-seeing. To clarify this fascinating fact, I have students read Owen Barfield's explanation of how it is that cognition depends on recognition. He asks the reader to suppose that

> he is standing in the midst of a normal and familiar environment . . .
> when suddenly he is deprived by some supernatural stroke of every ves-
> tige of memory—and not only of memory, but also of all those assimi-
> lated, forgotten experiences which comprise his power of recognition.
> He is asked to assume that, in spite of this, he still retains the full meas-
> ure of his cognitive faculty as an adult. It will appear, I think, that for
> the first few moments his consciousness—if it can bear that name—will
> be deprived not merely of all thought, but even of all perception. It is
> not merely that he will be unable to realize that that square, red and
> white object is a "house" . . . ; he will not even be able to see it *as* a
> square, red and white object.[6]

Seeing the point, my students speak of "Barfield's meaningless man." We can make meaning because we see in terms of what we have seen. Without re-membered forms to see *with*, we would not see at all. Seeing is thus the primal analogizing in which thinking has its origin.

Now these philosophical principles of perception—seeing is knowing; seeing is contingent on re-seeing; the intelligent eye forms by analogizing—provide the foundation for a pedagogy of knowing. How can we use what we can learn about perception in order to make observation not a preliminary exercise but a model of the composing process?

The atonceness of composing is well-represented by looking and writing in tandem. Since learning to record observations has a self-evident usefulness for everybody from nuclear physicists to nurses, from parents to doctors, and since observing our observations *requires* language, assignments which in-volve looking and looking again can rationally involve writing and writing again. Exercises which make recording and commenting correlative and vir-tually simultaneous have an authenticity which is unusal in composition as-signments. One procedure which helps writers enact revision as a mode of composing is what I call a dialectical notebook: notes, lists, statements, crit-ical responses, queries of all sorts are written on one side; notes on these notes, responses to these responses are written on the facing page. The inner dialogue which is thinking is thus represented as a dialectic, the beginning of thinking about thinking. This double-entry journal encourages a habit which is of immediate usefulness, since this format is the best there is for taking notes on lectures and reading. And it is easily adapted to what my colleague Dixie Goswami calls a "speculative draft," a procedure for writing papers which allows students to take advantage of atonceness by keeping notes and queries, formulations and re-formulations in continual dialogue on facing pages.

The dialectical notebook teaches the value of keeping things tentative. Without that sense, the atonceness of composing is dangerous knowledge that can cause a severe case of Writer's Block. Unless students prove to themselves the usefulness of tentativeness, no amount of exhortation will persuade them to forego "closure," in the current jargon. The willingness to generate chaos; patience in testing a formulation against the record; careful comparing of proto-statements and half-statements, completed statements and re-statements: these are all expressions of what Keats famously called "negative capability," the capacity to remain in doubt. The story is told of a professor of internal medicine who brought home to his students the value of this attitude in diagnosis by the slogan: "Don't just DO something: Stand there!"

Along with the value of tentativeness, practice in observation teaches the importance of perspective and context, which become ideas to think *with* as students practice observing natural objects, for instance, and observing their observations. A shell or pebble on the beach has one kind of appearance; if you bring it home, it has another. Such facts call for recognition, formulation, and articulation; in the practice of looking and looking again, of writing and writing again, as students learn to compare kinds of appearances, they are also learning that perception depends on presuppositions, remembrances, anticipations, purposes, and so on. In my own teaching, I hand out weeds and grasses, seeds and bones, feathers and beach combings because natural forms are themselves compositions, pedagogically useful emblems of historical process. Friends and colleagues have occasionally argued that Nature is an alien point of departure and that such an exercise as Ira Shor's examination of the contents of a wastebasket is more likely to engage the attention of Basic Writers.[7] Detective work (or archaeology) is certainly as useful a metaphor for interpretation as nature study: the point is to make the transformation of the familiar to the strange and the strange to the familiar an exemplification of what goes on in all interpretation: to foreground the process of "reading," of construing, of making sense of whatever is under observation, from different perspectives, in different contexts.

Freire shows us how. The peasants in his culture circles, who are learning *how* they make meaning and *that* they make meaning simultaneously with learning to recognize words and sounds, study pictures depicting familiar scenes, reading them as texts, translating and interpreting them and interpreting their interpretations in dialogue.[8] What Freire calls "problematizing the existential situation" is a critical act of mind by which historical contexts for objects and pictures are developed: Careful observation of what is depicted works together with the interpretation of its significance. Perception thus provides the point of departure for a pedagogy of knowing because it is through and through conceptual.

Problematic symbols and problem-posing pictures at one end; organic structures in the middle; at the other end, abstract designs and diagrams which we can ask students to observe, translating in the process from pictorial to verbal language. I. A. Richards, in a valuable essay called "Learning and Looking," suggests just how challenging that translation can be.[9] He is ostensibly discussing the problems of literacy training in societies in which depiction is not thought of as representational, but in the course of demonstrating how "reading" certain diagrams exercises the translation-transformation capacity necessary for handling the graphic code, he does much more. For one thing, he shows how comparing depends on the principle of opposition, which is essential to all critical inquiry into "what varies with what while the rest is treated as remaining constant." Even more importantly, he provides a superb demonstration of how perspective and context function heuristically by limiting. Careful looking and experimental translation teaches the observer to use oppositions to limit the range of choices. Just as learning to keep things tentative is an all-important support structure for the concept of the atonceness of composing, so learning the use of limits is essential if beginning writers are to understand that composing necessarily involves choosing. Limits are their means of defining and controlling choices: unless we teach the function of limits, no amount of exhortation will persuade our students to tolerate the risks which revision entails.

By keeping looking and writing together, we can teach revision as analogous to recognition in perception: if we can keep thinking and writing together, our students can learn how revision is analogous to the representation which language makes possible. Language has, of course, an indicative function, but it is its power to represent our interpretations of experience which is vital for a pedagogy of knowing. No thinking—no composing—could happen if we had no means of stabilizing images of what we have seen, of recalling them as forms to think about and to think *with*. Language is our means of *re*presenting images as forms: *forming* is our means of seeing relationships from one or another perspective and in different contexts.

Writing teachers have not, generally speaking, taken advantage of this power of language and mind—it was once called *imagination*—because linguistics, as institutionalized by current rhetorical theory, has no way of accounting for it. The conventional notion of thinking finds no room for the dialectic which language makes possible. It is based, rather, on the dichotomy of induction/deduction: either, it is thought, we go from "the data"[10] to one or another principle, or we go from "high level abstractions"[11] to the substantiating particulars. *Forming* is, I think, the working concept we need in order to benefit from the fact that everything that happens when we think, when we form concepts, has an analogue in the composing process. Consider the following passages, the first, Lev Vygotsky's formulation of the dialectical character of concept formation; the second I. A. Richards' characterization of what goes on when we compose.

> When the process of concept formation is seen in all its complexity, it appears a movement of thoughts constantly alternating between two directions, from the particular to the general, and from the general to the particular.[12]

> Composition is the supplying at the right time and place of whatever the developing meaning then and there requires. It is the cooperation with the rest in preparing for what is to come and completing what has preceded. It is more than this, though; it is the exploration of what is to come and of how it should be prepared for, and it is the further examination of what has preceded and of how it may be amended and completed.[13]

The logical ground for the analogy of thinking and writing is *forming*—seeing relationships, recognizing and representing them. Understanding that principle can show us how to start with thinking and writing together, and if we start with them together we will be more likely to keep them together. (The way to bridge from so-called personal writing to so-called expository writing, from creative to critical writing, and, I will argue, from writing to re-writing is not to allow a separation in the first place.) I want to concentrate now on one particular implication for classroom practice and course design of the premise that thinking and writing involve us in *seeing relationships*: how can that help us to teach revision not as a definite phase but as a dimension of the composing process?

From the idea that composing is a matter of seeing relationships we might profitably conclude that at the pedagogical center of any composition course there should be not the grammatical unit of the sentence but the rhetorical unit of the paragraph.[14] Cognition depends on recognition; the presence of experience is mediated by the representation of language; sentences depend on the relationships they bear to other sentences. It is therefore easier to construe several sentences than it is one. The writer as reviser is a writer reading: reading a paragraph, he has many points of entry; if he doesn't see a relationship as he starts to read, he might catch hold of another as he goes on. He can then re-read and apprehend the earlier sentence. Because it articulates a structure of relationships, the paragraph provides a more appropriate focus for learning revision than the single sentence does. Apprehending the logical and rhetorical relationships of sentences in a paragraph is analogous to perception and concept formation in a way that apprehending those articulated according to grammatical conventions within the sentence is not. That's why Gertrude Stein is right: "So paragraphing is a thing that anyone is enjoying and sentences are less fascinating."

Seeing relationships, as an idea to think with, can help offset the effects of certain theories of learning which, taking motor activity as the model, lead to the idea that because we must walk before we can run, we must therefore study sentences and paragraphs. Surely first things come first, but wherever language is concerned, that will always mean that complexity comes before the allegedly simple. That is because meanings are not elements but relationships. It is by virtue of its complexity that the paragraph is simpler to take hold of than the sentence. This kind of paradox is central to the pedagogy of knowing.[15] I do not mean that we ignore sentence structure when we teach revision: my point is that although errors are best identified in isolation, sentences are best revised in context, in the relational terms which the paragraph provides. Or which the would-be paragraph can be brought to the point of supplying: We are taking advantage of the atonceness of making meaning when we teach our students to compose paragraphs in the course of revising sentences.

Along with the dialectical notebook, "glossing" paragraphs can raise consciousness of the interdependence of saying and intending. I ask students to summarize their paragraphs in oppositional form, to represent in a double phrase in the margin what is being set over against what. Thus identified, the logical structure of the paragraph can be used as an Archimedean point from which to survey the individual sentences. If it is impossible to formulate a gloss, that will tell a student more than exhortatory comments on incoherence ever could. Or it may be that in the process of glossing, the student will express a hitherto unspoken intention which the paragraph can use. In that case, the gloss can be revised in sentence form and incorporated. Invention of needed sentences is contingent on recognizing the need; in my opinion, that recognition is inspired not by asking empty questions about what the audience needs to know but by seeing what the paragraph needs to say. To discover logical and rhetorical needs is to discover purpose, a process which is at once more complex and more manageable than trying to ascertain audience needs directly. They, of course, must be hypothesized and considered in conjunction, dialectically, with purposes, but to instruct the student to determine "the audience's needs" is frequently only an updated version of asking him to ask himself "What am I trying to say?" That is not, I think, a heuristically useful inquiry.

A way to encourage students to ask what a paragraph needs—what their argument or explanation or description or narrative needs—is to have them read their own paragraphs (a day or so after they've been written) a sentence at a time with the remaining sentences covered, anticipating at each period what the next sentence will be, will *do*, by writing one in its place. (The writer can do this on his own, of course, but it is best done in conference or in company with other readers, dialogue being the best model of dialectic there is.) The newly framed sentence can then be compared with the original sentence, of which it may, of course, be a replica; having two ways of saying (or one way twice) to work with is important in the practice of revision. The choice can be made, then, of which serves better in answering the perhaps newly-felt need, but nothing should be thrown away, since the paragraph might well require the old original sentence in a new setting.

Developing a sense of rhetorical and logical form is in large part a matter of anticipating what comes next, of knowing what is needed, recognizing its emergence. That is not a "skill" but a power of mind and it is exactly comparable to recognition in perception and representation with language. We do not need to teach this power, but we should assure that it is exercised. These simple techniques of paragraph review can serve that purpose because they keep the dialectic of intending and forming lively. Glossing and anticipating can help students see to it that the "what I mean" does not remain an amorphous, ghostly non-presence but is embodied over and over again. To find out if you've said what you meant, you have to know what you mean and the way to determine that is to say "it" again.

Only when a paragraph has been reviewed in the light of its gloss, the various sentences abandoned or rewritten, restored and reordered according to emerging criteria, is it the time to work on sentence correction. Error identification is often tantamount to error correction and, as I've noted, that is best carried out if the sentence can be "heard" in isolation from its support system, the context which makes meaning, rather than grammatical structure, predominate. The procedure I recommend is to read the paragraph backwards aloud, sentence by sentence—an old proofreader's trick. If the student stumbles or hesitates, that is a sign of recognition and actual re-writing can begin. Nothing will come of this or any other such procedure, of course, if the student cannot recognize a faulty sentence when he hears one. By assuring that there are occasions for reading good prose closely, carefully, and frequently aloud, we can help our students to develop an "ear" for syntax, like an "ear" for music, to expect the way a sentence will go or can go so that when it goes awry, they can hear the error. The remedy for a deficient "ear" is hearing good prose and that means that student writing will not be the exclusive "text" in a well-designed composition course.

When it is a simple matter of agreement, pronoun reference, tense consistency, or punctuation (in some cases), there is a role for grammatical instruction. But sentences which fail because of pleonasm, fauty paralellism, misused idiom or mixed constructions are, generally speaking, a different matter. They will yield to our grammatical analysis or the student's, but that analysis will serve no heuristic function.

Take, for instance, the following sentences:

—The elemental beach and the music of the sea was more preferable than that other summer beach.

—North Carolina is a state where the long straight roads that lead to small quiet places has an unusually loud bunch of inhabitants.

—I have always seen that as a silver lining behind the cloud.

—Teachers judge the quality of the student's performance much like that of the farmer's grading his beef.

In my opinion, the best use of time in working with sentences like these is for everybody in a small group, or for both student and tutor in conference, to revise the sentence by means of composing several interpretive paraphrases, using the parent paragraph as a sounding board. Restating, representing is a way to recognize intention: interpreting by means of paraphrase, rather than tinkering with the incorrect sentence as it stands, allows a student to call upon the resources he has for making meaning which are independent of any explicit knowledge of grammatical laws.

I do not mean that rhetorical and logical forms are simply "generated": written discourse is not natural in the way that speech, in a social setting, is. (The notion of a Language Acquisition Device is hazardous even as a model of the processes by which we learn language, let alone as a model of a model of how one learns to compose.) I have no faith that well-formed intentions will surface from the deeps, if only grammarians will step aside. Returning to intention is a hard journey, but it is profitable because of what can be learned on the way about the making of meaning.

Syntactical structures are linguistic forms which find conceptual forms: making them accessible to our students is one of our chief duties. Kenneth Koch's experiments are important to us all because they remind us of the value of teaching syntactical structures as generative form rather than as slots to be filled or inert elements to be combined. We can learn from Koch and others how to make syntax itself a heuristic. The procedure I have found most useful is called "persona paraphrase" and is described by Phillis Brooks in her important essay, "Mimesis: Grammar and the Echoing Voice."[16] Kenneth Burke's conception of recalcitrance explains the principles on which persona paraphrase is based: "A statement is an attitude rephrased in accordance with the strategy of revision made necessary by the recalcitrance of the materials employed for embodying this attitude."[17] Insofar as it recognizes the dialectics of recalcitrance; the paradox that complexity is simple; the fact that concept formation is dynamic; the fact that saying and intending inform one another—insofar as persona paraphrase is a technique which can teach revision as a mode of composing, it is the antithesis of sentence combining. This is not surprising: it presupposes a philosophy of language entirely foreign to the conceptions which underlie the manipulations of sentence combining.

Revising at this level in these ways means slowing things down: atonceness always does. Composing a persona paraphrase can take a full hour; composing interpretive paraphrases for a single conceptually faulty sentence can take up the entire class or conference time. It is time well-spent, but there is a very difficult pedagogical challenge in seeing to it that this necessarily slow, deliberate pace is not the only one at which the composition course moves. Others have probably long since discovered the paradox I've been slow to come to, viz., that atonceness requires a double track, if not a triple focus. Students should work independently on a long-term project for which the dialectical notebook is the enabling means of making meaning; they should continually be revising paragraphs with their fellow students; every day, in class or not, they should focus on the analysis and correction of a single sentence. The difference between the 101 section for Basic Writers, the noncredit course required of graduate students, and the Continuing Education Workshops in Writing should be a matter not of which elements are included but only of the ratios among them and the pace at which the entire course proceeds.

If we reject the linear model of composing and the pedagogy it legitimates—teaching the allegedly first things first; subskills before skills: the *know how* before the *know what*; walking (sentences) before running (paragraphs)—we will be free to invent courses which are consonant with the idea of the composing process as a continuum of forming. I have been claiming that recognition and representation, as the central operations of perception and concept formation, provide the models of forming which can help us teach revision as a way of composing.

Notes

1 This finding is reported by Susan V. Wall and Anthony R. Petrosky in an interesting and substantial paper read at the 1980 conference of the NCTE.

2 See *The Making of Meaning: Metaphors, Models, and Maxims for Writing Teachers* (Montclair, NJ: Boynton/Cook, 1981).

[3] "The Adult Literacy Process as Cultural Action for Freedom." *Harvard Educational Review*, 40 (1970), 217. Both Freire and Richards argue the importance of the learner's consciousness of his learning. It is the very opposite of the commonly held principle of letting well enough alone: if students can do something easily, naturally, why bother telling them how they do it? Conscientization does not depend on a teacher "telling" students what they are doing; Freire rejects this digestive theory of education. Richards comments in *Design for Escape* (NY: Harcourt, 1968), p. 111, that what learners need are *"assisted invitations . . . to find out just what they are trying to do and thereby how to do it."* I have used "assisted invitations" as a name for the exercises in my textbook, *Forming/Thinking/Writing* (Montclair, NJ: Boynton/Cook, 1978).

[4] Richard Coe brought to my attention the fascinating book with this title by R. L. Gregory (New York: McGraw-Hill, 1970). Coe's textbook, *Form and Substance* (New York: Wiley, 1981), is one of the few which present perception as profoundly conceptual, as an act of mind.

[5] *Visual Thinking* (Berkeley: University of California Press, 1969), p. 13.

[6] *Poetic Diction* (1928; rpt. Middletown, CT: Wesleyan University Press, 1973), p. 56. This passage appears, along with others, from works by Gombrich, Ogden, Burke, *inter alia,* in Part I of *Forming/Thinking/Writing.*

[7] Ira Shor's *Critical Teaching and Everyday Life* (Boston: South End Press, 1980) is a thoughtful adaptation of Freire to the Open Admission composition classroom. See especially "Re-Experiencing the Ordinary" and "Learning How to Learn." George Hillocks, in his NCTE pamphlet *Observing and Writing,* offers some excellent suggestions which keep interpretation at the center.

[8] An explanation of this procedure, together with a sequence of pictures, can be found in *Education for Critical Consciousness* (New York: Seabury Press, 1973). These passages are reprinted in *The Making of Meaning*, pp. 159-73.

[9] *Design*, pp. 93-124.

[10] The superscripts would be question marks in I.A. Richards' "Meta-semantic Markers," a signal indicating a highly problematic term. Nothing is given to us but a formless *Firstness*, in Peirce's terms.

[11] The positivist "Ladder of Abstraction," promulgated by the General Semanticists, is a muddle indeed, since it is not *abstraction* which is hierarchical but *generalization.*

[12] *Thought and Language*, tr. Eugenia Hanfmann and Gertrude Vakar (Cambridge, MA: M. I. T. Press, 1962), p. 80.

[13] *So Much Nearer* (New York: Harcourt, 1960), p. 119-20.

[14] I agree with those who argue that the paragraph is a rhetorical convention and that a single sentence may constitute a paragraph. See "The Logic and Rhetoric of Paragraphs," *F/T/W*, pp. 155-73. For the time being, I use the term to mean a sentence sequence which displays logical coherence.

[15] I have discussed this principle in "Tolstoy, Vygotsky, and the Making of Meaning," *College Composition and Communication*, 29 (October, 1978), 249-55.

[16] *Collge English*, 35 (November, 1973), 161-68. "We select a specific passage, illustrating a particular kind of structure, and require that the student copy its structure, phrase by phrase, sentence by sentence, but substitute a completely different subject matter." As Phyllis Brooks notes, persona paraphrase is highly adaptable. I have described certain uses my students have made of it in *F/T/W*, pp. 222-26.

[17] *Permanence and Change* (1935; rpt. Indianapolis: Bobbs-Merrill, 1954), p. 255.

PART TWO

Motivating Student Writing

"My first impetus to write came from a sixth grade English teacher who filled us with feeling that writing was a good thing to do and that there was something noble about the English language."

Anonymous

Since composing written language originates from very deep within, the teacher of writing must be sensitive not only to the surface features of student work but to the deep, underlying currents as well. In the past, the concept of motivation more often than not has stressed external matters. For example, some teachers believed that a provocative picture or quiet music would "inspire" writing, or that a field trip or a short story would "trigger" good writing. This view assumes that our students already have the technical competence for writing, and that the teacher's job is to find the right key for releasing their energy. Although these techniques do work on occasion, most current thinking about motivation emphasizes the intrinsic qualities of the composing process itself. All the essays in this section show that the highest level of student motivation grows out of good pupil-teacher relations, from strong peer relations within a class that over the course of a term becomes a *community* of learners, and out of discovering the reasons for writing within the wellspring of one's own life and personality. It is not simply "finding the right topic" but getting in touch with one's feelings that counts most and eventually produces the best writing.

When the personal element is missing from their writing, students are inclined simply to go through the motions, and the result is (we've all seen it) Engfish. But there is something even beyond this. What happens when motivation is reversed? What happens to the quality of writing when the primary motivation in the classroom is fear? What happens to the self concept? The human spirit? Certainly the current-traditional paradigm can point to its successes, yet one has to wonder to what extent the curriculum itself has contributed to the profound insecurity which so many people express about their writing ability. It is apparent now more than ever that the dynamics of personal relations operating within the composition class are not "neutral," not independent of so-called subject matter. As Norman Cousins has taught us in his 1979 best seller, *Anatomy of an Illness as Perceived by the*

Patient, the power of the mind and will are inextricably bound up with the drive for emotional and physical well-being. The essays in this section argue that the same is true for learning to write.

In the first essay, poet-teacher Jean Pumphrey describes how she moved her students away from "classroom writing" to more personally engaging work. The reader might observe that at the outset Pumphrey describes a personal conviction that has now become widespread in the profession—a dissatisfaction with the traditional approaches to teaching composition. The author goes on to explain, step by step, how she restructured her class to become a community of learners. The success of her method is revealed in an ironic student comment:

> At one point I asked a student if the five-minute write-ins were helping him. "No," he replied, "I want to keep writing."

Because it contains so much good common sense and at the same time penetrates the general academic sham, Lou Kelly's "Competence and Creativity in the Open Classroom" has become a classic in the field. She is not writing here about classrooms without walls, but about openness and honesty between people. This, she believes, must be the starting point for good writing. The reader might observe that almost every paragraph in the essay contains a poignant seed of wisdom about teaching and writing.

In "Writing, Inner Speech, and Meditation," James Moffett describes the benefits of meditation in the composing process. The author makes it clear that he is not describing a religious practice but a kind of psychological reality not fully understood by the Western World. Moffett describes in detail a variety of meditation techniques, showing how such techniques can assist the writer in transforming elusive inner speech into coherent written discourse.

Too often student writing is not an act of communication, argues Ken Macrorie, but simply an exercise to be graded. After years of teaching composition, the author "stumbled into a way to induce students to write so they excited each other and me." Macrorie's aim is clear: to make genuine communication the central focus of the writing class. "To Be Read" provides detailed accounts of how to accomplish that goal.

The concluding essay in this section has all the grace and good sense that only a writer could bring to the teaching of writing. Donald Murray, who is both teacher and writer, believes that we should involve our students in the "demanding, intellectual process" of writing. "How do you motivate your students to pass through this process?" he asks. The answer is clear: Let them write. Let students find their own subjects and discover their own stance. Let the only textbook be the student's writing.

In one sentence Murray captures the essence of what many believe to be the primary goal of the composition class. "We have to respect the student, not for his product, not for the paper we call literature by giving it a grade, but for the search for truth in which he is engaged." Involvement in the search for truth may indeed be the most powerful source of motivation available to us.

Teaching English Composition
as a Creative Art

JEAN PUMPHREY

If someone came up to you and said, "Go develop a sense of humor," I suppose you'd laugh if you had one, and go into a deeper depression if you didn't. This, I submit, is what happens all too often in the teaching of English composition. So much of what we say to students really amounts to "go write a good theme," and those who can, do; those who can't get depressed, frequently to the point of dropping out.

Even as there is too little meaningful teacher involvement in the process of writing, there is all too often too much involvement of the wrong kind. I think most teachers of composition will recognize the writing style which follows:

Each separate society is different from one another in their own way as individuals differ from each other. Every society is conditioned around what the people make it to be. The more people contained in a given area, the bigger the society and the greater the norms. And when you have these norms you can only do what is accepted by the people (who, of course, made up the norms) and if you violate the social expectations, you run into conflict.

If I seem to give too much credit to the author of this statement when I refer to her "style," I do not intend to. Credit must go to her teachers. I submit that no one writes this way naturally. Such a style of writing has to be learned. Few of us would like to think that this is what we're teaching, but when we stand outside the process, pushing the student too quickly into communicative language, leaping past the expressive function of language, I believe we are, unwittingly, teaching the style we then sit back and criticize.

Each fall we stagger under the barrage of such language from freshman college students. In an attempt to unscramble the student from such impossible "textbookeze," some may resort to a handbook, assuming the student is not ready for "great ideas" and must return to "go." Others may plead with or otherwise exhort the student to write in his own voice, write plainly about whatever he knows. "Write in your own voice," we tell him. "Pick a topic familiar to you, a theme you can support." We urge him to expose his private feelings. Surely that is something he knows something about. We tell him to give evidence, to be specific, to use examples, to be concrete, and, in *telling* him, we are doing exactly what we are telling him not to do. It is not surprising that students should do as we do, not as we say. It is not surprising

College English, 34 (February 1973), pp. 666-673. Copyright © 1973 by the National Council of Teachers of English. Reprinted by permission of the publisher and the author.

that they should learn more from *how* we teach than from what we teach.

The fact is that *no one*, in the decade of the seventies, is convinced by being told. Yet students and teachers go on telling with greater and greater embellishments as if extravagant rhetoric could obviate simple illustration. And we are all turned off, students and teachers alike.

The teacher, concerning himself primarily with the product rather than the process, grades in silence, grimly revising his transmogrifying comments. The student is expected to learn language by writing in silence, later by observing his "corrected" errors, often in contrast to an accomplished writer's "model essay." Alone in his study, suspecting somehow he is responsible, the teacher tries to devise means to help the student reorder his thoughts. Removed from the process, he is inclined to think in terms of form aside from content. Should he decide, in the name of Order or Expediency, to impose a pre-determined form upon his students' raw material, he runs the risk of alienating his students from language. Pleasure in language may be lost, and with it the opportunity to see writing as a process of discovery.

Much of the graceless language we are confronted with comes as a direct result of student attempts to put together too much too soon, using someone else's format. Much of this writing is simply a reflection of the degree to which the student has become alienated from language which should be as naturally his as love. Susanne Langer ("The Lord of Creation," *Fortune*, January, 1944) writes, "The process of transforming all direct experience into imagery or into that supreme mode of symbolic expression, language, has so completely taken possession of the human mind that it is not only a special talent but a dominant, organic need." If this be so, then why should writing be considered such an unpleasant task by so many students?

In the opinion of this writer, there can be no pleasure in language in the classroom so long as students write and teachers grade in painful isolation from one another. Yet teacher involvement in the process of writing has all too often meant interference, a dictating of form or content, a coming in with red pencil in hand, an approach which tends to separate teacher from student, form from content, and ultimately, student from language.

We need to get involved in the process together, all together, to mutually re-discover that language lives, that the word is alive, that writing is a process of discovery.

The sort of teacher involvement I am advocating brings teacher and students together in exploring the problems we all have in common when we try to write. It means sharing the pleasure we all can experience through writing. It means a shift in emphasis from teacher-student to student-peer evaluation, and an opening up of the classroom to let in real problems, as opposed to those artificially set up to "train" the student into logic or to "prepare" him for entrance into some other institution.

As a poet and as a teacher I have come to see the creative process as a process of scattering, then bringing together of various parts into a new whole. One does not know beforehand what form that whole will take, but that is how discoveries are made, and that is what makes writing, or any other creative act, exciting. It is the excitement of writing creatively which needs to be restored to the English classroom.

What follows is not a course description, but rather an attempt to illustrate some of the discoveries I and my students made while becoming involved together in the process of writing.

Attempting to illustrate a process is a little like trying to communicate a color in braille. I comfort myself with what I say to students: "All writing assignments are impossible. Though we can summon things to us with words (which is miracle enough), the word can never be the thing, and since writing is a process of selection, always we are compelled to leave things out, and to fear we have left the 'wrong' things out." With this *a priori* limitation in mind I shall try to illustrate the value of "spontaneous" writing in the classroom, and to show how certain techniques of fiction can be used to teach a multi-purpose writing skill to many who have become alienated from language, as well as to those who love language.

The class I refer to in the paragraphs which follow is a three unit freshman transfer composition class made up of students who placed themselves.

The class met three times a week. During the first week, after arranging our seats in a kind of circle, we began our discussion of writing. From the beginning we agreed that writing is a very complex and difficult task. I explained to the students that all of the writing assignments would be impossible; that I would not be looking for the perfectly executed assignment, but that I would be most concerned to see that each person had grappled in his or her way with the problem posed by the assignment. "What is it that makes writing so frustrating and so painful?" was the subject of the first of a series of five to ten minute write-ins designed to help students recover the excitement of using language expressively.

I suggested the students write on one side of the paper only, and with a smooth ball point pen. Much of the frustration connected with writing comes because the mind moves so much faster than the hand. Pencils move too slowly, and the process of erasing stops the forward movement. Often what has been erased turns out to be useful alter on. It is less frustrating and more productive to scratch out and later revise.

I wrote along with the students. This helped me to discover more about my own processes, and it served the purpose of encouraging the students, and of keeping me in closer touch with what was happening to them. I tried to make the most of my own "mistakes" to *reinforce* the idea that we were not aiming for perfection. Spelling, sentence structure, punctuation were all matters to be considered on a final draft, but not for now. Since we were not aiming for perfection the students were soon freer in their writing, and at the same time, less hesitant in reading aloud what they had written. Sometimes it was fun, sometimes serious, often it was both at the same time.

One student's response to the question "What makes writing so painful?" provoked a very serious and stimulating discussion. She wrote, "Writing is difficult because everything you write down is there forever. When you *say* something you get feelings back right away, and it's easier to know how to respond. But writing is stating something—not being able to take anything back."

We discussed whether or not it is true that we can't take back what we say in writing. We decided that although it is not true, most people act as if it were true. And that is part of what makes writing painful. We tend to write every moment as if every one of our words were to be published and immortalized. And so long as we are wondering "Am I saying the right thing? Am I saying it the right way?" that is the object of our concentration, and not the subject we are writing about. Our powers of observation are cut off to the extent to which we internalize a voice of authority which constantly demands a perfect product, even on a first draft. Our motto became "Write first, think later. Don't try to be the writer and the critic at the same time."

I asked the students to write the next assignment on white, unlined paper. This assignment was to write for five minutes without stopping, on any subject. Those who "couldn't find" a subject were asked to write on just that. The aim was pure quantity. After five minutes we did a word count. The record was 193. The girl who won had written about being fired from her job. She had more than enough to say on that subject. The students "without subjects" began to realize that, in actuality, they had a great wealth of material. It was a question of tapping the source, the flow. Who hasn't failed at something? And, sadly, we always have much to say about our failures. We wrote for another five minutes to see if anyone could beat the record. No one did, but we discovered that no had had time to be bored or intimidated by the prospect of writing.

I asked the students to hold up their papers. Facing each other, they made the not so surprising observation that nearly everyone had written as though his paper were lined, and as though the object were, not to expand thoughts, but to conserve paper. Thereafter, continuing to use unlined paper, and resolving to be more expansive and wasteful, we placed the waste paper basket in the center of the room, and used it freely as we wrote.

Released from the bondage of spelling, punctuation, erasers, and lined paper we were free wheeling. The students themselves began to provide the in-class writing assignments. We wrote on all sorts of objects, both strange and commonplace, and often grappled with unanswerable questions. If a hungry student began furtively to peel an orange so that the pervasive smell of rind reached us long before the sight of the orange, we wrote about that. Nothing was irrelevant, and thus much of the attention, the best concentration, which ordinarily goes out the window or toward some other "distraction," was caught and held.

The next planned assignment was to "put the classroom on paper" the way a novelist or short story writer puts a room into a sentence or a paragraph. After we had written for five minutes I asked the students what problems they were encountering. By this time they were aware of the great number of possibilities, angles of vision, open to the writer in describing any object or scene. The problem, they said, was where to begin. As we analyzed this problem it became clear the real problem was not where to begin, but *to begin*. The discovery that they could find so much to say had stopped them. We discussed writing as a process of selection. Selecting means making decisions, and the more importance we attach to each decision the more painful and difficult it becomes. The tendency to attach undue importance to each decision is minimized once the distinction between a first draft and a finished piece is clearly realized.

Gradually the students came to realize that it is more effective, more efficient, and less painful to write three drafts rapidly, each time adding and/ or subtracting detail, rather than painstakingly attempting a polished, all inclusive piece the first time through. I suggested they concern themselves, not absolutely, but generally, with *what* they have to say on a first draft, with the *order* in which they say it on a second draft, and with *how* they say it on a third draft.

Constantly we *tell* students to revise, revise, but not until they have been through the process, not once, but a number of times, do they clearly see the value of what we are telling them. This is partly because students are all too inclined to treat a first draft like a final draft; to approach it at the last minute, and with great intensity, until they exhaust themselves half way through. Perhaps this is because teachers themselves have tended to ask for "first drafts" while looking for neatly structured outlines, perfect sentence structure, precise punctuation, and perfect spelling. For whatever reason, most students initially rebel at the thought of going through, what seems to them, the very tedious process of writing a second or third draft.

Too often, I think, teachers have acted under the fear or the assumption that students, left to their own devices, will write sloppy, disorganized papers. One has only to leave them to their own devices to discover that students are no more resistant to the mind's need for order than the rest of us, and that their desire for order is, in fact, very great. It then becomes the function of the teacher, not to leap in with a magic formula five paragraph theme to assure the student of what will please him, the teacher, but rather to help the student through the wilderness of his own thought, to encourage him to use language expansively until he discovers what it is he wished to give order to. Free of any pressure to pre-order his thoughts, the student can then experience the excitement of seeing form evolve out of content as his scattered thoughts come together into a new whole.

By the time the students caught on to the advantage of writing freely and of doing several drafts, we were already into more sophisticated assignments related to their reading of literature. Thus far I have mentioned only in-class writing assignments and related discussion. The students were, at the same time, reading short stories and poems outside of class. The first few out-of-class writing assignments simply required the students to react in a personal way, positively or negatively, to the literature assigned. Gradually the in-class and out-of-class assignments came together. For example, having attempted to put a room on paper ourselves, we examined the way writers of fiction accomplish this.

One in-class assignment was to write from memory a description of a character from one of the stories. We then went through the story line by line listing all concrete details in order to determine what had been left out, or perhaps of greater interest, what had been added, by each of us. The next out-of-class assignment was to describe a person so everyone in the class would either like or dislike him. As we reacted to each description it soon became clear that the most convincing pieces of writing were those in which the writer paid close attention to concrete detail, attempting to show rather than tell. Increasingly the students grew to trust one another to evaluate and criticize constructively. Their writing improved as they continued to write for an audience beyond themselves or their teacher.

At one point I read the students the first few pages of Kafka's *The Metamorphosis*, up to the point where Gregor's mother calls to him from the other side of the door. I then asked the students to finish the story as they saw fit. This led to some hilariously funny writing, but they were able to see the limitless possibilities which confront, and at the same time offer themselves to the writer of fiction. We discussed how and why Kafka might have made certain decisions as he wrote, and how writing decisions in general are made. We played with the idea of a metamorphosis, trying to decide how other characters we had encountered would have reacted had each, like Gregor, found himself transformed into an insect. Or what if Gregor had turned into an antelope instead of an insect? The students could readily envision many variations on a single theme. Perhaps the most important discovery they made while tackling this assignment was how much easier it is to write when one has hold of a plot or a theme interesting enough to be self-propelling.

The next step was to prepare for a longer, more formal, out-of-class paper. I suggested possible themes, but recommended that the students develop their own. They were free to write a formal essay or to try writing a short story. The only requirement was that the paper must relate to the literature assigned. A short story, for example, could be modeled on Kafka's *The Metamorphosis.*

I asked the students on a Friday to bring in a statement of theme for Monday. Though they had been quite good about doing assignments, when Monday came, less than two thirds of the students had done the assignment. I asked how much time each of them had spent worrying about the assignment in the midst of weekend activities. That was another matter. One girl estimated she had spent as many as twelve hours worrying about, not doing the assignment. I suggested we take five minutes to write a statement of theme. In five minutes the student who had spent twelve hours worrying about the assignment had written a statement satisfactory to me. She had given herself a far more difficult assignment than I had because she unconsciously assumed, despite all indications to the contrary, that she would be held to her statement, tied to this one decision. Instead of writing a statement of theme she was attempting to write the entire paper in her head—

a little like trying to put a puzzle together in one's head without looking at the pieces. I pointed out that an initial statement of theme should be simply a tool to explore with, and added, somewhat didactically, "He who postpones the assignment, does it a hundred times."

Next I asked those who had statements to begin their first drafts. I reminded them that a first draft would simply amount to getting the pieces of the puzzle out on the table. I suggested they write only one set of ideas or images per page on one side of the page in order to achieve greater mobility when the time came to put their ideas back together in new form. Those who did not yet have a statement of theme I asked to write for five minutes at a time on several potential themes suggested by other students. When a student found something he wanted to continue writing on, I suggested he pursue that.

Though not every student found his theme that day, nearly everyone discarded a few dead ends. One by one the students were discovering that they had themes of their own, and could develop them. I wanted them to understand, also, that certain themes, unanswered questions, run through our entire lives, and that in writing a single paper, one only begins to tap a major theme.

Increasingly the students were coming to find they did not want to stop writing after five or ten minutes, that writing for "five" minutes was a good way to begin, a way to get past that time just prior to writing when the mind rebels. At one point I asked a student if the five minute write-ins were helping him. "No," he replied, "I want to keep writing."

Before the papers were due the students brought them into class for criticism. I suggested they divide into groups of three so that each student would have an audience of two. Each student read his paper aloud and was given general criticism. Then I asked them to exchange papers and to make specific comments in writing. I asked that the papers be typed, not just because a typed paper makes a better impression on the reader, but because I am convinced that typing a paper improves the quality of writing. The pen may be friendlier in the beginning, but typing a paper finishes it.

Despite student enthusiasm and the opportunity for much criticism beforehand, the papers were not all A's, and I would have been happier had I not had to put a grade on some of them. Some of the students had a problem with sentence structure until the very end, and I do not mean anywhere to imply that some of them would not have benefited from a grammatical approach. I will say that much of the rough sentence structure I encountered in the beginning had become smoother by the end of the course. I could particularly see a change in the writing of those who began with the sort of cramped style so evident in the piece of student writing first quoted in this paper. "Correcting" such writing is nearly impossible, and any attempt to do so is likely to produce more pain than anything else. It is not enough to *tell* such a student to be concrete, to give examples. She needs to discover the examples she needs by learning to explore ideas freely through writing.

I was generally pleased with the final papers the students turned in and also with the improvement I could see in their in-class writing. But more than that I was pleased to hear some of them say they were, for the first time, enjoying writing, that they were even beginning to write letters! I was pleased, not because I think learning must always be "fun," but because I know that one does more of what one enjoys and by doing more, one becomes better, and so enjoys doing more. A new and positive cycle is begun. Writing is, and always will be, one of the most diffiucult of human endeavors. This we understood and accepted from the beginning. The discovery, for some of the students, was that writing could be pleasurable and rewarding. . . .

The greatest problem I encountered throughout the course was that of evaluation. I postponed grading by making comments rather than corrections on the short out-of-class papers. In making comments I tried to re-enforce the positive, rather than emphasize errors. In addition, I told the students that I would, at any time, accept a paper to be graded, should anyone wish to know where he stood grade-wise. This worked for the better students who were more readily able to move from expressive to communicative language. But one semester is hardly enough time for the weaker student to make such a transition. It would have been better had these students been allowed to continue writing expressively without having to "get it altogether" for a grade. The course would have been more effective for all concerned, and more readily adaptable to individual needs, had it been offered on a credit, no-credit basis.

It could be asked at this point "Where and how will the student learn his basic grammar, his spelling and punctuation?" It is by no means my intent to discount this very real and valid concern. I can only say that if the student has not acquired his basic English in twelve years of schooling, it would be presumptuous to think that as college teachers we have the magic to teach him all this in one or two semesters. But we can, by *allowing* him to find pleasure in language, by encouraging him to expand his thoughts until they become interesting to him, help him to find the motivation to pursue the more mechanical aspects of language.

On the last day of class I asked the students to write for five minutes in response to the following question: "Has your attitude toward writing changed at all since the beginning of the semester?" I think the following anonymous response best illustrates how writing can be a process of discovery.

> Not really—If I have a good topic I get interested—If I don't it's just another assignment—I've always enjoyed writing when I'm interested in the subject. I've become a lot more critical of my writing. I guess my attitude has changed—I now feel that what I write must be a total expression of me—rather than just writing to fulfill the assignment—True, I am writing to fulfill this assignment but I'm also saying things I mean rather than a lot of the bullshit I'm capable of producing.

Toward Competence and Creativity in an Open Class

LOU KELLY

There's lots of optimistic talk these days about opening up the college classroom. The disparaging commentaries are also coming in. Not only from teachers committed to classical rhetoric and traditional grammar. Disillusioned innovators are publicizing their failures.

In *The New York Times*, July 22, 1971 (p. 33, col. 3), we hear of a man who bestowed upon his class the Rhetoric of Freedom. He read an excerpt from Jerry Farber's "The Student as Nigger" on the first day and delivered a sermon for the damned on the last day. The enslaved had not written up to the expectations of their liberator. In *College English*, December, 1971 (p. 293), we find a gloomy postmortem: "In a student-directed course it is the blind leading the blind."

At the end of the second year of a pilot study in an open approach to Rhetoric at the University of Iowa, we still face many problems, we still have many unanswered questions. We know we have not found the easy way out of frustration and boredom generations of freshmen have known in English 101, Communication Skills and Rhetoric. We know an open class is not achieved by casually deciding to try something new you've heard about. You can't walk in the first day, announce you're making no assignments and setting no requirements, then sit down and wait for something exciting and impressive to happen. The teachers who try, then denounce, the open class as another romantic educational myth may not be assuming their rightful share of responsibility for what doesn't happen. Maybe they invite their students *not* to learn. Maybe it's teachers—not students—who fail. Because they plunge into their little experiments with no self-examination, no clear notion of what we must give when we ask students to create something to replace the old ways we'd like to discard.

College English, 34 (February 1973), pp. 644-660. Copyright © 1973 by the National Council of Teachers of English. Edited by Lou Kelly especially for publication here. Reprinted by permission of the publisher and the author.

Twenty-one Iowa teachers know the agonizing it takes, alone and together, to achieve what we believe in. But we all agree with our new Writing Supervisor, Cleo Martin: in the open class the low days are lower and the high days are higher. And, we still believe we're into a better way of living.

My own convictions evolved from an experience where I was trapped—between departmental "standards" and all my despairing, sometimes hostile, students. For them the old ways of teaching composition meant failure. The freshmen were getting D's and F's on every theme they wrote for Rhetoric. Most of the sophomores had already flunked the departmental theme exam after completing one or two semesters of Rhetoric; the others were failing their first literature course because they were writing failing papers. The upperclassmen were failing a course because they had encountered a professor who not only required but graded papers. And the graduate students were living with the threat of failure as they struggled with their dissertations. For all these students, learning to write meant getting through a teacher's drudging assignments so they could turn out a finished product that would pass somebody's inspection. They rarely, if ever, thought of writing as human communication. For them, it was just a phony game, played for the chips called grades.

Working with these students changed my concept of myself as teacher, changed my concept of teaching composition. To put a little joy and a lot of reality into *my* teaching, into *their* learning—into *our* hours together—gradually became the goals of the Writing Lab at Iowa. And the voices I heard there, year after year, convinced me that the students' own language and the experiences—external and internal—that they wish to share make the best content for composition. Or to say it another way: the content of composition is the writer—the self that is revealed, thoughtfully and feelingly, in our own language, with our own voice. And while students are doing that for someone who responds to and questions what they're saying, they'll learn to analyze, limit, organize, and support whatever they write.

Our open-class project began and continues with teachers, experienced and inexperienced, who are somewhat or highly disillusioned with textbook-oriented, assignment-centered, teacher-dominated classes. We want to turn the sterile academic classroom into a place where everybody will *enjoy* sharing their knowledge and skills and opinions with other human beings. We want the class to become a *community of learners*. We want students to become responsible for their own learning. We want them to see writing as human behavior. Like talking. Talking to say whatever they are concerned about—whatever they think is worth saying.

And we believe people learn to write better by *talking*—in class and on paper—using the linguistic skills and the rhetorical strategies they have been learning and using, learning *by* using, all their lives. Young children not only learn to talk by living in a family of talkers. They learn to use words in meaningful contexts, they learn to accomplish things with words, by using what they have already learned in personal encounters with their families—with the group and with individuals in the group. These experiences prepare them to cope, with varying degrees of success, with the people and the situations they encounter in the world they discover beyond the family. On playground and street, in the homes of playmates, and at planned and unplanned gatherings of friends and strangers, they relate and interact with others in various ways, but in almost every instance they also use words to convey what they are thinking and feeling. And each experience helps them develop more competence in using language to connect with others.

That is learning through living. And I think learning to write at all educational levels should be an extension of that living-learning process. For it is the kind of learning that becomes a significant addition to the continuum of experience that is a person, that is a life. It is the kind of learning we value most. Because it changes us, our attitudes and our behaviors in some significant way. And that change has a lasting effect upon us.

The open class at Iowa attempts to help students experience that kind of learning. It is not an exercise in empty idealism, but a natural practical way for people to develop more competence in sending and receiving messages, oral and written. The help the teacher offers and the feedback students give each other are always part of somebody's effort to convey what they want to convey to the class, that is, the audience.

We are trying to make Rhetoric an extension of our learners and what they have already learned, what they have already experienced, instead of an extension of the teachers and their superior and special knowledge and experience. There are no lectures, handbooks, or class discussions "to cover" rhetorical principles or linguistic theories; no workbooks or programmed texts or learning systems "to clean up" the grammar, the misspelling, and the punctuation errors; no required readers "to supply" models for analysis and emulation or to generate ideas for significant papers; no prescribed assignments "to produce" a required number of specified kinds of papers.

Instead of all or any of that, we ask our students to share their own knowledge and skills, their own ideas and opinions, their own feelings—whatever they want to share with teacher and classmates. And that throws us into the endless debate over what the content of the course should be. A debate I do not expect to win. Not in my lifetime. Given the elitist humanism of professors of English and Rhetoric, any approach that makes the students' ideas more important than the teacher's, anyone who claims the resources the students bring with them are more important to their learning than the superior resources the teacher can provide, is bound to be labeled lowbrow. If not anti-intellectual. Because, they say, students have no ideas; students can't think; class discussions die in trivia and boredom when teacher does not feed in some structure, when teacher and text do not feed in some "college level" subject matter for discussion.

But we believe the knowledge our students bring with them, though it may not be as extensive or as academic as ours, is equally valid. Though they may not understand and cannot analyze all their experience, it is just as full of implications as ours is. So we stifle every impulse to fill the hour with our ideas when their talk—in class or on paper—seems simplistic or meaningless to us. Instead, we ask ourselves if they trust us and each other enough to share what they really think. And in discussions and papers that may sound superficial, in chatter that could become boring, we listen for insights into what each person's particular experience means to that person; we search for ways to help everybody see the implications they seem to be missing. If we are intent on *learning our students* instead of teaching them, if we want to know what's going on inside their heads instead of wanting to fill their heads with what we know, we never tune them out. Someone's frequent or occasional comment and all the nonverbal signals each person is always sending out become tiny pieces of a human jigsaw puzzle. And day after day, we try to fit it all together. So we can *see and respond* to the whole person. So we can *hear and respond* to the ideas everybody is trying to express. So we can help them express their ideas more fluently, more clearly, and more forcefully. So we can help them extend language, their ideas, and the self each of them is trying to express.

Instead of giving assignments to be graded by a teacher, we attempt to engage each one of our writers in a meaningful dialogue by asking them to talk on paper—in their own everyday language, about anything they want to talk about. The students begin cautiously, of course. No matter what we say, they still hear The Voice of Authority. They still feel The Threat of The Superior Intellect. They still see The Stranger who professes to know what The Educated need to know. And they hope they can psyche us out early, so they'll know how hard they must work to ace the course or merely get by.

But if we can convince them that we're listening for the sound of their voices instead of looking for errors or evaluating their ideas as we read what they write, if we can give them non-threatening feedback instead of normative grades, they will gradually begin to believe that we are receiving and trying to understand the message they are sending us. And they will begin to see us as a person who wants to know what they think and feel. Then the vast distance between student and teacher, though it may never be breached, is diminished. Dialogues that begin with skepticism—with student testing teacher, wondering if the whole approach is a gimmick, yet wanting to trust and be trusted—move along with refreshing candor. And they are soon talking freely about self and others, about the world they live in and the people they live with. Then we hear their keen awareness or their dull indifference, their egotism and confidence or their self-doubt and uncertainty, their passive acceptance or their constant questioning of the values they grew up on. We see some of the inner conflict, we feel some of the alienation and despair—whatever it is that fills the heads and hearts of our students. They are trying to analyze and understand their own personal problems, trying to search out the answers to their own questions, trying to express the complexities of their own lives.

It takes a lot of psychic strength to respond to that kind of writing. The teacher's comments can no longer be dominated by corrections, or by suggestions for turning an F paper into a C paper or a C paper into an A paper. Instead, we, too, must ask questions. Questions to help our writers find their own unique answers. Questions to move all of them toward writing that is a special way of defining, discovering, and knowing self—and others. But that does not mean you must turn your office into a confessional booth or try to become a swivel chair therapist. Hearing and responding to others is, I hope, natural human behavior which, I hope, we all engage in whenever we encounter another human being.

But hearing and responding every class day to forty or sixty—a *hundred*?—individual human beings is obviously impossible. At least for most of us. When we read of teachers who say they do it, when we listen to them tell how they do it, most of us feel like the young teacher who spoke quite despairingly at the evaluation session of a recent national convention. She had come with the hope of hearing, of finding something that would make her a better teacher. She was returning home with the feeling that all she had heard about successful teaching depended not upon anything she could learn and utilize in her classroom, but upon the personal attributes of one teacher. Though I admire and congratulate the great among us, their expertise, their genius, need not diminish the rest of us. For the teacher's greatness lies not in what he or she teaches, but in what the students learn.

They arrive unresponsive. Anticipating our required course with unloving words and equally expressive groans. But they are our only *indispensable* resource. We must let them, and help them, bring the realities of their own lives into the classroom. We must let them, and help them, respond to each other.

Because I have spent most of my teaching life working in one-to-one conferences with students, I believe any attempt to achieve an open class must begin with personal dialogue (talking on paper) between the teacher and each person in the class. It is, I think, the best way to let them know that we accept them as persons of worth, whose ideas and feelings are worth expressing, whose imperfections do not diminish them or their ideas. Our response to each person can give the initial sense of freedom and fulfillment that is so important, perhaps essential, to achieving competence and creativity in writing or speaking.

But every writer and every speaker needs an audience beyond the teacher, needs many responses to whatever they have to say on paper and in class. Everybody needs to be seen and heard by the group they are members of, needs to feel that they are identifiable and worthwhile members of that group. And that, I fear, shall never happen for all our students unless we abandon the old ways of class discussion.

Going from neat, straight rows-of-students with the teacher-at-center-front to teacher-sitting-with-students in a circle of chairs or around a ring of tables is an improvement *only* if all the people sitting in those chairs are really talking and listening to each other. While trying to face that challenge at Iowa, we are asking some questions that suggest some of the fundamental changes the open class hopes to achieve:

How many persons (or what proportion) participate, frequently and extensively, in my class discussion?

How many participate only when I directly invite them to?

How many really get involved?

Do I talk more than anybody else? more than everybody else?

Do I *direct* the discussion? Do I ask the questions and make the responses that take the class in the direction I want it to go? to the conclusion I want it to reach?

Do my students address most of their comments to me?

Do they raise their hands because it's just a habit or because I intimidate them?

Can my students talk freely when I am the discussion leader?

We believe teachers must learn to sit down and shut up. So students can get to know each other. So they can share what they know with each other. So they can learn from the feedback they give each other.

We keep no pedagogical secrets from our students because in the open class the pedagogical process is not the exlusive responsibility of the teacher. The distinctions between teaching and learning that are clear to everybody in the traditional classroom are not so clear; in fact, they gradually disappear as a class develops its own direction, its own structure and content. For the teacher also learns and each learner also teaches.

We never lose teacher-identity, we never become "just another student," but we see ourselves, and our students perceive us, as a participating member of the group, not the voice of authority that controls the group. Like all other members of the group, we give of our ideas, our knowledge, our competence. We give of self. By responding. To each person and to the group. But we never forget that in the open class the power lies in listening.

What we say and do on a particular day develops not from our past teaching experience but from whatever is happening in class on that day. Instead of following the sequence of assignments that worked *last* year, we respond to the experiences—external and internal—that students talk about, in class and on paper, day by day, *this* year. We respond by sharing a bit of our experience that seems relevant or by asking questions that will help everybody better understand their own ideas and the ideas of others, questions that will help them express their ideas more clearly and more forcefully. But we are always trying *not* to dominate everything that happens.

Very few students are prepared for that kind of learning. They arrive expecting to learn only from the teacher, sure that everything that is said in a classroom is a performance for the teacher, to be praised or criticized by the teacher. To most of them, class discussion means showing off what they know so they will get a good grade. The ones who have learned to do that talk a lot. The ones who haven't don't. Because they don't want to be compared with their glib and confident classmates. Because they are afraid of sounding stupid. When they try to put what's going on inside them onto paper, we hear the fears of the quiet ones and we get a glimpse behind the masks the easy talkers wear.

When I was sitting in class I could not express my feelings clearly. I just wasn't at ease. I felt trapped in a cage afraid to respond to anything around.

. . .

How can I write honestly about myself when I don't know who I am? I would like to know more why's. If something goes wrong, does that mean I shouldn't have done it or was it because I sinned the day before?

. . .

I'm really bothered with having to write things down and letting someone else read them or show them to the class. I feel that what I have written isn't good enough. I'm afraid if I say something wrong I will be laughed at. I don't want to be laughed at so I try to act like someone else and not be myself.

. . .

I like to see and hear what other people have to say before I show myself to them. I like to know where another person stands so that I might act in a way that would keep me up and even with that person. This I find is sometimes very hard to do.

. . .

My first time away from home. Watching my parents turn their backs and walk away. Watching security and guidance and love walk away. *God* am I lonely.

. . .

When Bill, Murphy and Melvin were talking about being black, I felt so ignorant. I had prepared a little speech but I just couldn't say anything. I feel so insignificant when I hear people talking about important world issues.

. . .

Even though no one knows you're on academic probation, you feel as though everyone is staring at you and thinking "boy are you stupid" and this makes me afraid to talk because then someone would know for sure that I am dumb and on probation.

. . .

You can never really know a person. A person can put on all kinds of fronts for you. You can dig a person for a lengthy time and still never know him. A person puts forth what he wants to put forth in any manner he chooses at any time.

To help students come to know each other, to help them come to trust each other, we begin by learning names and faces. Then for a day or two we visit together in groups of three to five persons. The teacher moves from group to group. Mostly listening but sometimes responding. Perhaps mentioning something somebody in the group has said in their first writing.

During the first few days I try to chat a moment with each person in the class. To express my delight in something he or she has written. To express my concern about some troubling thought shared with me. Or to ask why this writer has not written anything for this class.

Moving students from social chatter to more academic matters can be quite natural if, after the first or second day, the groups for conversation become "task" groups. For several days the tasks can be anything to ease the uneasiness, anything to fill the strained silence with people talking to each other. But it's important, no later than the second week, to talk about the concept of an open class. They need to understand the kind of learning we want them to experience; we need to understand their attitudes toward the approach. So we talk about their previous learning experiences and any misconceptions they seem to have about the open class we are asking them to help us create. And we talk about tentative goals and expectations.

From the beginning each person must try to understand the responsibilities that come with the freedom that comes with the open class. Though we make no *required* assignments for the whole class, no one is free to do nothing, no one is free *not* to learn, no one is free *not* to respond to classmates and teacher. If the dialogues do not develop, if there is no ongoing interchange of ideas, the class is not open. Instead it is a collection of closed mouths, closed ears, closed minds, and closed hearts.

But if we believe our students possess the youthful virtue Erik Erikson calls fidelity, then we can assume with confidence that they will respond to our faith in them and our concern for them. Not everyday, of course. Some will not respond on many days. Sometimes it may take several weeks, perhaps a whole term, to break through the walls that some people bring with them. But if we bring with us a full commitment to the concept of an open class, and patience—from a source that never runs dry; if we can live with the recurring frustration that closes in on the days when nothing's happening for nobody, and the recurring feeling of impotence that could be dispelled in an instant by simply asserting our authority; if our egos can stand the persistent, uncomforting feeling that we have not yet achieved what we hope to achieve, then we can keep on responding to the unresponsive ones. And eventually, either teacher or classmate will ask a question or make a suggestion that will evoke a response that will bring them into the *community of learners* the class is or hopes to become. But until and after that happens, the trusting teacher must also be a demanding teacher.

Usually the hour ends before we can consider all the questions and suggestions that grow out of class talk. And just as often it's obvious that nobody has the quick and easy answer or an obvious plan of action. Again it's time to form small task groups. The task: to explore some aspect of the situation being discussed, to search together for some answers to some of our questions. Next day, or a week or two later, the group can report their findings to the class and the class can ask more questions. We may never decide on the "right" answers, but shallow conversation becomes serious discussion as we explore the possibilities.

I hope it's clear that our small group work is not an attempt to turn the class into an encounter group, where all or most of the emphasis is on discovering and expanding self through *intensive* group experience. Fifty minutes a day, three or four times a week for one or two semesters gives us *ex*tensive time, not the kind needed for a group brought together solely for psychosocial purposes. Though I am obviously committed to an approach that centers on self and others, though I believe our best writing comes from intense awareness of self and a highly developed sensitivity to others, in the open class for rhetoric *that* emphasis can always be coordinated with the writing and talking students do in response to each other and the teacher.

Though every class sometimes wants and needs to analyze what's happening, the small groups are not for the purpose of *studying* group performance or interaction. All the research that has been completed and all the scholarly and popular books that have been published on group dynamics, communications theory, and interpersonal relations are certainly relevant. But if that became the content of the course, the emphasis could no longer be on each person and the group *talking*, in class and on paper, about their own ideas and concerns.

Breaking the class into small groups is only a means for releasing more talk, from everybody, and for giving each person maximum feedback on the ideas he expresses. Analyzing and evaluating group interaction is only a means of asking why we are not achieving what we are tyring to achieve. Mastering all the popular techniques of group interaction might make me a better composition teacher; it might make my students better composers. But whether or not we pursue that interest, we can go on interacting with each other. As a relating, communicating psychosocial being called teacher, I spend a lot of time trying to relate to and communicate with a lot of psychosocial beings called students. Which means, I hope, that we have learned *to ask each other why* when we feel we are not getting through to each other, as persons or as a group; *to ask each other how* we can break through the barriers that separate us from each other.

Any approach to composition that begins with free writing elicits one sure question: how do you get them to turn the corner to writing (or speaking) that is thematic, analytical, tightly organized, and fully substantiated?

To answer that question I must first be repetitious. Begin by *hearing and responding* to what each person is saying. I make no corrections, no comments on how the ideas are expressed or developed, no long response of any kind on the early writing. Maybe my Lab students' negative reactions to the teacher comments on the papers they bring with them have made me over-anxious. No matter how kind or cogent I sound to me, I wonder how the student will read me. Would any of them ever spend as much time thinking about my long comments as I would spend writing them? There's also the problem of *my* time. When students are talking to me on paper, I want to read every word everyone has written before I see them again. I want to hear how everyone is responding to the first days of class and to me. But I say enough in class and on paper to let them know that I'm connecting what they write with the persons I see and talk with in class, that I want to know each person better, that I enjoy their writing because I can visualize a unique human being and hear the sound of a unique human voice as I read the pages they fill with words. And I ask questions. First, the questions that say I want to hear more. Then, the ones that will, I hope, lead each person to a competent and creative telling of his or her own thoughts and feelings.

In the guidelines we offer young teachers the focus moves from "Voice" and "Perceptions" and "Values" to "Questions" which help writers see that the rhetorical structures many texts and syllabi prescribe are not unlike their own natural thought processes. But we do not make assignments on certain days to "teach" those concepts. Instead, we introduce linguistic and rhetorical principles whenever somebody's response to a piece of writing shared with the class, or somebody's question or dissatisfaction with their own writing, makes a little lesson by the teacher or a reference to the text relevant and therefore meaningful.

The traditional patterns of organization are easy "to cover" in the open class because much of the talking on paper that students do provides examples. They relate experiences or describe processes that can be classified as narration or time sequences; they describe people or places; they explain the cause of their joy or despair; they compare and contrast what's happening to them now with what happened to them last year. For some, of course, everything comes out hazy and confused. But for almost all of them, if it's something they are *ready* to share, what they say is forceful and coherent. When they *know* what they want to say, there is no hassle about organization or content. Each is part of their knowing.

To make the students' writing a part of the dialogues going on in class, we begin "publishing" excerpts or whole pieces as soon as possible. But I never share a piece of writing with the class without the writer's consent. And I never discuss writing as if I am grading it. I do not ask What do you think of the Introduction? or Does the writer include a sufficient number of representative examples to establish credibility? or What's wrong with this paper? Those questions and many others may be considered in personal conferences or in small groups later in the term, but we never talk in class about published writing unless someone, including the teacher, wants to respond to something somebody has said. Like, I know what you mean because this is what happened to me . . . or No, man, that's *not* the way it is because . . .

To ditto the lone A paper to show everybody else what the teacher wants, or to distribute inadequate papers so one student can tell another what's wrong with the writing or how to improve it, is asking students to talk to each other as teachers have always talked to them. It's asking them to evaluate each other as they think we would. It's asking them to compete with each other as they try to meet prescribed academic standards, as they try to fulfill teacher-imposed requirements. They learn far more, I think, by responding to each other's ideas as they would in a nonthreatening situation outside of class.

All students—the brilliant and the slow, the enthusiastic and the in-different, the aggressive and the meek—need to be assured that they know something that teacher and class will value. So we ask them to write and talk first about what they know best, what they enjoy most. I have never known a student who could not choose something that class and teacher knew very little about. Which means students become teachers. Explaining their special knowledge and skill. Answering the questions asked as they talk or as they read something they have written. Restating sentences that are not clear. Seeing the need for logical order if the audience cannot follow what they are saying. And when somebody says, "But I don't see what you mean," they can add some concrete details or visual images that will help us see what they are trying to explain. And when somebody says, "But I just don't get it. What is it really like?" they try to think of an analogy that will help us understand. And sometimes, even the ones labeled slow come up with a striking metaphor any writer would be proud of. When convinced that some-body wants to learn what *they know*, they learn what we want to teach them.

Wha'd'y'mean is the question our students ask each other most fre-quently if their writing is full of vague and ambiguous words or if their opin-ions are always stated in meaningless generalizations. When the person chal-lenged cannot come up with a satisfactory answer, a classmate may be able to help. Or the teacher can respond with a quick and easy lesson on defini-tion or supporting evidence. Or we can cite books, periodicals, or people who might be helpful in the search for answers that will help one person or the whole class extend and develop their ideas in well-supported essays.

When somebody makes a generalization, in class or on paper, that is obviously a strong conviction, an attitude fixed in and by their own experi-ence, our natural response to that question is an attempt to analyze what they've said. Which means they'll either state some supporting reasons for their opinion or they'll be going beyond their easy generalization to analyze what they think. They'll be organizing their thoughts. In the natural give and take of conversation, they'll be setting up a plan for an essay.

Instead of trying to teach everybody how to make outlines or giving them assignments that designate the way they must order their ideas, instead of giving them external forms to fill, we raise questions that we hope will help our students analyze and understand their own lives, their own beliefs, their own values. Questions that only they can answer. And with their answers they build coherent verbal structures; out of the meanings and the relationships they find, they learn to analyze, organize, and substantiate their ideas.

And they learn—through their own writing—that their attitudes toward self, subject, and audience can control (that is, help them, sometimes quite unconsciously, organize) whatever they want to say; that they can create the sound of their own voices on paper by re-creating their experiences—external and internal—with facts and details so graphic, with images so visual, that readers will *see* what they mean. They learn through the ongoing interaction with teacher and classmates without which an open class cannot be.

If we can break through the students' concept of English teacher as corrector-grader-judge of writing and writer, they can then see us as teacher-editor, the person who can help them learn to say, with clarity and force, whatever they want to say. Then they see how we can help them achieve a smoother flow of words, how we can help them see the implications of their own ideas and experiences, how we can help them develop a strong and clear voice that diverse, even hostile, readers will hear and understand.

For most people, talking on paper eliminates the phoniness that sets the tone for a lot of published and unpublished writing. It also exposes the stuffy and pompous writing many students think teachers want. They can hear the difference between the dull, dead papers that attempt to sound academic and the sound of their own voices on paper. But they learn to write graceful instead of cumbersome prose, they learn to write with clarity and force, only by working with their own writing. For me that means reading their writing aloud. First, so the class can hear and respond to what the writer is saying. Then, in student-teacher conferences or small nonthreatening groups, we talk about specific ways to make the ideas in specific pieces move from page to reader's mind. When the emphasis is always on *hearing* what they write, they become sensitive to the patterns and rhythms of their sentences. They also learn to spot the repetition that bores, the vagueness and ambiguity that confuses, the generalization that weakens, and the simplistic, limited point of view that expresses no awareness of how readers may disagree.

As writers cover a wide range of thought and feeling in their dialogues with teacher and classmates, they discover, if they don't already know, that they have many voices. They hear them as they read their writings aloud. And they learn that the voice that "comes naturally" in a given situation controls *what* and *how* we write about that situation. They learn from their own writing that they can define and enlarge their resources of self-expression by exploring and expanding all the possibilities that lie within the *self* each of them is or is becoming. And in their own unique way, within the limits of their own linguistic competence, they are beginning to develop their own personal style.

But the complex process of putting words together to say what we think and feel does not include spelling and punctuation and "correct" usage. We have not thrown out those social conventions. We have simply put them where they belong—in a totally separate and final stage of the human (or academic) activity that ends in a paper for somebody to read. We call that final stage *copyreading*. Our student writers learn "correctness," not from a book of rules, but by building their own Copyreading Guides with examples from their own writing.

If reading the papers your students write is a drudge instead of a joy, perhaps you should explore the possibilities for creative interaction the open class offers. When students are free to write about what's going on inside their own heads instead of hacking out 500-word themes, when everything they write is part of a dialogue with other human beings, the teacher's homework is not the boring, endless grind it used to be.

What would happen if I talked on paper the way I talk on the street? I somehow think of "blackmail" against me. Especially from English teachers.

. . .

When one is thinking, he shares his thoughts with no one but himself. When he has to put these thoughts down on paper for someone else to read, he tries to change them so that the other person will like him. It's almost impossible to put down on paper just what I think and not have my thoughts degraded.

. . .

When engaged in a conversation that I enjoy, the words just flow into sentences. This is so because I know what I want to say and without hardly thinking about it, it just comes out. But with writing, I sit and think about what I want to say and it always comes out wrong. Because it's not the real me. It's the me that has been conditioned through twelve years of school to form sentences the right way, to make sure spelling is correct, to make sure all punctuation is perfect. When I'm concentrating on these things my ideas just don't come out on paper like they do in conversation.

. . .

In high school if I liked the subject—Trig or Biology or Chemistry—I would look into the whys and wherefores of problems and see how the masterminds developed their hypotheses. But English was always a drag. I just didn't dig all those dumb-ass poets and all that hidden meaning. It was always the same old shit. My senior year was the worst because it was all those old English writers trying to write all that *elegant* shit. Now that I think about it, my junior year was worst because the whole year was spent on poems. *God* do I hate poems. I hate English and everyone keeps making me take it.

. . .

I've been watching everyone else as we sit here writing and they all have at least two pages. Do you really mean we can stop when we have nothing else to say?

. . .

I'm sweating something furiously writing this. As though I'm working in art. Letting myself go. Free as a bird. It's great. I can't believe how wound up I am. It's like racing against something or someone, going faster than I can get the words on paper. I feel like I'm being rushed— by myself. And I grow impatient trying to continue because I want to say so much.

. . .

When I was a little girl, I would always dream of going to faraway places . . . exotic countries. . . . Sometimes I would dream of going to a place where the people were living on clouds. These people were dressed in beautiful costumes and were handing out candy to all the boys and girls. Whenever I wanted to be near the water, I would turn on the television dream set in my head and be on a beach, wading in the water and building sand castles. Sometimes I would feed the birds on the beach and talk with them. After a while though, my dreams would end because I had to finish my math or do some chores around the house.

. . .

A patient at the University Hospital. This cat is nuts; he's sitting there having a debate with the opposition and there is no opposition. I went over and rapped with him. This cat thinks I'm a member of the House of Representatives. Man, we're debating whether or not 18-year-olds should be able to vote in major elections and I win.

Now he's a pastor and he's preaching to me about not running away from my master. If he calls me a nigger I don't know what I'll say. I think I better switch subjects before he gets out of hand. What can I change to? The cat's well educated so anything would probably be okay. Think. Girls! No, too old. I guess I better go; it's almost suppertime anyway.

Mom was just cracking her side all the time I was talking to him.

. . .

I'm sitting here trying to think of something that I have convictions about. But nothing is coming; I just feel null and empty. Is man capable of ever feeling nothing? Possibly I'm proving in these sentences that he cannot. When for a second I felt that I was thinking and feeling nothing, I suddenly started coming up with thoughts. It would be some accomplishment to be able to create nothingness in our minds. Like a vacuum. To flush everything out. To ease the mind of trouble, worry, and frustration. To momentarily establish peace and calm.

. . .

I'm confused. I wonder at what stage in a person's life he stops asking the questions and starts receiving the answers. I'm trying to establish the values that are really important and relevant to me. But about the time I decide what is most important, things change. I meet new people and experience new situations, then I change my mind.

. . .

You can learn by being helped—shown another way. But you must have the freedom to accept or reject that other way, or to modify it to fit you own style.

. . .

When I was learning to ride and race a motorcycle, a friend of mine showed me a better way to hold the clutch lever while starting the cycle. I was holding it back with my whole hand, at least the full four fingers. That made starting awkward, because as soon as the starting flag drops you must accelerate as quickly as you can and still keep the bike under control. Which means hanging on with both hands. And that's hard to do if you have a good grip in only one hand. My friend showed me that it is better to grip with three fingers and use my index finger to encircle the hand grip. I tried that way and it was better. But then I tried it using just two fingers on the clutch lever. That was better—for me. But not for him because he had shorter fingers. My friend helped me, even though I already had my own way. A poor way, but it was a place to be helped from. When he showed me his way, I tried it, found it better, adopted and adapted it. Then it was my way.

Can that kind of learning take place in this classroom? I'm skeptical. But hopeful.

Whatever level of competence your students have, whatever "track" the entrance exams place them in, I believe they will respond, and learn, in an open class—if you can engage them in student-student dialogues and student-teacher dialogues. But they won't learn unless we who would teach them start where they are. They can't understand new ideas unless they can relate them to their old ideas. They can't develop new attitudes and skills unless they can fit them into the whole set of attitudes and skills they bring with them.

The least competent may need to try to talk on paper two or three times a week for a full semester before they can fill a page with ease and confidence. But when teacher or classmate asks Why or What do you mean, they, too, can give clear and forceful answers—if they believe we really want to hear their answers. And if everybody becomes involved in finding the answers to the questions raised about the experiences shared, we do not have to "teach" them how to organize and support their ideas. They will learn to—experientially—in their dialogues with teacher and each other.

But changing the way we think and talk is a slow, sometimes painful, process. Some students may need a third semester of talking and writing in an open class. In fact, I believe we should provide the opportunities for them to continue the dialogues begun in English 101 in every course we offer. If we don't, college, like high school, will be little more than a place where they collect credits toward graduation, a place where they will again be denied the experiences that are essential to everyone's development as a thinking, feeling *literate* human being.

I like to think—perhaps only hope—that the open class offers a new direction—a new hope—for all people who dread freshmen English, especially the ones who might otherwise fail the course or drop out in frustration and despair because what they are being "taught" has little or no meaning for them. For I believe they will never learn what they need to know by sitting through lectures or class discussions dominated by the teacher and a few of their classmates; they will never learn to put their thoughts and feelings onto paper by filling blanks in workbooks and programmed texts; they will never know the joy of writing for others if they spend their class hours with learning systems and learning machines that provide "individualized" instruction in lonely carrels. We must reject all the software and hardware that offer us new or old ways of *pouring* grammar or rhetoric or great ideas into the student's head. We must permit, we must help *all* our students bring the reality of their own lives, their own language, into the classroom. No book can tell us how to do it. Nobody can answer all our questions about the open class. With the human resources our students bring with them, with the human situations that develop within the group, we make whatever we can. For teaching is a creative act.

The skeptical but hopeful writer quoted earlier offered another apt description of the kind of learning we hope for in all our writing classes:

As I browsed through a magazine yesterday, a full-page color photo of Sister Corita's striking painting of a Disraeli quote stopped me: "From the people and for the people all springs and all must exist."

Since I saw the quote first as a picture, I saw it as "From the people all springs." And I thought—all people are necessary for anything to develop. Or, for something to develop you need all people. Then I asked, why do you need all people? And I knew it was because all people see things differently and react differently to what they see.

Then I started thinking about our class and how each person is different and carries around with him a different set of thoughts. But all of us, all people, are interdependent on the thoughts that each expresses. It's like each person pulling something out of a box and offering it for consideration as part of a developing idea. So each person, all people, are responsible for everyone else's ideas. And the only way ideas can develop or change quickly is for all people to express their thoughts.

After thinking all that, I realized I am afraid of you all. Then I thought maybe someone is afraid of me. I am part of someone's fear. Which means I am inhibiting him and therefore I am inhibiting myself. I am hindering someone's development and therefore I am hindering my own development. . . .

Writing, Inner Speech, and Meditation

JAMES MOFFETT

Writing and meditating are naturally allied activities. Both are important for their own sake, and through each people can practice the other. Relating the two by means of a bridging concept, that of inner speech, brings out aspects of all three that can illuminate old educational goals and identify new ones. To work with this three-way interrelationship, we must construe writing in its highest sense—beyond copying and transcribing, paraphrasing and plagiarizing—as authentic *authoring*, because inner speech and meditation concern forms of thought, the composing of mind that constitutes the real art and worth of writing. Authoring is working up a final revision, for an audience and a purpose, of those thought forms that have surfaced to the realm of inner speech.

Inner and Outer Speech

Whatever eventuates as a piece of writing can begin only as some focusing on, narrowing of, tapping off of, and editing of that great ongoing inner panorama that William James dubbed the "stream of consciousness." What I will call here "inner speech" is a version of that stream which has been more verbally distilled and which can hence more directly serve as the wellspring of writing. We might ask someone suddenly to say what she is thinking and thereby learn the subject matter, the order or disorder of the thoughts and images, and perhaps some aura or vein characterizing this material, but until asked to tell us, the person may not even have been aware of her stream and, even if aware, may not have put it into words. And the selection, wording, and emphasis with which she verbalizes the material to us may not be the same as she did verbalize or would have verbalized it to herself. So we must understand "inner speech" as referring to an uncertain level or stage of consciousness where material may not be so much verbalized as verbalizable, that is, at least potentially available to consciousness if some stimulus directs attention there, and potentially capable of being put into words because it is language-congenial thought (discursive).

Inner speech distills not just *the* stream but a confluence of streams issuing from sensory receptors, memory, and a variety of more or less emotional or logical kinds of reflection. All the elements of this rich mixture trig-

College English, 44 (March 1982) pp. 231-244. This essay is an abridged version of an essay under the same title in the author's *Coming on Center: English Education in Evolution* (Montclair, NJ: Boynton/Cook Publishers, 1981). © 1981 Boynton/Cook Publishers. Used by permission of the author and publisher.

ger, interrupt, and reinforce each other. Sometimes they interplay rapidly, indicating perhaps that attention is free to skip more "randomly" or "spontaneously." Sometimes strong external influence or strong inner will sustains attention so steadily on one current that a clear continuity develops. Swordfighting, for example, holds consciousness to sensory information. An old person finished with striving may "dwell in the past," shutting out environmental stimulation and letting the memory current flow with little interruption—chronically, in some cases. Another person well into maturity may constantly forge generalizations from the matter of everyday occurrences or news, so that reflection stands in high ratio to memories and sensations. A teenager may spend much time replaying past incidents that he found to be ego wounding, or making scenarios to help meet trying situations he is busy foreseeing. At any moment this heady stuff can be tapped off and converted to ink.

The idea that most thinking, the discursive part, derives from internalized speech seems rather universally agreed on by specialists in cognition today, as shown by the enthusiasm of Jean Piaget and Americans for the work of Lev Vygotsky and A. R. Luria, whose school has for decades insisted that the sociohistorical origins of thought have not been adequately emphasized.[1] Society peoples the heads of most individuals via speech, which is learned from and for others but in shifting inward merges with universal inborn logical faculties, biologically given, and with idiosyncratic penchants of mind to result in thinking that is at once personal and cultural. As Hans Furth reminds us from his work with the education of the deaf, not all thinking is verbal, and conceptual maturation may occur among people who cannot speak.[2] The Russian psycholinguists accept that thought and speech originate separately, but they play down the independence of innate mentation because they believe that human psychosocial evolution ("historical dialectic") determines individual thinking more than the biological givens. Surely, we have here a serpent with its tail in its mouth: mind and society feed in and out of each other.

It may be helpful for teachers to regard listening or reading, say, as assimilating someone else's outer speech into one's ongoing inner speech, the effect being something like a garbled script or heavily annotated and superscribed text. Evidences of this hearing or reading may evince themselves minutes or years later when our receiver becomes sender in turn and synthesizes his own continuity for others to introject, naturally drawing on what he has heard and read along with other experience and his unique creativity. The circles keep turning over. People learn to talk and write by listening and reading as much as by anything else.

Writing as Revised Inner Speech

However personal or impersonal the subject matter, *all* writing as authoring must be some revision of inner speech for a purpose and an audience. This is not at all to say that writing is solipsistic thinking about narcissistic content, or even that it favors "personal experience." Because of the circularity just discussed, one's revised inner speech may reflect convention so much as hardly to bear a personal mark. "Off the top of the head," as we say. In Samuel Beckett's play *Waiting for Godot* a slavish character called Lucky gives a remarkable soliloquy that starts as a surface verbal stream full of stock stuff and familiar phrases straight out of ads and folk talk and official promulgations, then moves downward to poetic and original verbalization of the deeper self, à la Molly Bloom or Anna Livia Plurabelle. (Beckett was not Joyce's secretary for nothing.) I saw the Trinidad dancer Geoffrey Holder perform this soliloquy by dancing out this descent into the self at the same time he vocalized the deepening verbal stream, creating an unforgettable audio-visual emblem as he bucked and spluttered his way down through tensions into the grace of unconflicted fluency.

Egocentricity is merely a localization within the larger circles of ethnocentricity, biocentricity, and geocentricity that are concentric to it. This is why "subjectivity" is not so personal as it is usually made out to be and not the only issue to consider in adapting inner speech to public communication. So much of the dullness, awkwardness, shallowness, and opacity that teachers object to in student writing owes to skimming along in the froth instead of plunging into the current, where intuition lines up with intelligence and particularities of experience correct for cliché. Seldom has anyone shown students how to work their way down, like Lucky. Most discourse in society today follows the now notorious circuit of the computer, "garbage in, garbage out." Something really significant has to happen inside—mediation by mind. If "output" differs from "input" mainly in being more amateurishly put together, then subjectivity has little meaning, and objectivity cannot be an authentic enough issue to be dealt with.

What really teaches composition—"putting together"—is disorder. Clarity and objectivity become learning challenges only when content and form are *not* given to the learner but when she must find and forge her own from her inchoate thought. Now, *that* is hard, not the glorified book-reporting or the filling in of instances to fit someone else's generalization (topic). All this traditional school and college writing only *looks* mature because it is laced with highly abstract generalizations—quotations from the greats, current formulations of issues, and other ideas received from books or teachers. Such haste to score, to make a quick intellectual killing, merely retards learning, because those writers have not worked up those generalizations themselves. This short-circuits the natural circularity between thought and society, bypasses any true mediation by mind, and results in a simply more insidious form of inculcation. I invite the reader to think of writing not only as Lucky's descent into self but also as the ascent from chaos to cosmos. I certainly do not mean to equate the self with chaos, but the inner speech that boils off the self represents some sort of confused concoction of self and society. Through ordering this chaos we may use composition to achieve composure.

The subject matter of student writing, then, needs to be material not previously interpreted or abstracted by others—the writer's own eyewitnessing, memories, interviews, experiments, feelings, reflections, and reactions to reading. But central is the process of *expatiation* that takes the interplay of inner voices back out into the social world, where the give-and-take of minds and voices can lift each member beyond where he or she started. This requires enormously more small-group interaction than classrooms now foster—task talk, improvisation, and topic discussion.

Some other advantages of teaching writing from inner speech regard therapy and general self-development. The processes of psychotherapy and of writing both require maximum synthesizing of this firsthand and secondhand knowledge into a full, harmonious expression of individual experience. This calls for the removal of spells to which the person has not agreed and of which he is unconscious. Freud asked the patient to start talking about anything and just keep uttering as fluently, fully, and spontaneously as possible everything that came into his head—in other words, to attempt to verbalize aloud his stream of consciousness or externalize his inner speech. This technique presupposes that from the apparent chaos of all this disjointed rambling will emerge for analyst and patient an order, eventually "betrayed" by motifs, by sequencing, by gradual filling in of personal cosmology. Thus, if successful, the subject's cosmologizing processes, the idiosyncratic ways of structuring and symbolizing experience, stand more clearly revealed and presumably more amenable to deliberate change, if desired. The most important thing a writer needs to know is *how he or she does think and verbalize and how he or she might.*

Not for a moment do I suggest that the teacher play psychiatrist. The therapeutic benefits from writing are natural fallout and nothing for a school teacher to strive for. They inhere in the very parallelism described here. Good therapy and composition aim at clear thinking, effective relating, and satisfying self-expression. Precisely because it is not thought of as therapy and works toward another goal, writing can effect fine therapy sometimes. At any rate, selfawareness is the means in both cases, and this requires focusing attention on one's inner speech.

Most of all, keeping inner speech as the matrix of all writing keeps teaching of writing centered on authentic authorship, so that all these other benefits of writing accrue to the novice as well as to the professional. The novice needs, after all, not fewer but more kinds of motivation. The student needs to enjoy and value the benefits of self-expression, communication, therapy, and art. The more evident all these benefits are the more easily learners can muster the strength it takes to stick at practice. If practiced as real authoring, not disguised playback, writing *discovers* as much as it communicates, and this basic benefit must ever be held out and made clear to students. Writing is hauling in a long line from the depths to find out what things are strung on it. Sustained attention to inner speech reveals ideas one did not know one thought, unsuspected connections that illuminate both oneself and the outside objects of one's thought. No better motivation exists, because young people do want to find out what they and the world are like. But only if we construe writing as its maximum meaning will the discovery aspect of it become real for students. Instead of using writing to test other subjects, we can elevate it to where it will *teach* other subjects, for in *making sense* the writer is *making knowledge.* Certainly I am not alone in arguing that writing should appear to students as a serious learning method itself to discover things about external subjects as well as oneself. Paradoxically, writing does not become an instrument of investigation and discovery of external things until it is acknowledged to be grounded in inner speech, because only when the individual brings some consciousness to the monitoring of the stream of experience does she start to become the master instead of the dupe of that awesome symbolic apparatus that, ill or well, creates her cosmos.

Meditation as Control of Inner Speech

It is best to head off at the outset the common notion that meditation comes from another culture, that it is a practice only of strange and dangerous cults, or that it inculcates a particular religious doctrine. Meditation has always been and never ceased to be practiced in Western culture. All cultures of all times, in fact, have included some forms of it.

The modern meaning of meditate—"to turn over in the mind, reflect on"—represents a much more cerebral version of former practices. It seems clear that the meaning of meditation has changed as our culture has shifted to an emphasis on the new-brain, left-hemisphere, literate, technical, abstract modes of knowing. Consider the reference in Psalms 19:14, "Let the words of my mouth, and the meditation of my heart, be acceptable in thy sight." The Tibetan Rinpoche Thartang Tulkhu once said at a meditation workshop that "Meditation is nonconceptualization," that is, a bypassing of the whole cultural system for filtering reality based on logic and language.[3] My own yoga teacher, Swami Sivalingam, once said meditation was relaxation, by which he meant a total release of both muscles and thoughts right down practically to the cellular level of functioning.[4] Surely, central to any definition of meditation would be some notion of transcending intellectual knowledge. By itself the intellect will indeed proceed on the basis, as John Locke stated for the modern age, that "nothing is in the mind that was not in the senses." (Recent physics has certainly put this notion to rout.)

The variety of meditation techniques we are confronted with today represents not only alternatives preferred by individuals or cultures but also a gradation in depth owing to historical changes. Accordingly, meditation varies all the way from highly focused discursive reflection (close to the current Western meaning of the word) to rare mystic experiences of ectasy ("being outside" oneself).

My own practical definition of meditation states it as some control of the inner stream ranging from merely *watching* it to *focusing* it to *suspending* it altogether. This range of meditative techniques suggests a rough developmental sequence of teaching methods relevant to writing. It starts in the pre-verbal, with gazing, ends in the post-verbal, with silence, and runs from uncontrolled to controlled mind.

Researchers at Harvard's Pre-School Project reported that the children they observed whom adults described later, in school, as the "brightest, happiest, and most charming" had spent as much as twenty percent of their pre-school time "staring" with absorption at some object or another, the largest amount of time the children had allotted to any single activity.[5] "Staring" is the small child's meditation and a chief way he or she learns. This action affords direct knowledge, not yet mediated by discourse, and should be encouraged in school. Many bright thinkers and writers do not talk much in the early years but pay such rapt attention that when they do start talking they have a lot to say and know how to say it well. ("Contemplation" basically means "gazing.") Spontaneous gazing of the preschool years can easily continue as a pleasant school activity if children are furnished with engaging materials and encouraged to get deep into them individually, as they are in some Montessori schools.

A variation of gazing is visualization. The meditator closes his eyes and transfers the image inward to the middle of the forehead. Alternately gazing outward and visualizing inward teaches one to develop inner attention and imagination without forcing verbalization. Other pure visualization meditations can follow. Staying focused either in or out frees the meditator a while from the excitations of the environment and lets him or her feel the strength of the self, the deeper self that abides at least somewhat independently of the outside. Writing presupposes just such inner strength. A writer of whatever age has to feel full of herself and have a degree of confidence, belief that she has something to say, faith in her will, and control of her attention. Gazing and visualizing, finally, develop *vision*—seeing and perceiving in both outer and inner ways prerequisite for writing. These first meditation techniques should help develop selfhood, control, and perception. From here on the techniques run from most discursive to least discursive.

The next simplest and easiest meditation technique consists of letting inner speech flow spontaneously but of *witnessing* it. Instead of floating along on this stream and being borne away from the center of the self, one sits on the bank, so to speak, and watches it flow by, staying separate from it, not trying to influence it, but above all not being "carried away" by it.

The other techniques require and also develop increasing control of inner speech. Once able to still himself, turn inward, and witness his thoughts, the meditator may deliberately attempt to narrow down and focus his inner speech, to exert some control over it. Will comes more into play. Now even to observe is to alter, so maintaining the witness distance and not getting "lost in thought" already asserts some influence no doubt on the direction and content of inner speech. The present step consists, however, of setting a subject, holding the mind to it without distraction, focusing on it with special intensity, and developing it to an understanding not achievable by ordinary, relatively wayward reflection. Inasmuch as this discursive meditation consists of a given subject and a stipulated procedure for focusing inner speech on that subject, it offers a remarkable analogy to school composition assignments, which we call, significantly, "themes," the same term by which church manuals commonly referred to meditation subjects.

Providing a splendid historical parallel between this discursive meditation and composition, Louis Martz developed during the 1950s the thesis that the traits that our century came to recognize and admire in the so-called "metaphysical poets" of the seventeenth century derived rather directly from very popular meditation practices initiated by Saint Ignatius Loyola, spread by the Jesuits as part of the Counter-Reformation, and taken to heart by these poets.[6] This Jesuitical meditation may best represent what I am calling discursive meditation, the sort most obviously related to writing as a finished product.

The Ignatian meditation structure that Martz says accounts for the traits of the poetry of John Donne, George Herbert, Henry Vaughan, and others comprised 1) a prelude called the "composition of place," 2) a point-by-point analysis of the subject, and 3) a concluding "colloquy." Sometimes more preliminaries were recommended, and sometimes the number of analytic points or colloquies might be five, say, instead of three, but the main format was this trinity. During the famous "composition of place" or "seeing the spot" the meditator tried to create as vividly as possible in his mind some scene or situation such as an incident from the life of Christ, the Judgment Day, the agonies of Hell, the miseries of his own life, the hour of death, or the glory and felicity of the kingdom of heaven. On this spot he brought to bear all the powers of his memory, imagination, and intelligence, to fill out the scene in fullest sensory detail and make it as real as if he were there or it existed in him. An important specific suggestion of the manuals was to employ "similitudes" of various sorts to enable the meditator to feel the reality of the conjured moment and to relate it to his familiar world. Within this mental stage setting, virtually a controlled hallucination, the intellect made several distinct points by analyzing the scene or situation into components, aspects, causes, effects, and so on. Such points, stimulated by the dramatic and graphic intensity of "seeing the spot," not only deepened the meditator's spiritual understanding but brought on in turn a swelling of "affections" or feeling, a shift from head to heart, that the "colloquies" expressed. These seem to have been not so much dialogue as direct address or petition from the meditator to God, some other spirit or figure, other earthly creatures such as animals, or his own soul or self. In poetic rhetoric the equivalent, I assume, would be called "apostrophe." It was "familiar talke," as St. Francis of Sales called it, "colloquial," as we would say today. We have here in Martz' demonstration a relatively clear instance from history of efforts to control inner speech affecting writing.

To continue further along the meditation scale I am delineating, we have to move backward in history. During the first few centuries of Christianity certain of the so-called "Church Fathers," especially in the Eastern or Byzantine church, practiced non-discursive meditations, as they described and prescribed in the collection called *Philokalia*.[7] The central meditation of this Christian strain—called Hesychast and focused on the so-called "Jesus prayer of the heart"—will exemplify non-discursive meditation. It still survives in certain Greek and Russian traditions, has been revived recently in the United States as part of the Charismatic Movement, and was attempted by Frannie in Salinger's story "Frannie."[8] The Jesus prayer of the heart typifies the meditation method that consists of repeating over and over to oneself a *single* idea put in a *single* piece of speech until the focus of that idea and the incantation of that verbal sound induce transcendence of the usual state. Consciousness is then altered beyond thought and speech. The "prayer" is, "Lord Jesus Christ, have mercy upon me!" A word or phrase intoned repeatedly in exactly the spirit the Christian Fathers did the Jesus prayer of the heart is what the Hindus call a *mantra*. But how can just saying something over and over reveal the highest truths about life? And what if you do not happen to believe in Jesus, or even in God?

To answer that I will ask a third question: How does meditation differ from prayer? The astonishing healer Edgar Cayce answered that prayer is talking to God; meditation is listening to God.[9] Discourse versus silence. Among other things, people are transmitter/receiver sets, which means they are made both to transmit and receive but not *at the same time.* If you want to listen, you have to switch the channel over to receiving and keep still. If God or Nature or Cosmic Intelligence is transmitting at the other end, and the individual is holding the line muttering and squawking and debating and petitioning, she is missing a lot! Missing perhaps what she most wants to know, for lack of which she must mutter, squawk, debate, and petition. But as every one knows who has ever tried to stop thinking, it is very difficult indeed. The mind is a drunken monkey, say the yogis. But one way to cure the habit of ceaselessly speaking to ourselves is—homeopathically—to go ahead and speak to ourselves but to say the same thing over and over.

To understand non-discursive meditation we have to consider both what the mind is aimed at and what it is aimed from. The root meaning of "discourse" is "running to and fro." The meaning of "mystic" derives from *mystos*, "keeping silence," derived in turn from the Greek *myein,* "to keep closed" (of eyes and lips). The repeated phrase or mantra substitutes for inner speech which "runs to and fro" in usual discursive fashion and relatively so even in the focused devotional. During mantra repetition inner speech continues, in a sense, but changes profoundly from *serial* thoughts, a *train* of thoughts, to a *point* of thought. The voice moves on in time, repeating the same words, but the mind becomes, as yogis say, "one-pointed." Repeating the phrase suspends or at least mitigates inner speech so that non-conceptual intuition can take over in an altered state of consciousness both more receptive and more perceptive. Not only does the idea or object contemplated reveal itself more deeply, but it is as if a whole new and finer attunement occurs, enabling the individual to detect signals from within and from the environment that the ordinary mind drowns out or filters out.

All these meditation techniques may be summarized in the form of a scale progressing from nonverbal to verbal and then, within the verbal, from babble to silence. Put another way, it goes from external focus to internal focus and then, within the internal focus, from uncontrolled to controlled inner speech.

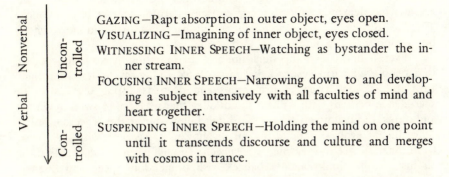

GAZING—Rapt absorption in outer object, eyes open.

VISUALIZING—Imagining of inner object, eyes closed.

WITNESSING INNER SPEECH—Watching as bystander the inner stream.

FOCUSING INNER SPEECH—Narrowing down to and developing a subject intensively with all faculties of mind and heart together.

SUSPENDING INNER SPEECH—Holding the mind on one point until it transcends discourse and culture and merges with cosmos in trance.

If we think of gazing as that of the small child, then this progression comes full circle in the sense that it begins and ends in silence and rapture, but the circling rises—spirals—rather than closes because the child's gazing is spontaneous and unaware, whereas the meditator who has succeeded in suspending inner speech goes into conscious voluntary rapture.

The Grand Paradox

The reader can see already the paradox that we have been engaging with. If discourse is "running to and fro," why encourage it—especially if people desire composure? If the deepest and most desirable "meditation" is silence, "nonconceptualization," then why think? If suspending inner speech opens the gate to higher knowledge, who wants to *develop* inner speech? If language just distorts reality through a social lens, what good will it do to learn to write well? Doesn't successful verbal expression conflict with the very goal of expression—to speak the truth? Or is writing just a parlor game, to entertain and blandish, not to symbolize reality?

Certainly we have to face the negative aspects of speech, and even of conceptual thought itself. To do so, however, seems to undermine the main aims of schooling. If we are not trying to teach students to think and to express themselves, then, hell's bells, what are we up to anyway? How can we old poetry-loving English teachers with our rich inner life and our great investments in language turn around and talk it down? Because, precisely, we have to say the truth, and the truth is that speech is double-edged, a curse and a blessing. (The root of *sacred* means both holy and cursed.)

The teaching of writing must rise to a new sophistication consonant with a new stage in human evolution. A paradox is literally a "double teaching," and that is exactly what we must do—teach two apparently contradictory things at once. Youngsters need to develop inner speech as fully as possible and at the same time learn to suspend it. They must talk through to silence and through stillness find original thought. A paradox is not a real but an apparent contradiction. To develop and undo discourse at the same time would not be working against ourselves. Teaching both ways at once, double teaching, has its reason. People are at once both human and what we call divine, that is, participate in the social subsystem which in turn participates in the total cosmic system. The new stage of evolution at which we are arriving demands education for conscious attunement to both at once. This means the ability to switch deliberately back and forth and know where one's mind is all the time.

Even if one rejects this dual aim and dual method, it is a practical fact that people who can suspend discourse think and speak better when they turn it back on. Thought straightens and deepens during the hiatus, in accordance perhaps with William James' idea that we learn to swim in winter and ice-skate in summer, that is, by lying fallow during the off-season. Like other highly evolved people, Swami Sivalingam can switch with great ease from inner silence to very energetic speech. Though given to long meditation all his life, he thinks and verbalizes with tremendous speed and fluency though seldom does he have the opportunity today to speak in his native Tamil. It is difficult to keep up with his thoughts and words even though he may be using a recently learned language. When Swami Sivalingam puts pen to paper he writes virtually without pause in a smooth transcription of inner flow. His own guru was the renowned Swami Sivananda, a Western-trained medical doctor turned yogi who wrote over 300 books, most on subtle and difficult subjects. Because the will is lined up behind the mind, and the thought is resolved, advanced meditators talk and write with a combination of depth and fluency that writing teachers should pay attention to; their ability demonstrates very convincingly the benefits of suspending inner speech.

Harder to believe perhaps is that this truth holds for so-called nonverbal or inarticulate people. Such people do in fact have a busy inner life, but they are less conscious of it, and they are talking to themselves in far more restricted, compulsive ways, telling themselves the same few things over and over, or re-running in a mental twilight things others have said or shown them. Such people desparately need release from this limiting and uncontrolled repetition, which narrowly programs what they can see, say, and do about the circumstances of their life. So even for the "speechless" person the mind works better if it can be turned down or off from time to time.

Counter-Spell

It should be clear at this point that learning to write well, in the view developed here, is nothing less than learning to discourse well, and that educationally, speaking up and shutting up have to be considered together. This means that we would do well not only to take a very broad view of what teaches writing but also to recognize then that many of the best ways of teaching writing may be themselves ends as much as means. In any sensible set of values, meditation deserves a place in schools for its own sake, regardless of its value to writing, and writing might well be regarded as adjunct to meditation rather than the reverse. Aside from clerical maintenance that may be done by computers, what is writing for anyway? Let's keep this perspective in mind as we approach the question of what methodology may best act as counter-spell to teach paradoxically.

First of all, *language* may be used as a counter-spell to itself. The incantatory use of language, which is non-discursive or only half discursive, resolves most directly the paradox of teaching and unteaching discourse at the same time. Rhythm, rhyme, repetition, imagery, sheer sound and beat and vocal play—these take a minimum of meaning and charge it with a mental energy that works below the level of symbols and communication (and best appeals to the "nonverbal" or "inarticulate" person). Incantation makes words operate like music or dance or graphic arts. The tense emphasis school usually places on communication alone not only misses the proper entrance point into writing for less verbal people but also misses a key solution to the limitations of discourse, for the incantatory uses of language can undo language and cast a counter-spell. Schools need to emphasize, in parity with the symbolic uses of language to express ideas, the forms of language that transcend ideas and alter consciousness. This means far more time devoted to song and poetry and to drama and fiction as rhythmic influences, not merely as thematic vehicles. And students should write more in these forms and *perform* such writings of others, not always read them silently. By organizing specialties like "creative drama" and "creative writing," schools have effectively placed them out of bounds for most students most of the time, whereas writing and performing these art forms of language should occur constantly at all ages as a daily staple. Other educators and I have written much about this elsewhere—to no great avail so far because of government doctrines favoring lower goals falsely regarded as utilitarian.

But of course I am suggesting that forms of meditation are the main counter-spells. To connect meditation more directly with schooling, let's look again at the scale of meditation techniques sketched earlier. This array can serve to find the best meditation for a given writer and topic. The point on the scale closest to the finished composition lies near the middle, where we found the discursive meditation of the Jesuits. But if fluency comes hard, maybe one should babble first, just witness the spontaneous production of ideas, words, and images. If depth is needed, perhaps one should aim for silence, try to get beyond what one has already heard and said and read about something and just focus on the subject non-discursively—that is, just hold centered in consciousness some idea, emblem, or phrasing of the subject, and sink deep in without trying to have thoughts about it. Then the meditator could back up on the scale toward discourse and begin to permit trains of thoughts of build up about her subject. More generally, where on this scale, a teacher might ask, can a certain student find herself at the moment, given her verbal and nonverbal development so far?

Gazing, contemplating, may be done at any age as a way to know most fully some object of the material world. The famous biology professor Louis Agassiz at Harvard would ask a student to describe a certain fish and then send the student back repeatedly to look at it until the observer began to see *internal* features that he would normally not perceive. Here is an example of a teacher wise enough to demand his students return to the rapt gazing of the child in order to experience his subject more fully and directly. He saw that intellect alone was not a profound enough observer to yield the kind of knowledge necessary for science. Let a learner visually lock into some object he or she has chosen either out of curiosity or deep involvement or as part of a project requiring further knowledge of the object. As a meditation, gazing slips the limits of conceptualization and enables one to see more and hence have more to say when back in the discursive mode.

Students can practice visualizing in connection with many imaginative activities in school, including the already popular "guided fantasy" technique some teachers have adopted. Alone, the meditator imagines, with eyes closed, an inner picture at the "third eye" (Cyclopean) position in the middle of the forehead. Though common to probably all cultures, including Christian, the conjuring and holding of an image before the inner vision has been especially developed in Tibetan meditation, which draws on Buddhism and yoga, especially tantric yoga.[10] Tantra emphasizes transcending rather than shunning the senses as a means to development. This means that the aspirant subtilizes his sensory vision right onto a higher plane, partly by gazing at "art objects" especially made for this (as indeed was much Christian art) and then by introjecting these, eyes closed, and continuing to see the object. Sometimes one uses a visual construction, called a *yantra*, that is especially designed to be contemplated for its effect on consciousness, being a schema of cosmos as both unity and miltiplicity. Carl Jung's mandalas, some Persian rug patterns, and Navajo sand paintings are yantras. Found or student-made yantras can serve to establish visualization as a general practice for imagining anything at will. Schools can also borrow a practice rapidly catching on in circles of "the new medicine," which is to imagine and hold a picture of something as one would *like* it to be, such as an illness or impairment improved. Clinical statistics are documenting that this often works, corroborating one older meaning of meditation relating to healing.[11]

Since television may well cause some atrophying of the visualizing faculty, as some of us educators have conjectured in regard, usually, to reading problems, visualization practice may improve both comprehension and composition at once. Visualization played an important role in the "composition of place" in Ignation meditation, and no doubt also in the production of "similitudes," which entail *seeing* similarities between points in one's subject and comparable concrete items.

The way in which the Jesuitical sort of discursive meditation might be applied to writing found a spokesman in Gordon Rohman over a decade ago.[12] Rohman lifted out of the eccesiastical context the essential process that worked for meditators and writers of the seventeenth century and offered it to teachers as one pre-writing technique, leaving subject matter open and capturing the spirit rather than the letter of the procedure. Doing the same thing in my own way, I would recommend that teachers coach students on how to get themselves into a meditative state of unusual absorption in a subject that interests them and then to visualize, imagine, feel, and think everything they can about that subject without at first concerning themselves about writing something down. After students have brought to bear on a subject all their faculties and thus focused intensively for a time their inner speech, then they would write down some version of these thoughts and proceed from there to work up a composition, presumably with mid-writing responses from others and as much repetition of these inner and outer processes as is appropriate for student and subject. So the aim of discursive meditation is to channel and intensify inner speech in a state of heightened consciousness and self-communication that enables the writer to summon all he or she is capable of saying about the subject. Previous or concurrent practice in visualization will greatly aid this summoning.

The yogic or Hesychast type of non-discursive meditation does not have to be done with a mantra. Virtually any focal point that is powerful and positive for the meditator can serve well. When using mantras, students should make or choose their own. Making and discussing mantras should, in fact, become an important classroom activity. What is a good thing to keep saying to yourself? Are we already repeating, consciously or unconsciously to ourselves, certain key words or magic phrases? Are they good or bad for us? What ideas are "elevated" or spiritual? What aspects of language form make for good mantras? Word? Phrase? Sentence? Stanza? Work with mantras can become of part of writing and performing song and poetry.

Alternatives to mantras are yantras and other tantras, that is, all arts and sensory avenues. Repetitive external sound may work well to help some individuals to stay one-pointed. Verbal or nonverbal, visual or auditory, physical or imaginary—these are good choices to have for individualizing. A phrase may be sung aloud or intoned within. A verbal person may start to still his inner chatter *only* by vocalizing something. A nonverbal person may achieve good focus best on an image. An unimaginative person may do well to transfer an image by alternately gazing and visualizing. A lonely person may release some anxious "running to and fro" by chanting to others.

Zen Buddhist practitioners of the meditation technique called za-zen focus on their normal breathing, which moves in time but stays the same in the sense that in even respiration one breath is like another. In this respect breath is like a mantra, and in some meditation practices, like the Hesychast, breathing and repetition of the mantra are coordinated. Za-zen emphasizes the here-and-now in contrast with conceptualization, which by its abstract nature necessarily refers out of the present. Holding attention on regular breathing is perfectly safe and may be an easy, fitting focus for many students, offering an alternative to visual and auditory focuses. For this as for all other techniques a quiet location and a comfortable sitting position are essential. Sitting cross-legged on the floor or sitting on a chair (preferably without touching the back of the chair), one keeps the spine erect but not stiff, releases muscles, and slows and deepens breathing. The key to meditation is a relaxed body and an alert awareness.

Breath has a very close connection to thought, almost entirely unsuspected in our era, that I think science will soon begin to rediscover. Though za-zen is simply attending to breathing without altering it, some of the most powerful consciousness-altering exercises entail slowing, holding, or patterning the breath. *Pranayama* or breath control has for thousands of years been associated by yogis with mind control, in keeping with the etymological connection in all languages I have heard of between breath and spirit.[13] Pranayama is the specialty of my own teacher, Swami Sivalingam, who has said that it is a "shortcut meditation." So powerful is breath control, in fact, that it can be dangerous without a teacher when carried beyond the more elementary exercises. Some day soon educators should work out with wise specialists like Swami Sivalingam just which exercises can be safely done at which ages and with how much or little monitoring by others.

Because meditation techniques are the closest to writing, I have featured them, but suspending inner speech as a means to greater knowledge and power underlies a prodigious array of activities of all cultures of all times that may suggest how teachers might go about finding and devising counter-spells in lieu of or in league with meditation. The "techniques of ecstasy," as the scholar Mircea Eliade has called them,[14] may be physiological as well as psychological. Physical activity calling for totally external focus of attention or total bodily involvement can make inner speech virtually impossible. In writing about "sports highs" that athletes report, Michael Murphy has made this connection.[15] This explains why martial arts are considered spiritual disciplines. (As my younger daughter said of her high-school fencing class, "Your mind doesn't wander!") Think now of the real meaning of Shakers, Quakers and Holy Rollers, who attempt to bring on this state by dancing of a sort as do the Sufi Whirling Dervishes, whom I have seen do authentically their gradually accelerating revolving movement with eyes closed and to the accompaniment of chanting. All of the arts originally aimed at trance induction for purposes of enlightenment, as typified by some of the Greek Mysteries, the main source of Western drama, music, art, and dance to the extent that these did not derive more directly from the mysteries of earlier civilizations.

Other bodily activities are also relevant to teaching methods. Pleasantly monotonous craft movements like knitting and weaving or work activities like hauling a rope or wielding a pickaxe or shovel or thrusting seedlings into mud tend to "entrance" the ordinary mind and constitute a natural kind of meditation. Crafts, arts, sports, and many practical self-help activities hold inner speech in abeyance or mute it and thus help attune us beyond the discursive thought. Since these possible counter-spells should be curriculum candidates anyway, in keeping with the principle that worthy means are also worthy ends, they will offer opportunities to integrate writing with many other kinds of learning to which it is organically related by way of regulating and balancing one's own mind and body.

Some teachers teach meditation under other names or have initiated related activities. *The Centering Book* and its successor *The Second Centering Book*, pioneering works by education professors, contain many verbatim directions for leading youngsters in exercises of relaxation, concentration, breathing, visualizing, centering, and inner attention.[16] Other books are coming out all the time on the teaching of meditation to young people, usually based on experience in school or community settings. The most educational experimentation with meditation has occurred outside of school, however, in workshops for adults. In his Intensive Journal workshops Ira Progoff, a psychotherapist, teaches people how to use writing to discover what they really feel and think and want and are.[17] I have been greatly struck, as have some others, by the similarities between the kinds of writing and the climate for writing of my own approach for school teaching of language arts and Progoff's approach for adult therapy, both developed independently at about the same time. I am struck too that Progoff has also come to use meditation as a method of engaging people in writing.

But to teach meditation one must practice meditation. Though I am always suprised by how many teachers "come out of the closet" when I talk about meditation, the profession needs far more practitioners. To the extent that schools have the money, projects for changing teachers and the "facilitative behaviors" movement in staff development have tried to improve curriculum by arranging experiences in self-awareness and personal growth for the teachers. Since meditation naturally fulfills this aim, if staff development included it, then schools would simultaneously prepare teachers to improve writing while fostering their general adult growth.

Meditation techniques show how to witness one's own mind, direct one's own mind, and silence one's own mind. Then the mind can be better shared. Teachers can give no greater gift to their students than to help them expand and master inner speech. Good writing will ensue, whereas fiddling with form alone will teach, if anything, only how to carpenter better the craziness of themselves and their world. Let's direct discourse toward its own self-transformation and self-transcendence. In doing so we will also accomplish better the traditional curriculum goals.

Notes

[1] First see Lev Vygotsky, *Thought and Language* (Cambridge, MA: MIT Press, 1962). Included in this volume is an insert, "Comments," by Jean Piaget, that gives Piaget's main views of inner speech, especially as related to Vygotsky's. Then see Piaget's *Mind and Society* (Cambridge, MA: Harvard University Press, 1978) and A. R. Luria, *Cognitive Development: Its Cultural and Social Foundations* (Cambridge, MA: Harvard University Press, 1976).

[2] Hans Furth, *Thinking Without Language: Psychological Implications of Deafness* (New York: Free Press, 1966).

[3] Founder and head llama of the Nyingma Tibetan Meditation Center in Berkeley, CA and author of many books published there.

[4] Swami Sivalingam, a life-long yogi from South India, is founder of the Prana Yoga Ashram, based in Berkeley with other centers around the world, and author of *Wings of Divine Wisdom*, published by the Ashram, 1977.

[5] Reported in Burton White, *The First Three Years of Life* (Englewood Cliffs, NJ: Prentice-Hall, 1975).

[6] *The Poetry of Meditation* (New Haven: Yale University Press, 1954). As an appendix to his *The Meditative Poem: An Anthology of 17th Century Verse*, Martz included a typical manual of the time, Edward Dawson's "The Practical Methode of Meditation" (1614).

[7] *Writings from the Philokalia on Prayer of the Heart*, trans. E. Kadloubovsky and G. E. H. Palmer (London: Faber & Faber, 1951). For current material see George Maloney, *The Jesus Prayer* and Father David Geraets, *Jesus Beads* (Pecos, NM: Dove Publications, 1974 and 1969 respectively). These two books are published by the Benedictine Abbey at Pecos, which also publishes on the Charismatic Movement, in which the abbey is active.

[8] Salinger's Glass family had been reading *The Way of a Pilgrim* and *The Pilgrim Continues His Way*, trans. Helen Bacovcin (Garden City, NY: Doubleday, Image, 1978). *The Spiritual Instructions of Saint Seraphim of Sarov*, ed. Franklin Jones (San Francisco: Dawn Horse, 1973) puts this tradition in relation to yoga and oriental thought.

[9] *A Dictionary: Definitions and Comments from the Edgar Cayce Readings*, comp. Gerald J. Cataldo (Virginia Beach, VA: A.R.E. Press, 1973), p. 52.

[10] Phillip Rawson, *The Art of Tantra* (Greenwich, CT: New York Graphic Society, 1973).

[11] Carl Simonton, et al., *Getting Well Again* (New York: J. P. Tarcher, 1978), and Irving Oyle, *The Healing Mind* (New York: Pocket Books, 1976).

[12] "Pre-Writing: The Stage of Discovery in the Writing Process," *College Composition and Communication*, 16 (1965), 106-112.

[13] For both specific references to connections between thought and breath and to general doctrines of Tibetan yogic techniques of enlightenment see W. Y. Evans-Wentz, *The Tibetan Book of the Great Liberation or the Method of Realizing Nirvana through Knowing the Mind*, commentary by C. G. Jung (New York: Oxford University Press, 1954).

[14] See *Shamanism: Archaic Techniques of Ecstasy*, Bollingen Series 76 (Princeton, NJ: Princeton University Press, 1964). Eliade's remarkable scholarship combines with rare personal understanding to make him one of the most valuable contemporary explainers and presenters of spiritual disciplines. See also his *Yoga: Immortality and Freedom*, Bollingen Series 56 (Princeton, NJ: Princeton University Press, 1958).

[15] Michael Murphy and Rhea White, *The Psychic Side of Sports* (Reading, MA: Addison-Wesley, 1978).

[16] Gay Hendriks and Russel Wills, *The Centering Book* (Englewood Cliffs, NJ: Prentice Hall, 1975). Also Gay Hendriks and T. Roberts, *The Second Centering Book: More Advanced Awareness Activities for Children, Parents, and Teachers* (Englewood Cliffs, NJ: Prentice Hall, 1977).

[17] *At a Journal Workshop: The Basic Text and Guide for Using the Intensive Journal* (New York: Dialogue House, 1975). For a useful incorporation of some of Progoff's practices into schools see Mark Hanson, *Sources* (Box 262, Lakeside, CA 92040: Interact).

To Be Read

KEN MACRORIE

We ask students never to judge ideas or events out of context, but fail to see our composition classes in any larger world. That is why they are such astonishing failures. For decades we have been smearing the bloody marks (*sp, awk, gr*) in the margins of what we call "themes." These papers are not meant to be *read* but *corrected*.

Now we are living in a great series of revolutions, testing whether the present forms of school, church, state, family, and relationships between blacks and whites will endure. Already high school students are following the lead of college students—publishing underground newspapers, asking for a voice in making the rules of their schools. Tomorrow they will be suggesting or forcing changes in the classroom—in what they are asked to read, to write, and how their work is to be evaluated.

A textbook named *Correct Writing, Forms A, B, C, and D* is likely to receive only a hoot of derision from students who are communicating with each other and with administrators and teachers in dozens of new ways. As the television generation, they are not any longer going to suffer learning in grade school that the White House is where the President lives, in junior high what the President's name is, and in senior high that the house is located on Pennsylvania Avenue. Many of them have been there, and to the Pentagon as well.

These are perilous moments for American establishments. They will be destroyed or they will reform. We have a small chance to keep our students from turning our schools into the shambles remaining after revolutions in Watts, Newark, and Detroit. But it is a chance.

Four years ago I stumbled into a way to induce students to write so they excited each other and me. Now that I have worked out a program and seen it elicit lively and valuable writing from all levels of students (from

English Journal 57 (May 1968), pp. 686-692. Copyright © 1968 by the National Council of Teachers of English. Reprinted by permission of the publisher and the author.

81

seventh grade through graduate school) and all ranges of students (from "remedial" to "honors"), I know trying to reform writing in the schools and colleges makes sense.

Here is the program:

1. Ask students to place themselves outside of class anywhere they can be alone and quiet. Then write for ten minutes as fast as they can, putting down whatever comes to mind. If they can't think of a word, they should start by reporting what they see in front of them. Let the mind and pencil go until they fill a large-sized notebook page. Twice, so they have two papers to bring to the next class.

2. Ask for honesty. Say you know school doesn't often nurture it, that at times you will be dishonest, as everyone is without realizing—but you will try to speak truth. Pass out an example of phony writing—pretentious, empty:

> But the area which caused Henry and I to become steadfast friends was outdoor sports.

Also pass out an example of honest writing, like this:

> He doesn't have legs. Not ones that feel or move. It's been that way almost four years now. Wheels. I was scared to talk at first, felt like a kid asking what it is that everyone's talking about. But we did. We used to goof around and tell dirty jokes. I always felt a little fake. Dan and I took him to the bathroom every day. Had to be done in a special way. We were there once, Dan asked a question—I don't remember what it was—something involving my ability to work.
>
> "What do you think I am, a cripple?" That's what I said. I didn't look at anyone, just the wall. For about half an hour. I felt very whole, but my stomach was tin foil. They were quiet, both of them. Quiet as being alone. I wished someone would cut off my arms.

3. Ask students to keep all papers in a folder. At the end of the semester you will choose the six to ten best papers and give a course grade on them. If the student needs a grade earlier—to convince his father he should buy him a car or so he can apply for college—you will grade his folder as of the moment. His classmates and you will be constantly commenting on his papers in this seminar-style class, and some papers will be reproduced as examples of fine writing; so he will know how he is doing.

If students' free writings turn out too personal or confessional, they should try others. Ask them not to submit writing that embarasses them because of its intimacy. If they write close to their heart, they may ask you to withhold their names when their papers are presented to the class.

4. Ask students to bring two free writings to the second meeting and to exchange papers with another student. They should underline (or indicate in the margin) any phrases or sentences they like for content or expression, or both.

5. Discuss the marked passages with students. Ask students to comment on some before you praise them. Look for truth and liveliness. Take papers

home, mark passages or phrases you like. Ditto these excerpts. Write nothing on the papers.

6. At the third meeting continue discussion of good passages. Tell students that for the first month or so they should make only positive comments on each other's writing. If the class numbers no more than twenty, begin the first few meetings with the group seated in a circle, or around a giant table made from a number of tables. If the class is more than twenty, for part of the period separate students into smaller groups. Seven is good because it puts pressure on writers so they cannot dismiss criticism—good or bad—as merely a gesture from friend or enemy. Do not visit the groups. In the first month ask no student to read his paper aloud to others unless you think it a smashing success. Otherwise, you read it to the class or ask students to exchange papers several times so they may be read aloud without the class knowing who wrote them.

7. Ask students to write two fifteen-minute free papers trying to focus on one subject, not letting the mind skip as freely as in the first writing. If they get off the subject and are going marvelously, they should continue on the detour.

8. As you and the students discuss the writing, allow them to react even when they can't say what they like about the writing. Twelve heads nodding up and down in appreciation will charge any writer's batteries. Begin now occasionally to point out why a writing is good: strong metaphor, rhythmic sentences, tension between two ideas or facts, fresh expression instead of clichés, insight, memorable sensuous details. Don't feel obliged to offer all the papers to class criticism, even if you have a two-hour period in which to work.

9. Show students how to tighten writing. Ask them to choose their best free writing and cut all wasted words—outside of class. Urge what professional editors suggest (not necessarily what English textbooks emphasize): for example, eliminating unnecessary uses of *which, that,* and *who.* Show students where they have repeated words powerfully.

10. Ask students to write a forty-five minute free paper focusing on one subject.

11. Encourage and encourage, but never falsely. When you get a fine piece of writing with a weak beginning and ending that need chopping, type it on a ditto master in the most powerfully cut version you can arrange without changing any words, and then—if the author approves—post it on the bulletin board in the hall. Correct all spelling errors and mechanical weaknesses before publishing it in any way. Publishers never knowingly embarrass their writers.

Try to place several writings in the student newspaper or magazine early in the semester. Don't expect students to take that initiative. For years they have been indoctrinated to believe they can't write. Their papers have been massacred—all that blood in the margins.

12. Ask students to write an informal case history of a day or hour (or several days, hours, or weeks condensed into one) on a job, or in a process or

activity they've gone through many times. Or to tell what happens during a half-hour in the school library at a certain spot. They should put the reader there, not try for clinical detachment unless they need it. If they wish, they can write freely several times about the experience and then try to find a center (some tension, meaning, or lack of meaning) in the activity that helps tell them which details to discard and which they need more of. This paper may run two pages or ten.

13. Read aloud a few of these case histories the day they are due. Ask students to point out anything they like. Take them home, read them, try not to comment unless you have a major suggestion. Do not correct. Do not mark mistakes. Ditto two to four (one or three if your class lasts only fifty minutes) that you think compelling.

Occasionally during the semester you will find a paper that becomes excellent when cut massively. Ditto the cut version, then append the cut paragraphs or sentences. Remind students that this surgery is only one possibility and that the author has the *authority* to restore any of the material cut. After class discussion of case histories, ask all students to take their papers home and do their own revising and adding to. Let them know reworking of papers is expected in all major assignments, except when a paper seems strong all the way through upon first writing. Tell students that the wastebaskets of professional writers are full of discarded pages.

14. Ask students to record short fabulous realities in a notebook or journal. Examples:

   a. Boy and girl talking, he standing in gutter, she on curb, for better eye-to-eye contact.
   b. Sign downtown: "Four Barbers, No Waiting," and then below: "Television While You Wait."

Written skillfully these fabulous realities embody six essentials of most good writing: The writer (1) makes an event happen before the reader, (2) locates it significantly, (3) presents materials that create a tension or point, (4) uses only details that bear upon that tension or point, (5) does not waste words, and (6) saves the punch till the end, where it gains from suspense. The first fabulous reality above could be improved by reordering:

   Boy and girl talking—for better eye-to-eye contact she stands on the curb, he in the gutter.

The surprise is now at the end.

15. Ask students to think of expanding one fabulous reality into a little story. If they have nothing expandable, they needn't try. Conduct this class for writers, not hothouse scholars. When writers have worked hard and nothing goes right, they give up a project and start another. Good writing usually is produced half by civil engineering and half by hidden springs that suddenly start flowing.

16. Ask students to write a longer paper remembering some childhood incident that shook them up. They should put the reader there, not generalize about feelings. Start with "One day—" and recreate that young

world. In this, and in all writing, do not allow clichés. If students can't think of another way of saying "It rained cats and dogs"—one that hits precisely the mood and intensity they want—let them say, "It rained hard." In casual conversation cliches are to be expected and endured; in writing—inexcusable. A writer asks his reader to look at his sentences. His first duty is not to bore him.

17. When childhood papers come in, introduce the elementary kinds of organization—Before-After, The Journey (we did this or went here and then did that and went there—whether this is a movement in ideas or action), and The Hook (at the end tying back to the beginning, perhaps with irony). Suggest that students may want to use one of these patterns in reshaping their childhood papers. (Call writing "writing" or "papers," never "themes." Whoever would voluntarily read something called a "theme"?) From now on in seminar sessions point out weaknesses in students' writing as well as strengths, but in front of the class don't be hard upon the paper of a student not yet praised by the group.

18. Ask students to keep a journal for three weeks or more, making entries only when they see or think of something striking. Present excerpts from strong journals, like Thoreau's, to show range and diversity of entries.

Ask students to try several short free writings in their journals, and not to worry if they don't hit a subject that goes beautifully. A journal is a place for many failures and a few successes. Ask that entries be communications to others, not Dear Diary private statements. In five or ten years the student looking at this journal should be able to put himself back in his experience. He can't do that with comments like these: "What a terrible week it has been. Tommy just isn't the sort of guy I thought he was going to be. I'm really miserable." He can with an entry like this:

We went for a ride in the fog last night, out on Ravine Road, There are no lights and no houses. So in the fog we were isolated. All that existed in the universe was about ten yards of yellow ribbon and my eyes, and that curving conveyor belt which I had to steer my eyes along—very much like my life at times.

19. Ask students to try word play in journals. Read Lewis Carroll's *Through the Looking Glass*, the text for word play. Make words speak to each other, as Shakespeare or a good newspaper headline writer does. Puns, rhymes. Revive dead metaphors. Record good word play heard in TV commericials or seen in advertisements, or around school. Examples:

a. Love Is a Many Splintered Thing. [student word play]

b. Watch how Gossard [girdles] makes tummies disappear in ten seconds flat.

20. Ask students to write an article for the school magazine or newspaper. They must think of readers and give them news in fact or expression—something that hits the writer and will hit the reader. At the outset, the article should grab and hold and tell the reader enough to satisfy his need

for completeness. What persons say should be exploited, but only the words that strike hard in what they say or how they say it.

21. In assigning the article suggest that students try and discard and try again. Let them know you expect some of the articles to be published. Ask them to study campus publications for length of story, style, and kinds of responsibility shown by the writer. Don't restrict students to a tight, "straight" news article. Allow feature stories or columns of personal opinion if the writing seems to move in that direction.

22. Let students know that at any time in the semester you will allow them to depart from an assignment if they have motive and materials boiling. This freedom must be balanced with discipline. About halfway through the course, when students are apt to slough off (feeling wearied and harried, like you) by using rewriting possibilities as an excuse for not turning in work, begin the practice of requiring two pieces of writing every week, even if only short free writings. You are developing writers. They are persons who write.

23. When you use professional models, whenever possible point out how students have employed the techniques you are pointing to. You have dittoed student work to refer to. For example, this paper—

I had always wanted a BB gun, but I never had one until now. We were going out to a friend's farm near Paw Paw and my dad bought me one to take along. At first I took it home to practice. I thought it was a big thing to hit an empty Joy bottle from twenty feet.

After I got to the farm, the owner asked me to shoot some black-birds for him. For a long time no blackbirds came around. At last one landed in a walnut tree in the yard. I walked under it quietly so I wouldn't scare it. The stupid thing just sat there begging to be shot. I fired my first shot. I saw the little gold BB fly past his head. Dumb bird. It still didn't move. I shot again and the bird's face reacted with pain. It fell over, hanging upside down by one foot from its branch. I shot again. It still hung there. I could see blood on its feathers even from where I stood. With the fourth shot, it fell, its black feathers red.

The last phrase, "its black feathers red," exhibits poetic concentration and carries the weight of the boy's revelation. During the experience he changed his feelings from sadism to sympathy, but he lets the reader infer the change. He does not tell him. He speaks no joy or condescension after "the bird's face reacted with pain." Like a professional writer, he allows some of the smallest details to rise to the surface, and they turn out aptly ironic and symbolic. Practicing to kill, he is shooting a Joy [name of a detergent] bottle. He uses gold BB's for blackbirds. He probably did not intend these extra meanings, but they are present, they work, and he did not excise them.

Because this paper on shooting blackbirds is a small piece of literature, it embraces many of the qualities of good explanatory or persuasive writing, while carrying a different intention and purpose. Show students how "personal" writing usually makes up part of all good critical essays and descriptions and explanations, like those written by Emerson, Bernard Shaw, or E. B. White. The sharply chosen details of the story about the blackbird constitute evidence for its large and unexpressed assertions. "Too subjective," says one teacher. Nonsense. The writer here looked hard at himself over a period of time that gave him distance, recreated the thoughtless killer he once was, took the reader inside his sadistic attitude, and then revealed the change through action rather than explanation. Subjectivity and objectivity are both present and never confused. A trainer of literary critics could ask for no more. (The stories about the boy in the wheelchair and the shooting of blackbirds were written in classes of John Bennett, teacher at Central High School in Kalamazoo, who has used this approach to teaching writing.)

24. After three weeks of journal keeping, ask students to turn in journals. Excerpt from them some of the best writing and ditto it for students. You need not look at journals again if you do not want to. You may suggest to students that journals make useful banks for ideas and beginning pieces of writing.

25. Ask students to write a paper about something they have read. They should tell how and why some part of the work delighted, enraged, or stamped itself onto their memories. At the beginning and end of the paper they may present experience from their lives that illuminates the work. They may discuss book, magazine, short story, poem, sign, instruction sheet, letter, whatever. For this assignment one boy wrote of how successful Truman Capote had been in making the murderers in *In Cold Blood* seem human. The boy showed that in many ways they lived and thought like his own acquaintances and friends, who were not violent, sadistic, or murderous. Students should make their experience touch the experience in what they read, but not distort the author's world. Sometimes only part of this paper will go well. That part may be so good it can be lifted out to stand by itself.

26. Call attention to sound effects in both professional and student writing. Ask for several free writings (in journals or elsewhere) that experiment with sounds.

27. Ask students to write an indirect paper, in which they say the opposite of what they mean, create a fantasy that parallels some life situation, or speak in a pompous or otherwise false voice in order to satirize. Remind them frequently that they use these techniques in conversation with other students when they mimic, speak praise when they mean blame, or talk roughly to convey admiration or love. Don't use the word "satire." In this writing they must maintain one approach and tone. They cannot write "straight" part of the time and ironically the rest of the time.

Explain that some contemporary writers and artists using what has been called the "Put-On" mix tone and approach so the audience is never sure where the communicator stands. This ploy is sometimes appropriate and effective but more often irresponsible. In every activity of this course, except the assignments on word play and indirect writing, a few sophisticated students may feel they are being pushed into an old-fashioned, traditional mold. If you sense this reaction, say that most artists master the traditional techniques and forms of their art before significantly breaking them.

28. Throughout the course take up matters of usage and dialect when occasions present themselves. Language styles change. Today what we teachers once considered unpublishable vulgarity and obscenity is being printed, frequently by good writers and editors. Make students justify any use of material that shocks you. Does the material, the occasion, the audience, seem to the students to call for the language employed? You don't have to like it yourself, but don't inhibit the student's language to the point that he loses the rhythms inherent in his voices. Remember he has many voices. Frequently he should be able to find one that speaks clearly and excitingly to his classmates, to you, and to him.

By reading aloud passages from students' writing, constantly remind them of the differences between rhythmic sentences and stiff, flat, awkward sentences—the authentic and the badly borrowed. This emphasis on genuine voice does not mean you need to encourage only one style—informal, conversational, of the alley. Most good writers of ideas and experience—Shakespeare, Emerson, James Baldwin—employ a style which alternates between homely, kitchen language and elevated words. This alternation provides variety and tension and insures precision without artificiality.

29. Tell students that if they attend this seminar-style class regularly and write and criticize others' writing, they will write several, perhaps half a dozen, pieces that deserve to be published to the whole school community. That is a promise.

Expect student seminar criticism to improve slowly. Students need to test your assertion that you want truth. They need to discover ways of helping writers rather than injuring them. They need your more sophisticated and experienced judgment. Several times a week for periods of fifteen to twenty minutes, talk about writing clearly and authoritatively. If you do not know a great deal more about the craft than most students, you should learn or quit teaching. In valuable seminars the teacher lets the students do most of the talking but comes forward strongly when he feels he can inform or lead. He is never the authoritarian but often authoritative.

In general, do away with individual conferences with students about their papers. Most teachers dominate those sessions. Few such conferences provide the long-term support a writer needs to improve on his own. The teacher-student dialogue in the office has bad connotations for the student. In this course you are doing something different for him: providing praise from both his fellow students (whom he must trust more than you at the outset) and the most convincing approval—publication of one kind or another.

When you find a student who is not improving, take him aside and ask for four or five free writings again. Look for what is good in them. If nothing, try again. Bring him out of his doldrums or fear by honest praise for what he has done well, if only a sentence or paragraph.

30. Finally, the students' writing will be as good as the amount of discovery and wonder it contains. Old ideas, if held dearly, are valuable when expressed in new ways. Otherwise, the materials students present to others and to you should be news. The surest way for a writer to find newness is to try almost unbearably for truth. Last year in *The Reporter* magazine, Gene Baro said of Edward R. Murrow: "He told the truth in order to see it."

Teach Writing as a Process not Product

DONALD M. MURRAY

Most of us are trained as English teachers by studying the product: writing. Our critical skills are honed by examining literature, which is finished writing; language as it has been used by authors. And then, fully trained in the autopsy, we go out and are assigned to teach our students to write, to make language live.

Naturally we try to use our training. It's an investment and so we teach writing as a product, focusing our critical attention on what our students have done, as if they have passed literature in to us. It isn't literature, of course, and we use our skills, with which we can dissect and sometimes almost destroy Shakespeare or Robert Lowell to prove it.

Our students knew it wasn't literature when they passed it in, and our attack usually does little more than confirm their lack of self-respect for their work and for themselves; we are as frustrated as our students, for conscientious, doggedly responsible, repetitive autopsying doesn't give birth to live writing. The product doesn't improve, and so, blaming the student—who else?—we pass him along to the next teacher, who is trained, too often, the same way we were. Year after year the student shudders under a barrage of criticism, much of it brilliant, some of it stupid, and all of it irrelevant. No matter how careful our criticisms, they do not help the student since when we teach composition we are not teaching a product, we are teaching a process.

And once you can look at your composition program with the realization you are teaching a process, you may be able to design a curriculum which works. Not overnight, for writing is a demanding, intellectual process, but sooner than you think, for the process can be put to work to produce a product which may be worth your reading.

What is the process we should teach? It is the process of discovery through language. It is the process of exploration of what we know and what we feel about what we know through language. It is the process of using language to learn about our world, to evaluate what we learn about our world, to communicate what we learn about our world.

Instead of teaching finished writing, we should teach unfinished writ-

The Leaflet, (November 1972) pp. 11-14. Copyright © by The New England Association of Teachers of English. Reprinted by permission of the editor.

ing, and glory in its unfinishedness. We work with language in action. We share with our students the continual excitement of choosing one word instead of another, of searching for the one true word.

This is not a question of correct or incorrect, of etiquette or custom. This is a matter of far higher importance. The writer, as he writes, is making ethical decisions. He doesn't test his words by a rule book, but by life. He uses language to reveal the truth to himself so that he can tell it to others. It is an exciting, eventful, evolving process.

This process of discovery through language we call writing can be introduced to your classroom as soon as you have a very simple understanding of that process, and as soon as you accept the full implications of teaching process, not product.

The writing process itself can be divided into three stages: *prewriting, writing,* and *rewriting.* The amount of time a writer spends in each stage depends on his personality, his work habits, his maturity as a craftsman, and the challenge of what he is trying to say. It is not a rigid lock-step process, but most writers most of the time pass through these three stages.

Prewriting is everything that takes place before the first draft. Prewriting usually takes about 85% of the writer's time. It includes the awareness of his world from which his subject is born. In prewriting, the writer focuses on that subject, spots an audience, chooses a form which may carry his subject to his audience. Prewriting may include research and daydreaming, note-making and outlining, title-writing and lead-writing.

Writing is the act of producing a first draft. It is the fastest part of the process, and the most frightening, for it is the commitment. When you complete a draft you know how much, and how little, you know. And the writing of this first draft—rough, searching, unfinished—may take as little as one percent of the writer's time.

Rewriting is reconsideration of subject, form, and audience. It is researching, rethinking, redesigning, rewriting—and finally, line-by-line editing, the demanding, satisfying process of making each word right. It may take many times the hours required for the first draft, perhaps the remaining fourteen percent of the time the writer spends on the project.

How do you motivate your student to pass through this process, perhaps even pass through it again and again on the same piece of writing?

First by shutting up. When you are talking he isn't writing. And you don't learn a process by talking about it, but by doing it. Next by placing the opportunity for discovery in your student's hands. When you give him an assignment you tell him what to say and how to say it, and thereby cheat your student of the opportunity to learn the process of discovery we call writing.

To be a teacher of a process such as this takes qualities too few of us have, but which most of us can develop. We have to be quiet, to listen, to respond. We are not the initiator or the motivator; we are the reader, the recipient.

We have to be patient and wait, and wait, and wait. The suspense in the beginning of a writing course is agonizing for the teacher, but if we break first, if we do the prewriting for our students they will not learn the largest part of the writing process.

We have to respect the student, not for his product, not for the paper we call literature by giving it a grade, but for the search for truth in which he is engaged. We must listen carefully for those words that may reveal the truth, that may reveal a voice. We must respect our student for his potential truth and for his potential voice. We are coaches, encouragers, developers, creators of environments in which our students can experience the writing process for themselves.

Let us see what some of the implications of teaching process, not product, are for the composition curriculum.

Implication No. 1. The text of the writing course is the student's own writing. Students examine their own evolving writing and that of their classmates, so that they study writing while it is still a matter of choice, word by word.

Implication No. 2. The student finds his own subject. It is not the job of the teacher to legislate the student's truth. It is the responsibility of the student to explore his own world with his own language, to discover his own meaning. The teacher supports but does not direct this expedition to the student's own truth.

Implication No. 3. The student uses his own language. Too often, as writer and teacher Thomas Williams points out, we teach English to our students as if it were a foreign language. Actually, most of our students have learned a great deal of language before they come to us, and they are quite willing to exploit that language if they are allowed to embark on a serious search for their own truth.

Implication No. 4. The student should have the opportunity to write all the drafts necessary for him to discover what he has to say on this particular subject. Each new draft, of course, is counted as equal to a new paper. You are not teaching a product, you are teaching a process.

Implication No. 5. The student is encouraged to attempt any form of writing which may help him discover and communicate what he has to say. The process which produces "creative" and "functional" writing is the same. You are not teaching products such as business letters and poetry, narrative and exposition. You are teaching a product your student can use—now and in the future—to produce whatever product his subject and his audience demand.

Implication No. 6. Mechanics come last. It is important to the writer, once he has discovered what he has to say, that nothing get between him and his reader. He must break only those traditions of written communication which would obscure his meaning.

Implication No. 7. There must be time for the writing process to take place and time for it to end. The writer must work within the stimulating tension of unpressured time to think and dream and stare out windows, and pressured time—the deadline—to which the writer must deliver.

Implication No. 8. Papers are examined to see what other choices the writer might make. The primary responsibility for seeing the choices is the student. He is learning a process. His papers are always unfinished, evolving, until the end of the marking period. A grade finishes a paper, the way publication usually does. The student writer is not graded on drafts any more than a concert pianist is judged on his practice sessions rather than on his performance. The student writer is graded on what he has produced at the end of the writing process.

Implication No. 9. The students are individuals who must explore the writing process in their own way, some fast, some slow, whatever it takes for them, within the limits of the course deadlines, to find their own way to their own truth.

Implication No. 10. There are no rules, no absolutes, just alternatives. What works one time may not another. All writing is experimental.

None of these implications requires a special schedule, exotic training, extensive new materials or gadgetry, new classrooms, or an increase in federal, state, or local funds. They do not even require a reduced teaching load. What they do require is a teacher who will respect and respond to his students, not for what they have done, but for what they may do; not for what they have produced, but for what they may produce, if they are given an opportunity to see writing as a process, not a product.

PART THREE

The Sentence:
A Reluctant Medium

"No class hour should pass without attention to sentences."

J. N. Hook

After catching a vision of what needs to be said, the writer begins to give that vision form, reinforcing those places which are most important, filling out the missing parts, erasing the blemishes and inconsistencies. Out of that fragile web of thought emerge the shape and color and texture of written discourse. The primary unit for giving the vision substance and form is the sentence. Individually, a single sentence can reveal the craftsmanship, the technical competence of a writer. Taken together as a whole, all the sentences in a piece of writing portray the writer's overall pattern of thought.

Since the sentence is the basic unit of written discourse, it should receive primary attention in the composition classroom. Teachers of English should, of course, help their young charges with problems of conceptualization and discovery, but they cannot stop there. They must go on to a task which is not as glamourous yet just as important, for those beginners must learn how to become consummate craftsmen of language. They must learn how to weigh every word, every mark of punctuation, how to develop an eye and ear for the language, how to bring to their written work all the care and concentration within their power. "But style shows through an accumulation of small particulars, and the artist in language may ponder a long while . . ." writes Richard M. Weaver in the lead essay "Some Rhetorical Aspects of Grammatical Categories." Weaver shows that each sentence type—the simple, the complex, the compound—creates its own distinct rhetorical effect. In the next essay, Daiker, Kerek, and Morenberg show how "open" sentence-combining exercises can be used to teach a variety of rhetorical strategies and techniques. Indeed, almost all the rhetorical nuances described by Weaver can be explored in the classroom through sentence-combining exercises.

The next two essays continue to focus on the traditional elements of style. In Francis Christensen's "A Generative Rhetoric of the Sentence," the reader is introduced to the concept of symmetrical form, particularly the cumulative sentence with its short base clause and appended non-clausal modifiers. In "Symmetrical Form and the Rhetoric of the Sentence" I have tried to provide a counterpoint to Christensen's generative rhetoric by showing that symmetrical form is also vital in composition and can be as dynamic in its own way as asymetrical form.

In "The Syntax of Error" Valerie Krishna has identified an error which has long eluded description, "a more serious, more fundamental mistake than the classical errors of verb agreement, punctuation, pronoun case, and so on . . . " Krishna argues that students often waste the important subject-verb relation by putting their main ideas into grammatically minor slots, such as prepositional phrases and dependent clauses. Krishna's work is important because it shows how the writer's ideas are related to grammatical functions.

The concluding two essays explore the world of Grammar B, those constructions outside the usual realm of style, constructions such as the crot, the labyrinthine sentence, the fragment, the list, double voice, refrains, and synchronicity. In "Grammars of Style: New Options in Composition," Winston Weathers makes a convincing argument that these new ways of expression are legitimate and powerful and should be included in the composition class alongside the regular constructions. Students should be "exposed to, and informed about, the full range of compositional possibilities," Weathers writes. In arguing for a reevaluation of the fragment sentence, Kline and Memering offer support for Weathers' thesis.

Helping our students gain control of "the full range of compositional possibilities" within the sentence is no small task. It is slow, time-consuming work, but one suspects most composition teachers find it downright exciting.

Some Rhetorical Aspects of Grammatical Categories

RICHARD M. WEAVER

We soon realize that different ways of saying a thing denote different interests in saying it, or to take this in reverse as we do when we become conscious of language, different interests in a matter will dictate different patterns of expression. Rhetoric in its practice is a matter of selection and arrangement, but conventional grammar imposes restraints upon both of these. All this amounts to saying what every sensitive user of language has sometimes felt; namely, that language is not a purely passive instrument, but that, owing to this public acceptance, while you are doing something with it, it is doing something with you, or with your intention.[1] It does not exactly fight back: rather it has a set of postures and balances which somehow modify your thrusts and holds. The sentence form is certainly one of these. You pour into it your meaning, and it deflects, and molds into certain shapes. The user of language must know how this counterpressure can be turned to the advantage of his general purpose. The failure of those who are careless, or insensitive, to the rhetoric of grammar is that they allow the counter force to impede their design, whereas a perspicacious use of it will forward the design. One cannot, for example, employ just any modifier to stand for a substantive or just any substantive to express a quality, or change a stabilized pattern of arrangement without a change in net effect, although some of these changes register but faintly. But style shows through an accumulation of small particulars, and the artist in language may ponder a long while, as Conrad is said to have done, over whether to describe a character as "penniless" or "without a penny."

In this approach, then, we are regarding language as a standard objective reality, analyzable into categories which have inherent potentialities. A knowledge of these objective potentialities can prevent a loss of force through friction. The friction we refer to occurs whenever a given unit of the system of grammar is tending to say one thing while the semantic meaning and the general organization are tending to say another. A language has certain abilities or even inclinations which the wise user can draw into the service of his own rhetorical effort. Using a language may be compared to riding a horse; much of one's success depends upon an understanding of what it *can* and *will* do. Or to employ a different figure in illustration, there is a kind of use of language which goes against the grain as that grain is constituted by the categories, and there is a kind which facilitates the speaker's projection by going with it. Our task is an exploration of the congruence between well understood rhetorical objectives and the inherent character of major ele-

from Richard M. Weaver, *The Ethics of Rhetoric* (Chicago: Henry Regnery Company, 1953), pp. 116-131. Copyright © 1953 by Henry Regnery Company.

ments in modern English.

The problem of which category to begin with raises some questions. It is arguable that the rhetoric of any piece is dependent upon its total intention, and that consequently no single sentence can be appraised apart from the tendency of the whole discourse. Our position does not deny that, since we are assuming merely that within the greater effect there are lesser effects, cooperating well or ill. Having accepted that limitation, it seems permissable for us to begin with the largest unit of grammar, which is the sentence. We shall take up first the sentence as such and then discriminate between formal types of sentences.

Because a sentence form exists in most if not all languages, there is some ground to suppose that it reflects a necessary operation of the mind, and this means not simply of the mind as psychologically constituted but also as logically constrained. . . .

As we turn now to the different formal types of sentences, we shall follow the traditional grammatical classification and discuss the rhetorical inclination of each in turn.

Through its form, the simple sentence tends to emphasize the discreteness of phenomena within the structural unity. To be more specific, its pattern of subject-verb-object or complement, without major competing elements, leaves our attention fixed upon the classes involved: "Charles is King." The effect remains when the simple sentence compounds its subject and predicate: "Peaches and cantaloupes grew in abundance"; "Men and boys hunted and fished." The single subject-predicate frame has the broad sense of listing or itemizing, and the list becomes what the sentence is about semantically.

Sentences of this kind are often the unconscious style of one who sees the world as a conglomerate of things, like the child; sometimes they are the conscious style of one who seeks to present certain things as eminent against a background of matter uniform or flat. One can imagine, for example, the simple sentence "He never worked" coming after a long and tedious recital which it is supposed to highlight. Or one can imagine the sentence "The world is round" leaping out of a context with which it contrasts in meaning, in brevity, or in sententiousness.

There is some descriptive value in saying that the simple sentence is the most "logical" type of sentence because, like the simple categorical proposition, it has this function of relating two classes. This fact, combined with its usual brevity and its structural simplicity, makes it a useful sentence for beginnings and endings (or important meaning-groups, not so much of formal introductions and conclusions). It is a sentence of unclouded perspective, so to speak. Nothing could be more beautifully anticipatory than Burke's "The proposition is peace."

At the very minimum, we can affirm that the simple sentence tends to throw subject and predicate classes into relief by the structure it presents them in; that the two-part categorical form of its copulation indicates a positive mood on the part of the user, and that its brevity often induces a

generality of approach, which is an aid to perspicuous style. These opportunities are found out by the speaker or writer who senses the need for some
synoptic or dramatic spot in his discourse. Thus when he selects the simple
sentence, he is going "with the grain"; he is putting the objective form to
work for him.

The complex sentence has a different potentiality. Whereas the simple
sentence emphasizes through its form the co-existence of classes (and it must
be already apparent that we regard "things existing or occurring" as a class
where the predicate consists only of a verb), the complex sentence emphasizes a more complex relationship; that is to say, it reflects another kind
of discriminating activity, which does not stop with seeing discrete classes as
co-existing, but distinguishes them according to rank or value, or places them
in an order of cause and effect. "Rome fell because valor decined" is the
utterance of a reflective mind because the conjunction of parts depends on
something ascertainable by the intellect but not by simple perception. This
is evidence that the complex sentence does not appear until experience has
undergone some refinement by the mind. Then, because it goes beyond simple observation and begins to perceive things according to a standard of
interest, it brings in the notion of dependence to supplement that of simple
togetherness. And consequently the complex sentence will be found nearly
always to express some sort of hierarchy, whether spatial, moral, or causal,
with its subordinate members describing the lower orders. In simple-sentence
style we would write: "Tragedy began in Greece. It is the highest form of
literary art." There is no disputing that these sentences, in this sequence,
could have a place in mature expression. But they do not have the same
effect as "Tragedy, which is the highest form of literary art, began in
Greece" or "Tragedy, which began in Greece, is the highest form of literary
art." What has occurred is the critical process of subordination. The two
ideas have been transferred from a conglomerate to an articulated unity, and
the very fact of subordination makes inevitable the emergence of a focus of
interest. Is our passage about the highest form of literary art or about the
cultural history of Greece? The form of the complex sentence makes it unnecessary to waste any words in explicit assertion of that. Here it is plain
that grammatical form is capital upon which we can draw, provided that
other necessities have been taken care of. . . .

In summation, then, the complex sentence is the branching sentence,
or the sentence with parts growing off other parts. Those who have used it
most properly have performed a second act of analysis, in which the objects
of perception, after being seen discretely, are put into a ranked structure.
This type of sentence imposes the greatest demand upon the reader because
it carries him farthest into the reality existing outside self. This point will
take on importance as we turn to the compound sentence.

The structure of the compound sentence often reflects a simple artless-
ness—the uncritical pouring together of simple sentences, as in the speech of
Huckleberry Finn. The child who is relating an adventure is likely to make it
a flat recital of conjoined simple predications, because to him the important

fact is that the things were, not that they can be read to signify this or that. His even juxtapositions are therefore sometimes amusing, for now and then he will produce a coordination that unintentionally illuminates. This would, of course, be a result of lack of control over the rhetoric of grammar.

On the other hand, the compound sentence can be a very "mature" sentence when its structure conforms with a settled view of the balance it presents. When a sentence consists of two main clauses we have two predications of similar structure bidding for our attention. Our first supposal is that this produces a sentence of unusual tension, with two equal parts (and of course sometimes more than two equal parts) in a sort of competition. Yet it appears on fuller acquaintance that this tension is a tension of stasis, and that the compound sentence has, in practice, been markedly favored by periods of repose like that of the Eighteenth century. There is congeniality between its internal balance and a concept of the world as an equilibrium of forces. As a general rule, it appears that whereas the complex sentences favors the presentation of the world as a system of facts or as a dynamisim, the compound sentence favors the presentation of it in a more or less philosophical picture. This world as a philosophical cosmos will have to be a sort of compensatory system. We know from other evidences that the Eighteenth century loved to see things in balance; in fact, it required the idea of balance as a foundation for its insitutions. Quite naturally then, since motives of this kind reach into expression-forms, this was the age of masters of the balanced sentence—Dryden, Johnson, Gibbon, and others, the *genre* of whose style derives largely from this practice of compounding. Often the balance which they achieved was more intricate than simple conjunction of main clauses because they balanced lesser elements too, but the informing impulse was the same. That impulse was the desire for counterpoise, which was one of the powerful motives of their culture.

In this pattern of balance, various elements are used in the offsettings. Thus when one attends closely to the meanings of the balanced parts, one finds these compounds recurring: an abstract statement is balanced (in a second independent clause) by a more concrete expression of the same thing; a fact is balanced by its causal explanation; a statement of positive mode balanced by one of negative mode; a clause of praise is balanced by a clause of qualified censure; a description of one part is balanced by a description of a contrasting part, and so on through a good many conventional pairings. Now in these collocations cause and effect and other relationships are presented, yet the attempt seems not so much to explore reality as to clothe it in decent form. Culture is a delicate reconciliation of opposites, and consequently a man who sees the world through the eyes of a culture makes effort in this direction. We know that the world of Eighteenth century culture was a rationalist world, and in a rationalist world everything must be "accounted for." The virtue of the compound sentence is that its second part gives "the other half," so to speak. As the pattern works out, every fact has it cause; every virtue is compensated for by a vice; every excursion into generality must be made up for by attention to concrete circumstances and vica versa.

The perfection of this art form is found in Johnson and Gibbon, where such pairings occur with a frequency which has given rise to the phrase "the balanced style." When Gibbon, for example, writes of religion in the Age of Antonines: "The superstition of the people was not embittered by any mixture of theological rancor; nor was it confined by the chains of any speculative system,"[2] we have almost the feeling that the case of religion has been settled by this neat artifice of expression. This is a "just" view of affairs, which sees both sides and leaves a kind of balanced account. It looks somewhat subjective, or at least humanized; it gives us the gross world a little tidied up by thought. Often, moreover, this balance of structure together with the act of saying a thing equivocally—in the narrower etymological sense of that word—suggests the finality of art. This will be fround true of many of the poetical passages of the King James Bible, although these come from an earlier date. "The heavens declare the glory of God; and the firmament sheweth his handiwork"; "Man cometh forth as a flower and is cut down; he fleeth also as a shadow and continueth not." By thus stating the matter in two ways, through balanced clauses, the sentence achieves a degree of formal completeness missing in sentences where the interest is in mere assertion. Generally speaking the balanced compound sentence, by the very contrivedness of its structure, suggests something formed above the welter of experience, and this form, as we have by now substantially said, transfers something of itself to the meaning. In declaring that the compound sentence may seem subjective, we are not saying that it is arbitrary, its correspondence being with the philosophical interpretation rather than with the factual reality. Thus if the complex sentence is about the world, the compound sentence is about our idea about the world, into which some notion of compensation forces itself. One notices that even Huxley, when he draws away from his simple expositions of fact and seeks play for his great powers of persuasion, begins to compound his sentences. On the whole, the compound sentence conveys that completeness and symmetry which the world *ought* to have, and which we manage to get, in some measure, into our most satisfactory explanations of it. It is most agreeable to those ages and those individuals who feel that they have come to terms with the world, and are masters in a domain. But understandably enough, in a world which has come to be centrifugal and infinite, as ours has become since the great revolutions, it tends to seem artificial and mechanical in its containment.

Notes

[1] To mention a simple example, the sarcasm uttered as a pleasantry sometimes leaves a wound because its formal signification is not entirely removed by the intonation of the user or by the speech situation.

[2] *Decline and Fall of the Roman Empire* (Bury's ed., London, 1900), I, 28.

Using "Open" Sentence-Combining Exercises in the College Composition Classroom

DONALD A. DAIKER, ANDREW KEREK, and MAX MORENBERG

Can sentence combining be made the center of a college composition course, a recent contributor to *College Composition and Communication* asks, without causing students to revolt out of sheer boredom? That this question is asked in a major professional journal may reveal a widespread misunderstanding of the evolution of sentence-combining exercises; at least, it implies that the questioner has not yet become aware of *open* sentence-combining exercises or does not know how to use them in the classroom. Perhaps he knows only the useful but limited form of sentence combining called *closed* or signalled exercises. A typical closed exercise consists of two or more sentences with a set of instructions so specific that there is usually but one wholly correct way of making one sentence from several. Here, borrowed from John Mellon, is a sample closed exercise:

SOMETHING would be almost unbearable.
The rocket fails in its final stage. (T:infin)

By transforming the second sentence into an infinitive phrase and substituting it for SOMETHING in the first sentence, the student is expected to reach the one correct answer:

For the rocket to fail in its final stage would be almost unbearable.

Although closed exercises help students at any grade level practice specific constructions like infinitive phrases, they seem too mechanical and too restrictive ever to become the center of a college composition course. Indeed, their exclusive use might well justify revolt.

But when open sentence-combining exercises are made the organizing principle of a college composition course, they are more likely to excite student imagination than incite student revolution. Open exercises, like those found in William Strong's pioneering textbook *Sentence Combining: A Composing Book* or in our own *The Writer's Options: College Sentence Combining*, essentially differ from closed exercises in their degree of freedom and their range of options. If closed exercises specify what structures are to be used and how they are to be made, open exercises are accompanied by more general instructions like "combine these sentences into an effective paragraph." It is the open exercise which most clearly illustrates that sentence-combining—despite its name—involves units of discourse larger than the sentence and provides practice in writing skills that go far beyond mere combining, even beyond syntax in its broadest sense. The open exercise demonstrates that a more accurate term for sentence combining might be "disciplined writing practice."

Here is an open exercise from *The Writer's Options*:

THE HOME FRONT

Combine the following sentences into an effective essay. The spaces between groups of sentences indicate where one of your sentences may end and another begin, but feel free to ignore the spaces whenever you choose.

1. "Rosie the Riveter" was the symbol for the civilians.
2. The civilians worked for the war effort.
3. The work was during World War II.

4. She was like all of them.
5. All of them rode to work at a war factory.
6. The riding was in a '38 Studebaker.
7. The Studebaker had bald tires.
8. The car was filled to capacity.
9. But the car was short on gas.

10. She put up blackout curtains at night before she did this.
11. She turned on the lights.
12. And she tuned in the radio.
13. She wanted to hear Gabriel Heatter or H. V. Kaltenborn.
14. They had the latest reports from the European Theater of Operations.
15. They had the latest reports from the Pacific Theater of Operations.

16. She made supper.
17. At the same time, she was listening to "Amos 'n Andy" or "The Hit Parade."
18. She was listening to "Gangbusters" or "Lux Radio Theater."

19. But mostly she thought about her husband.
20. Her husband was "somewhere in the Pacific."
21. The censored letters always said "somewhere in the Pacific."

22. This was it.
23. Millions of Americans spent the war years somehow.
24. They were waiting for loved ones in uniform.
25. They were listening to the news on the radio.

26. And they were taking part in this.
27. It was the greatest production effort a people have ever made.

28. Women like Rosie learned how to do this.
29. They soldered.
30. They ran lathes.
31. They drove buses for this reason.
32. They wanted to replace men.
33. The men were needed for combat.

34. High-school kids worked evenings.
35. They worked in tank factories.
36. They worked in steel mills

37. Old people took up trades.
38. The old people were in retirement.
39. The trades were half-forgotten.

40. They produced the weapons.
41. The weapons fought the Axis powers.
42. They produced 296,029 airplanes.
43. They produced 86,333 tanks.
44. They produced 319,000 artillery pieces.

45. They raised steel production by 70 percent over prewar years.
46. They increased the production of aluminum by 429 percent.
47. They increased the production of magnesium by 3358 percent.

48. They saved tin cans.
49. They brushed their teeth with half-brushfuls of toothpaste.
50. They worked at the local U.S.O.

51. They walked the darkened streets in the evenings.
52. They were air-raid wardens.
53. Or they strained their eyes.
54. They were peering through the night skies.
55. They were aircraft-warning watchers.

56. They waited.
57. They worked.
58. They lined up.
59. The lining up was for hard-to-get-items.
60. Sugar was a hard-to-get-item.
61. Nylons were a hard-to-get-item.
62. Tires were hard-to-get-items.
63. Coffee was a hard-to-get-item.
64. Their ration coupons were in hand.

65. They were a people.
66. The people were united against totalitarianism.
67. The people were united to win a war.
68. They wanted to win a war.
69. They believed in the war.

Although the stated instructions for "The Home Front" are simply to create an effective essay from the given sentences, you have nearly as many options in assigning an open exercise as your students have for completing it. For example, you can require your students to use, at points in their essay that they determine for themselves, the specific constructions emphasized in recently assigned closed exercises, constructions like appositives or absolutes or paired coordinators. You can instruct your students to add several details of their own or, conversely, to eliminate from their finished version the two or three details least relevant to their thesis. You can direct them to add an introduction or a conclusion, or to restructure the essay so as to focus less on American unity and more on the importance of the radio. Or, whenever you choose, you can specify an audience for your student writers—perhaps a group of World War II veterans or of ERA supporters, perhaps readers of the *Encyclopaedia Britannica* or of *Playboy* magazine.

However you modify the instructions, open exercises like "The Home Front" always challenge the student writer to make a series of effective rhetorical choices. So that students learn both to recognize the range of their choices and to evaluate the relative effectiveness of each choice, you *must* make some completed student versions available to the entire class. To do so, try using the blackboard, an overhead projector, or dittoed or mimeographed copies. If you had assigned "The Home Front" as homework and selected several students to submit their completed assignments on ditto masters, you could then distribute to your class versions like the following three:

THE HOME FRONT

[Student version # 1]

"Rosie the Riveter" was the American symbol for the civilians working for the war effort during World War II. She rode to work in a crammed '38 Studebaker with bald tires and an empty gastank. At night she would put up blackout curtains, then turn on the lights and tune in the radio so she could listen to Gabriel Heatter or H. V. Kaltenborn, who broadcast the latest reports from the European and Pacific Theater of Operations. Later, while making supper, she listened to popular radio shows such as: "Amos 'n Andy" or "The Hit Parade," "Gangbusters" or "Lux Radio Theater." But her thoughts rarely strayed from her husband who was "somewhere in the Pacific."

This was how millions of Americans spent the war years, waiting for loved ones in uniform, listening to the news on the radio, and unknowingly taking part in the greatest production effort ever.

Everyone pitched in. Women learned to drive buses, solder machinery, and run lathes; high-school kids worked long evenings in tank factories and steel mills, old people took up half-forgotten trades; all because men were needed for combat. Together, they raised the production of steel, aluminum, and magnesium by overwhelming percentages. Which enabled them to produce a total of nearly three-fourths of a million artillery pieces, tanks, and airplanes: weapons that fought the

Axis powers. They saved tin cans, brushed their teeth with half-brush-fuls of toothpaste and worked at their local U.S.O. In the evenings, air-raid wardens walked the darkened streets as aircraft-warning watchers strained their eyes peering into the night skies.

Waiting in lines for those hard-to-items: sugar, nylons, tires, and cof-fee, they held on tightly to their ration coupons. They were a people united against totalitarianism. United in their desire to win a war, a war they believed in.

THE HOME FRONT
[Student version # 2]

The civilians who worked for the war effort during World War II were symbolized by the figure of "Rosie the Riveter." She like all of them rode to the war factory where they worked in a '38 Studebaker, filled to capacity but short on gas, with bald tires.

At night before she turned on the light and tuned in the radio she put up blackout curtains. She wanted to hear Gabriel Heatter or H. V. Kaltenborn because they had the latest news from the European and Pacific Theater of Operation. While making supper she listened to either "Amos 'n Andy," "The Hit Parade," "Gangbusters," or "Lux Radio Theater" but mostly she thought about her husband whose censored letters always said he was "somewhere in the Pacific."

Millions of Americans spent the war years this way: listening to news on the radio, waiting for loved ones who were in uniform, but they were all taking part in the greatest production effort a society had ever engaged in. Women like Rosie learned how to solder, run lathes, and drive buses to replace men who were needed for combat.

While high-school kids worked evenings in tank factories or steel mills, retired people again took up their half forgotten trades. They pro-duced a total of 296,029 airplanes, 86,333 tanks and 319,000 artillery pieces, all weapons which fought the Axis powers. They raised produc-tion of steel by 70 percent, aluminum by 429 and magnesium by 3358 percent over prewar years.

Everyone helped out in their own way: saving tin cans, brushing their teeth with half-brushfuls of tooth paste, working at the U.S.O. They waited and worked. With their ration coupons in hand they lined up for Sugar, Nylons, Tires, and other hard to get items.

They were a people, united in their desire to suppress totalitarianism. They were a people united to win a war they believed in.

THE HOME FRONT
[Student version # 3]

In most World War II texts and movies, glorious American soldiers are idolized as they conquer shattered cities and raise victory flags over half-standing battlements. It is easy to give credit to these men for their ac-complishments, but it is even easier to neglect the people in their shadows—the people on the "homefront." Uniting together, millions of American "homefronters" helped contribute substantially to overseas victories.

"Rosie the Riveter," the nickname for civilian women working for the war effort, represented the vast number of dedicated housewives who sacrificed comfortable lives for long days of work, worry, and sweat. Many had the same schedule. They rode to work early in the morning in a '38 Studebaker filled with too many people and too little gas. At night, after a long hard day of work, they would put up blackout curtains, turn on the lights and tune in the radio to hear Gabriel Heatter's or H. V. Kaltenborn's latest reports from both the European and Pacific Theater of Operations. But mostly they thought about their husbands who, according to the censored letters, were "somewhere in the Pacific."

During these years of waiting for loved ones in uniform and listening to the news on the radio, Americans took part in the greatest production effort a people have ever engaged in. To replace men needed for combat, women like Rosie learned how to solder, run lathes and drive buses. In the evenings high-school students worked in tank factories and steel mills, and even old people in retirement took up half-forgotten trades.

All together, U.S. citizens produced 296,029 airplanes, 86,333 tanks, and 319,000 artillery pieces which were used by the Allies to thwart the spread of Fascism. They raised the production of steel by 70%, aluminum 429%, and magnesium 3358% over prewar years. Civilian air-raid wardens walked the darkened streets in the evenings and aircraft-warning watchers strained their eyes to peer through the night skies. During the day, people lined up, ration coupons in hand, for the hard-to-get items like nylons and tires, coffee and sugar.

These were a people united—united against totalitarianism and united in their desire to win a war they believed in.

Once the three versions of "The Home Front" have been read aloud, class discussion can move in whatever direction you and your students choose. You might begin with broad questions about thesis and organization. Is one version most effective in clearly stating its central idea? Is version #3 strengthened because its thesis is stated in the first paragraph? Is anything lost from version #1 and #2 because their thesis statements are delayed until the final paragraph? From questions about thesis placement you might turn to supporting details. Does version #3 improve with the names of the radio programs eliminated? What about its omitting the tin cans, half-brushfuls of toothpaste, and the U.S.O.? Does version #3 gain from the original details added at its beginning? Does version #1 improve with the specific production numbers and percentages converted into round figures? Do students with unreproduced versions of "The Home Front" want to volunteer some of their own additions or omissions for class reaction? Finally, are there general standards for determining which details to include and which to omit.

You might next consider organizational questions. Since all three versions follow the order of the original sentences—some open exercises consist of deliberately misarranged sentences that must be reordered—discussion will probably emphasize paragraphing and coherence. You might ask whether the short concluding paragraphs of versions #2 and #3 are more effective than the longer concluding paragraph of version #1. Are the details of people waiting in line more appropriate to the essay's last or next-to-last paragraph? What should the last paragraph of an essay accomplish? The same as the first? Does the first paragraph of #1 improve when it is divided into two separate paragraphs, as in #2? How effective is the one-sentence second paragraph of version #1?

Of course, open exercises allow for more than asking questions of your students. They furnish concrete examples of writing strategies and techniques that will be more readily and successfully imitated by your students than will the faultless prose of E. B. White or Henry David Thoreau. For example, the student versions of "The Home Front" illustrate several effective techniques for creating coherence. One such technique is the short transitional sentence: "Everyone pitched in" in version #1 or "Many had the same schedule" in version #3. Another technique is the transitional word or phrase like "Later" or "But" in the first paragraph of #1, "All together" and "During the day" of #3. With these examples, your students are better prepared to improve the coherence of version #2. Its first two paragraphs can be more tightly connected by the kind of transitional phrase found in the same position in version #3, "after a long hard day of work." With this suggestion, the second paragraph of version #2 becomes "At night, after a long, hard day of work, she put up the blackout curtains before turning on the light and tuning in the radio." A different strategy of coherence might be used to strengthen the connection between the third and fourth paragraphs of version #2. One possibility is a short transitional sentence like "But it wasn't only women who helped" or "Young and old contributed." Another effective strategy of coherence is the repetition of a sentence pattern. If you remove *while* from the opening of the fourth paragraph, the subject-verb-object pattern of "High-school kids worked evenings in tank factories or steel mills" repeats the pattern of "Women like Rosie learned how to solder, run lathes, and drive buses" in order to join the two sentences more tightly together.

Whenever you finish with problems of coherence and organization, the fifth paragraph of version #2 offers a smooth transition to questions of punctuation and grammar. The paragraph opens with a sentence that is at once a highly effective transition and an example of grammatical error: "Everyone helped out in their own way. . . . " After acknowledging the excellence of the transition—praise is especially welcome now because you earlier called attention to weaknesses of coherence in this version—you may want to identify and then correct the error in pronoun-antecedent agreement. If you ask for student suggestions, someone will probably revise the sentence to read "Everyone helped out in his own way." Depending on your own attitudes, you will either approve the suggestion or begin a lecture on the non-sexist use of pronouns. Instructors who highly value grammatical correctness will find a way to shift discussion to the sentence fragments in the last and next-to-last paragraphs of version #1. From there, they are likely to go to examples of faulty parallelism in versions #1 and #2, then to the misplaced modifier and vague pronoun reference of #2. But sentence combining as a method no more implies an attitude toward traditional grammar than it favors the cumulative sentence over the periodic or long sentences over short ones. Despite the research that has linked training in sentence combining to increased T-unit and clause length, sentence combining can as easily teach students to write in the style of the early Hemingway as the later James. It all depends on the values instructors communicate to their students.

Had you begun with the full sentence "Everyone helped out in their own way: saving tin cans, brushing their teeth with half-brushfuls of toothpaste, working at the U.S.O.," discussion might have turned to questions of punctuation instead of grammar. Is the colon used correctly here? What about the colon in the last paragraph of version #1? Are the colon and the dash (used in the first and last paragraphs of #3) interchangeable? Why not? What is the difference between them? And how does each relate to the semi-colon? Is the semi-colon appropriate in the third paragraph of #2? Is there a comma problem in the first paragraph of #2? In the first paragraph of #3? In teaching punctuation, grammar, or any other writing element, you can always move beyond the student versions to introduce examples of your own, to suggest options that your students have not chosen, or—so that students can practice what they've just discussed—to assign short, in-class writing exercises on anything from the comma splice and the colon to figurative language and tone. Occasionally, you may want to reproduce your own version of an open exercise to be read and evaluated with the student versions.

If any class time remains, you can begin a discussion of diction by explaining the appropriateness of *battlements* in the first paragraph of #3 and the inappropriateness of *suppress* in the last paragraph of #2. When you eventually move from words to phrases, you might ask for examples of wordiness. One student may suggest that *rode to the the war factory where they worked* in the first paragraph of #2 becomes more concise as *rode to work at a war factory*. Another student may show that, in the second paragraph of #2, the sentence "She wanted to hear Gabriel Heatter or H. V. Kaltenborn *because they had* the latest news from the European and Pacific Theater of Operations" improves as "She wanted to hear Gabriel Heatter or H. V. Kaltenborn *with* the latest news. . . ." Perhaps a third student will ask about the middle paragraph of #3. Can't its opening be shortened? With the help of your students, you might conclude that *During these years of working and waiting* is more forceful than the longer *During these years of waiting for loved ones in uniform and listening to the news on the radio.*

Making sentences and phrases more concise may lead, perhaps in a later class, to a full discussion of syntax. Actually, the sentences in the three student versions of "The Home Front" are so varied and so rich that you could easily spend an entire class commenting on nothing but syntax. Appositives, participles, absolutes, balanced phrases, subordinate clauses, interrupted coordination, series variation, complex prepositional phrases, noun substitutes—all these constructions and more are here to be recognized, contrasted, evaluated, and—as often as possible—held up for imitation. You would certainly want to call attention to the very best sentences: in #1, the last sentence of the first paragraph; in #2, the first sentence in the fourth paragraph; and in #3, the last sentence of the first and fourth paragraphs. Such excellent student sentences are most likely to be imitated if they are read aloud more than once and then recited aloud by the whole class.

But the syntax of some student sentences should be improved, not imitated. Look for example, at the conclusions of the three versions of "The Home Front":

1. They were a people united against totalitarianism. United in their desire to win a war, a war they believed in.
2. They were a people, united in their desire to suppress totalitarianism. They were a people united to win a war they believed in.
3. These were a people united—united against totalitarianism and united in their desire to win a war they believed in.

All three student writers apparently realize that repeating key terms or sentence elements, especially at the conclusion of an essay, is an effective means of emphasis. But all have problems making repetition work. In the first version, the fragment is more disruptive than emphatic, and the repeated *a war* sounds too artificial to be forceful. The second version is adequate but undistinguished, even if the misplaced comma is removed. The third version is good, but something is wrong with its rhythms. After you have praised all three students for experimenting with repetition, you might request suggestions for improvement. If you are greeted with silence, venture the generalization that repeated words usually work most effectively when they are separated from each other by at least one intervening word. With this hint, one of your students may volunteer a sentence like this:

These were a united people—united against totalitarianism, united in their desire to win a war they believed in.

Now that the sentence has been improved, you can choose whether to have it recited aloud, to request additional student suggestions for improvement, to assign a related in-class writing exercise, or to move to a totally new area of discussion.

Because of such choices, an open sentence-combining exercise like "The Home Front" gives composition teachers relevant material for at least two fifty-minute classes. More important, a single open exercise can help teach just about any significant writing skill or strategy.

In part because students sense their growing mastery of skills and strategies, they generally enjoy working out the open exercises and then discussing them—often heatedly—with their classmates and instructor. It's hardly surprising, after all, that they would rather discuss their own writing than locate topic sentences in a Walter Lippmann essay, or review the four indispensable properties of all respectable paragraphs. Of course, sentence combining does more than spark student enthusiasm for writing; as experimental studies have shown, training in sentence combining enhances syntactic maturity and improves overall writing quality. One plausible explanation for such success is that sentence combining places student writing at the psychological and physical center of the composition course. What becomes psychologically most important in a sentence-combining course is not the prose of George Orwell or James McCrimmon but the sentences, paragraphs, and essays of Kathy Huber who sits in the second row and Jon Barnes who sits in the fourth. Making immediately clear that nothing counts more than the writing of your students helps in subtle but perceptible ways to increase their interest in writing and to build their confidence as writers. But making student writing the physical center of the course is equally important: sentence-combining teachers keep the focus on student writing by consistently assigning writing exercises as homework and by occasionally assigning writing exercises in the classroom. In a sentence-combining course, the act of writing is usually not reduced to equality with reading about writing, reading essays by professional writers, or studying language and grammar. In fact, a major premise of sentence combining is that you learn a skill by practicing a skill. That is, you learn to write best not by writing for one day, reading about it for two days, and then watching others demonstrate it for three more; you learn to write best by writing all six days.

Once your students realize that a sentence-combining course built around open exercises confronts them with a variety of interesting and meaningful writing decisions, they will have little time left for boredom. And once they understand that the skills learned from the exercises do in fact transfer to their original compositions, helping them to become better writers and to receive higher grades, they will surely have no desire for revolt.

A Generative Rhetoric of the Sentence

FRANCIS CHRISTENSEN

If the new grammar is to be brought to bear on composition, it must be brought to bear on the rhetoric of the sentence. We have a workable and teachable, if not a definitive, modern grammar; but we do not have, despite several titles, a modern rhetoric.

In composition courses we do not really teach our captive charges to write better—we merely *expect* them to. And we do not teach them how to write better because we do not know how to teach them to write better. And so we merely go through the motions. Our courses with their tear-out work books and four-pound anthologies are elaborate evasions of the real problem. They permit us to put in our time and do almost anything else we'd rather be doing instead of buckling down to the hard work of making a difference in the student's understanding and manipulation of language.

With hundreds of handbooks and rhetorics to draw from, I have never been able to work out a program for teaching the sentence as I find it in the work of contemporary writers. The chapters on the sentence all adduce the traditional rhetorical classification of sentences as loose, balanced, and periodic. But the term *loose* seems to be taken as a pejorative (it sounds immoral); our students, no Bacons or Johnsons, have little occasion for balanced sentences; and some of our worst perversions of style come from the attempt to teach them to write periodic sentences. The traditional grammatical classification of sentences is equally barren. Its use in teaching composition rests on a semantic confusion, equating complexity of structure with complexity of thought and vica versa. But very simple thoughts may call for very complex grammatical constructions. Any moron can say "I don't know who done it." And some of us might be puzzled to work out the grammar of "All I want is all there is," although any chit can think it and say it and act on it.

The chapters on the sentence all appear to assume that we think naturally in primer sentences, progress naturally to compound sentences, and must be taught to combine the primer sentences into complex sentences—and that complex sentences are the mark of maturity. We need a rhetoric of the sentence that will do more than combine the ideas of primer sentences. We need one that will *generate* ideas.

For the foundation of such a generative or productive rhetoric I take the statement from John Erskine, the originator of the Great Books courses,

from *Notes Toward a New Rhetoric: Six Essays for Teachers* by Francis Christensen (pp. 1-17). Copyright © 1967 by Francis Christensen. Originally appeared in *College Composition and Communication*, October 1963. Reprinted by permission of Francis Christensen and Harper & Row, Publishers, Inc.

himself a novelist. In an essay "The Craft of Writing" (*Twentieth Century Writing*, Philosophical Library, 1946) he discusses a principle of the writer's craft which, though known he says to all practitioners, he has never seen discussed in print. The principle is this: "When you write, you make a point, not by subtracting as though you sharpened a pencil, but by adding." We have all been told that the formula for good writing is the concrete noun and the active verb. Yet Erskine says, "What you say is found not in the noun but in what you add to qualify the noun. . . . The noun, the verb, and the main clause serve merely as the base on which meaning will rise. . . . The modifier is the essential part of any sentence." The foundation, then, for a generative or productive rhetoric of the sentence is that composition is essentially a process of *addition*.

But speech is linear, moving in time, and writing moves in linear space, which is analogous to time. When you add a modifier, whether to the noun, the verb, or the main clause, you must add it either before the head or after it. If you add it before the head, the direction of modification can be indicated by an arrow pointing forward; if you add it after, by an arrow pointing backward. Thus we have the second principle of a generative rhetoric—the principle of *direction of modification* or *direction of movement.*

Within the clause there is not much scope of operating with this principle. The positions of the various sorts of close, or restrictive, modifiers are generally fixed and the modifiers are often obligatory—"The man who came to dinner remained till midnight." Often the only choice is whether to add modifiers. What I have seen of attempts to bring structural grammar to bear on composition usually boils down to the injunction to "load the patterns." Thus "pattern practice" sets students to accreting sentences like this: "The small boy on the red bicycle who lives with his happy parents on our shady street often coasts down the steep street until he comes to the city park." This will never do. It has no rhythm and hence no life; it is tone-deaf. It is the seed that will burgeon into gobbledegook. One of the hardest things in writing is to keep the noun clusters and verb clusters short.

It is with modifiers added to the clause—that is, with sentence modifiers —that the principle comes into full play. The typical sentence of modern English, the kind we can best spend our efforts trying to teach, is what we may call the *cumulative sentence*. The main clause, which may or may not have a sentence modifier before it, advances the discussion; but the additions move backward, as in this clause, to modify the statement of the main clause or more often to explicate or exemplify it, so that the sentence has a flowing and ebbing movement, advancing to a new position and then pausing to consolidate it, leaping and lingering as the popular ballad does. The first part of the preceding compound sentence has one addition, placed within it; the second part has 4 words in the main clause and 49 in the five additions placed after it.

The cumulative sentence is the opposite of the periodic sentence. It does not represent the idea as conceived, pondered over, reshaped, packaged, and delivered cold. It is dynamic rather than static, representing the mind thinking. The main clause ("the additions move backward" above) exhausts the mere fact of the idea; logically, there is nothing more to say. The additions stay with the same idea, probing its bearings and implications, exemplifying it or seeking an analogy or metaphor for it, or reducing it to details. Thus the mere form of the sentence generates ideas. It serves the needs of both the writer and the reader, the writer by compelling him to examine his thought, the reader by letting him into the writer's thought.

Addition and direction of movement are structural principles. They involve the grammatical character of the sentence. Before going on to other principles, I must say a word about the best grammar as the foundation for rhetoric. I cannot conceive any useful transactions between teacher and students unless they have in common a language for talking about sentences. The best grammar for the present purpose is the grammar that best displays the layers of structure of the English sentence. The best I have found in a textbook is the combination of immediate constituent and transformation grammar in Paul Roberts' *English Sentences*. Traditional grammar, whether over-simple as in the school tradition or over-complex as in the scholarly tradition, does not reveal the language as it operates; it leaves everything, to borrow a phrase from Wordsworth, "in disconnection dead and spiritless." *English Sentences* is oversimplified and it has gaps, but it displays admirably the structures that rhetoric must work with—primarily sentence modifiers, including nonrestrictive relative and subordinate clauses, but, far more important, the array of noun, verb, and adjective clusters. It is paradoxical that Professor Roberts, who has done so much to make the teaching of composition possible, should himself be one of those who think that it cannot be taught. Unlike Ulysses, he does not see any work for Telemachus to work.

Layers of structure, as I have said, is a grammatical concept. To bring in the dimension of meaning, we need a third principle—that of *levels of generality* or *levels of abstraction*. The main or base clause is likely to be stated in general or abstract or plural terms. With the main clause stated, the forward movement of the sentence stops, the writer shifts down to a lower level of generality or abstraction or to singular terms, and goes back over the same ground at this lower level.[1] There is no theoretical limit to the number of structural layers or levels, each[2] at a lower level of generality, any or all of them compounded, that a speaker or writer may use. For a speaker, listen to Lowell Thomas; for a writer, study William Faulkner. To a single independent clause he may append a page of additions, but usually all clear, all grammatical, once we have learned how to read him. Or, if you prefer, study Hemingway, the master of the simple sentence: "George was coming down in the telemark position, kneeling, one leg forward and bent, the other trailing, his sticks hanging like some insect's thin legs, kicking up puffs of snow, and finally the whole kneeling, trailing figure coming around in a beautiful right curve, crouching, the legs shot forward and back, the body leaning out against the swing, the sticks accenting the curve like points of light, all in a wild cloud of snow." Only from the standpoint of school grammar is this a simple sentence.

This brings me to the fourth, and last, principle, that of texture. *Texture* provides a descriptive or evaluative term. If a writer adds to few of his nouns or verbs or main clauses and adds little, the texture may be said to be thin. The style will be plain or bare. The writing of most of our students is thin—even threadbare. But if he adds frequently or much or both, then the texture may be said to be dense or rich. One of the marks of an effective style, especially in narrative, is variety in the texture producing the change in pace. It is not true, as I have seen it asserted, that fast action calls for short sentences; the action is fast in the sentence by Hemingway above. In our classes, we have to work for greater density and variety in texture and greater concreteness and particularity in what is added.

I have been operating at a fairly high level of generality. Now I must downshift and go over the same points with examples. The most graphic way to exhibit the layers of structure is to indent the word groups of a sentence and to number the levels. The first three sentences illustrate the various positions of the added sentence modifiers—initial, medial, and final. The symbols mark the grammatical character of the additions: SC, subordinate clause; RC, relative clause; NC, noun cluster; VC, verb cluster; AC, adjective cluster; A + A, adjective series; Abs, absolute (i.e., a VC with a subject of its own); PP, prepositional phrase. The elements set off as on a lower level are marked as sentence modifiers by junctures or punctuation. The examples have been chosen to illustrate the range of constructions used in the lower levels; after the first few they are arranged by the number of levels. The examples could have been drawn from poetry as well as from prose. Those not attributed are by students.

1

1 He dipped his hands in the bichloride solution and shook them,
   2 a quick shake, (NC)
      3 fingers down, (Abs)
         4 like the fingers of a pianist above the keys. (PP)

Sinclair Lewis

2

   2 Calico-coated, (AC)
   2 small-bodied, (AC)
      3 with delicate legs and pink faces in which their mis-
         matched eyes rolled wild and subdued, (PP)
1 they huddled,
   2 gaudy motionless and alert, (A + A)
   2 wild as deer, (AC)
   2 deadly as rattlesnakes, (AC)
   2 quiet as doves. (AC)

William Faulkner

3

1 The bird's eye, / , remained fixed upon him;
   2 / bright and silly as a sequin (AC)

1 its little bones, / , seemed swooning in his hand,
  2 wrapped . . . in a warm padding of feathers. (VC)
                                        Stella Benson

4

1 The jockeys sat bowed and relaxed,
  2 moving a little at the waist with the movement of their horses. (VC)
                                        Katherine Anne Porter

5

1 The flame sidled up the match,
  2 driving a film of moisture and a thin strip of darker grey before it.
       (VC)

6

1 She came among them behind the man,
  2 gaunt in the gray shapeless garment and the sunbonnet, (AC)
  2 wearing stained canvas gymnasium shoes. (VC)
                                        Faulkner

7

1 The Texan turned to the nearest gatepost and climbed to the top of it,
  2 his alternate thighs thick and bulging in the tight-trousers, (Abs)
  2 the butt of the pistol catching and losing the sun in pearly gleams.
       (Abs)
                                        Faulkner

8

1 He could sail for hours,
  2 searching the blanched grasses below him with his telescopic eyes,
       (VC)
  2 gaining height against the wind, (VC)
  2 descending in mile-long, gently declining swoops when he curved
       and rode back, (VC)
  2 never beating a wing. (VC)
                                        Walter Van Tilburg Clark

9

1 They regarded me silently,
  2 Brother Jack with a smile that went no deeper than his lips, (Abs)
    3 his head cocked to one side, (Abs)
    3 studying me with his penetrating eyes; (VC)
  2 the other blank-faced, (Abs)
    3 looking out of eyes that were meant to reveal nothing and to stir
         profound uncertainty. (VC)
                                        Ralph Ellison

10

1 He stood at the top of the stairs and watched me,
  2 I waiting for him to call me up, (Abs)

    2 he hesitating to come down, (Abs)
        3 his lips nervous with the suggestion of a smile, (Abs)
        3 mine asking whether the smile meant come, or go away. (Abs)

                            11

1 Joad's lips stretched tight over his long teeth for a moment, and
1 he licked his lips,
    2 like a dog, (PP)
        3 two licks, (NC)
            4 one in each direction from the middle. (NC)
                            Steinbeck

                            12

1 We all live in two realities:
    2 one of seeming fixity, (NC)
        3 with institutions, dogmas, rules of punctuation, and routines,
            (PP)
            4 the calendared and clockwise world of all but futile round on
                round; (NC) and
    2 one of whirling and flying electrons, dreams, and possibilities, (NC)
        3 behind the clock. (PP)
                            Sidney Cox

                            13

1 It was as though someone, somewhere, had touched a lever and shifted
    gears, and
1 the hospital was set for night running,
    2 smooth and silent, (A + A)
    2 its normal chatter and hum muffled, (Abs)
    2 the only sounds heard in the whitewalled room distant and unreal:
        (Abs)
        3 a low hum of voices from the nurses' desk, (NC)
            4 quickly stifled, (VC)
        3 the soft squish of rubber-soled shoes on the tiled corridor,
            (NC)
        3 starched white cloth rustling against itself, (Abs) and, outside,
        3 the lonesome whine of wind in the country night (NC) and
        3 the Kansas dust beating against the windows. (NC)

                            14

1 The beach sounds are jazzy,
    2 percussion fixing the mode—(Abs)
        3 the surf cracking and booming in the distance, (Abs)
        3 a little nearer dropped bar-bells clanking, (Abs)
        3 steel gym rings, / , ringing, (Abs)
        /4 flung together, (VC)
        3 palm fronds rustling above me, (Abs)
            4 like steel brushes washing over a snare drum, (PP)
        3 troupes of sandals splatting and shuffling on the sandy cement,
            (Abs)

4   their beat varying, (Abs)
5   syncopation emerging and disappearing with changing
    paces. (Abs)

15

1   A small Negro girl develops from the sheet of glare-frosted walk,
2   walking barefooted, (VC)
3   her bare legs stiking and coiling from the hot cement, (Abs)
4   her feet curling in, (Abs)
5   only the outer edges touching. (Abs)

The best starting point for a composition unit based on these four principles is with two-level narrative sentences, first with one second-level addition (sentences 4, 5), then with two or more parallel ones (6, 7, 8). Anyone
sitting in his room with his eyes closed could write the main clause of most
of the examples; the discipline comes with the additions, provided they are
based at first on immediate observation, requiring the student to phrase an
exact observation in exact language. This can hardly fail to be exciting to a
class: it is life, with the variety and complexity of life; the workbook exercise is death. The situation is ideal also for teaching diction—abstract-
concrete, general-specific, literal-metaphorical, denotative-connotative. When
the sentences begin to come out right, it is time to examine the additions for
their grammatical character. From then on the grammar comes to the aid of
the writing and the writing reinforces the grammar. One can soon go on to
multi-level narrative sentences (1, 9-11, 15) and then to brief narratives
of three to six or seven sentences on actions with a beginning, a middle, and
an end that can be observed over and over again—beating eggs, making a cut
with a power saw, or following a record changer's cycle or a wave's flow and
ebb. (Bring the record changer to class.) Description, by contrast, is static,
picturing appearance rather than behavior. The constructions to master are
the noun and adjective clusters and the absolute (13,14). Then the descriptive noun cluster must be taught to ride piggy-back on the narrative sentence, so that description and narration are interleaved: "In the morning we
went out into a new world, a glistening crystal and white world, each skele-
ton tree, each leafless bush, even the heavy, drooping power lines sheathed in
icy crystal." The next step is to develop the sense for variety in texture and
change in pace that all good narrative demands.

. . . The same four principles can be applied to the expository paragraph. But this is a subject for another paper.

I want to anticipate two possible objections. One is that the sentences
are long. By freshman English standards they are long, but I could have produced far longer ones from works freshmen are expected to read. Of the sentences by students, most were written as finger exercises in the first few
weeks of the course. I try in narrative sentences to push to level after level,
not just two or three, but four, five, or six, even more, as far as the students'
powers of observation will take them. I want them to become sentence
acrobats, to dazzle by their syntactic dexterity. I'd rather have to deal with

hyperemia than anemia. I want to add my voice to that of James Coleman (*CCC*, December 1962) deploring our concentration on the plain style.

The other objection is that my examples are mainly descriptive and narrative—and today in freshman English we teach only exposition. I deplore the limitation as much as I deplore our limitation to the plain style. Both are a sign that we have sold our proper heritage for a pot of message. In permitting them, the English department undercuts its own discipline. Even if our goal is only utilitarian prose, we can teach diction and sentence structure far more effectively through a few controlled exercises in description and narration than we can by starting right off with exposition (Theme One, 500 words, precipitates *all* the problems of writing). There is no problem of invention; the student has something to communicate—his immediate sense of impressions, which can stand a bit of exercising. The material is not already verbalized—he has to match language to sense impressions. His acuteness in observation and in choice of words can be judged by fairly objective standards—is the sound of a bottle of milk being set down on a concrete step suggested better by *clink* or *clank* or *clunk*? In the examples, study the diction for its accuracy, rising at times to the truly imaginative. Study the use of metaphor, of comparison. This verbal virtuosity and syntactical ingenuity can be made to carry over into expository writing.

But it is still utilitarian. What I am proposing carries over of itself into the study of literature. It makes the student a better reader of literature. It helps him thread the syntactical mazes of much mature writing, and it gives him insight into that elusive thing we call style. Last year a student told of rereading a book by her favorite author, Willa Cather, and of realizing for the first time *why* she liked reading her: she could understand and appreciate the style. For some students, moreover, such writing makes life more interesting as well as giving them a way to share their interest with others. When they learn how to put concrete details into a sentence, they begin to look at life with more alertness. If it is liberal education we are concerned with, it is just possible that these things are more important than anything we can achieve when we set our sights on the plain style in expository prose.

I want to conclude with a historical note. My thesis in this paragraph is that modern prose like modern poetry has more in common with the seventeenth than with the eighteenth century and that we fail largely because we are operating from an eighteenth century base. The shift from the complex to the cumulative sentence is more profound than it seems. It goes deep in grammar, requiring a shift from the subordinate clause (the staple of our trade) to the cluster and the absolute (so little understood as to go almost unnoticed in our textbooks). And I have only lately come to see that this shift has historical implications. The cumulative sentence is the modern form of the loose sentence that characterized the anti-Ciceronian movement in the seventeenth century. This movement, according to Morris W. Croll,[3] began with Montaigne and Bacon and continued with such men as Donne, Browne, Taylor, Pascal. To Montaigne, its art was the art of being natural; to Pascal, its eloquence was the eloquence that mocks formal eloquence;

to Bacon, it presented knowledge so that it could be examined, not so that it must be accepted.

But the Senecan amble was banished from England when "the direct sensuous apprehension of thought" (T. S. Eliot's words) gave way to Cartesian reason or intellect. The consequences of this shift in sensibility are well summarized by Croll:

> To this mode of thought we are to trace almost all the features of modern literary education and criticism, or at least of what we should have called modern a generation ago: the study of the precise meaning of words; the reference to dictionaries as literary authorities; the study of the sentence as a logical unit alone; the careful circumscription of its limits and the gradual reduction of its length; . . . [4] the attempt to reduce grammar to an exact science; the idea that forms of speech are always either correct or incorrect; the complete subjection of the laws of motion and expression in style to the laws of logic and standardization—in short, the triumph, during two centuries, of grammatical over rhetorical ideas.

Here is a seven-point scale any teacher of composition can use to take stock. He can find whether he is based in the eighteenth century or in the twentieth and whether he is consistent—completely either an ancient or a modern—or is just a crazy mixed-up kid.

Notes

[1] Cf. Leo Rockas "Abstract and Concrete Sentences," *CCC*, May 1963. Rockas describes sentences as abstract or concrete, the abstract implying the concrete and vice versa. Readers and writers, he says, must have the knack of apprehending the concrete in the abstract and the abstract in the concrete. This is true and valuable. I am saying that within a single sentence the writer may present more than one level of generality, translating the abstract into the more concrete in added levels.

[2] This statement is not quite tenable. Each helps to make the idea of the base clause more concrete or specific, but each is not more concrete or specific than the one immediately above it.

[3] "The Baroque Style in Prose," *Studies in English Philology; A Miscellany in Honor of Frederick Klaeber* (1929), reprinted in *Style, Rhetoric and Rhythm: Essays by Morris W. Croll* (1966) and A. M. Witherspoon and F. J. Warnke, *Seventeenth-Century Prose and Poetry*, 2nd ed. (1963). I have borrowed from Croll in my description of the cumulative sentence.

[4] The omitted item concerns punctuation and is not relevant here. In using this scale, note "what we should have called modern a generation ago" and remember that Croll was writing in 1929.

Symmetrical Form and the Rhetoric of the Sentence

RICHARD L. GRAVES

Historically, the style of writing attributed to Gorgias has been regarded as artificial and contrived. Indeed, the adjective derived from his name carries with it a strongly pejorative connotation; whaterever is "Gorgianic" is said to be there only for effect or to make an impression, a thin veneer with no substance at all. In the *Art of Persuasion in Greece*, George Kennedy reminds us that one of the problems with the Gorgianic figures—"antithesis, isocolon, parison [parallelism of form], homoeoteleuton, and others of that sort"—is that they are too conspicuous. "Most ancient and modern critics," he writes, "have regarded them with disfavor; if the highest art is to conceal art, as has often been claimed, the devices hardly qualify, for they are extraordinarily conspicuous."[1] One of those ancient critics which Professor Kennedy cites as looking upon the figures with disfavor is Quintilian, whose full commentary on the subject deserves our attention: "The old orators were at great pains to achieve elegance in the use of words similar or opposite in sound. Gorgias carried the practice to an extravagant pitch, while Isocrates, at any rate in his early days, was much addicted to it. Even Cicero delighted in it, but showed some restraint in the employment of a device which is not unattractive save when carried to excess, and, further, by the weight of his thought lent dignity to what would otherwise have been trivialities. For in itself this artifice is a flat and foolish affectation, but when it goes out hand in hand with vigour of thought, it gives the impression of natural charm, which the speaker has not had to go far to find."[2]

The central thrust of Quintilian's comment is that it is not the figures themselves but their excessive use which can lead to foppish writing. Quin-

from *Classical Rhetoric & Modern Discourse: Essays in Honor of Edward P. J. Corbett*, edited by Robert Connors, Lisa Ede, & Andrea Lunsford (Carbondale, IL: Southern Illinois University Press, forthcoming).

tilian rightly condemns their merely ornamental use as "flat and foolish affectation," yet his criticism is mixed. There are times, that last cryptic sentence implies, when their use is justified, notably when the style grows "naturally" out of the subject matter at hand. Kennedy himself seems to reserve a modicum of praise: "Yet in his own age the style of Gorgias did not seem in poor taste. There was then a general desire to create a literary prose . . . "[3] The tendency of our age, it seems to me, has been to accept the negative connotation of Gorgianic figures uncritically and not give due consideration to the possible positive effects. In order to gain a full understanding of the figures, I believe it is necessary to see them not in a narrow, restricted way but as part of a larger perspective. It is necessary to see them as part of the continuing human concern with the idea of symmetry, an idea which is rooted in our physiological being and touches many aspects of our collective lives.

It may be that the worst examples of Gorgianic figures represent a kind of imperfect individuation of the Greek idea of symmetry, an idea which was so well expressed in their architecture. But although a particular individuation may be flawed, the concept itself may still be valid. The concept of symmetry seems to be a part of what Kenneth Burke calls "the innate forms of the mind." Burke suggests that certain basic thought patterns such as contrast, comparison, balance, repetition, and so on, parallel "certain psychic and physical processes which are at the roots of human experience."[4] Burke's basis for calling them "innate" is that they are closely tied up with the rhythm of bodily processes: "The appeal of form as exemplified in rhythm enjoys a special advantage in that the rhythm is more closely allied with 'bodily' processes. Stystole and diastole, alternation of the feet in walking, inhalation and exhalation, up and down, in and out, back and forth, such are the types of distinctly motor experiences 'tapped' by rhythm. Rhythm is so natural to the organism that even a succession of uniform beats will be interpreted as a succession of accented or unaccented beats."[5]

Moreover, we see the concept of symmetry expressed everywhere, all around us in all kinds of human institutions. For example, the idea of justice carries with it the idea of balance and symmetry. We believe that the punishment should always be related to the crime. This idea is reflected in the maxim "An eye for an eye, and a tooth for a tooth." At least part of the success of this maxim is derived from the condition laid down by Quintilian: the symmetry in the form reflects the "vigour of thought," or what we may describe as the psychological symmetry inherent in the concept. It is not surprising then that symmetry should also be a major concern of the arts. Suzanne Langer describes symmetry as a fundamental principle of art. "The second great function of design," she writes, "which may be more important, at least if we measure its importance by its influence on the further potentialities of art, is the establishment of symmetry, or correlation of counterparts, which creates the axis as a structural element."[6] Langer goes on to explain the role of right and left in relation to a median, and the function of vertical and horizontal planes. However, her most interesting contention is that symmetrical form is not only fundamental to human experience but capable of expressing "our deepest vital feeling." She writes, " The safest device to achieve living form is symmetrical composition." Thus seen, symmetry is not merely a cold, static form but, rather, a potentially dynamic, life-giving force.

It is important to note that the ideas about symmetrical form which have been discussed thus far—ideas from classical rhetoricians as well as from Kenneth Burke and Susanne Langer in our own time—are all based on personal experience, or more accurately, in personal intuition. They appeal to our experience and sense of logic for corroboration, and they are supported by the weight of scholarly prestige, tradition, and authority. It is possible, however, to express these same philosophical constructs in quantitative terms, put them into a research design, and test their validity empirically.[7] Although these same constructs may appear foreign to us when they are expressed quantitatively, the results of empirical testing can yield untold benefits for our field. A series of studies conducted by the perceptual psychologist Fred Attneave, for example, sheds further light on the question of the function of symmetrical form.[8] His research deserves our careful attention.

Attneave was interested in studying, in quantitative terms, a belief long held by Gestalt psychologists, namely, that symmetry has a positive effect on memory. "Are regular figures better remembered than irregular ones simply because they contain less information to be remembered," he asked, "or does their superiority persist even when information is held constant? In other words, which is remembered more accurately; a large, well-organized figure, or a small, poorly-organized figure containing the same amount of information?"[9] In order to test that theory, Attneave devised a series of three experiments in which subjects were asked to recall certain non-verbal patterns ("patterns of dots presented in rectangular matrices") which had been presented to them. Two kinds of variables were included in the experiments: (1) the amount of information, i.e., the size of the pattern, and (2) the level of symmetry.

In the first experiment, labeled "Immediate Reproduction," Attneave presented 149 subjects divided into five groups a series of patterns. The patterns were arranged as follows: (1) a 12 cell grid with 6 dots randomly arranged, (2) a 20 cell grid with 9 dots randomly arranged, (3) a 20 cell grid with 10 dots symmetrically arranged, (4) a 35 cell grid with 19 dots randomly arranged, and (5) a 35 cell grid with 17 dots symmetrically arranged. Each group was shown a different class of patterns, and subgroups within each were shown reverse image patterns as well as the patterns in reverse order.

In the first experiment Attneave found that slightly fewer errors occurred with the symmetrical patterns. However, in the second experiment, labeled "Delayed Reproduction" (which increased the length of the viewing time), the symmetrical patterns were clearly easier to remember, even when the amount of information was increased. The clear superiority of the symmetrical patterns was also evident in the third experiment ("Identification"), which required subjects to identify the various patterns with arbitrarily chosen names.

Although Attneave was cautious in reporting his findings, he did observe what might be called a consistent tendency toward the symmetrical pattern being easier to remember. He writes: "The further finding that symmetrical patterns are more accurately reproduced than random patterns with the same number of elements (and accordingly more information) may be taken to indicate that some perceptual mechanism is capable of organizing or encoding the redundant pattern into a simpler, more compact, less redundant form."[10] The implications of studies such as these for comprehending, and therefore composing, a text are intriguing. It seems only a matter of time before we gain a fuller understanding of not only the subtle influence of symmetrical form on the learning process but the nature of the "perceptual mechanism" itself.

Let us now consider briefly the role of symmetry in the teaching of written composition. During the past twenty years, three major theories of the sentence have been advanced, all of which offer significant help to the young writer. Since all three are concerned with control of elements inside the sentence, it is appropriate to classify them as *syntactic rhetorics*. The first of these is the generative rhetoric advanced by Francis Christensen in 1963. The major importance of this work is that it illustrates so well the function of asymmetrical form—the cumulative sentence with its short base clause and jungle of appended, non-clausal modifiers. The second major theory appears in Edward P. J. Corbett's well-known text, *Classical Rhetoric for the Modern Student*. In that text Corbett reminds us of the classical concept of form which appears in sentence schemes, and especially of the power which can be derived from repetition and rhythm within the sentence. The third major theory is that inherent in sentence-combining activity, an activity which makes students aware of the dynamics of the embedment process within the sentence. Although all three of these syntactic rhetorics employ the idea of symmetry, none (with the exception of Corbett) treats it directly.

Even though these syntactic rhetorics fail adequately to emphasize symmetry, their strategies are clearly superior to more traditional approaches, which typically present students with examples of flawed parallelism and ask them to mend them. The difficulty, as we know, is that simply asking students to correct examples often does not stimulate a genuine understanding of a concept. More importantly, such exercises rarely promote the kind of active learning that the teaching of writing requires.

Attneave's experiments and Burke's comments on innate form suggest the potential fruitfulness of efforts to develop a syntactic rhetoric based on symmetry and parallelism—one which could, in combination with other related activities, serve as a powerful heuristic tool. As a beginning for this obviously demanding project, I offer here a tentative outline of the structure of parallelism in the English language. Using this simple guideline, the resources already provided by current syntactic rhetorics, such as sentence-combining, and other activities such as imitation, teachers can themselves develop direct exercises designed to increase students' understanding and control of this powerful linguistic resource.[11]

Below is an outline of the structure of parallelism in the English language. The outline and accompanying examples are the raw material for fashioning a curriculum which is both compassionate and intellectually honest. Parallelism is shown as consisting of four major categories: (1) the repetition of key words; (2) the use of opposite words; (3) the repetition of grammatical elements; and (4) combinations of these, in which selected elements function together. The examples below are drawn from a broad range of the resources of the English language and are intended to be representative. The italicized words in each example illustrate the kind of parallelism being described; in the examples of combinations the first element mentioned is italicized except where noted.

I. THE REPETITION OF KEY WORDS

1. Basal Repetition—the repetition of key particles, especially prepositions and articles.

   I have a dream my four little children will one day live in a nation where they will not be judged *by the* color *of their* skin but *by the* content *of their* character.

   Martin Luther King, "I Have a Dream"

2. Conceptual Repetition—the repetition of major conceptual terms, particularly nouns, verbs, or adjectives.

   There warn't no color in his face, where his face showed: it was *white*; not like another man's *white,* but a *white* to make a body sick, a *white* to make a body's flesh crawl—a tree toad *white*, a fish-belly *white*.

   Mark Twain, *The Adventures of Huckleberry Finn*

3. Parallel Modification—the same word modifying two different words in the sentence.

   False face must hide what the *false* heart doth know.

   Shakespeare, *Macbeth*

4. Isocolon—precise word-for-word repetition of two or more members (phrases, clauses, etc.) with the exception of one or two words.

   . . . He did not know the Somali proverb that says a brave man is always frightened three times by a lion; *when he first* sees his track, *when he first* hears him roar and *when he first* confronts him.

   Hemingway, "The Short Happy Life of Francis Macomber"

II. THE USE OF OPPOSITE WORDS (ANTHITHESIS)

   The *rich* ruleth over the *poor*, and the *borrower* is servant to the *lender.*

   Proverbs 22.7

III. REPETITION OF GRAMMATICAL ELEMENTS

1. Nominal

The hazy *sunlight*, the warm and drowsy *air*, the tender *foliage*, the opening *flowers*, betokened the reviving life of nature.

Mark Twain, *Life on the Mississippi*

2. Verbal

Suddenly one of these gypsies, in trembling opal, *seizes* a cocktail out of the air, *dumps* it down for courage and, moving her hands like Frisco, *dances* out alone on the platform.

Scott Fitzgerald, *The Great Gatsby*

3. Participial

They move in orderly lines around the box, *crowding* one another precisely, without injury, *peering* down, *nodding,* and then *backing* off to let new people in.

Lewis Thomas, *The Lives of a Cell*

4. Infinitival

Manny Greenhill is hoping to get Miss Baez *to write* a book, *to be* in a movie, and *to get around* to recording the rock 'n roll songs.

Joan Didion, "Where the Kissing Never Stops"

5. Gerundive

And with her cries came the sound of hoofs, and the *beating* of wings and the *roaring* of lions.

Kahlil Gibran, *The Prophet*

6. Adjectival

His features are *strong* and *masculine*, with an Austrian Lip, an arched Nose, his Compexion *olive,* his Countenance *erect*, his Body and Limbs well *proportioned*, all his Deportment *majestick*.

Swift, *Gulliver's Travels*

7. Adverbial

The Bible's account of Moses is, alas, as *geographically* perplexing as it is *spiritually* enlightening.

National Geographic

8. Prepositional

To counteract any evil result of that bad conjunction he walked quickly *past* the ranch house, *through* the chicken yard, *through* the vegetable patch, until he came at last *to* the brushline.

John Steinbeck, *The Red Pony*

9. Clausal

There are thousands *who* are in opinion opposed to slavery and to the war; *who* yet in effect do nothing to put an end to them; *who*, esteeming themselves children of Washington and Franklin, sit down with their hands in their pockets, and say that they know not what to do, and do nothing; *who* even postpone the question of freedom to the question of free-trade . . .

Thoreau, "On the Duty of Civil Disobedience"

IV. COMBINATIONS

1. Basal and Conceptual Repetition (both italicized)

As men's prayers *are a disease of the* will, so *are* their creeds *a disease of the* intellect.

Emerson, "Self Reliance"

2. Parallel Participles and Basal Repetition (both italicized)

Blinded by the glare *of the* headlights and *confused by the* incessant groaning *of the* horns, the apparition stood swaying for a moment before he perceived the man in the duster.

Scott Fitzgerald, *The Great Gatsby*

3. Parallel Participles and Anthithesis

. . . We have before us a blameless and noble spirit *stricken* to the earth by malign powers, *but not conquered; tempted, but grandly putting the temptation away: emeshed by subtle coils, but sternly resolved to rend them* and march forth victorious, at any peril of life or limb.

Mark Twain, "In Defense of Harriet Shelley"

4. Antithesis in Isocolon

Power corrupts the *few*, while *weakness* corrupts the *many*.

Eric Hoffer, *The Ordeal of Change*

5. Parallel Nouns and Verbs in Isocolon

With mine own *tears* I *wash* away my *balm*,
With mine own *hands* I *give* away my *crown*,
With mine own *tongue deny* my sacred *state*.

Shakespeare, *Richard II*

6. Antithetical Adjectives in Isocolon

Now am I *humble*, who was once *proud*;
Now am I *silent*, who was once *loud*.

Janis Ian, "Light a Light"

7. Antithesis and Parallel Verbs in Isocolon

If a free society cannot *help* the many who are *poor*, it cannot *save* the *few* who are *rich*.

John F. Kennedy, "Inaugural Address"

8. Parallel Modification and Parallel Nouns, with Antithesis and Basal Repetition

> Let us focus instead on a *more* practical, *more* attainable peace based not on a sudden *revolution* in *human nature*, but on a gradual *evolution* in *human institutions* . . .
>
> John F. Kennedy, "What Kind of Peace Do We Want?"

9. Antithetical Infinitives in Isocolon

> It takes some little time to find out that phrases which seem intended *to guide* the reader aright are there *to mislead* him; that phrases which seem intended *to throw light* are there *to throw darkness*; that phrases which seem intended *to interpret* a fact are there *to misinterpret it*; that phrases which seem intended *to forestall prejudice* are there *to create it;* that phrases which seem *antidotes* are *poisons* in disguise.
>
> Mark Twain, "In Defense of Harriet Shelley"

Even this brief description for the four major categories of parallelism reveals how pervasive principles of symmetry are in our language. And their pervasiveness argues strongly for our including the study of parallelism and symmetry in our writing curriculum. We must be certain, however, that such principles are taught not as sterile forms to be imposed, willy nilly, on the "content" of sentences, but as major means through which we perceive and structure reality.

Greek art, architecture, and oratory all reflect the importance of balance and symmetry. And the Greek rhetoricians gave us our first full accounting of these principles in language. We can learn much by returning to these ancient authors' discussions and using their insights to inform our teaching of sentence rhetoric. Students can begin, perhaps, by discovering examples of parallelism in newspapers, magazines, and even textbooks. They can then go on to create symmetrical structures, seeing for themselves how parallelism—and purposeful "faulty" parallelism[12]—focus our attention and influence our understanding of particular sentences. Extensive *exercitatio*, accompanied by instruction in the *ars* of symmetry, can lead students back to the principles adumbrated by Greek rhetoricians, and forward into new areas of language play. Thus does the work of the classical rhetoricians nicely balance our teaching of modern discourse.

Notes

[1] George Kennedy, *The Art of Persuasion in Greece* (Princeton: Princeton University Press, 1963), pp. 65-66.

[2] *The Institutio Oratoria of Quintilian, Vol. III.*, trans. H. E. Butler (Cambridge: Harvard University Press, 1921), p. 489.

[3] Kennedy, p. 66

[4] Kenneth Burke, *Counter-Statement* (Los Altos, CA: Hermes Publications, 1953). p. 46.

[5] Burke, p. 140

[6] Susanne K. Langer, *Mind: An Essay on Human Feeling, Vol. I* (Baltimore: The Johns Hopkins University Press, 1967), p. 125.

[7] The direction which the field of psycholinguistics has taken supports Kenneth Burke's contention that psychology has replaced metaphysics as a foundation of aesthetic theory. See *Counter-Statement*, p. ix.

[8] Fred Attneave, "Symmetry, Infomation, and Memory for Patterns," *The American Journal of Psychology*, 68 (1955), 209-222.

[9] Attneave, p. 209.

[10] Attneave, p. 220.

[11] I have not included in this outline such essential cues to parallelism as "both . . . and," "not only . . . but also," etc. Most teachers of composition already recognize, I believe, their significance.

[12] In *Artful Balance: The Parallel Structure of Style,* Mary P. Hiatt encourages a broader view of parallelism: ". . . let us no longer insist on 'parallel ideas,' whatever they may be. Let us not jump too hastily at 'faulty' parallelism. Let us become aware of the rhetorical patterns of repetition that add emphasis to parallelism. Let us, in other words, encourage more flexibility in our approach to parallelism and indulge in less didacticism." (New York: Teachers College Press, 1975), p. 9.

The Syntax of Error

VALERIE KRISHNA

Perhaps the most vexing problem that teachers of basic writing face is the fact that the most serious errors that appear in student papers are those that we are the least equipped to handle, those that are in fact next to impossible to deal with by traditional methods. Unfortunately, the mistakes that students make are not always those clear-cut and predictable errors that are the most precisely described and categorized in the grammar books—errors of punctuation, spelling, agreement, tense, case, and so on. Important as these details are, they dwindle in significance next to problems of incoherence, illogicality, lack of conventional idiom or clear syntax—amorphous and unpredictable errors involving the structure of the whole sentence that are difficult to pinpoint, define, and analyze. The fact is that the most serious and most intractable mistakes are those that do not fit into neat categories and defy analysis. Here are a few examples.

1. In regard to the Watergate affair and the recent problems that the White House is involved with, it is of concern to all citizens.
2. The use of the pilgrimage was created to make the scene more realistic.
3. His concern for outward appearances is mainly to use it to convey the inner character.
4. Man has invented various types of poisons to kill insects; among the surviving insects, they have all become immune to these poisons.
5. By limiting the open enrollment program won't help to solve the problem.

A teacher who discovers a sentence of this type in the student's paper is hard put to know how to begin to deal with it. It is clear that the student has committed some sort of error. It is also clear that the error is a more serious, more fundamental mistake than the "classical" errors of verb agreement, punctuation, pronoun case, and so on that are systematically set out in the grammar books. A conscientious teacher will recognize the gravity of the problem and will wish to deal with it before moving on to work on conventional errors of detail. However, it is not exactly clear just what the error is that has been committed. The sentence might be labeled "illogical" or "incoherent"; the writer might be said to have "shifted syntax" in mid-sentence.

Journal of Basic Writing, I (Spring 1975), pp. 43-49. Copyright © 1975 by The English Department, City College of New York. Reprinted by permission of the editor.

Grammar books caution against illogicality and incoherence, and some of them even give a name to this type of syntax shift—the "mixed construction"—but most offer little help in correcting any of these problems. They offer little help because gross structural errors of this type are not amenable to correction by the method that is used for errors of detail.

We eradicate errors of detail by concentrating on them. Grammar books isolate, define, categorize, and in general supply us with a great deal of information about them. We know, for example, exactly where an error involving verb agreement is likely to occur (in sentences in which the subject and the verb are separated by a prepositional phrase, the verb comes before the subject, or the subject is a collective noun, and so on). Thus an error such as this is comprehensible, predictable, and amenable to correction. We can anticipate such errors and try to head them off, either by having students do exercises that duplicate the kinds of sentences that we know are likely to give rise to such errors or by training students to be especially alert for verb agreement errors in these kinds of sentences when they proofread.

We have no such guidelines for errors such as the mixed construction and other errors involving problems of structure, coherence, and logic. For one thing, labels like "illogical" and "incoherent" and terms like "mixed construction" are vague: they do not isolate and define an error clearly. For another, there are so many different ways in which a writer can shift syntax in the middle of a sentence or "mix his constructions" that such errors simply cannot be categorized and predicated in precisely the way that errors of verb agreement can. Similarly, no one can possibly anticipate all of the different ways in which a piece of writing might be illogical or incoherent. Errors of verb agrrement can almost be thought of as one error—or several very well understood variations on one error—that is committed over and over again. Every mixed construction, every incoherence, every illogicality seems to be a unique and original creation. Therefore, because grammar books cannot deal with them in the same way they deal with errors of detail, they lack information on structural errors. Hence, the teacher despairs as he feels that such errors are random, unpredictable, and impossible to handle at the same time that he recognizes that they are the most serious problems that can appear in a student's papers.

The impossibility of classifying structural errors per se and of dealing with them in the traditional way forces us into another approach. Rather than concentrating on the errors themselves as finished products and attempting to define them as such, I believe that we can understand and deal with them best by understanding the type of approach to the sentence that stands behind such errors. That is, though I do not believe that structural errors in themselves can be categorized, I do believe that the sentences in which they appear can. Many of these structural errors are not the random aberrations that they seem to be, but instead are the direct outgrowth of what I call a *weak structural core* that is disjoined from the idea that a writer is trying to express. Students who are making structural errors, though they are committing mistakes that are unique and unclassifiable in themselves, are often following a stereotyped formula in constructing sentences in which these mistakes appear. Such writers habitually "back into" their sentences, putting the heart of their idea into prepositional phrases, object noun clauses, adjectives, adverbs, or other ancillary parts of the sentence, wasting the subject and/or the verb position on indefinite, evasive expressions such as *it is, it appears, this seems to be the case*, or on other general, abstract, imprecise words (or omitting the subject or verb entirely), and finally joining the ancillary part of the sentence to the main clause awkwardly and illogically. This habitual wasting of the subject-verb position, along with the frantic struggle to fit a central thought into a peripheral expression and then to fit the expression to the main clause is the source of many, perhaps most, of the structural errors that appear in student papers, and, I believe, contributes to idiomatic, stylistic, and grammatical errors as well. The structural errors that are the most difficult to fit into a neat category and thus the most difficult to deal with are especially likely to occur in sentences that have this feeble structure: an anemic main clause too weak or indefinite to hold up modifiers and a clumsily attached, overburdened prepositional phrase into which the writer has attempted to cram the central idea of his sentence. The way to correct such mistakes, as well as to avoid them, is to strengthen the main clause, to move the central idea into the subject and/or the verb.

This common thread runs through the examples cited above, which seem at first glance idiosyncratic and baffling. Let us look again at the first sentence.

In regard to the Watergate affair and the recent problems that the White House is involved with, it is of concern to all citizens.

In this sentence, whatever the student wants to put forward as his central idea (and the teacher, of course, cannot be sure what it is) is very far from the core of the sentence—the subject and the verb—which is occupied by the vague expression *it is*. A teacher can help a student to rewrite this sentence by instructing him to move his central idea into the core of the sentence. Generally, if one asks the writer of such a sentence what the subject of the sentence is, he will answer "Watergate affair," "recent problems" (or both), or "White House"; that is, he will name the *logical* subject of the sentence. The teacher can then point out that the logical subject is not in the position of grammatical subject, which is occupied by the uninformative word *it*. The teacher can then explain to the student that the logical subject and the grammatical subject ought to coincide and instruct the student to recompose the sentence, using the logical subject as the grammatical subject. I have found that, when students recompose sentences in this way, structural errors frequently disappear. For example, if the student decides that both "Watergate affair" and "recent problems" are his subject and moves them out of the prepositional phrase and into the position of subject, there is no longer any place for the indefinite *it* (which happens also to be a pronoun without a clear reference), which is messing up the structure of the sentence, and the student will have little difficulty in restructuring the whole sentence since the source of the problem has been removed (though he may run into a verb agreement problem because of the compound subject):

The Watergate affair and the recent problems that the White House is involved with are [or is, as the case may be!] of concern to all citizens.

If the student is instructed to do the same thing with the verb that he has done with the subject, the sentence improves stylistically:

The Watergate affair and the recent problems that the White House is involved with concern all citizens.

Similarly, the second sentence cited above is easy for a student to finish, once the student has moved whatever he considers his logical subject into the position of grammatical subject, occupied in the original sentence by the vague word *use*:

The *pilgrimage* was created to make the scene more realistic.

or

The *writer* (or *Chaucer*) created the pilgrimage to make the scene more realistic.

The third sentence may be rewritten in several ways, depending again on what the student decides is his logical subject. The important point is that when a word that expresses his idea more precisely is moved into the position of subject, the rest of the sentence follows easily:

Outward appearances are used to convey inner character.

or

The author (or a proper name) uses outward appearances to convey inner character.

The fourth and fifth sentences seem at first glance to exemplify errors that are very different: one of faulty pronoun reference and the other a missing verb. However, in both cases, what appears to be the logical subject has been buried in a prepositional phrase and needs to be elevated to the position of grammatical subject:

Man has invented various types of poisons to kill insects; the surviving insects have all become immune to these poisons.

Limiting the open enrollment program won't help to solve the problem. problem.

Idiomatic errors, also difficult for teachers to deal with, may also be eliminated when the main clause is strengthened. Many idiomatic errors involve prepositions, and these often appear in sentences in which the writer has similarly put his central thought into a prepositional phrase, rather than into the subject and verb, and then joined this phrase with the wrong preposition to the main clause. The following sentence is an example:

Everybody in the world tries to make money, but everybody thinks differently in using it.

When I questioned the student who wrote this sentence, she said that she had felt uneasy about the prepositional phrase but didn't know how to go about "fixing it." I asked her what action she wanted to talk about in the second part of the sentence, whether she really wished to say something about *thinking*. She replied that she had actually wanted to say something about *using*, and then went on immediately to *but everybody uses it differently*, automatically eliminating the unidiomatic preposition.

Some conventional grammatical errors, such as dangling participles, can also be corrected by this method, as in the following example:

By paying directly, it is assured that we get better service.

Once a student substitutes a noun that expresses his thought more precisely than the indefinite *it*, the core of the sentence is strengthened, and the dangling participle disappears:

Paying directly assures us better service.

By paying directly we are assured better service.

We cannot help but wonder why students write in this way. Three possibilities suggest themselves to me.

1. It may simply be that students have a habit of attacking sentences in this roundabout way because they have the mistaken notion that simplicity and directness are the mark of the simple-minded and are trying to "dress up" their writing. These introductory circumlocutions may appear impressive to them, and they may be using them to make their writing look profound. If so, this habit may be nothing more than a variation of the pompous, inflated writing affected by writers of all types (with the difference, of course, that basic writing students have a hard time pulling it off without making structural and grammatical errors).

2. Perhaps students write in this way to disguise the fact, from the reader and from themselves, that they are not thinking clearly or that they actually have nothing to say. It could be that, when ideas fail them, they take refuge in this construction simply as a means of filling up the page, hoping that the reader will not notice the difference. (There is a kind of wild logic in this process, because if one has nothing to say, it makes sense for the subject and the verb to be as nearly empty of meaning as possible.) . . .

3. A third possibility is that students write in this way because they find writing painful and words treacherous and are trying to tread as lightly as possible in the world of the written word in order not to make fools of themselves. If this is so, then attacking errors indirectly through sentence structure in the way described here, rather than directly through teaching students everything we know about errors and daily painting a bleaker and bleaker picture of all the possible ways their writing might go wrong, might be even more important than I have so far suggested. Teaching students what *to do*, if it could be worked out as completely and systematically as has our traditional method of teaching them what *not* to do, how to construct a sentence rather than how not to, may be the only kind of craftsmanship that we can present without inhibiting our students so much that we drive them into the very errors that we are trying to teach them to avoid.

Grammars of Style:
New Options in Composition

WINSTON WEATHERS

One of our major tasks as teachers of composition is to identify compositional options and teach students the mastery of the options and the liberating use of them. We must identify options in all areas—in vocabulary, usage, sentence forms, dictional levels, paragraph types, ways of organizing materials into whole compositions: options in all that we mean by style. Without options, there can be no rhetoric for there can be no adjustment to the diversity of communication occasions that confront us in our various lives.

To identify options we must not only know about those already established in the language but we must also be alert to emerging ones, and in some cases we must even participate in creating options that do not yet exist but which would be beneficial if they did. We must never suppose that the options in front of us represent the complete and final range of possibilities and that now we can relax: that because we have options enough to avoid rigidity and totalitarianism that we have thus fulfilled our obligations to do all we can to free the human mind and the communication issuing from it.

Most of us do, of course, make options available to our students. Most of us have long shucked off the prescriptions and strictures of an earlier day that gave us "no choice" in how to write but insisted only upon the "one good way." Most of us who teach writing attempt to provide our students with a repertoire of writing styles—from the plain to the elegant, from the tough to the sweet, from the colloquial to the formal, from the simple to the complex—in order that our students may make more refined stylistic decisions in consideration of subject matter, audience, occasion, and so forth. Many of us have argued for many years now that our task is to reveal to our students a full range of styles and to provide our students with a rationale for making appropriate selections from that range.

Yet even in our acceptance and inculcation of pluralism and diversity, we stay—if we stop and think about it—within the safe confines of a general "grammar of style," a grammar within which our options are related one to another, all basically kin, none of which takes us outside a certain approved and established area.

By "grammar of style" I mean the "set of conventions governing the

The essay here is an abridged version of the one under the same title appearing in *Freshman English News*, 4 (Winter 1976), pp. 1-4, 12-18. Copyright © 1976 by Winston Weathers. Reprinted by permission of the author and publisher. The full, text-length treatment of Grammar B appears in Winston Weathers, *An Alternate Style: Options in Composition* (Montclair, NJ: Boynton/Cook Publishers, 1980).

construction of a whole composition; the criteria by which a writer selects the stylistic materials, method of organization and development, compositional pattern and structure he is to use in preparing any particular composition." This "grammar" defines and establishes the boundaries in which a composition must take place and defines the communication goals to which a composition is committed.

Any number of such "grammars" may theoretically exist and be available to a writer at any one time. Yet on a practical level, in today's classroom we keep all our stylistic options within the confines of one grammar only—a grammar that has no particular name (we can call it the "traditional" grammar of style/ or maybe even call it Grammar A) but has the characteristics of continuity, order, reasonable progression and sequence, consistency, unity, etc. We are all familiar with these characteristics for they are promoted in nearly every freshman English textbook and taught by nearly every English teacher.

Our assumption—regardless of liberality so far as diversity of styles is concerned—is that every composition must be well-organized and unified, must demonstrate logic, must contain well-developed paragraphs; that its structure will manifest a beginning, middle, and end; that the composition will reveal identifiable types of order; that so far as the composition deals with time it will reveal a general diachronicity; etc. Our teaching and texts will be concerned, almost without exception, with "subject and thesis," "classification and order," "beginning and ending," "expansion," "continuity," "emphasis," and the like. All remains, in other words, within a particular grammar of style that leads to compositions that "make sense": it is a grammar that cannot tolerate a mixed metaphor because a mixed metaphor is not "reasonable," and cannot tolerate a mixture of the impersonal third-person "one" and the impersonal "you" because that would be "inconsistent" and contrary to "unity."

We allow options "within reason." We allow options, but only those that fit within a particular box. In our charity, we allow our students to write in one style or another—

> Arriving in London in the spring of 1960, when crocuses were first blooming in Regency Park, I went directly to the Mount Royal Hotel (the hostelry that many an American tourist knows very well, located as it is on Oxford Street, near the Marble Arch and Hyde Park and conveniently located near everything the American tourist wants to see) where I registered for a room and indicated my intention to stay for seven or eight weeks at least.

> I arrived in London in the spring of 1960. Crocuses were blooming in Regency Park. I went directly to the Mount Royal Hotel. It's located on Oxford Street, near Marble Arch and Hyde Park, and it's convenient to a lot of things the American tourist wants to see. I checked in at the hotel and told the clerk I was going to stay in London seven or eight weeks at least.

but both must do just about the same thing. You can try to write like Henry James or you can try to write like Ernest Hemingway, but you must not forget that both James and Hemingway, quite different in their literary styles, wrote within the same "grammar of style"; neither of them went beyond the parameters that Grammar A provides.

It is as though we told a card-player that his deck of fifty-two cards (equal let's say to the "things we can do with language, our stylistic materials") is good only for playing the game of bridge. As good teachers, we explain the rules of bridge and at the same time point out to the student/player his options within bridge: he can play the Culbertson system or the Goren system or the Jacoby system. And indeed he can play his bridge hands even contrary to best advice if he himself so decides, though tradition and good sense usually suggest that he draw trumps early in the hand and play second hand low. We teach him to play bridge, to practice a certain freedom within it (he can conceivably play "high style" or "low style" or "middle style") but there is no way under the sun that he can, in playing bridge, meld a pinochle or "shoot the moon."

Not that anyone really argues that while playing bridge one should not play bridge. But our fault is that we teach students to play bridge only and to have access only to the options that bridge provides. We teach only one "grammar" and we only provide square/rectangular boxes. We don't teach students other games with other options. And in our teaching, when someone does "meld a pinochle" at the bridge table, all we know to do is to mark it in red ink and say "wrong," without ever suggesting to the student that if he wants to meld pinochle he might like to know about *another game* where it would be very "right."

We identify our favored "grammar of style," our favored game and box, as the "good" grammar of style, and we identify what it produces as "good writing." And anything that looms upon the horizon as a distinctly different possibility we generally attack as "bad writing," or identify as "creative writing which we don't teach in this class" or ignore altogether, claiming it is a possibility that only rare persons (like James Joyce or Gertrude Stein) could do anything with and that ordinary mortals should scrupulously avoid.

Yet there it is. The beast sniffing outside the door. And ultimately we must deal with it.

It is, of course, *another* grammar of style, another set of conventions and criteria, another way of writing that offers yet more options and offers us yet further possibilities for rhetorical adaptations and adjustments. It is not just another "style"—way out on the periphery of our concerns—but is an altogether different "grammar" of style, an alternate grammar, Grammar B, with characteristics of variegation, synchronicity, discontinuity, ambiguity, and the like. It is an alternate grammar, no longer an experiment, but a mature grammar used by competent writers and offering students of writing a well tested "set of options" that, added to the traditional grammar of style, will give give them a much more flexible voice, a much greater communication capacity, a much greater opportunity to put into effective language all the things they have to say.

And be assured: Grammar B in no way threatens Grammar A. It uses the same stylistic "deck of fifty-two cards" and embraces the same English language with which we are familiar. Acknowledging its existence and discovering how it works and including it in our writing expertise, we simply become better teachers of writing, making a better contribution to the intellectual and emotional lives of our students.

The writer who wishes to practice the alternate grammar—for whatever reasons—will want to master a number of stylistic maneuvers and conventions from which he may select, just as he does in the traditional grammar, the particular devices/schemes/techniques that seem useful in a particular communication/rhetorical situation and that he can combine into the "style" appropriate, as he so judges, to the composition he is writing. The following presentation of such maneuvers/conventions/devices is not complete, of course, but is representative of the sort of writing practices found in the alternate grammar and does provide a writer with a basic and beginning set of "things to do":

The *Crot*. A crot (crots, plural) is an obsolete word meaning "bit" or "fragment." The term was given new life by Tom Wolfe in his "Introduction" to a collection of *Esquire* magazine fiction, *The Secret Life of Our Times*, edited by Gordon Lish (New York: Doubleday, 1973). A basic element in the alternate grammar of style, and comparable somewhat to the "stanza" in poetry, the crot may range in length from one sentence to twenty or thirty sentences. It is fundamentally an autonomous unit, characterized by the absence of any transitional devices that might relate it to the preceding or subsequent crots and because of this independent and discrete nature of crots, they create a general effect of metastasis—using that term from classical rhetoric to label, as Fritz Senn recently suggested in the *James Joyce Quarterly* (Summer, 1975), any "rapid transition from one point of view to another." In its most intense form, the crot is characterized by a certain abruptness in its termination: "As each crot breaks off," Tom Wolfe says, "it tends to make one's mind search for some point that must have just been made—*presque vu!*—almost seen! In the hands of a writer who really understands the device, it will have you making crazy leaps of logic, leaps you never dreamed of before."

The provenance of the crot may well be in the writer's "note" itself—in the research note, in the sentence or two one jots down to record a moment or an idea or to describe a person or place. The crot is essentially the "note" left free of verbal ties with other surrounding notes.

Very brief crots have the quality of an aphorism or proverb, while longer crots may have the quality of descriptive or narrative passages found in the traditional grammar of style. The crots, of whatever kind, may be presented in nearly random sequence or in sequences that finally suggest circularity. Rarely is any stronger sense of order (such as would be characteristic of traditional grammar) imposed upon them—though the absence of traditional order is far more pronounced when the grammar is used in fiction and poetry. The general idea of unrelatedness present in crot writing suggests correspondence—for those who seek it—with the fragmentation and even egalitarianism of contemporary experience, wherein the events, personalities, places of life have no particular superior or inferior status to dictate priorities of presentation.

Nearly always crots are separated one from the other by white space, and at times each crot is given a number or, upon rare occasion, a title. That little spectrum—white space only, white space plus a numbering, white space plus a titling—provides a writer with a way of indicating an increase in separation, discreteness, isolation. Occasionally, but rarely, crots are not separated one from the other typographically but the reader is left to discover the "separation" while he seems to be reading a linear, continuous text; jamming crots against each other becomes a fourth option in presentation, one that provides a greater sense of surprise (or perhaps bewilderment) for the reader.

The effect of writing in crots is intensified, of course, as the number increases. Since each crot is not unlike a "snapshot" or a color slide, the overall composition, using crots, is similar to a "slide" show, especially if the slides have not been arranged into any neat and tidy sequence. "My Trip to New Orleans" written in traditional grammar will have some sort of orderly quality to it: the trip will be presented chronologically, spatially, or what have you. But "My Trip to New Orleans," written in the alternate grammar, will depend, not upon the order in which the "slides" appear, but upon the sharp, exceptional quality of each crot or "slide" and upon the "crazy leaps of logic" that Wolfe mentioned, with the reader jolted from one snapshot to the next, frequently surprised to be given an "aerial view of New Orleans as the plane begins its descent to the airport" and immediately after that "a close-up of an antique candelabrum used in a Louisiana antebellum mansion and now on sale in a New Orleans antique store" followed by "a broad shot of Canal Street" followed by a picture of "Marge and Myrtle getting into the taxicab at the airport to come into the city."

Crots at their best will not be all that banal of course in content, but will have some sharp, arresting, or provocative quality to them. Even if they are unable to stand alone as mini-compositions (sometimes they actually are capable of that) and gain their full effect in association with others, each one should have a certain integrity and interestingness about it. Crots may be written in any dictional style deemed appropriate to the communication occasion, with a single dictional style prevailing, usually, throughout an entire composition. On rare occasions, dictional level may shift from one crot to another, but usually the level of diction is a constant.

Crots are akin, obviously, to a more general kind of "block" writing— the kind of writing found, for instance, in E. M. Forster's *Two Cheers for Democracy* and in Katherine Anne Porter's essay "Audubon's Happy Land." In such block writing, the authors have strung together short, fairly discrete units of composition to make whole compositions. Likewise, a series of crots is not unlike a collection of aphorisms—say those of Eric Hoffer who, in a book like *The Passionate State of Mind and Other Aphorisms*, has brought together brief compositional units, some a sentence long, some several paragraphs long, each quite distinct from the other, yet grouped into a whole composition on the basis of a certain attitude and view of life common to them all. These compositions of "blocks" or "aphorisms" are so much in the spirit of crot writing that they may be considered a part of its development out of a traditional grammar of style into the alternate grammar. The writing of Forster, Porter, and Hoffer—in fiction *and* nonfiction—gives evidence of the usefulness of something other than the ordered, linear procedure of traditional grammar even to writers who would not be identified as especially experimental or stylistically daring.

The *Labyrinthine Sentence* and the *Sentence Fragment.* Though the alternate grammar of style uses the ordinary range of sentence types, it makes use also, and more frequently, of two radical sentence types: the labyrinthine sentence and the sentence fragment. And it tolerates a certain mixture of sentence types that would not be found in the traditional grammar of style. The alternate grammar tolerates great leaps from the long, labyrinthine sentence to the short fragmentary sentence, creating a sharp, startling effect at times. Yet it is not committed entirely to the startling juxtaposing: often enough a composition in the alternate style will be wholly labyrinthine or wholly fragmentary. Or at times, a most ordinary traditional sentence "style" will prevail. Usually, if traditional sentence types are to be mixed with the more radical forms, the mix will involve only traditional types and sentence fragments. Rarely do the traditional sentences and labyrinthine sentences mix successfully.

The labyrinthine sentence is a long complex sentence, with a certain "endless" quality to it, full of convolutions, marked by appositives, parentheses, digressions. A parody through exaggeration of the highly structured Johnsonian sentence of the eighteenth century, the labyrinthine has immediate ancestry in the long, radical sentences of twentieth-century fiction—such as the famous Molly Bloom one-sentence soliloquy that ends Joyce's *Ulysses.* The current master of the labyrinthine sentence is John Barth—but there are numerous other practitioners: one interesting (and perhaps unlikely) example that comes to mind is the opening sentence of *Rousseau and Revolution* by Will and Ariel Durant.

This long, almost picaresque sentence—through which an author rides picaro like—works for many writers as a correspondence to the complexity, confusion, even sheer talkativeness of modern society. When a writer talks about Walt Whitman this way—

Walt Whitman, born on Paumanok (that is: Long Island), saw in that island's shape (understandably, when you look at the map) the fish that, in the context of Western-Christian iconography, equals Christ equals rebirth equals, especially for Whitman, messianic connotations and (given Whitman's translation of biological events and conditions into transcendental mythological patterns) therefore portend for "I, Walt Whitman" (to be born later, again, with the writing of *Leaves of*

Grass) a divine dimension and a capacity for illuminating the masses who, though they never read him, remained always his projected audience, and revealing, to the enslaved (more than "the slaves," of course; all of us at one time or another) a certain kind of liberation, freedom, escape from the prison.

—he is suggesting, via style, the entangling environment in which the masses and the enslaved live and are living and from which Whitman sought to rescue them.

In contrast with this kind of labyrinthine sentence but often its companion (a la Quixote and Panza), the sentence fragment—frequently a single word or a very short phrase of only two or three words—suggests a far greater awareness of separation and fragmentation: not entanglement but isolation. It is also a highly emphatic kind of sentence and, in conjunction with other sentence types, creates a variegated, more sharply pointed kind of reading line. Gertrude Stein was a great pioneer in the use of the single word/word phrase/sentence fragment unit: as Robert Bartlett Haas says in an introductory note to Stein's essay on "Grant or Rutherford B. Hayes": "During the late 1920's and early 1930's, Gertrude Stein seems to have been dealing with . . . what the sentence was . . . as seen from the standpoint of an American syntax. Another concern was the description of events by protraying movement so intense as to be a thing in itself, not a thing in relation to something else.

" 'Grant or Rutherford B. Hayes' attempts to do this by replacing the noun and the adjective and emphasizing the more active parts of speech. Here a driving pulse is created by syncopating the sentence. The thrust comes from a concentrated use of verb and verb phrases." (Gertrude Stein, *How Writing is Written*, ed. R. B. Haas; Los Angeles: Black Sparrow Press, 1974, p. 12).

Only a few words from Stein's essay are needed to indicate her method:
Grant or Rutherford B. Hayes.
Jump. Once for all. With the praising of. Once for all.
As a chance. To win.
Once for all. With a. Chance. To win.

The farther reach of sentence types in the alternate grammar of style provides the writer with a much greater number of options. He can write the crots of the alternate grammar (a) in the traditional sentence types, (b) in the labyrinthine sentence, (c) in sentence fragments, or (d) in combinations of (i.) traditional sentences and sentence fragments or (ii.) labyrinthine sentences and sentence fragments.

The *List*. To create a list, a writer presents a series of items, usually removed from sentence structure or at least very independent of such structure. Usually a list contains a minimum of five items, the items being related in subject matter but presented in list form to avoid indicating any other relationship among the items than that they are *all there at once,* that they are parts of the whole. Presenting a list of items is comparable to presenting a "still life" of objects without indication of foreground or background, without any indication of relative importance, without any suggestion at all of cause-effect, this-before-that, rank, or the like. Obviously the items on the list must be presented one first, one second, one third—but the sequence is generally arbitrary and meaningless.

Adapted from the plethora series found in traditional grammar of style, and antedated by "catalogues" such as appear in Whitman's poetry, the list stands in stark simplicity—a list of objects, observations, or what have you— to give a quick representation of a character, a situation, a place by the simple device of selecting items to represent the subject under discussion. Donald Barthelme, a frequent user of lists, can range—as he does in a short story, "City Life,"—from a list dealing with television viewing ("On 7 there's 'Johnny Allegro' with George Raft and Nina Foch. On 9 'Johnny Angel' with George Raft and Claire Trevor," all the way through a total of eight variations to the final "On 31 is 'Johnny Trouble' with Stuart Whitman and Ethel Barrymore") to a "list" description of a wedding with such items as "Elsa and Jacques bombarded with flowers" to "The minister raises his hand" to such a simple item as "Champagne."

Though lists may be presented in a straight reading line, they are usually presented in columnar form, the items arranged typographically one beneath the other just as one writes a grocery list.

One of the attractions of the list to the contemporary writer is that— disregarding the fact that bias may have entered into the selection of the items in the first place—the list is basically a presentation of items without commentary, seeming to say, "Consider these items without any help from the writer. The writer is keeping his mouth shut. He is simply giving you the data, the evidence, the facts, the object. You, the reader, must add them up and evaluate them." Or there is the suggestion that there are no "values" at all that can be imposed upon the list, that reality stands before us neutral, amoral, and that if we do impose values upon a list it is an arbitrary act upon our part.

Whereas in the traditional grammar of style, one might write—

Whitman grew up as a boy on Long Island, absorbing all the images of sea and sky and shore, all the images of the pastoral world that were always to be a part of his poetry even as he later celebrated the urban glories of Manhattan.

—in the alternate grammar one might well write—

Whitman grew up as a boy on Long Island.

Sea.
Gulls.
Sky.
Shore.
Stones.
Roses.
Salt air.

Tides.
Farms.
Dusty Roads.
Mockingbirds.
Horses.
Summer Clouds.
Later: Brooklyn. Later: Manhattan. But always: Sea. Stones. Cattle.
Birds. Lilacs. Even as the metropolis paved its way toward mercantile
grandeur and urban glory.

The difference between the two is not a matter of "quality," but is a
matter of differing effects, differing reader involvement, differing authorial
voice. One is no more creative than the other; one is no more fictional than
the other.

Double-Voice. Even in nonfiction, as in fiction, a writer speaks with a
"voice"—if not always the same voice in all his writing, certainly a given
voice in a given composition. Indeed, the creation of "voice" is one of the
tasks of "style," and the traditional grammar of style has always been used
for that purpose among others. In the alternate grammar, however, voice is
not always considered a singular characteristic, but often enough a plural
characteristic—not a surprising consideration in an age of stereophonics and
multi-media dispositions in general.

Writers use double-voice many times when they feel that they could say
this *or* that about a subject; when they feel that two attitudes toward a subject are equally valid; when they wish to suggest that there are two sides to
the story (whatever the story may be); when they wish to distinguish
between their roles as (a) provider of information and data, and (b) com-
mentator upon information and data; or when they wish to effect a style
"corresponding" to ambiguous realities.

The double-voice may be presented in straight-line form—

Whitman was born on Long Island in 1819. Are island children marked
for a certain sense of individuality, or separation? He was the Whitman's second child. Do "second" children make a greater struggle for
identity than the oldest or the youngest? Whitman moved with his
parents to Brooklyn when he was four years old. Have children, by the
age of four, absorbed most of their primary images, established their
essential attitudes and feelings toward life regardless where they move?

Straight-line presentation of double voice is what John Barth uses, for
instance, in "Lost in the Funhouse": one example occurs in the opening
paragraph of the story:

For Ambrose it is *a place of fear and confusion.* He has come to the seashore with his family for the holiday, *the occasion of their visit is Inde-
pence Day, the most important secular holiday of the United States of
America.* A single straight underline is the manuscript mark for italics
which in turn is the printed equivalent to. . . .

The shift of voice that comes with the words "A single straight underline" provides Barth with a way of writing both as story-teller and as "observer" of the story-teller.

Obviously, one effective way for writers to present double-voice is to present parallel passages in column form, simply running two tracks of composition down the page, side by side. John Cage does this often enough, notably in his essay "Erik Satie," in *Silence* (Wesleyan University Press, 1961; M.T.T. Press, 1966). In this essay, Cage alternates two voices, one indicated by italics to the left of the page, the other by roman type to the right of the page. In another essay, "Where Are We Going? And What Are We Doing?" Cage sets up double-voice, at times even triple-voice, by writing this way—

The candles at the Candlelight Concert are
One New Year's Eve I had too
electric. It was found dangerous
many invitations. I decided to
for them to be wax. It has not yet

and so forth.

By far, though, the standard way of presenting double-voice is simply to present the columns without any further complications:

Whitman was born in 1819 on Long Island. When he was four, his parents moved to Brooklyn where Whiman grew up and went to school. All his youth he spent, one place or another, in town or in country, betwixt East River and the Atlantic Ocean.	We are born by accident in a certain location, yet the location impinges upon our soul and psyche, and we absorb the shapes and sounds and sights peculiar to that location and our view of reality is constructed from this primary, childhood material.

And obviously, two *lists* can run parallel to each other—doing all that lists themselves do and at the same time creating the double voice:

Sea	Atlantic/Womb & Tomb/Such Mystery
Gulls	Arcs of whiteness/plaintive screams
Sky	Endless/one should not stare into space too long a time
Shore	Boundaries/the line between
Stones	Foundation & Crushing Force
Roses	Perfume & Thorn
Salt Air	Wake me up! Sting against my face!
Tides	Of blood
Farms	Pastoral themes/dirty labor in barns
Country Roads	Delicate tracks/muddy ruts
Mockingbirds	Music & Irony
Horses	I stare into their eyes & wonder about the universe.

Summer Clouds   Like every child, I Walt Whitman,
                     lie & stare into their magic
                     shapes, their shifting forms,
                     and see men and beasts.

(Double-voice embraces, actually, what might be called double-percep-
tion or double-thought, and it is sometimes difficult to distinguish between a
dual vision and a dual sound. Many times the writer, in juxtaposing two
statements, gives less attention to distinguishing his "voices" and concen-
trates upon the fact that he is seeing two scenes at once or is approaching a
subject from two different angles at once.)

Repetitions/Repetends/Refrains. Repetitions play a more important
part in the alternate grammar than they do in the traditional; repetitions are
used to achieve a kind of momentum in composition when traditional continuity has been suppressed, eliminated, or handled with such subtlety that it
scarcely seems present at all. The repetitions come in all forms: simple *repetitions* of individual words; phrases and sentences used as *refrains*; words,
phrases, or sentences used as *repetends.* The repetitions are mostly devoted
to binding and holding together, creating even at times a certain rhythm that
carries a reader through disjointed sentences and passages. Perhaps the concern with repetitions in the alternative grammar is compensatory for a pervasive acceptance of fragmentation and discontinuity.

In the recent volume, *Style and Text* (ed. Hakan Ringbom, issued by
the Abo Akademie, Finland), Irma Ranavaara notes, in her essay on Virginia
Woolf's style, that Woolf makes great use of repetition, a use that ranges
through all parts of speech. Some examples given by Professor Ranavaara are
these, taken from Woolf's last novel, *Between the Acts*:

> She had come into the stable yard where the dogs were chained; where
> the buckets stood; where the great pear tree spread its ladder of
> branches against the wall.
> what a cackle, what a raggle, what a yaffle—as they call the wood-
> pecker, the laughing bird that flits from tree to tree.
>
> Faster, faster, faster, it whizzed, whirred, buzzed.
>
> The cook's hands cut, cut, cut.

Woolf was concerned in all her writing, of course, with answering the
question, "How can we combine the old words in new orders so they survive,
so that they create beauty, so that they tell the truth?" And she foraged into
the alternate grammar of style, trying this and trying that, with repetiton
being one of the stylistic devices she used heavily to escape the very economy of the traditional grammar and all the implications of that economy.

Woolf's repetitions, though of high incidence, are essentially limited to
an easily achieved epizeuxis. Gertrude Stein, in such an essay as "American
Food and American Houses" (1938), uses a slightly more subtle kind of
repetition and in ways more typical of the alternate grammar. Stein writes
such sentences as "salads fruit salads have immensely taken their place,"

with the "salad" repetition being quite different from ordinary epizeuxis. Likewise, her repetition of the word "pancake" in this sentence—

> Then there used to be so many kinds of pancakes, every kind of pancake, that too has disappeared the pancake has pretty well disappeared and I imagine that there are lots of little Americans who have never even heard of them never even heard of the word pancakes. (Haas, ed., Gertrude Stein, *op. cit.*)

The efforts of a Stein or a Woolf are simply preludes to the full use of repetition that we find in full-blown examples of the alternate grammar. When we come to Tom Wolfe's essay "Las Vegas!!! (What?) Las Vegas (Can't Hear you! Too Noisy!) Las Vegas!!!" we find him opening with a tremendously exaggerated super-epizeuxis, repeating the word "hernia" thirty times in a row; then—after a slight interruption for the phrase "eight is the point, the point is eight"—repeating the word "hernia" another seven times, pausing for the phrase "hard eight," then finishing out the opening paragraph with another sixteen "hernia"'s.

Wolfe's repetition in this case suggests movement and energy, and probably most repetitions, when presented in tightly concentrated form this way, are "corresponding" to a certain "throb of life." Sometimes, though, repetitions are less concentrated, more scattered—as in this passage from John Dos Passos' *U.S.A.*—

> Thomas Edison at eighty-two worked sixteen hours a day; he never worried about mathematics or the social system or generalized philosophical concepts; in collaboration with Henry Ford and Harvey Firestone who never worried about mathematics or the social system or generalized philosophical concepts;
>
> he worked sixteen hours a day trying to find a substitute for rubber; whenever he read about anything he tried it out; whenever he got a hunch he went to the laboratory and tried it out.

In such repetition the correspondence is probably more with the idea of inevitable recurrence of experience, the "sameness" and "inevitability" of reality, a recognition that in reality there are both stabilizing "things we count on" and boring things that never go away. Different writers will find different values in the repetition, some writers using it sparingly but some writers creating, with it, a great sense of saturation and density. Once again, the writer has options.

Given such stylistic maneuvers and devices as these (there are many more, of course—including the many that are shared with traditional grammar and including more exceptional devices absolutely beyond the pale of traditional grammar, e.g. the non sequitur and the mixed metaphor) the contemporary writer can mix and match as his own compositional inclinations and rhetorical commitments determine. He may, in his use of such maneuvers and devices, achieve, as he often does, two stylistic effects quite characteristic of compositions in the alternate grammar. They are the effects of (a) synchronicity and (b) collage-montage.

Synchronicity. In the traditional grammar of style all "time" considerations are diachronic or chronological. Even the devices of "foreshadowing" and "flashback" are still part of a diachronic conceptualization. In the alternate grammar, however, there is an acceptance of "all things present in the present moment" with many of the devices already mentioned implying this effect: double-voice implies a certain simultaneity in reality: two things going on at once. Repetitions/repetends/refrains also imply recurrence: certain material occurs in the composition; one reads it and passes on, assuming *those words* to be in the "past" of the composition; but no—we meet the material again; it was not a prisoner of the "past" but is present now, the same as it was, transcending a past/present/future sequence.

If the desire of the writer is to suggest synchronicity, he can indeed make use of double-voice and repetition. He can make use of the double-column list. He can make use of the labyrinthine sentence, especially when it emphasizes circularity (borrowing epanalepsis from the traditional grammar and making heavy, exaggerated use of it).

Much use is made also of the present tense to achieve synchronicity since the present tense can equal both the real present and the historical present; without moving from one verb to another, synchronicity can be created —as in such a passage as this—

Whitman is crossing East River on the Brooklyn Ferry. A woman is giving birth on a farm on Long Island on the thirty-first of May. He observes the reflections in the water. Whitman is dying in Camden. Peter Doyle conducts the trolley through the broad streets of Washington and the old man stares out the window, stares at the American people. The woman calls her second child Walter. And crossing on the ferry with him are all types of people, all the diverse faces, all the diverse parts of the American whole. So he walks through Camden. So he walks through Washington, D.C. He climbs up on the trolley and visits with Peter Doyle. He shortens his name to Walt. He tells his mother he is going to cross on the ferry, make his way to Manhattan, he has things to say. Thus Whitman is born on Paunmanok, 1819. Thus he is dying, carefully, in the spring of 1892. He is making a kind of journey through the flow of people and across the broad river.

(Note: In synchronicity, use is often made of transitional and relating words—such as "so," "therefore," "thus," "then"—in a kind of "binding of time," parodying the traditional grammar of syle wherein transition/relationship is accepted and expected. The resulting non-sequiturs are a by-product, yet become an important characteristic of the alternate grammar, since the non-sequiturs cut through old logical patterns and question the validity of old connections.)

Synchronicity is often achieved simply through the scrambling of sentences or paragraphs or crots, scrambling them out of ordinary time sequences, so that one keeps encountering them again and again in a certain time period. For instance, if one had crots dealing with (a) one's arrival in

New Orleans, (b) one's visit to the French Quarter, (c) in particular one's dining at Antoine's, and (d) one's departure from New Orleans, synchronicity would be achieved by scrambling the crots to present now one from group b, now one from group c, now one from group a, now one from group b, now one from group d, now one from group c, now one from group d, etc. Even if the individual crots use appropriate verb tenses (past tense primarily, with some past perfect) still the effect of the scrambling would be synchronic—all events indistinguishable within one large time frame.

Synchronicity is, of course, a stylistic effect used to support a writer's concern with the "here and now," the contemporary. Synchronicity also allows the writer to concentrate upon the immediate moment and yet include matter from the past without having to compromise the discussion of the present. If, in the opinion of a writer, the only reality is what stands in front of him here and now, then his knowledge of the past is best presented in present terms. With appreciative nods toward such a history theorist as R. G. Collingwood, the writer conceives his very "knowledge of the past" as a current knowledge: knowledge *in* the present *of* the past is a synchronous situation. All in all, synchronicity provides stylistic correspondence to the "timelessness of events."

Collage/Montage. Another frequent effect of the alternate grammar is collage/montage in which diverse elements are patched together to make the whole composition. Easily achieved with crots and the other stylistic devices so far identified, collage/montage reacts against the "categorizing" of traditional grammar and insists on packaging together into a heterogenous community all those matters that in traditional grammar would be grouped into homogenous units. Quite compatible with and similar to synchronicity, the collage/montage effect (which in traditional grammar would be considered random, hodge-podge, patchwork) is a stylistic effort at synthesis, distinguishable from traditional grammar's effort, nearly always, at analysis.

In extreme form, collage/montage can mean something as radical as William Burroughs's famous cut-up method, whereby texts written in traditional grammar are arbitrarily cut up, horizontally and vertically, and converted into near-unintelligible scraps of text. The scraps are then shuffled (or folded in) and joined randomly. Sometimes Burroughs carries his cut-up method so far as to cut up individual sentences into fragments, then paste the fragments back into new sentences. He does this for instance in *A Distant Hand Lifted*, wherein a typical sequence reads: " . . . remember/my/ messages between remote posts of/exploded star/fold in/distant sky/example agent K9 types out a/distant hand lifted. . . . " Burroughs says this collage "method can approximate walky talky immediacy."

Less radical, and more useable, are methods of collage that use larger and more intelligible units of composition, each unit—like the crot—communicative within itself, simply being joined in the collage to other communication units, perhaps from different periods, perhaps dealing with different subject matter, perhaps even containing different sentence/dictional style, texture, tone. Collage at its best actually countermands much of the discontinuity and fragmentation of the alternate style by revealing, by the time a composition ends, a synthesis and a wholeness that might not have been suspected at any station along the way.

As the compositional units to be "synthesized" become larger, more substantial, and more complete within themselves, we come to the sense of montage—a presentation in sequence, side by side, of compositional units less fragmental, yet fairly disparate so far as form or content are concerned. Frequently the disparate units are actually examples of various established compositional forms—e.g. poem, aphorism, letter, description, narration, anecdote, interview, questionnaire, etc. William Blake achieved such a montage effect in the prefaces to the various chapters of *Jerusalem*: In the preface to the first chapter, for instance, he presents (a) a prose apologia for the writing of *Jerusalem*, (b) a verse apologia and address to readers, (c) a verse quatrain, (d) a brief prose theological essay, (e) a thirty-five line poem in a rough kind of iambic pentameter, (f) a three-stanza hymn-like poem made up of four-lined stanzas in generally rhymed tetrameters.

In current montage effects, writers create multi-genre compositions, using as Dylan Thomas does, for instance, in his essay "Reminiscences of Childhood," a sequence of (a) description, (b) an original poem, (c) more prose description containing (d) passages of dialogue, and ending with (e) an aphoristic-like statement, "The memories of childhood have no order, and no end."

This kind of multi-genre montage effect in the alternate grammar replaces, somewhat, the more traditional method of citation and quotation, though quotations themselves—in isolated forms—are often used in montage.

The use of various genres within the prose nonfiction composition— (e.g. the "mimeographed schedule" in Terry Southern's "Twirling at Ole Miss"; the dramatic "scene" complete with dialogue, along with song lyrics and individual "testimonial" statements by Frank Sinatra's family in Gay Talese's "Frank Sinatra Has a Cold"; tape transcripts of earth-to-moon conversations in Norman Mailer's *Of a Fire on the Moon*)—is valued by contemprorary writers because it suggests that there is little difference between genres, between fiction/nonfiction in the verbal response to reality, that the category lines separating "literary forms" in the traditional areas do not really make sense if we begin to perceive reality and the verbal response to that reality in new and different ways. Hence: Norman Mailer's *The Armies of the Night*: History as a Novel, The Novel as History; Truman Capote's nonfiction novel *In Cold Blood*.

Formal Fragments:
The English Minor Sentence

CHARLES R. KLINE, JR. and W. DEAN MEMERING

Linguists have made much progress in the description of English syntax, leaving the prescription of usage to rhetoricians and composition teachers. Sometimes linguistic insights prove useful to those of us who teach writing, as various studies concerning "syntactic maturity" attest (Loban, 1963; Hunt, 1965; O'Donnell, Griffin, and Norris, 1967; Mellon, 1969; Emig, 1971; and O'Hare, 1973). If nothing else, the linguists have shown us how to describe with great precision the sentences our students produce.

Descriptions and Judgments of Fragments

Linguists have also noted that writers sometimes write "incomplete" sentences; Fries relates completeness to formality:

> Apparent, too, although less obvious are the differences between conversation and formal writing in the matter of sentence completeness. Conversation abounds in groups of words that do not form conventionally complete and logical sentences. Many verbs are omitted; clauses are uttered which are to be attached to a whole context of conversation rather than to any particular word in a parsable sentence; single words stand for complete ideas. In formal writing the situation demands much more logical completeness of expression, and most of the sentences appear to satisfy the demands of conventional grammatical analysis. (Fries, 1940)

Here we find Fries talking about the same thing that English teachers mean when they say "fragment." And Fries talks about it in the same way that teachers do; it occurs in speech, but not in "formal writing." The problem remains for the present study: what must English teachers do about students (native speakers, usually) who write fragments? We could make the inference from Fries that in formal writing, students *should* not write fragments, but such a decision is rhetorical, not linguistic. We would do well to consult the rhetoricians here.

Unfortunately, we find several answers to the question from different authors. Bell and Cohn (1972) advise just *don't* write fragments, period. The *Harbrace College Handbook* (1972) explains that some fragments are effective and some are not. Specifically, the fragment is "not only standard but

Research in the Teaching of English, 11 (Fall 1977), pp. 97-110. Copyright © 1977 by the National Council of Teachers of English. Reprinted by permission of the publisher and authors.

desirable" in questions and answers, exclamations, written dialogue, and "assertions containing elliptical elements." But the editors of the Harbrace handbook agree with Fries:

> Despite their suitability for some purposes, however, sentence fragments are comparatively rare in formal expository writing.

Hans P. Guth (1972) also finds some fragments permissible. According to Guth, fragments are permissible when they are employed for "special effects": common transitional expressions ("So much for past developments. Now for a look at our present problems."), answers to questions, impressionistic descriptive passages, narrative passages suggesting random, disconnected thought, transcripts of conversation or dialogue, and afterthoughts deliberately delayed for ironic effect (Man is the only animal that blushes. Or needs to.—Mark Twain). Guth thinks enough of these fragments to call them non-sentences. Still, he says students commonly write fragments as "afterthoughts," and that they are commonly appositives, adjectives or adverbs, prepositional phrases, verbs, and verb phrases, and dependent clauses. These fragments, he suggests, should be hooked up to the preceding sentence or developed as separate sentences, e.g.:

> These are my relatives. A fine group of people.

> These are my relatives, a fine group of people.

William Irmscher (1972) in *The Holt Guide to English* gives much the same advice. When a fragment is "ineffective" it should be removed, and a fragment is apparently "effective" when it is used for "special effect." It begins to sound as if the rhetoricians are talking in circles. Irmscher cites a few "effective" fragments.

1. Any number of eloquent tributes were made to Eleanor Roosevelt at her death. The most eloquent by Adlai Stevenson, a former Democratic candidate for President, her friend, and admirer.
2. I think we must set up priorities among values. Human beings first. Yes. No doubt about the first priority.
3. The radical left. There's a group that may change the whole structure of things if they have staying power.

J. N. Hook (1972) suggests that the fragment is only a stylistic variation and students *may* use them:

> Some rather bright student will probably ask the old question, "Why can't we use sentence fragments? Professional writers do." You may give the old answer that professional writers sometimes consciously use sentence fragments for special effects. It is the unconscious use that is to be condemned. If a student, or a whole class, has consistently demonstrated mature ability in sentence construction, encouragement may indeed be given to stylistic experimentation, including use of fragments. For less mature students it may be appropriate to ask them to put a star in the margin opposite a fragment to show that the use was intentional.

We wonder how serious Hook is about this and what the effect would be on a writer who interrupted his thoughts to star his sentence fragments.

Brooks and Warren (1972) make no mention of fragments except as a feature of impressionistic style, e.g.:

From a second-story window the sign, "W. P. Kennicott, Physician and Surgeon," gilt on black sand, a small wooden motion-picture theater called "The Rosebud Movie Palace." Lithographs announcing a film called, "Fatty in Love." (Sinclair Lewis, *Main Street*)

Richard M. Weaver (1974) admits that fragments occasionally appear in serious writing, but he prefers to call them "minor sentences." Where they are well employed, he says, no incoherence results. But he cautions students not to overuse them:

Although it is not entirely avoided, its use is restricted. Expository writing sprinkled with minor sentences is likely to be a sign of illiteracy.

James M. McCrimmon (1972) suggests that we can classify writing as *colloquial, informal,* and *formal* and that fragments appear in each of these respectively: frequently, infrequently, and never. In formal writing, he says, the fragment constitutes a "period fault," except where the intention is to imitate speech.

A new movement in the teaching of writing suggests that the student's writing is too personal for the teacher to tamper with. Not only do the writers in this movement urge that informal (or, at least, *more* informal) student writing be considered entirely acceptable, but they also write in the manner they advocate for students. Ken Macrorie (1968) makes statements like these:

But enough of these errors. The good writer masters grammar in order to control his words, and meaning is his target.

. . . .

To write fully, you must use all your senses. Remember how places and objects smell, the taste of the back of your hand, the touch of concrete, the sound of a laugh—an American's laugh, a Southerner's laugh, a Northerner's. Such variety.

. . . .

As you dash off these writings ["Free writings"], don't plan ahead. Write. Spill out whatever comes to mind and eye. Put down honestly what you feel and see.

In the kind of writing stressed by Macrorie, and others, the frequency of non-sentences is likely to be higher since the writing is less formal (at least as the word is commonly used by composition teachers).

From the rhetoricians, then, we get a range of answers from "never use a fragment," to "use them infrequently." And when they are used, they must be used deliberately, in certain kinds of writing, to achieve an effect, and without causing incoherence. The advice of those who suggest that the fragment is entirely taboo may be easiest for students to understand, but it seems unreasonable to ask students to work with greater restriction than those imposed on skilled adults—if it is true that skilled adults do sometimes write fragments. Of those authors who suggest that fragments are used deliberately, in certain kinds of writing, and so on, we should ask how they know this. The answer may be that a lifetime of reading so informs them, but in that case the disagreements among rhetoricians make a problem. Apparently, each one's intuition tells one something different about the literature one has read.

Fragments in the Sample

We suggest that we should investigate whether and under what conditions fragments occur by looking at some writing. We know beforehand that some writers do use fragments, in impressionistic description, in imitation of dialogue, to achieve irony and emphasis, to ask and answer questions, to make assertions and exclamations, and to achieve transition. And we know further that fragments occur in informal and colloquial writing. Therefore, we can exclude all such fragments from our investigations. The chief disagreement among teachers seems to be over *formal writing*, or serious writing. We can, then, ask three questions.

1. Do fragments occur in formal written English?
2. Under what conditions (if any) do they occur, excluding those already mentioned?
3. With what frequency do they occur?

The Sample—We may have some difficulty defining a body of writing as "formal" English, although McCrimmon suggests that formal sentences are relatively long and complex in structure. Perhaps we can do no better than to suggest that "Formal English" is the writing of well-educated adults who write to an audience of similarly well-educated adults. Using this definition, we selected at random fifty books and magazines which we believed represented formal English. We found concatenated dependent clauses, the comparative structure (the more . . . the better . . .), the "not" construction, the "added thought," answers to rhetorical questions, the appositive, elliptical clauses and phrases, deletion of redundant elements, the infinitive as fragment, loose final free modifier, the questionable "for" fragment, and paragraph beginning fragments other than transitional devices.

Illustrative Items from the Sample

We hold these truths to be self-evident, that all men are created equal, that they are endowed by their Creator with certain unalienable Rights, that among these are Life, Liberty, and the pursuit of Happiness. That to secure these rights, Governments are instituted among Men, deriving their just Powers from the consent of the governed.

English teachers with a good memory may recall that the next "sentence" from the Declaration begins "That, whenever any form of Government becomes destructive of these ends. . . . " We will assume that the declaration represents the *most* formal English. We are not sure what constitutes "sprinkled with minor sentences," but the second paragraph of *The Declaration of Independence* contains two of them. We cannot discern what "effect" Jefferson was striving for. In view of the length and complexity of the main clause, the many commas, and the repetition of *that*—it appears that Jefferson made an editorial choice in favor of his readers; i.e., it's easier to read this way. It is possible, of course, that each one of these noun clauses is in fact a separate sentence, each one beginning with "We hold. . . . " In that case, Jefferson made a stylistic choice—to delete the redundant main clauses, perhaps to relieve the monotony they would have produced. But in this case we are proposing a linguistic theory of some complexity: the writer holds in his mind a proto-string of sentences which bear common elements; he deletes the common elements (in this case both the subject and the verb of the subsequent strings) and then writes the resultant strings as *separate sentences* instead of as embeddings within a single sentence? The prospect has a certain mind-boggling attractiveness, but no linguistic theory—not to mention a parsimonious one—can account completely for such a phenomenon.

The comparative—The comparative construction is idiomatic in English, and it is one of the reasons why "fragment" may not be a good term in these investigations:

> They then determined the number of these unrelated words recalled when the subject attempted to repeat the sentence and the sequence of words. The more words recalled, the less memory used to store the sentence. The fewer words recalled, the more memory used to store the sentence. (Noam Chomsky, "Language and the Mind")

In this case it is difficult to see the "fragments" as part of the preceding sentences or as in any way incomplete or as written for effect. If anything at all suggested to Chomsky that his "sentences" should be written this way, it may have been that that's the way English goes. It could be argued that Chomsky here emphasizes the results of an experiment by stating them in this form. But we would suggest that the emphasis derives from the balanced structure more than from the absence of any necessary component of the syntax.

> *The Not Fragment*— Emily Dickinson's poems, because they have such tension, are much more authentically in the metaphysical tradition than Emerson's are. Not, however, that many of his values were hers also—especially where they concerned the integrity of the mind and the sufficiency of inner resources. (F. O. Matthiesen, *American Renaissance*)

> In a country like Italy, where the kitchen is still a kind of sacred cave presided over by a mother-goddess, the design of a cooking module that can be rolled about and plugged in anywhere has profound implica-

tions. Not, perhaps, the immediate death of the nuclear family—but certainly a substantial critique of it. (*Time*)

The *Not* fragment is very common, and we cannot see that it would read with less emphasis if punctuated as one sentence. The only apparent effect of many of these fragments is the effect of afterthought.

True, there are architects so called in this country, and I have heard of one at least possessed with the idea of making architectural ornaments have a core of truth, a necessity, and hence a beauty, as if it were a revelation to him. All very well from his point of view, but only a little better than the common dilettantism. (Henry David Thoreau, *Walden*)

The world is mind precipitated, and the volatile essence is forever escaping again into the state of free thought. Hence the virtue and pungency of the influence on the mind of natural objects, whether inorganic or organized. (Ralph Waldo Emerson, *Nature*)

It is possible, to be sure, that a thing precisely observed can be poorly rendered. Or that it may be poorly received by the reader. (John Ciardi, "The Art of Maxine Kumin," *Saturday Review*)

What is impressive about these non-sentences by Thoreau, Emerson, and Ciardi is their coherence. The reader is occasioned no reading difficulty at all. In fact, it takes a special kind of reading even to find some of these fragments. We found that if we began *reading*, following the thoughts of the writer, we could not attend to his syntax. It became necessary to *skim* rapidly, paying very little attention to the content of what we were skimming, in order to find the fragments. It is possible that the impression some teachers have that these fragments do not occur in formal writing is the result of the fragments' complete naturalness and appropriateness in context. They are so coherent that the reader is not aware of their presence.

The Dependent—I am sure no other civilisation, not even the Roman, has showed (sic) such a vast proportion of ignominious and degraded nudity, and ugly, squalid, dirty sex. Because no other civilisation has driven sex into the underworld, and nudity to the w.c. (D. H. Lawrence, *Pornography and Obscenity*)

Like the Emerson example above, Lawrence's is clearly a dependent clause, and just as with Emerson, we would hestiate to ascribe any conscious effect-striving to Lawrence.

So what was missing from little Saalbach on that bright February morning? Snow. *Schnee*. The same thing missing from so many other Alpine ski resorts this winter. (David Butwin, "Booked for Travel, The Pleasant Slush of Saalback," *Saturday Review*)

Butwin's first two non-sentences—"Snow. Schnee."—represent a widely accepted usage, answers to rhetorical questions. But the third is an appositive. Here we think the writer does achieve emphasis, but it is not easy to ascribe the emphasis to syntax alone. (The question and answer device and

the use of three fragments in a row, one of which is a German word . . . italicized for emphasis, have a great deal to do with it.) It could be argued that
the final fragment tends to tone down the over-emphasis achieved by the
preceding fragments.

Another common usage is the listing of elliptical clauses and phrases, as
in this by Sir Winston Churchill:

> The spirit of the long-vanished Roman Empire, revived by the Catholic
> Church, returned once more to our Island, bringing with it three dom-
> inant ideas. First, a Europe in which naturalism or even the conception of
> nationality had no place, but where one general theme of conduct and
> law united the triumphant martial classes upon a plane far above race.
> Secondly, the idea of monarchy, in the sense that Kings were the
> expression of the class hierarchy over which they presided and the
> arbiters of its own frequently conflicting interests. (Winston Churchill,
> *The Birth of Britain*)

If we care to speculate about why Churchill wrote this way, a good
speculation might simply be to make the reading easier. Connected up as one
sentence, these clauses produce a very long and complex sentence to read.
Developed into full sentences, the passage might have contained a redundancy that Churchill would find inelegant (First, there was a Europe . . .
Secondly there was the idea of monarchy . . .?). But it might be better to
speculate that Churchill simply wrote good idiomatic English, in which lists
of things are commonly stated elliptically. (A native speaker could say, but
probably wouldn't: "Bring me three things from the store. Bring me a dozen
eggs. Bring me a quart of milk. And bring me a loaf of bread.") As Jefferson
did in the Declaration, Churchill performed a very simple transformation by
deleting the redundant element, but instead of imbedding the resultant trans-
forms in the main clause, he wrote them as separate sentences. The same
thing can be observed in the following:

> New schools sprang up on all sides. In Italy, Futurism; in Switzerland
> and New York, Dada; in Hollywood, *De Stijl* (the style). (William
> Snaith, "The Anguish of Modern Art")

> His last whim had been to bring with him, on his weekly visits, some
> new, useful, and ingenius article for the young housekeeper. Now a bag
> of remarkable clothespins; next a wonderful nutmeg-grater, which fell
> to pieces at the first trial; a knife-cleaner that spoilt all the knives; or a
> sweeper that picked the nap neatly off the carpet, and left the dirt;
> labor saving soap that took the skin off one's hands; infallible cements
> which stuck firmly to nothing but the fingers of the deluded buyer; and
> every kind of tin-ware; from a toy savings bank for odd pennies, to a
> wonderful boiler which would wash articles in its own steam, with
> every prospect of exploding in the process. (Louisa May Alcott, *Little
> Women*)

The Infinitive   It is fairly easy to find infinitives written as fragments
such as this one:

That is why I started to write. To save myself. (Eldridge Cleaver, *Soul on Ice*)

Here again it appears that the fragment adds emphasis, but again it is no easy thing to convince every reader that such is the case. Consider:

> When its wearer reached for a taxi door one morning, only a part of the sheep went with her; the left sleeve tore away from the arm hole. A fluke perhaps, but not if the sour suspicions of a swelling number of retailers and their customers are correct. (*Time*)
>
> The relative clause does not allow for the thought-pause, as follows: "This using of 'whiches' is a practice which . . . leads to wordiness and flabbiness in writing." Excusable in conversation or an impromptu speech and even in a dictated letter or the first draft of an article. Inexcusable in the final draft. (H. L. Anshutz, "College *English? College English?*")

Here we find a college professor, writing in a professional journal, in an article on the quality of writing in that journal, doing the same thing as the editors of *Time*—dispensing with both the subjects and the verbs of some of his sentences. Why? It may be that Anshutz has given the answer: avoid wordiness and flabbiness in writing. The "effect" then is one of economy, but this is an effect of slightly different order than irony, emphasis, or other such literary effects. In these examples, and in all the other examples in this collection, the "fragments" or "non-sentences" invariably sound right. One of the implications of this study may be that formal written English is not very far removed from oral English after all. The spoken English of the highly educated, when they are speaking to other highly educated people in formal situations, may not be strikingly different from formal written English. College professors we have known tended to speak very formally even when speaking aside from the prepared lecture or discussing a question in class. If it could be shown that formal oral English is not very unlike formal written English, then we could simply abandon the pejorative connotation of the "fragment." The appearance of a fragment in writing could be explained as idiomatic in formal English—the spoken language of the highly educated. Unfortunately, we do not now have such research.

Other Fragments—We also found fragments related to the first sentence in a paragraph and as the first sentence in a paragraph:

> I would like to deal with two of the most profound of these misrepresentations. First, concerning the nonscientists' impression that scientists are blankly optimistic. (C. P. Snow, "The Conflict of Two Cultures")
>
> For aspect is one of the most disputed notions in linguistics, and tense, at least the "essence" of some of the oppositions found in it, only slightly less so. (O. Szemerinyi, "Unorthodox Views of Tense and Aspect," *Archivum Linguisticum*)

"For" is often a borderline conjunction in terms of fragments or sentences: in one case it can be read as a coordinating conjunction—which allows for some flexibility in starting sentences—and in another case it can be read as a subordinating conjunction. The Szemerinyi example seems to us clearly a case of the paragraph (and sentence) starting with a *subordinating,* not a coordinating element. At least one text on usage describes *for* in this fashion.

> Dependent clauses that explain or give a reason for the main clause are sometimes set off by commas:
>
> > Ortega rejects this definition, for he believes "mass" is not a matter of number but a mental habit. (Martin, Ohmann, and Wheatley, *The Logic and Rhetoric of Exposition*)

The reader must decide for himself. If the reader agrees that *for* can be a subordinate conjunction, the number of fragments in any corpus will disproportionately increase, because the "for" fragment is very common.

Conclusions from the Sample

At least we can say that in *this* sample, the sentence fragment does occur in the writing of highly educated adults. Fragments are relatively easy to find; five minutes of skimming will usually produce one, if the writer uses them at all. It is very hard to find one in these: Bruce Catton, *Terrible Swift Sword; The Encyclopaedia Britannica*; Will Durant, *The Reformation;* Arnold Toynbee, *A Study of History;* Edward Gibbon, *The History of the Decline and Fall of the Roman Empire.* There may be a fragment or two in that group of books (the odds favor it), but we couldn't find any after a much more taxing search than it took to produce the others that we did find. It cannot be claimed that these writers are more formal than every one of those in the sample. It might be argued that except for the encyclopedia, they are all scholarly historians, but the reader will find the sample above represented well both scholars and historians. The only rule we can make from this evidence is that some writers use fragments and some don't.

The Conditions for Fragments

Having established that fragments occur in formal written English (our first question) and that the frequency of occurrence (our second question) is higher than generally assumed, we must attempt to answer our other question: Under what conditions do fragments occur? As a starting point, we used earlier work.

A study of the non-sentence carried out in the last decade corroborates our findings and allows us to move toward a schema of the non-sentence. In the Bowman (1966) study the frequency and type of minor and fragmentary sentences in a corpus of spoken language were studied. Based on the results of her work and ours, it is possible to make some assertions about the non-sentence and its place in writing classes' assignments.

Bowman's monograph is the report of a study she conducted by taping and transcribing the language of one family whose English was described as "local standard." We can use the classification she evolved as a point of comparison for our previous examples. As a result of such a classification, we will have a matrix of sentences, non-sentences, and fragments—according to linguistic criteria (elements and dependency) and rhetorical criteria (occurrence, position, and context).

Bowman divided the taped language into Sentences, Minor sentences, and Fragments. Of her total 4245 utterances, she found 1258 minor sentences and 157 fragments. In terms of proportion, she found that one-third of the corpus was either minor sentences or fragments. The latter she defined as ". . . utterances in the corpus which do not end with a terminal juncture." The difference between minor and major sentences is based on A) the presence of both subject and predicate and B) the absence of any element(s) which would cause the sentence to be grammatically linked to any other utterance (and be therefore *not* independent). Under this classification, then, subjectless sentences are to be considered minor sentences, as are predicateless ones and ones which are linked to another utterance by grammatical dependence.

As a further classification, Bowman divided minor sentences into either Dependent or Independent minor sentences. Figure One portrays that division and the various components of each. A subjectless sentence is considered an independent minor sentence. An utterance which is a repetition of an element from a previous sentence is an example of a dependent minor sentence. (Such an item might be "Can you imagine that? He went to town. To town.")

Obviously, since Bowman's corpus was taken from spoken English, and since we do not consider written English to be just "talk written down," some of her categories are not directly applicable. By combining some categories and eliminating others (those not applicable to written English), we have arrived at the schema presented in Figure Two. (Bowman considered omitted verbs and verbal auxiliaries under "Subjectless Minor Sentences." We consider both of these as part of the category "Ellipsis.")

As we mentioned earlier, certain words and phrases which teachers commonly call "fragments" may be perceived as incorrect usage since they are similar to *informal speech*, and informal speech clearly has no place in written pieces, according to these teachers. We believe we have eliminated categories in which such usage would occur.

Another observation, although simplistic, seems warranted: many of the classifications dropped from Figure One because Figure Two contains categories for written English only might be perfectly acceptable to the English teacher who is principally concerned with urging the student to express himself in a "natural voice."

Using the schema presented in Figure Two as a basis, the examples of non-sentences presented earlier in this study fit into the diagram nicely, but not perfectly.

Most of the examples we presented fit into Dependent Minor Sentence-

FIGURE ONE
Bowman's Classificatory Schema

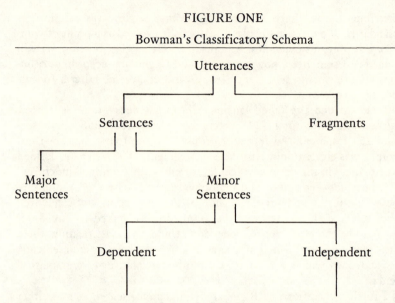

1. Otherwise major, but needs an element from previous sentence repeated to be major sentence
2. A repetition of item(s) from previous sentence
3. Minor sentence or a fragment completed by the speaker or other speaker
4. Minor sentence is last element of previous utterance ("Unless . . . . ")
5. First part of following sentence started, interrupted, started again and completed

1. Sentence abandoned before completion
2. Subjectless minor sentence
   a. Imperative
   b. Elliptical (omitted ART, POSS, CONJ, PREP, V, Vaux, Vbe, and "there")
   c. Non-imperative, non-elliptical, simple verb ("Just get away from the city.")
3. Nominal phrase
4. Material read from written matter
5. Accepted literary ("Oh, for summer.")
6. Exclamations
7. Polite words
8. "How about" and "What about" constructions
9. ADJ and ADJ phrases ("Very nice.")
10. "How" and "What" constructions ("How revolting.")
11. Interrogatives ("What?" or "Why?")

FIGURE TWO

Minor Sentence Schema for Written English

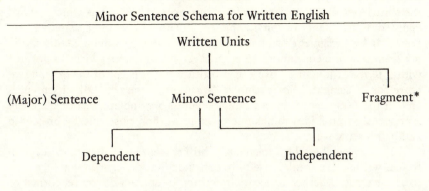

| 1. Key element of sentence in previous unit, but not repeated in minor sentence
2. Repetition of element(s) from the previous sentence
3. Dependent element of previous sentence but not attached ("Unless...." or "For .... ")
4. Adjectival or adverbial phrase which confirms or qualifies aspect of previous unit | 1. Imperatives, exclamations, one word interrogatives, and one word or phrase length answers to question posed in previous unit
2. Ellipsis based units (missing ART, POSS, etc.)
3. Literary ("Oh, for summer.")
4. Phatic discourse elements
5. Nominal, adjectival, or adverbial phrases not in #4 of Dependent classification (esp., appositive)
6. "How" and "What" constructions
7. Subjectless, non-imperative, non-elliptical units ("Just to get away.") |

*The fragment would be defined in this schema as a unit which would not fit into any of the above categories or which is a dependent minor sentence with no context.

Dependent Element of Previous, Dependent Minor Sentence-Confirming Adjectival or Adverbial, or Independent Minor Sentence-Ellipsis-based. Taken together these data provide evidence that we use several types of minor sentences more often than other types.

Towards a Redefinition

Having established the presence of fragments in formal written English, it seems that the question of the Fragment (Non-sentence) is really two-fold: 1. What is the *nature* of the non-sentence and what is the nature of the fragment? 2. What criteria may be advanced regarding the linguistic/rhetorical classification of the non-sentence and the appropriateness of the non-sentence?

The nature of the "fragment" in both Bowman's study and ours is such that we need to devise a new concept and perhaps a new term to account for the shift from "fragment" to "minor sentence." Those items which we had counted as fragments in our sample should now be counted as minor sentences. If by "fragment" we mean (as Bowman does) fragmented, discontinuous, and/or non-continuous *thought*, " . . . utterances which do not end with a terminal juncture," we can substitute the concept of the *broken sentence* for "fragment." For example: "We went to the . . . " Minor sentences and all the "fragments" in our sample express a complete idea or complete a previously stated idea minus one or more of the items typically present in an English sentence.

It is clear that the "fragment" (broken sentence) does not occur in formal writing. We think it useful to conclude that the broken sentence is always an error, whether it occurs in written or spoken discourse, formal or informal.

The minor sentence (including those we called "fragments") is a stylistic feature of many writers and should be acceptable in any student writing. We can postulate only one rule about its use:

Dependent and Minor Sentences should be contiguously placed and related to either an Independent Minor Sentence or a (Major) Sentence.

This rule seems defensible to us. In the first place the interests of clarity and continuity demand that written units which are not Sentences be obviously related to either the last previous or the next written unit; otherwise, the unit or the entire passage may be misunderstood. In the second place, our sample—which, though small compared to all the literature available, has no examples of elements which would not meet the rule—gives us no occasion for believing that any other rules or conditions of use are needed. We found no discontinuous, noncontiguous minor sentences, so we cannot state that, in formal written English, such occur.

Practically, however, this rule means that teachers of composition should have much less use for the pejorative term "fragment," the incidence of which is very slight, even in student writing. We suggest as a general rule that "fragments" will largely disappear if teachers will read student papers rapidly, attending to the substance of the sentences. Given such a reading, only blatant incoherence caused by non-interpretable units will announce the presence of a "fragment," i.e., a broken sentence. If, however, teachers ignore substance and search instead for incomplete utterances punctuated as sentences, the likelihood is that teachers will find—and erroneously label as "fragments"—many perfectly acceptable minor sentences.

References

Bell, J. K., and Cohn, A. A. *Handbook of Grammar, Style, and Usage.* Beverly Hills, CA: Glencoe Press, 1972.

Bowman, E. "The Minor and Fragmentary Sentences of a Corpus of Spoken English." *International Journal of American Linguistics,* Part II, 1966, *33*, 3.

Brooks, C., and Warren, R. P. *Modern Rhetoric* (Shorter, 3rd ed.). New York: Harcourt Brace Jovanovich, 1972.

Emig, J. *The Composing Processes of Twelfth Graders.* Urbana, IL: National Council of Teachers of English, 1971. (NCTE Research Report No. 13.)

Fries, C. C. *American English Grammar.* New York: Appleton-Century-Crofts, Inc., 1940.

Guth, H. *Words and Ideas.* Belmont, CA: Wadsworth Publishing Co., Inc., 1972.

Hodges, J. C. and Whitten, M. E. *Harbrace College Handbook* (7th ed.). New York: Harcourt Brace Jovanovich, 1972.

Hook, J. N. *The Teaching of High School English* (4th ed.). New York: The Ronald Press, 1972.

Hunt, K. W. *Grammatical Structures Written at Three Grade Levels.* Urbana, IL: National Council of Teachers of English, 1965. (NCTE Research Report No. 3.)

Irmscher, W. F. *The Holt Guide to English.* New York: Holt, Rinehart and Winston, Inc., 1972.

Loban, W. D. *The Language of Elementary School Children.* Urbana, IL: National Council of Teachers of English, 1963. (NCTE Research Report No. 1.)

Macrorie, K. *Writing to Be Read.* Rochelle Park, NJ: Hayden, 1968.

McCrimmon, J. *Writing with a Purpose* (5th ed.). Boston: Houghton Mifflin, 1972.

Mellon, J. *Transformational Sentence Combining: a Method for Enhancing the Development of Syntactic Fluency in English Composition.* Urbana, IL: National Council of Teachers of English, 1969. (NCTE Research Report No. 10.)

O'Donnell, R. C., Griffin, W. J. and Norris, R. C. *Syntax of Kindergarten and Elementary School Children: A Transformational Analysis.* Urbana, IL: National Council of Teachers of English, 1967. (NCTE Research Report No. 8.)

O'Hare, F. *Sentence Combining: Improving Student Writing Without Formal Grammar Instruction.* Urbana, IL: National Council of Teachers of English, 1973. (NCTE Research Report No. 15.)

Weaver, R. M., and Beal, R. S. *A Rhetoric and Composition Handbook.* New York: William Morrow & Co., 1974.

PART FOUR

Beyond the Sentence

"The paragraph, indeed, is the microcosm of the discourse and admits and demands a very extended study in any scheme of instruction in English"

Alexander Bain

At a large university, a student was brought before the academic honesty committee for cheating. Going into the final exam with a D- average, the student wrote out an essay on a yellow pad (the topic for the exam had been given), tore off the top page, and then brought the pad to the exam. During the exam the student was caught going over the indentions on the imprinted pad. At the hearing, the committee asked the student what help the teacher had offered during the course.

"She didn't offer much help," the student replied. "She just kept saying over and over: 'Make it coherent. Make it coherent.'"

The teacher, who was quite young, was asked if she were familiar with the recent work on teaching coherence. She responded that she was not. She went on to explain that she was a new Ph.D. graduate, but during the course of her graduate study she had never encountered anything on how to teach coherence. The young teacher was obviously well-grounded in literature, but she was totally uninformed about that important work on coherence which began appearing in the journals in the mid-sixties. One has to wonder how many times this tragedy has been repeated in our nation's classrooms. How many composition teachers are still unfamiliar with the skills for teaching one of the most important components of the composition curriculum?

The first essay, which is from the mid-sixties, is a cornerstone work. Becker's tagmemic approach emphasizes the three elements, topic, restriction and illustration (TRI), which may occur in a variety of sequences. His description of equivalence classes and lexical markers is extremely useful. It gives the writer a guideline for repeating key words and for indicating cognitive shifts, which in turn leads toward improvement in the reading comprehension of the passage.

Whereas Becker's work appeared two decades ago, the essay "Something Old, Something New: Functional Sentence Perspective" by William J. Vande Kopple illustrates some current insights into stretches of prose beyond the sentence. Vande Kopple's work is full of germinal ideas for teaching techniques and will likely become a classic in the field.

The same is true of "Coherence, Cohesion, and Writing Quality" by Stephen P. Witte and Lester Faigley. First, the authors summarize the varieties of cohesion which appear in an important 1976 publication by Halliday and Hasan, *Cohesion in English*. Then they go on to describe the results of applying that system of analysis to ten of the highest rated and lowest rated essays from freshmen enrolled at the University of Texas. They conclude by distinguishing between coherence and cohesion, and by discussing how these factors are related to the quality of writing.

Patterns of organization which occur in paragraphs and longer stretches of prose are concerned with invention as much as they are with arrangement, says Frank J. D'Angelo in "Paradigms as Structural Counterparts of *Topoi*." D'Angelo argues that "invention, arrangement, and style are parts of an organic whole," not discrete entitities. According to a unified theory of composing, the emergence of coherence within a given text is a dynamic, creative act which grows out of the subject itself; it is not simply a series of boxes to be filled.

In the concluding essay, C. H. Knoblauch reminds us that the analysis of texts is not the same as the creation of texts. Knoblauch reviews several schemes of classification and points out that though they may differ in specifics, they do not differ "in aspiration or methodological focus." The beginning of writing, Knoblauch argues, lies in intentionality, in the complex network of the sometimes conflicting purposes of the writer and the expectations of the reader. The major implication here is that we still do not fully comprehend the relation between analytic thinking and synthetic thinking, the taking-apart and the putting-together. Most would agree, however, that both kinds of thinking are necessary in learning to write, and that as teachers of writing the more fully we understand both processes, the greater our chances for success will be.

A Tagmemic Approach to Paragraph Analysis

In order to be of more than peripheral interest to rhetoricians and literary scholars, linguistic research must move beyond the sentence, even though passing over this threshold vastly complicates linguistic theory. However, the initial steps toward a theory of language which explains both grammatical and rhetorical patterns can probably be made by extending grammatical theories now used in analyzing and describing sentence structure. The purpose of this paper is to illustrate how one such theory, tagmemics, can be extended to the description of paragraphs.[1]

Tagmemic theory can be characterized in many different ways depending upon one's primary assumptions about language. Among the various linguistic theories currently respectable—signals grammar, slot and substitution grammar, finite-stage grammar, phrase structure grammar, and transformational grammar—tagmemics is probably closest to slot and substitution grammar, the sort of grammar exemplified in Charles C. Fries' *The Structure of English* and A. S. Hornby's *A Guide to Patterns and Usage in English* (to mention two works known to most English teachers), although it would be false to describe tagmemics as merely a slot and substitution grammar, for it includes features of all these grammars and is probably the broadest and most flexible of them—and it is the only one of them which contains theoretical motivation for carrying language description beyond the sentence.

In tagmemic theory, the central concept in the process of partitioning patterns is the tagmeme, which can be defined as the class of grammatical forms that function in a particular grammatical relationship. . . . Another way of defining tegmemes might be to say that they are spots or slots in a system where substitution is possible, and they include both the functional spot or slot and the set of substitutable forms. As composites of both form and function, tagmemes reflect an important axiom in tagmemic theory: that meaning cannot be separated from form or form from meaning without serious distortion. Put in terms of partitioning, this means that a whole is not the sum of its parts (if by "parts" we mean only the isolated segments), but only of its parts plus their relationships.

The concept of the tagmeme is useful in the rhetorical analysis of structures beyond the sentence. It gives us criteria for partitioning discourse in a significant way, though it is by no means a completely new idea to

College Composition and Communication, 16 (December 1965), pp. 237-242. Copyright © 1965 by the National Council of Teachers of English. Reprinted by permission of the publisher and the author.

divide a sequence of discourse into functional slots and filler classes. The traditional syllogism can be viewed as a system of slots and filler classes; there are rigid restrictions on how each slot (or term in a premise) can be filled, and only a limited number of patterns (or moods) are correct. Also the strategies of argumentation and the forms of definition have traditionally been conceived of as something like functional slots and classes in a larger pattern in which expectations are aroused and fulfilled.

Before I illustrate the use of the tagmeme in describing paragraph structure, let me first emphasize that partitioning a paragraph into functional parts reveals only one aspect of its structure. Like sentences, paragraphs are multisystemic. In addition to its systems of functional parts, a paragraph has two other structural features in the tagmemic approach: there is continuity or concord between the parts, and there is a system of semantic relationships in which the reader's expectations are aroused and fulfilled.[2] Each of these three perspectives on the paragraph is necessary for a complete description, and the isolation of only one perspective tends to distort the description somewhat by suppressing other features of paragraph structure.

To further limit my focus, I will discuss only the structure of expository paragraphs. Narrative, descriptive, and argumentative paragraphs have quite different structures from those I will present, though the methods of analysis I use are the same, and the grammatical markers of paragraph slots are nearly identical for all types of paragraphs.

There seem to be two major patterns of paragraphing in expository writing. These two patterns can be derived experimentally by giving students samples of expository paragraphs and asking them to partition them in ways that seem significant. There are disagreements about how particular paragraphs ought to be partitioned, but also a striking percentage of agreement, especially after students have partitioned enough paragraphs to recognize recurring patterns.

The first expository pattern has three functional slots, which can be labelled T (topic), R (restriction), and I (illustration). In the T slot the topic is stated, in the R slot the topic is narrowed down or defined, and in the I slot the topic, as restricted in R, is illustrated or described at lower level of generality. These slots seem to reflect what Kenneth Burke calls "an internal form," a natural way of talking or writing about something.[3]

These three slots usually correspond to three levels of generality in the paragraphs, and one of the signals of a new slot is a noticeable shift in level of generality. The recent work of Francis Christensen emphasizes this aspect of paragraph structure;[4] indeed, he makes layers of generality central to his theory. It is, however, extremely difficult to be very precise about one's ability to recognize, say, *Hereford* as a particular instance of *cow*—difficult, that is, without a lexical theory which makes levels of generality explicit.

Each of the slots in a TRI paragraph can be filled in various ways; that is, certain rhetorical types of sentences typically occur in certain slots. For instance, the T slot can be filled by a simple proposition, or a proposition implying a contrast, comparison, partition, etc. The R slot is frequently a re-

statement of T at a lower level of generality, a definition of T or a term in
T, a metaphoric restatement of T, etc. The I slot can be filled by one or
more examples (often in a narrative or descriptive pattern), an extended
analogy, a series of specific comparisons, etc. For each slot there is a general
function and a set of potential fillers. Each slot and its fillers constitute,
therefore, a paragraph-level tagmeme.

The following paragraph is an example of the TRI pattern:

(T) The English Constitution—that indescribable entity—is a living
thing, growing with the growth of men, and assuming ever-varying
forms in accordance with the subtle and complex laws of human character. (R) It is the child of wisdom and chance. (I) The wise men of
1688 moulded it into the shape we know, but the chance that George I
could not speak English gave it one of its essential peculiarities—the system of a Cabinet independent of the Crown and subordinate to the
Prime Minister. The wisdom of Lord Grey saved it from petrification
and set it upon the path of democracy. Then chance intervened once
more. A female sovereign happened to marry an able and pertinacious
man, and it seemed likely that an element which had been quiescent
within it for years—the element of irresponsible administrative power—
was about to become its predominant characteristic and change completely the direction of its growth. But what chance gave, chance took
away. The Consort perished in his prime, and the English Constitution,
dropping the dead limb with hardly a tremor, continued its mysterious
life as if he had never been.

Lytton Strachey, *Queen Victoria*

In this paragraph we note that the T slot is filled by a metaphoric proposition (*The English Constitution . . . is a living thing . . .*); the R slot by a mere
specific instance of that metaphor (*living thing* —> child); and the I slot by a
set of examples ordered historically in one dimension and categorically
according to the "parentage" (*wisdom and chance*) of the "child" (the Constitution) in the other.

The second major pattern of expository paragraphs has two slots, which
can be labelled P (problem) and S (solution). The P slot, often in question
form, is the statement of a problem or an effect which is to be explained,
and the S slot states the solution or cause of P. If it is extended, the S slot
very often has an internal structure of TRI (an example of embedding at the
paragraph level). This second pattern is shown in the following paragraph,
which also illustrates two other features of paragraph structure (which will
be considered later)—that is, the combining of what could be two paragraphs
into a single paragraph (i.e., the slot S occurs twice, giving two contrasting
answers to the question in P), and the appending of transitional sentences to
formally unified paragraphs. These transitional sentences make paragraphs
indeterminate units, for, as transitions, they are shared by two paragraphs
and usually could occur as well at the end of one paragraph as at the beginning
of the next. The majority of the disagreements in experimental student parti-

tioning of paragraphs involved transitional sentences.

(P) How obsolete is Hearn's judgment? (S$_1$) (T) On the surface the five gentlemen of Japan do not themselves seem to be throttled by this rigid society of their ancestors. (R) Their world is in fact far looser in its demands upon them than it once was. (I) Industrialization and the influence of the West have progressively softened the texture of the web. Defeat in war badly strained it. A military occupation, committed to producing a democratic Japan, pulled and tore at it. (S$_2$) (T) But it has not disappeared. (R) It is still the invisible adhesive that seals the nationhood of the Japanese. (I) Shimizu, Sanada, Yamazaki, Kisfi and Hirohito were all born within its bonds. Despite their individual work, surroundings and opinions, they have lived most of their lives as cogs geared into a group society. Literally as well as figuratively speaking, none of them has a lock on his house door. [transition] In 1948, after Hearn had gone to his grave, a Japanese sociologist, Takegi Kawashima, could write with much justice about the behavior of his contemporaries: [A long quotation follows, beginning a new paragraph.]

Frank Gibney, *Five Gentlemen of Japan*

Although there are more kinds of expository paragraphs than these two, I would say that the majority of them fall into one of these two major types. Many expository paragraphs which at first appear to be neither TRI or PS can be interpreted as variations of these patterns. In this sense these two patterns can be called kernel paragraph patterns. Furthermore, narrative, descriptive, and argumentative paragraphs occur in expository works and sometimes combine with expository paragraphs to produce mixed patterns. There are also minor paragraph forms (usually transitional paragraphs or simple lists)—and, finally, there are "bad" paragraphs, like poorly constructed, confusing sentences.

The variations of these two patterns (TRI and PS) can be seen as the results of four kinds of operations: deletion, reordering, addition, and combination. Slots may be deleted, especially the R slot—though this slot appears to be deleted more often in poor student paragraphs than in high quality expository writing. Frequently, especially at the beginnings and endings of essays, the pattern is recorded by inversion, e.g. TRI $\rightarrow$ IRT. Inversion gives the paragraph a completeness or closure that is lacking in the more open-ended TRI order. Students, asked to evaluate paragraphs *out of context*, prefer IRT paragraphs almost exclusively when the choice is between TRI and IRT. Another way of making a TRI paragraph less open-ended is by addition—for example, repeating the T slot at the end (e.g. T$_1$RI $\rightarrow$ T$_1$RIT$_1$ in which the fillers of the two T slots are semantically equivalent). This exanded form of the TRI pattern seems to occur most frequently when the discourse is complex or long and the reader is not likely to retain the controlling idea of the paragraph. And, finally, two paragraphs may be combined, especially when they are either contrastive or parallel semantically. The paragraph by Gibney above contains an illustration of paragraph combination.

So far in this article the procedures for partitioning paragraphs have been pretty much intuitive; that is, I have not talked about formal markers of paragraph structure. I have generalized about the patterns my students and I find, and I have sketched out the basis for a taxonomy of expository paragraph patterns. Now I would like to describe the formal markers of paragraph tagmemes.

The formal signals of the internal tagmemic structure of paragraphs are both rather indeterminant and redundant. For instance, there are almost no markers of paragraph slots similar to the relatively simple plural or tense markers in English grammar. The markers of paragraph tagmemes are complex—usually redundant combinations of graphic, lexical, grammatical, and phonological signals.

The simplest of these is the graphic marker, indentation, which, like other punctuation marks, is related to all three linguistic hierarchies (i.e. lexical, grammatical, and phonological). Indentation sets off a unit which has a certain kind of internal structure allowable by the rules of the language, just as an independent clause is punctuated by a period or a period substitute. At the paragraph level, however, the grammatical constraints are much looser than, say, at the phrase level. This greater grammatical freedom allows the writer to create interesting tensions in paragraphing by skewing the lexical, grammatical, and graphic markers of the paragraph—similar to enjambment in poetry where the poet uses the end of a line (a graphic marker) as a device to achieve emphasis in counterpoint with regular grammatical and lexical emphasis.

The lexical markers of paragraphs are of two sorts, equivalence classes[5] and lexical transitions. In the Strachey paragraph above, the lexical *head* of the paragraph is the term *English Constitution*, which designates an equivalence class that occurs throughout the paragraph (*English Constitution, indescribable entity, It, it, . . . , English Constitution*). The domain of this equivalence class is the entire paragraph. Other lexical equivalence classes in the paragraph are dependent on this head class, and their domains extend over only parts of the paragraph. For instance, the domain of the class which includes the human forces which shaped the constitution (*wise men of 1688, George I, . . . , The Consort*) covers only the I slot and is a lexical marker of the I slot—that is, a feature of the structure of the paragraph which allows readers to partition it in predictable ways. A further study of the lexical equivalence classes in the paragraph reveals that the domains of these classes clearly distinguish the three slots (TRI) of the paragraph.

Lexical transitions are words and phrases which mark the semantic concord of the paragraph, words like *but* and *then* in slot I of the Strachey paragraph. Certain of these words are closely associated with particular slots: slot I is often marked by *for example*, slot R by *in other words*, etc. Lexical transitions may also signal continuation of a slot, e.g. such words as *furthermore, likewise,* or (as in the Strachey paragraph) *then*.

Although the paragraph seems most clearly marked as a lexical unit, chiefly by the equivalence classes, paragraph tagmemes are also marked by numerous grammatical constraints with domains beyond the sentence. There are clear, though not yet adequately defined, relationships between the domains of the lexical equivalence classes and the grammar of the sentences in the paragraph. Though these relationships are many and complex, a few of the more interesting and subtle relationships can be mentioned here. I will concentrate on grammatical parallelism and the sequence of verbs.

A sequence of lexical units in an equivalence class, including substitutes like pronouns and demonstratives, establishes what might be called lexical parallelism. These lexical units have certain grammatical roles (e.g. subject, object, agent, locative, etc.) in the sentences of a paragraph, and, to a great extent, these grammatical roles are maintained throughout the paragraph. Consequently, major changes in the grammatical roles of equivalence classes, especially the head classes, signal either new slots or new paragraphs. In the Strachey paragraph, for instance, the head class (the *English Constitution* class) fills the subject slot in the first two sentences, which are grammatically and lexically parallel. Then, in the I slot, this lexical class shifts to the object slot (*The wise men of 1688 moulded it. . . .*) and remains there in the following sentence (*The wisdom of Lord Grey saved it. . . .*), while a new lexical class (human agents of change) fills the subject slot in these sentences. This shift is another marker of the I slot in the paragraph, and it illustrates the clear relationship of grammatical patterns in a sequence. One particular pattern which seems to have as its chief function the continuance of lexical and grammatical parallelism (though it does not appear in the illustrations I have given) is the passive transformation; the passive allows the writer to retain grammatical focus on a particular lexical class in a discourse.

Verb sequences are also important markers of paragraph structure. A shift in verb form frequently marks a slot in a paragraph. Expanded verb forms (e.g. the "progressive" and "perfect" forms) seem especially important in marking major shifts in focus in a discourse, particularly in paragraphs, and shifts in tense likewise usually mark new paragraph slots. The I slot in the Strachey paragraph is marked by a shift to past tense, and the changes in verb form in the Gibney paragraph also correspond to the slot structure. These constraints on verb form, however, need to be specified more precisely; we appear to have but scratched the surface of a very subtle area of inquiry, the sequence of verb forms in English.

Finally, there are the phonological markers of paragraph structure. Paragraph tagmemes seem to be marked by shifts in pitch register, tempo, and volume when paragraphs are read aloud.[6] While these signals can be perceived by a trained phonetician, they have not been adequately described in the laboratory, and their written counterparts have not been identified.

This paper rests on the evidence that readers can partition paragraphs in a consistent and predictable way, that there are shared conventions of grouping sentences into higher-level units, and that there are structural cues which signal these patterns beyond the sentence. In outlining the tagmemic approach to paragraph analysis, however, I have made at least two major omissions. I have not, first of all, acknowledged our debts to traditional rhetoric, though the reader has undoubtedly recognized them. The similarities are many; it would be surprising if one were to find something entirely new in a field as old and as diligently studied as rhetoric. What is new, I think, is the attempt to relate rhetorical and grammatical patterns and to use a few general concepts to describe language patterns from phonemes to paragraphs and, hopefully, beyond paragraphs.

The second major omission is that I have not discussed rhetorical field structure—the network of semantic categories that, for instance, allows us to add to Strachey's paragraph: we carry his illustrations into the twentieth century without any difficulty, continuing to specify the alternating forces of wisdom and chance that have shaped the historical development of the English Constitution. It is through field analysis that we begin to understand the organic nature of the paragraph, its ability, like a poem's, to shape itself once its dimensions have been specified.[7]

Notes

[1] This work is the result of my collaboration with Kenneth L. Pike and Richard Young in research on rhetoric, sponsored in part by the Center for Research on Language and Language Behavior, University of Michigan, under a grant from the Language Development Branch, U.S. Office of Education. Tagmemic theory is developed in Kenneth L. Pike, *Language in Relation to a Unified Theory of the Structure of Human Behavior* (Glendale: Summer Institute of Linguistics, Part I, 1954; Part II, 1955, Part III, 1960). See also Robert E. Longacre, *Grammar Discovery Procedure: A Field Manual* (The Hague: Mouton and Co., 1964); for a brief description using English examples, Robert E. Longacre, "String Constituent Analysis," *Language*, 36 (1960), pp. 63-68.

[2] This three-part definition of the paragraph reflects the assumption in tagmemic theory that three perspectives are necessary to a complete description of behavior: a *particle* perspective, which views behavior as made up of discrete contrasting parts; a *wave* perspective, which emphasizes the unsegmentable continuum of behavior; and a *field* view, in which units are seen in context (sequence, class, or ordered set). This article focuses on paragraph tagmemes as particles in sequence. For a fuller explanation of tagmemic trimodalism, see Kenneth L. Pike, "Language as Particle, Wave, and Field," *The Texas Quarterly*, 2 (Summer 1959), pp. 37-54; and Pike, "Beyond the Sentence," *CCC*, 15 (October 1964), pp. 129-135.

[3] Kenneth Burke, *Counter-Statement* (Chicago: University of Chicago Press, 1957), pp. 45-46.

[4] Francis Christensen, "A Generative Rhetoric of the Paragraph," *CCC*, 16 (October 1965), pp. 114-156. See also Christensen, "A Generative Rhetoric of the Sentence," *CCC*, 14 (October 1963), pp. 155-161.

[5] The theory of equivalence classes or equivalence chains is from Zellig S. Harris, *Discourse Analysis Reprints* (The Hague: Mouton and Co., 1963), pp. 7-10. Tagmemic discourse analysis is developed in Kenneth L. Pike, "Discourse Analysis and Tagmeme Matrices," *Oceanic Linguistics*, 3 (Summer 1964), pp. 5-25.

[6] These phonological signals are discussed in Kenneth L. Pike, *Language*, Part I (Glendale: Summer Institute of Linguistics, 1954), pp. 66-72.

[7] Field theory is described broadly in Edward R. Fagan, *Field: A Process for Teaching Literature* (University Park, Penn.: The Penn. State University Press, 1965), and it is applied to problems of rhetoric in Kenneth L. Pike, "Beyond the Sentence," *CCC*, 15 (October 1964), pp. 129-135.

Something Old, Something New:
Functional Sentence Perspective

WILLIAM J. VANDE KOPPLE

Functional Sentence Perspective (FSP) is a theory that predicts how units of information should be distributed in a sentence and how sentences of information should be related in a discourse.[1] The theory originated in Europe in the work of Weil (1878). In this century his work inspired Mathesius, who with several other linguists, many of whom are associated with the Prague linguistic circle, further developed the principles of FSP, primarily by analyzing the interworking syntax with semantics in German, Russian, and Czech. In America, linguists such as Chomsky (1965), Fillmore (1970), Chafe (1970), and Lakoff (1971) have tried to account for FSP distinctions and constraints in various components of an adequate grammar. Others, including Gundell (1974), Keenan and Schieffelin (1976), and Kuno (1978) have used the theory to explain such linguistic phenomena as gapping, forward and backward pronominalization, and left and right dislocation sentence patterns. And several rhetoricians, such as Strunk and White (1962), Tichy (1966), McCrimmon (1967), Macrorie (1968), Elsbree and Bracher (1972), and Williams (1970) have written about principles for cohesion and emphasis that are consistent with FSP.

In brief, for Functional Sentence Perspectivists a sentence conveys its message most effectively if its two major parts, the topic and comment, perform specific semantic and communicative tasks. In English, the topic usually includes the grammatical subject and its adjuncts. The comment usually includes the verb and objects or carries primary sentence stress.

For each part theorists posit slightly different but often corresponding communicative functions. They claim that the topic should express either the theme of the sentence, the elements with the least communicative dynamism (a measure of how much an element contributes to the development of a communication), the least important information, or the old information. They assert that the comment should express either information about the theme, the elements with the most communicative dynamism, the most important information, or the new information.

However, most assign the topic the role of expressing the old information in a sentence, that which is either stated in, recoverable from, or relatively more accessible in the prior context. And most assign the comment the role of expressing the new information, that which is not expressed in, is difficult to derive from, or is relatively less accessible in the prior context.

Research in the Teaching of English, 17 (February 1983) pp. 85-99. Copyright
© 1983 by the National Council of Teachers of English. Reprinted by permission
of the publisher and the author.

Although these specific functions sometimes correspond to the others that are posited for the topic and comment, they do not correspond in every case. This does not mean that the other functions are insignificant. It does mean that many scholars believe that the distinction between old and new information is the principal one underlying the topic/comment articulation (see Chafe, 1970) and that a more objective decision can probably be made about what is old and new information than about what information the other communicative functions would subsume.

My primary question in research was whether an English discourse that is consistent with FSP as detailed above has cognitive advantages over one with the same content but that is contradictory to FSP. Weil has claimed that the movement from topic to comment "reveals the movement of the mind itself" (cited by Firbas, 1974, p. 12). If this is true, a discourse consistent with FSP should be more readable and memorable than one contradictory to FSP. But we have all probably encountered writers who consistently place new information early in their sentences. Is this style due to carelessness or impatience to express new information? Or could this order actually be easier for us to process?

Clearly, we need to test FSP. But what should the tests be like?

First, they should use connected discourses as materials. After all, almost every time we encounter writing, we process connected discourse, not nonsense syllables, individual words, isolated sentences, or pairs of sentences. And in order to decide what is old and new information in a sentence, we must know what information precedes the sentence in discourse.

Second, the discourses should be entirely natural. No one should question whether they could occur in normal language situations. They should be clear, natural, even "well-written."

Third, the discourse should vary only along the old-new dimension. The sentences of one discourse should express the old and new information in accord with FSP; sentences in the variant should reverse the positions of old and new information.

Although some semanticists might disagree, I believe that such discourses have the same truth values; thus truth value should not be a relevant variable. For some evidence, I refer to Sachs's finding that "two sentences can have different forms but express the same meaning" (1967, p. 438). And it is probable that even if there were slight differences in truth values, very few people reading normally would notice them.

These comments do not apply to discourses composed of different orderings of the same simple statements or sentences. For even if we vary the order of sentences in a passage carefully, we probably affect the logical connections within the passage as well as its overall semantic structure. However, researchers might claim that some of these differences are not cognitively significant. Yet discourse consisting of sentences that can be moved around freely must at least verge on the unnatural or rare.

Is such research reported in the scholarly journals? The studies that come closest to meeting our needs are de Beaugrande's (1979), Clements'

(1979), and Rothkopf's (1962). Yet these fail to provide the specific help we need for one or more reasons.

De Beaugrande's passages were composed of different orders of the same sentences. And he varied the position of sentences and paragraphs, not just bits of information within sentences, without an explicit principle. Clements also composed passages by varying the order of the same sentences without a detailed principle. Furthermore, he assumed that the FSP principle for distributing information in a sentence is justified in itself and applies to the distribution of information in an entire discourse. Finally, Rothkopf's passages also were composed of the same sentences in different orders, his experimental sentences "are probably not a representative sample of the population of instructional sentences" (p. 673), and he did not vary the location of the same bit of information according to FSP.

Therefore, the applicability of FSP to continuous natural discourse remains unproved. To begin testing it, I performed three readability and three retention experiments on paragraphs that I wrote by following or contradicting the FSP principles that Daneš presents (1974, p. 118). In general, each sentence of a rule-governed form expresses old information in its topic and new information in its comment. In each sentence of a variant, the positions of old and new bits of information are reversed.

More specifically, the rule-governed forms are topically linked. Their topics are identical or closely related through pronoun substitution, synonym substitution, specification, additional characterization, slight qualification, or enumeration of set members. For an example, consider paragraph 1 (with main topics italicized):

Currently *the Marathon* is the best waxless ski for recreational cross-country skiing. Its weight is a mere two pounds. Yet *its two-inch width* allows the skier to break a trail through even the heaviest snow. *Its most unique characteristic* is the fishscale design for its bottom. *The Marathon* is almost as effective as most waxable skis. In fact, *it* is even better than some waxable skis when the snow is very wet. *The Marathon* can be used with most conventional bindings. However, *it* works best with the Suomi double-lock. Finally, *the Marathon* is available in six different colors.

In the variation of paragraph 1, most of the topics are only remotely related. Consider paragraph 2 (with main topics italicized):

Currently *the best waxless ski for recreational cross-country skiing* is the Marathon. *A mere two pounds* is its weight. Yet *the skier* can break a trail through even the heaviest snow with its two-inch width. *The fishscale design for its bottom* is its most unique characteristic. *Most waxable skis* are only slightly more effective than the Marathon. In fact, *some waxable skis* are not as good as it when the snow is very wet. *Most conventional bindings* can be used with the Marathon. However, *the Suomi double-lock* works best with it. Finally, *six different colors* are available for the Marathon.

However, paragraph 2 contains exactly as many topics and the same propositional information as paragraph 1. And I examined both of these paragraphs, as well as all experimental paragraphs, to ensure that they were identical or very similar in numbers of words, clauses, sentences, nominalizations, reversible and non-reversible passives, as well as in introductory conjunctions, adverbs, and prepositional phrases. I also established that the corresponding sentences in each paragraph were about the same length and contained many of the same words and full verbs.

After this was established, a colleague who was familiar with FSP underlined the topics in the paragraphs. In all cases her judgments agreed with mine. To ensure that no words or sentences in the paragraphs were markedly awkward, I asked several colleagues to evaluate them. Usually nine read a rule-governed paragraph and nine others read its variant, commenting on any words or sentences that they considered awkward. If one evaluator objected to a word or sentence, I changed it to what he suggested. Therefore, one of a pair of paragraphs should not have had an advantage in experiments because it contained fewer inappropriate words or awkward sentences than the other. Finally, I selected and distributed all subjects at random.

Descriptions of the three readability and three retention experiments follow:

Readability Experiment 1:

Subjective Judgments of Readability with Subjects Alerted Before a Single Reading

Materials used were the topically linked paragraph 3a and its variant, 3b. (3a and 3b are slightly altered versions of paragraphs 1 and 2, printed above. Copies of these and all other experimental paragraphs and materials are available upon request.) Subjects were 72 high-school sophomores and 59 high-school seniors. I told them that they would read two paragraphs identical in subject matter but different in form, that after reading them once they should indicate on the separate answer sheet whether one paragraph was easier to read or whether they could detect no significant difference in readability between them, and finally, that they should try to justify their decision in writing. Then I gave them a copy of 3a and 3b, which I had prepared almost identically. I decided which subjects read one paragraph before the other by flipping a coin and correcting for equal numbers at the end.

Eighty-six of the 131 total subjects chose paragraph 3a, twenty-seven chose paragraph 3b, and eighteen saw no difference between the two. Testing the hypothesis that the probability of subjects favoring 3a is less than one-half by using the normal approximation to the binomial distribution leads to a z for these figures of 3.58, significant at the .0002 level. These and additional data appear in Table 1.

TABLE 1

Subjective Judgments of Readability with
Subjects Alerted Before a Single Reading

	3a	3b	no difference	z	p
total subjects	86	27	18	3.58	.0002
sophomores	50	16	6	3.30	.0005
seniors	36	11	12	1.69	.05

Readability Experiment 2:
Subjective Judgments of Readability with Subjects Alerted After a Single Reading

Again I used paragraphs 3a and 3b. My subjects were 73 different high-school sophomores and 67 different high-school seniors. I proceeded as I did in the first experiment except that I waited until immediately after the students had read the paragraphs once to inform them that they should judge readability. If a significant number of students favored 3a, we would have stronger evidence of its greater readability than that from the first experiment because of the advantages of 3a must have persisted in memory.

Of the 140 total subjects, 87 indicated that 3a was easier to read than 3b, 38 decided that 3b was easier than 3a, and 15 felt that there was no difference between the two. The z for the number preferring 3a is 2.87, significant at the .002 level. These and additional data appear in Table 2.

TABLE 2

Subjective Judgments of Readability with
Subjects Alerted After a Single Reading

	3a	3b	no difference	z	p
total subjects	87	38	15	2.87	.002
sophomores	45	20	8	1.99	.02
seniors	42	18	7	2.08	.02

Readability Experiment 3:
Subjective Judgments of Readability After Many Readings

Materials were the topically linked paragraph 5a and its variant, 5b. I designed this experiment to compensate for the possibility that one reading of paired paragraphs might not have allowed subjects to make the most careful judgments of readability. My subjects were 118 high-school sophomores and 66 high-school seniors, all of whom had also participated in one of the first two experiments. I gave them a sheet on which 5a and 5b appeared. One-half of the subjects saw 5a above 5b; the other half saw 5b on top. I told them to read the paragraphs as often as they wished within eight minutes. After eight minutes, they had to indicate on the bottom of the sheet whether one paragraph was easier to read, or whether they could detect no significant difference in their readability. Also, they were supposed to comment on their decision. They all finished this task easily.

Most students favored 5a over 5b. 121 of the 184 total subjects preferred 5a over 5b, 41 preferred 5b over 5a, and 22 said they perceived no difference between the two. The z for these figures, that is, the normal approximation to the distribution of those who preferred 5a is 4.28, significant at less than the .0001 level. These and other data appear in Table 3.

TABLE 3
Subjective Judgments of Readability After Many Readings

	5a	5b	no difference	z	p
total subjects	121	41	22	4.28	<.0001
sophomores	74	31	13	2.76	.006
seniors	47	10	9	3.45	.0006

Retention Experiment 1:
The Double-distractor Recognition Test

I used the topically linked paragraph 11a and its variant, 11b. My subjects were 74 high-school sophomores. I first gave them all a three-page practice booklet. The first page, the instructions, informed them that on a signal they should flip to the second page and read the practice paragraph printed there carefully but only once. For the practice paragraph, I adapted a paragraph from the *Encyclopaedia Britannica* so that one-half of the sentences could provide a target from their topic and the other half could provide a target from their comment. However, I did not alternate sentences with topic targets with those with comment targets since trying that seemed to make the paragraph awkward. In this way, I tried to avoid predisposing subjects to look for targets in only certain parts of sentences. After the subjects read the paragraph, they were to flip to the third page, on which were randomly ordered numbers, words, and short phrases. Ten of these were in the practice paragraph; twenty were distractors. The subjects were to circle the targets and avoid the distractors.

I allowed them ample time for the practice test. When they were finished, we corrected it together, tabulating scores by subtracting the sum of distractors circled and targets omitted from the number of targets circled. Other scoring methods are possible. For example, one can simply count the number of targets circled. But Klare et al. (1957) demonstrated that the method I used is good to compensate for guessing and to measure what subjects retain.

Immediately after the practice, I gave the students another three-page booklet. All students saw identical first pages (instructions) and third pages (10 targets and 20 distractors in random order). However, 37 of them saw 11a on their second page, while 37 saw 11b. All of them proceeded as they had on the practice sheet.

Each of the 10 targets expressed new information that was contained in a comment in 11a and in a topic in 11b. Two colleagues helped me select the two distractors for each target. I asked them to work individually, looking for items which were likely to be confused with targets because they were associated with them, sounded like them, or meant something similar to them. If both of them suggested the same distractor, I automatically accepted it. When they suggested different ones, I chose the one I thought could more easily be confused with the target. And occasionally I used a distractor which neither had suggested but which occurred to me because of their suggestions.

The 34 subjects who had read the topically linked paragraph 11a performed somewhat better than did the thirty-four who had read 11b. Those who had read 11a had an average score of 7.16 on the recognition task, and those who had read 11b had an average score of 6.54. Using a *t*-test on these data produced a *t* of 1.01, which is significant between the .15 and .2 levels.

Retention Experiment 2:
The Short-answer Test

Materials were the topically linked paragraph 9a and its variant 9b. Seventy-four high-school sophomores participated. I first gave them a three-page practice booklet. The first page informed them that on a signal they should flip to the second page, read the practice paragraph (adapted from the *Encyclopaedia Britannica* so that one-half of the sentences could provide an answer from their topic and one-half could provide an answer from their comment) found there once, and then flip to the third page and provide short answers to the 10 randomly ordered questions printed there. All the answers appeared in the practice paragraph.

I gave them as much time as they needed. When they had answered the questions, we corrected the tests together, subtracting the number of incorrect answers from the number correct. To be scored as correct, answers had to appear exactly as they had in the paragraph.

Then we moved to the actual test. I gave each subject another three-page booklet. All saw identical first pages (instructions) and third pages (randomly ordered questions). However, 37 found 9a on their second page, while 37 found 9b. All proceeded as they had on the practice test.

I wrote the 10 questions myself, avoiding any words found in only one of the two paragraphs. The answers were numbers, words, or short phrases, each of which expressed new information and appeared in a comment in 9a and in a topic in 9b.

Those who had read the topically linked paragraph 9a answered significantly more questions correctly than did those who had read 9b. The former averaged 7.03 correct answers; the latter averaged 5.62 correct responses. A *t*-test applied to these data produced a *t* of 2.8, significant between the .0005 and .005 levels.

Retention Experiment 3:
The Immediate Recall Test

I used the topically linked paragraph 3a and its variant, 3b. Seventy-two high-school sophomores took this test. Again I first gave them a three-page practice booklet. From instructions on the first page they learned that on a signal they were to flip to the second page and read the paragraph (from *Time*) printed there once, and then immediately flip over to the blank third page and write a recall protocol for the paragraph. I gave them as much time as they needed, and then I simply collected the booklets.

Immediately after the practice test, I gave them another three-page booklet. All saw identical first pages (instructions) and blank third pages. But 36 found 3a on their second page, while 36 found 3b. They proceeded exactly as they had in the practice test.

In scoring the protocols, I followed the guidelines of King (1960). That is, in each protocol I counted the number of function words, content words, and three-word sequences. (ABCDE contains the following three-element sequences: ABC, BCD, CDE.) I accepted misspelled words only if they were unambiguous.

Students who had read 3b recalled an average of 4.66 function words, while those who had read 3a recalled an average of only 4.57 function words. However, those who had read the topically linked 3a excelled in the other two categories. They recalled an average of 22.72 content words, and those who had read 3b recalled an average of 19.81 content words. Also, readers of 3a recalled an average of 11.19 three-word sequences, as contrasted to the average of 8.28 recalled by the readers of 3b. These data as well as the results of the *t*-test are in Table 4.

TABLE 4

The Immediate Recall Test

	mean function words	t/p	mean content words	t/p	mean 3-word sequences	t/p
paragraph 3a	4.566		22.722	1.399/ .1<p<.15	11.194	1.918/ .025<p<.05
paragraph 3b	4.661	insignificant	19.806		8.278	

We will have to wait for additional tests using both older and younger subjects on these and other paragraph forms before we can come to a definite conclusion about the validity of FSP, but, taken together, these six experiments provide strong evidence for the theory.

A very probable explanation why linked forms were superior to their variants is that they probably facilitated Haviland and Clark's (1974) proposed given-new strategy of comprehension. According to Haviland and Clark, when we read a sentence, we first divide it into its given (what we already know) and new information. We view the given as a pointer to a matching antecedent in memory and search for it. If we cannot find an antecedent, we either construct one with an inferential bridge, view all the information as new and begin a new and separate memory structure, or try to reanalyze what is given and new in the sentence. Thus a sentence will be easy to comprehend if the given information is clearly marked and obviously matches an antecedent in memory. A sentence will be difficult if the given information is not clearly marked, does not match an antecedent in memory, or demands an inference for identification.

Now consider how subjects probably process a topically linked form. Since they see the paragraph in no special context, they should view all information in the first sentence as new. When they reach the second sentence, however, they probably try to relate it to information in the first. That should be easy since the given information is either identical or closely related to information in the first and since the given appears early in the sentence. While reading only the beginning of the second sentence, therefore, subjects can already know what antecedent to look for and can feel confident that the rest of the sentence probably expresses new information. Moreover, since the bits of given information are identical or related and are expressed in topics throughout the paragraph, subjects can reinforce the old information in memory. And after a number of sentences, perhaps they can even predict that the next sentence will have the identical old information in its topic. This would help them since it would decrease time they need to process the old and increase the amount of attention they can give to the new.

Contrasting how subjects probably process a variant provides a good explanation why such forms did not test out as well. Again, subjects probably regard all information in the first sentence as new. When they begin to read the second sentence, they immediately encounter more new information. They then must decide whether to begin a new memory structure or to continue into the sentence before deciding that it expresses no given information. They decide to continue reading, which leads them to given information. They then can search for the antecedent in the first. But before adding the new information to it, they might have to re-scan the first part of the second sentence to refresh their memory about what was new. They probably repeat this process in the subsequent sentences, although after a certain number of sentences they might begin expecting the given to be expressed in the comment. Such mental hesitations and shifts in direction must take time and probably prevent subjects from reinforcing the old and new information in memory to the extent possible in a linked paragraph. Therefore, I hypothesize that the topically linked forms were more readable and memorable in experiments than their variants because they facilitated the given-new strategy of comprehension while the variants frustrated this strategy to some degree.

The best empirical evidence that subjects actually added new information to an anchor of old information emerged from the protocols in the immediate recall test on paragraph 3b. Many of the 36 subjects who read and recalled 3b actually rearranged the information in its sentences, writing protocols that resembled the topically linked 3a. That is, they often took the identical old information expressed in the comments of 3b and topicalized it. Doing this gave them a common reference point near the beginning of each sentence. For example, one student's protocol for 3b, printed with its mechanical errors, reads as follows:

Currently the best wax-less ski is the Marathon. It is only four pounds in weight. Yet, it can go thru heavy snow with its mere 3 inch width. It is good for both kick and glide. The Marathon can be used in wet snow where other waxed skis aren't as good. It can take any kind of binding but the Adidas binding is the best. Last of all, the Marathon comes in 4 colors.

To determine the extent of this tendency, I first counted how many grammatical sentences after the opener were in the 36 protocols. I omitted the first since it usually appeared exactly as in 3b. Then I counted the number of these which expressed the old information not in their comment but in their topic. Sixty of the 101 grammatical sentences did. Twenty-five of the 36 subjects switched the old and new information around in at least one sentence. Thus the tendency in protocols to topicalize identical or related old information was strong indeed. It shows that subjects were very dependent on identical reference points when storing information from 3b.

As I noted earlier, I believe that experimental evidence for FSP has important implications for discourse analysts. That the experiments justified FSP for English might surprise some of them. Some have assumed that the rigid control that syntax exercises over word order in English severely restricts the operation of FSP principles. Indeed, Mathesius characterizes English as "so little susceptible to the requirements of FSP as to frequently disregard them altogether" (cited in Firbas, 1974, p. 17). It would follow from this claim that English writers and speakers are not very sensitive to or significantly affected by the position of old and new information in sentences. However, the tests reported here provide evidence that when syntax allows us to express old information in the topic and new information in the comment, we definitely should. Accordingly, discourse analysts should try to discover how we can systematically relate the morpho-phonological and syntactic structures of English to topic and comment (see van Dijk, 1977, p. 115).

Evidence for FSP also has important implications for teachers of writing. We should teach both the principles of FSP and the ways in which our students can reconcile them with English syntax. Doing this would be beneficial in several ways.

First, we would be teaching principles that are founded in experiments, with implications about how we process and store information. Some of the principles we inculcate now are not justified by empirical evidence.

Second, once our students learn and work with the principles of FSP, their discourses should become more readable and memorable.

Third, our students should develop a more thoughtful approach to their writing processes. Many of them seem to record and leave information as they think of it. And many, perhaps because of impatience, customarily express bits of new information in sentence topics. If they knew the principles of FSP, they could learn to identify old and new bits of information and position them according to the theory.

Fourth, their discourses should also become more cohesive. After all, students trained in the principles of FSP should become highly skilled at identifying and relating appropriate bits of old and new information in discourses. And this skill should be helpful in recognizing, interpreting, and using many of the devices of cohesion that researchers such as Williams (1970), Fowler (1977), van Dijk (1972, 1977), and perhaps most notably, Halliday (1968, 1970) and Halliday and Hasan (1976) have investigated and described recently. If we examine Halliday's (1977) most recent summary of his and Hasan's work on cohesion, we shall see that many of the devices of cohesion he describes are based on connections between bits of old information in the sentences of discourse. Many of the devices are anaphoric; they depend on our recognizing that older, more derivable information is being referred to, substituted for, or repeated.

For example, consider the elements that Halliday says function by reference. These elements include the personals (*she*), the demonstratives (*this*), and the comparatives (*earlier*). All of these are "interpretable only by reference to something other than themselves" (1977, p. 188). The "something other" is frequently information that is expressed earlier in the text. And Halliday notes that when we connect personals, demonstratives, and comparatives to older information, cohesion is established between the two points in a text (1977, p. 189).

Similar comments apply to the linguistic devices Halliday says function by substitution. These "function as alternatives to the repetition of a particular item and hence cohere with the passage in which the item occurs" (1977, p. 189). For example, in the text "Last week I called on my neighbor. Having done so, I feel quite cheerful," *Having done so* substitutes for the first sentence. We must relate *Having done so* to the older information in order for the text to cohere and make sense.

Finally, another way that we can create cohesion in a text is by reiteration or collocation. Halliday calls this lexical cohesion. For example, in texts we often repeat the same word, substitute a synonym for a word, or replace a word with one that is closely associated with it or has a more general meaning than it. In doing so, we again link elements to older information.

Students who have worked with the principles of FSP should be especially adept at recognizing and interpreting such cohesive devices. Perhaps they will become more sensitive to the possibilities for cohesion in their own discourses and more apt to use cohesive devices. And they should also be able to add insights to the work on cohesion. For on the basis of the empirical evidence we have, they would know that in order to facilitate processing of texts, they should express elements that are linked to older information in sentence topics whenever possible and whenever there is no good reason not to. If students had an anaphoric element in each sentence and expressed each element in a sentence topic, their discourses would be quite similar to the topically linked paragaphs I used in experiments. I believe we can consider such forms cohesive not only because they contain many devices of cohesion but also because they relate information in accord with F SP, thereby probably facilitating processing.

Are there other forms of discourse which we might consider cohesive on these same grounds? Daneš (1974) shows that there are at least two others, both of which we should examine with our students when we work on cohesion. In one, which we can for convenience call rhetorically linked, the topic of each sentence except the first repeats or is closely related to information in the comment of the preceding sentence. In other words, the information in the comment of each sentence carries over to the topic of the next sentence. This pattern produces a chain of old and new information throughout the discourse. One of Daneš's short examples of this form is the following: "The first of the antibiotics was discovered by Sir Alexander Fleming in 1928. He was busy at the time investigating a certain species of germ which is responsible for boils and other troubles" (p. 118).

In the other form, the topic of the first sentence introduces a general subject or hypertheme, and the topics of subsequent sentences express sub-themes that are derivable from the hypertheme. Often, given the hyper-theme, the subthemes are predictable. Daneš says that this form of discourse has derived topics. His English example is as follows:

New Jersey is flat along the coast and southern portion; the north-western region is mountainous. The coastal climate is mild, but there is considerable cold in the mountain areas during the winter months. Summers are fairly hot. The leading industrial production includes chemicals, processed foods, coal, petroleum, metals and electrical equipment. The most important cities are Newark, Jersey City, Pater-son, Trenton, Camden. Vacation districts include Asbury Park, Lake-wood, Cape May, and others. (p. 120)

Daneš notes that the choice and sequence of the derived topics will be con-trolled primarily by various extralinguistic constraints.

Of course, we must stress with our students that it is rare to find a discourse that conforms perfectly to any of these patterns. Daneš himself points out that some discourses are made up of combinations of these patterns, and that others omit parts of the sequence or disrupt the sequence by insertions. And obviously there are many discourses with structures that we have not been able to describe adequately yet. But helping our composi-tion student identify such patterns in discourse should both reinforce the principles of F SP and alert them to possibilities for cohesion in texts, cohe-sion dependent on what seems to be proper information flow.

In addition to the benefits discussed above, teaching composition stu-dents the principles of F SP and exploring their relationships to other aspects of texts might lead to some significant insights about discourse and the writ-ing process in the future. It is possible, for example, that if we examine the progression of topics in a text, we might be able to develop an explicit method to determine what topic of discourse (see van Dijk, 1977) is entailed by the sentence topics. It is also possible that if we examine how the comments of a discourse relate to each other, we might be able to formulate a method to describe how certain kinds of discourses are generated. And we might even be able to relate paragraphing practices in English to amounts of and relationships between new information.

I conclude by noting that several important questions related to FSP remain to be answered. For example, in how many different ways can new information relate to old? How can we determine what the topic and comment of initial sentences in discourse are? To answer that, how much will we have to know about the situation in which a discourse occurs? Does such a posited function as transition have cognitive reality? Do complex sentences have a topic-comment structure that we can describe? Do certain kinds of writing differ in the amounts of new information they contain? When do we develop the ability to relate new information to old, or when does this ability show itself? Finally, do people of similar educational and cultural backgrounds develop similar cognitive hierarchies, schemata, or sets of old and new information?

Notes

[1] The author wishes to thank Janel Mueller and Joseph M. Williams for advice.

References

Chafe, Wallace. *Meaning and the Structure of Language.* Chicago: The University of Chicago Press, 1970.

Chomsky, Noam. *Aspects of the Theory of Syntax.* Cambridge, MA: MIT Press, 1965.

Clements, Paul. "The Effects of Staging on Recall from Prose." In Roy O. Freedle (Ed.), *Advances in Discourse Processes.* Vol. II. Norwood: Ablex, 1979, pp. 287-330.

Daneš, František. "Functional Sentence Perspective and the Organization of the Text." In Daneš (Ed.), *Papers on Functional Sentence Perspective.* The Hague: Mouton, 1974, pp. 106-128.

De Beaugrande, Robert. "Psychology and Composition." *College Composition and Communication,* 1979, *30,* 50-57.

Elsbree, Langdon, & Bracher, F. *Heath's College Handbook of Composition.* Eighth ed. Lexington, MA: D.C. Heath, 1972.

Fillmore, Charles J. "Types of Lexical Information." In Kiefer (Ed.), *Studies in Syntax and Semantics.* Dordrecht: D. Reidel, 1970. Pp. 109-137.

Firbas, Jan. "Some Aspects of the Czechoslovak Approach to Problems of Functional Sentence Perspective." In Daneš (Ed.), *Papers on Functional Sentence Perspective.* The Hague: Mouton, 1974. Pp. 11-37.

Fowler, Roger. "Cohesive, Progressive, and Localizing Aspects of Text Structures." In van Dijk and Petöfi (Eds.), *Grammars and Descriptions.* New York: Walter de Gruyter, 1977. Pp. 64-84.

Gundell, J. *The Role of Topic and Comment in Linguistic Theory.* Doctoral dissertation, University of Texas, 1974.

Halliday, M. A. K. "Notes on Transitivity and Theme in English, Part 2." *Journal of Linguistics,* 1968, *3,* 199-244.

Halliday, M. A. K. "Language Structure and Language Function." In Lyons (Ed.), *New Horizons in Linguistics.* Harmondsworth: Penguin Books, 1970. Pp. 140-165.

Halliday, M. A. K. "Text as Semantic Choice in Social Contexts." In van Dijk and Petöfi (Eds.), *Grammars and Descriptions.* New York: Walter de Gruyter, 1977. Pp. 176-225.

Halliday, M. A. K., & Hasan, R. *Cohesion in English.* London: Longman, 1976.

Haviland, Susan E. & Clark, H. H. "What's New? Acquiring New Information as a Process in Comprehension." *Journal of Verbal Learning and Verbal Behavior,* 1974, *13*, 512-521.

Keenan, E. O., & Schieffelin, B. B. *Foregrounding Referents: A Reconsideration of Left Dislocation in Discourse.* Mimeographed paper, 1976.

King, David J. "On the Accuracy of Written Recall: A Scaling and Factor Analytic Study." *The Psychological Record,* 1960, *10*, 113-122.

Klare, George R., *et al.* "The Relationship of Style Difficulty, Practice, and Ability to Efficiency of Reading and to Retention." *Journal of Applied Psychology,* 1957, *41*, 222-226.

Kuno, Susumu. "Generative Discourse Analysis in America." In Wolfgang U. Dressler (Ed.), *Current Trends in Textlinguistics.* New York: Walter de Gruyter, 1978. Pp. 275-294.

Lakoff, George. "On Generative Semantics." In Steinberg and Jakobovits (Eds.), *Semantics. An Interdisciplinary Reader in Philosophy, Linguistics and Psychology.* Cambridge: Cambridge University Press, 1971. Pp. 232-296.

Macrorie, Ken. *Writing to Be Read.* New York: Hayden Book Co., 1968.

McCrimmon, James M. *Writing with a Purpose* (Fourth ed.). Boston: Houghton Mifflin, 1967.

Rothkopf, Ernst Z. "Learning from Written Sentences: Effects of Order of Presentation on Retention." *Psychological Reports,* 1962, *10*, 667-674.

Sachs, Jacqueline S. "Recognition Memory for Syntactic and Semantic Aspects of Connected Discourse." *Perception and Psychophysics,* 1967, *2*, 437-442.

Strunk, William Jr., & White, E. B. *The Elements of Style.* New York: Macmillan, 1962.

Tichy, Henrietta J. *Effective Writing for Engineers, Managers, Scientists.* New York: Wiley & Sons, 1966.

Van Dijk, T. A. *Some Aspects of Text Grammars.* The Hague: Mouton, 1972.

Van Dijk, T. A. *Text and Context Explorations in the Semantics and Pragmatics of Discourse.* London: Longman, 1977.

Weil, Henri. *The Order of Words in the Ancient Languages Compared with That of the Modern Languages.* Trans. C. W. Super. Boston, 1878.

Williams, Joseph M. *The New English.* New York: The Free Press, 1970.

Coherence, Cohesion, and Writing Quality

STEPHEN P. WITTE and LESTER FAIGLEY

A question of continuing interest to researchers in writing is what internal characteristics distinguish essays ranked high and low in overall quality. Empirical research at the college level has for the most part taken two approaches to this question, examining errors[1] and syntactic features[2] while generally ignoring the features of texts that extend across sentence boundaries.[3] Neither the error approach nor the syntactic approach has been entirely satisfactory. For example, Elaine Maimon and Barbara Nodine's sentence-combining experiment suggests that, as is true when other skills and processes are learned, certain kinds of errors accompany certain stages in learning to write.[4] Because the sources of error in written discourse are often complex and difficult to trace, researchers can conclude little more than what is obvious: low-rated papers usually contain far more errors than high-rated papers. With regard to syntax, Ann Gebhard found that with few exceptions the syntactic features of high- and low-rated essays written by college students are not clearly differentiated. Indeed, research in writing quality based on conventions of written English and on theories of syntax, particularly transformational grammar, has not provided specific directions for the teaching of writing.

Such results come as no surprise in light of much current research in written discourse. This research—published in such fields as linguistics, cybernetics, anthropology, psychology, and artificial intelligence—addresses questions concerned with extended discourse rather than with individual sentences, questions about how humans produce and understand discourse units often referred to as *texts*.[5] One such effort that has attracted the attention of researchers in writing is M. A. K. Halliday and Ruqaiya Hasan's *Cohesion in English*.[6] Although Halliday and Hasan do not propose a theory of text structure or examine how humans produce texts, they do attempt to define the concept of *text*. To them a text is a semantic unit, the parts of which are linked together by explicit cohesive ties. Cohesion, therefore, defines a text as text. A *cohesive tie* "is a semantic relation between an element in a text and some other element that is crucial to the interpretation of it"

College Composition and Communication, 32 (May 1981), pp. 189-204. Copyright © 1981 by the National Council of Teachers of English. Reprinted by permission of the publisher and the author.

(p. 8). The two semantically connected elements can lie within the text or one element can lie ouside the text. Halliday and Hasan call within-text cohesive ties *endophoric* and references to items outside the text *exophoric.* An example of an exophoric reference is the editorial "we" in a newspaper. Such references are exophoric because no antecedent is recoverable within the text. Exophoric references often help link a text to its situational context; but, as far as Halliday and Hasan are concerned, exophoric references do not contribute to the cohesion of a text. For Halliday and Hasan, cohesion depends upon lexical and grammatical relationships that allow sentence sequences to be understood as connected discourse rather than as autonomous sentences. Even though within-sentence cohesive ties do occur, the cohesive ties across "sentence boundaries" are those which allow sequences of sentences to be understood as a text.

Halliday and Hasan's concept of textuality, defined with reference to relationships that obtain across "sentence boundaries," suggests a number of possibilities for extending composition research beyond its frequent moorings in sentence-level operations and features. The major purpose of the present study is to apply two taxonomies of cohesive ties developed by Halliday and Hasan to an analysis of essays of college freshmen rated high and low in quality. Because *Cohesion in English* is a pioneering effort to describe relationships between and among sentences in text, we anticipate that cohesion will be studied in future research addressing the linguistic features of written texts. We are particularly interested in identifying what purposes Halliday and Hasan's taxonomies can serve in composition research and what purposes they cannot serve.

Halliday and Hasan's System for Analyzing and Classifying Cohesive Ties

Cohesion in English specifies five major classes of cohesive ties, nineteen subclasses, and numerous sub-subclasses. In the analysis of cohesion which follows, we will be concerned with only the five major classes—*reference, substitution, ellipsis, conjunction,* and *lexical reiteration and collocation*—and their respective subclasses. Two of the major classes—*substitution* and *ellipsis*—are more frequent in conversation than in written discourse. *Substitution* replaces one element with another which is not a personal pronoun, and *ellipsis* involves a deletion of a word, phrase, or clause. The effect of both substitution and ellipsis is to extend the textual or semantic domain of one sentence to a subsequent sentence. The word *one* in sentence 2 illustrates cohesion based on substitution and the word *do* in sentence 4 illustrates cohesion based on ellipsis.

   Substitution
1. Did you ever find a lawnmower?
2. Yes, I borrowed *one* from my neighbor.
   Ellipsis
3. Do you want to go with me to the store?
4. Yes, I *do*.

The remaining three categories include the bulk of explicit cohesive ties in written English. The categories of *reference* and *conjunction* contain ties that are both grammatical and lexical. *Lexical reiteration and collocation* is restricted to ties which are presumably only lexical.

 Reference cohesion occurs when one item in a text points to another element for its interpretation. Reference ties are of three types: *pronominals, demonstratives and definite articles,* and *comparatives.* Each of the sentence pairs below illustrates a different type of reference cohesion.

 Reference Cohesion (Pronominal)
 5. At home, my father is himself.
 6. He relaxes and acts in *his* normal manner.
 Reference Cohesion (Demonstratives)
 7. We question why they tell us to do things.
 8. *This* is part of growing up.
 Reference Cohesion (Definite Article)
 9. Humans have many needs, both physical and intangible.
 10. It is easy to see *the* physical needs such as food and shelter.
 Reference Cohesion (Comparatives)
 11. The older generation is often quick to condemn college students for being carefree and irresponsible.
 12. But those who remember their own youth do so *less* quickly.

The interpretation of the italicized elements in sentences 6, 8, 10, and 12 depends in each case upon presupposed information contained in the sentences immediately above it.

 A fourth major class of cohesive ties frequent in writing is *conjunction.* Conjunctive elements are not in themselves cohesive, but they do "express certain meanings which presuppose the presence of other components in the discourse" (p. 226). Halliday and Hasan distinguish five types of conjunctive cohesion—*additive, adversative, causal, temporal,* and *continuative.* Examples of these subclasses of conjunctive cohesion appear below and illustrate how conjunctive cohesion extends the meaning of one sentence to a subsequent one.

 Conjunctive Cohesion (Additive)
 13. No one wants to be rejected.
 14. *And* to prevent rejection we change our behavior often.
 Conjunctive Cohesion (Adversative)
 15. Small children usually change their behavior because they want something they don't have.
 16. Carol, *however,* changed her behavior because she wanted to become part of a new group.
 Conjunctive Cohesion (Causal)
 17. Today's society sets the standards.
 18. The people more or less follow it [sic].
 19. *Consequently,* there exists the right behavior for the specific situation at hand.

Conjunctive Cohesion (Temporal)

20. A friend of mine went to an out-of-state college.
21. *Before* she left, she expressed her feelings about playing roles to win new friends.

Conjunctive Cohesion (Continuative)

22. Different social situations call for different behaviors.
23. This is something we all learn as children and we, *of course,* also learn which behaviors are right for which situations.

Coordinating conjunctions (such as *and, but,* and *so*), conjunctive adverbs (such as *however, consequently,* and *moreover*), and certain temporal adverbs and subordinating conjunctions (such as *before, after,* and *now*) supply cohesive ties across sentence boundaries.

The last major class of cohesive ties includes those based on *lexical* relationships. *Lexical* cohesion differs from *reference* cohesion and *conjunctive* cohesion because every lexical item is potentially cohesive and because nothing in the occurrence of a given lexical item necessarily makes it cohesive. If we were to encounter the word *this* in a text, we would either supply a referent from our working memory of the text or reread the text to find a referent. Similarly, when we encounter a conjunctive adverb such as *however,* we attempt to establish an adversative relationship between two text elements. In contrast, lexical cohesion depends on some "patterned occurrence of lexical items" (p. 288). Consider the following sentences adapted from a mountaineering guidebook:

24. The ascent up the Emmons Glacier on Mt. Rainier is long but relatively easy.
25. The only usual problem in the climb is finding a route through the numerous crevasses above Steamboat Prow.
26. In late season a *bergschrund* may develop at the 13,000-foot level, which is customarily bypassed to the right.

Three cohesive chains bind together this short text. The first chain (*ascent, climb, finding a route, bypassed to the right*) carries the topic—the way up the mountain. The second and third chains give the setting (*Glacier, crevasses, bergschrund*)(*Mt. Rainier, Steamboat Prow, 13,000-foot level*). These chains give clues to the interpretation of unfamiliar items. For most readers, *Steamboat Prow* is unknown, but one can infer that it is a feature on Mt. Rainier. Similarly, *bergschrund* is a technical term referring to a crevasse at the head of a glacier where the moving ice breaks apart from the stationary ice clinging to the mountain. In this text, a reader can infer that *bergschrunds* are associated with glaciers and that they present some type of obstacle to climbers, even without the final clause in 26.

Lexical cohesion is the predominant means of connecting sentences in discourse. Halliday and Hasan identify two major subclasses of lexical cohesion: *reiteration* and *collocation. Reiteration* is in turn divided into four subclasses, ranging from repetition of the *same item* to repetition through the use of a *synonym or near-synonym,* a *superordinate item,* or a *general item.*

Lexical reiteration is usually easy to identify. An example of synonymy occurs in 25 and 26 with the pairing of *ascent* and *climb.* The three other subclasses are illustrated in the following student example:

Lexical Reiteration (Same Item), (Superordinate), and (General Item)

27. Some professional tennis players, for example, grandstand, using obscene gestures and language to call attention to themselves.

28. Other *professional athletes* do similar *things,* such as spiking a football in the end zone, to attract *attention.*

In 28, *professional athletes* is, in this case, a superordinate term for *professional tennis players.* Professional athletes in other sports are encompassed by the term. *Things,* in contrast, is a general term. Here *things* is used to refer anaphorically to two behaviors, "using obscene gestures and language." While superordinates are names of specific classes of objects, general terms are even more inclusive, not restricted to a specific set of objects. The other type of lexical reiteration, illustrated by sentences 27 and 28, is same-item repetition: *attention* is simply repeated.

All the lexical cohesive relationships which cannot be properly subsumed under lexical reiteration are included in a "miscellaneous" class called *collocation.* Collocation refers to lexical cohesion "that is achieved through the association of lexical items that regularly co-occur" (p. 284). Lexical cohesion through collocation is the most difficult type of cohesion to analyze because items said to collocate involve neither repetition, synonymy, superordination, nor mention of general items. What is important is that the items said to collocate "share the same lexical environment" (p. 286). The following student example illustrates this principle:

Lexical Cohesion (Collocation)

29. On a camping trip with parents, teenagers willingly do the household chores that they resist at home.

30. They gather *wood for a fire,* help put up the *tent,* and carry *water from a creek or lake.*

Although the italicized items in 30 are presented as the "camping trip" equivalents of *household chores,* the cohesion between sentences 29 and 30 results more directly from the associations of the italicized items with *camping trip.* The italicized items in sentence 30 collocate with *camping trip* in sentence 29. The mountaineering guidebook passage, however, is much more difficult to analyze. For one of the authors of the present article, antecedent knowledge of mountaineering allows *Steamboat Prow* to collocate with *Mt. Rainier* and *bergschrund* to collocate with *glacier.* For the other author, neither pair is lexically related by collocation apart from the text where they are connected by inference. We will return to this problem later in this essay.

In addition to the taxonomy that allows cohesive ties to be classified according to function, Halliday and Hasan introduce a second taxonomy.

This second taxonomy allows cohesive ties to be classified according to the amount of text spanned by the *presupposed* and *presupposing* elements of a given tie. Halliday and Hasan posit four such "text-span" classes. Membership in a class is determined by the number of T-units a given cohesive tie spans.[7] Taken together, the two taxonomies Halliday and Hasan present allow any given cohesive tie to be classified in two different ways, one according to function and one according to distance. The four "text-span" classes contained in Halliday and Hasan's second taxonomy are illustrated in the following paragraph from a student paper:

Text-Span Classes (Immediate, Mediated, Remote, Mediated-Remote)

31. *Respect* is one reason people change their behavior.
32. For example, one does not speak with his *boss* as he would talk to a friend or co-worker.
33. One might use four-letter words in talking to a co-worker, but probably not in talking to his *boss.*
34. In talking to teachers or *doctors*, people also use bigger words than normal.
35. Although the situation is different than when one speaks with a *boss* or a *doctor*, one often talks with a minister or priest different [sic] than he talks with friends or *family.*
36. With a *family,* most people use a different language when they talk to their parents or grandparents than when they talk to younger brothers and sisters.
37. People's ability to use language in different ways allows them to show the *respect* they should toward different people, whether they are professionals, *family* members, clergy, friends and co-workers, or *bosses.*

Immediate cohesive ties semantically linked adjacent T-units. The repetition of *doctor* in sentences 34 and 35 creates an *immediate* tie, forcing the reader to assimilate the content of 34 into the content of 35. In contrast, the repetition of *family* in sentences 35, 36 and 37 forms a *mediated* tie. The semantic bridge established by the occurrence of *family* in 35 and 37 is channelled through or mediated by the repetition of *family* in 36. The cohesive tie involving the repetition of *family* is not simply a series of immediate ties, because once a lexical item appears in a text all subsequent uses of that item presuppose the first appearance. *Immediate* and *mediated* ties join items in adjacent T-units. Such ties enable writers to introduce a concept in one T-unit and to extend, modify, or clarify that concept in subsequent and successive T-units.

Remote ties, on the other hand, result when the two elements of a tie are separated by one or more intervening T-units. The tie between *respect* in 31 and 37 is *remote;* here the repetition of the word signals to the reader that the semantic unit represented by the paragraph is now complete. Finally, ties which are both mediated and remote are called *mediated-remote.* An example of this type of cohesive tie appears in the repetition of *bosses* in sentences 32, 33, 35 and 37. Here the presupposing *bosses* in 37 is separated from the presupposed *boss* in 32 by intervening T-units 34 and 36 which contain no element relevant to the particular cohesive tie. Thus the tie is *remote*. However, the presupposing *bosses* is also *mediated* through repetitions of *boss* in 33 and 35. Hence the term *mediated-remote*. Skilled writers use mediated-remote ties to interweave key "themes" within the text.

Analysis of Student Essays

To explore the usefulness of Halliday and Hasan's theory of cohesion in writing research, we used their two taxonomies in an analysis of ten student essays. These essays were written by beginning University of Texas freshmen on the "changes in behavior" topic used in the Miami University sentence-combining experiment.[8] From 90 essays which had been rated holistically by two readers on a four-point scale, we selected five essays given the lowest score by both raters and five essays given the highest score. We analyzed these ten essays according to categories of error and according to syntactic features, as well as according to the number and types of cohesive ties. Our analyses of error and content variables yielded results similar to those other researchers have reported—that high-rated essays are longer and contain larger T-units and clauses, more nonrestrictive modifiers, and fewer errors.[9]

We anticipated that an analysis of cohesive ties in the high- and low-rated essays would reveal similar gross differences. The results of our analysis confirmed this expectation. At the most general level of analysis, the high rated essays are much more dense in cohesion than the low-rated essays. In the low-rated essays, a cohesive tie of some type occurs once every 4.9 words; in the high-rated essays, a tie occurs once every 3.2 words, a difference in mean frequency of 1.7 words. Likewise, a large difference in the mean number of cohesive ties per T-unit appears, with 2.4 ties per T-unit in the low-rated essays and 5.2 ties per T-unit in the high rated essays. The figures for this and the preceding index, however, are not precisely comparable because the T-units in the high-rated essays are, on average, 1.64 words longer than those in the low-rated essays. By dividing the number of cohesive ties in an essay set by the number of words in that set, we arrived at another general index of cohesive density. In the high-rated essays, 31.7% of all words contribute to explicit cohesive ties while only 20.4% of the words in the low-rated essays contribute to such ties.

The ways in which writers of the high- and low-rated essays form cohesive ties also distinguish the two groups of five essays from each other. Writers of the high-rated essays use a substantially higher relative percentage of *immediate* (High: 41.6%/Low: 32.8%) and *mediated* (High: 7.6%/Low: 0.8%) cohesive ties than do the writers of the low-rated essays. On the other hand, writers of the low-rated essays use more *mediated-remote* (High: 25.9%/Low: 36.7%) and *remote* ties (High: 26.9%/Low: 29.7%). These percentages allow us to focus on some crucial differences between the two essay sets. The larger relative percentage of *immediate* cohesive ties in the high-rated essays suggests, among other things, that the better writers tend to establish stronger cohesive bonds between individual T-units than do the writers of the low-rated essays. Analyses of *reference* and *conjunctive cohesion* support this observation. Writers of high-rated essays employ reference cohesion about twice as often, 84.1 times to 47.8 times per 100 T-units, as the writers of low-rated papers. The largest difference in the occurrence of referential cohesion is reflected in the higher frequency of third-person pronouns in the high-rated essays (High: 25.1 per 100 T-units/Low: 5.1 per 100 T-units). This lower frequency of third-person pronouns in the low-rated essays may be a direct result of the less skilled writers' attempts to avoid errors such as ambiguous pronoun reference. Because third-person pronouns usually refer back to the T-unit immediately preceding, we can infer that the wrtiers of high-rated essays more often elaborate, in subsequent and adjacent T-units, topics introduced in a given T-unit.

Also contributing importantly to the greater use of *immediate* cohesive ties is the frequency with which the more skillful writers use *conjunction* to link individual T-units. Conjunctive ties most often result in *immediate* cohesive ties between T-units. It is not surprising, then, to find that the writers of high-rated essays employ over three times as many conjunctive ties (High: 65.4 per 100 T-units/Low: 20.4 per 100 T-units) as the writers of low-rated essays. Neither is it surprising to discover that the more skillful writers employ all five types of conjunction while the less skillful writers use only three. As is the case with pronominal references that cross T-unit boundaries, conjunctives are most often used to extend concepts introduced in one T-unit to other T-units which follow immediately in the text. Thus the more skillful writers appear to extend the concept introduced in a given T-unit considerably more often than do the less skillful writers. One major effect of such semantic extensions is, of course, essay length; and this finding helps to explain why the high-rated essays are, on the average, 375 words longer than the low-rated essays.

The relative frequency of *lexical cohesion* gives another indication that the writers of high-rated essays are better able to expand and connect their ideas than the writers of low-rated essays. By far the largest number of cohesive ties, about two-thirds of the total ties for both the high and low samples, fall into the general category of *lexical cohesion*. Writers of the high-rated essays create some type of lexical tie 340 times per 100 T-units or every 4.8 words. Writers of the low-rated essays, however, manage a lexical tie just 161 times per 100 T-units or every 7.4 words. The majority of lexical ties (65%) in the low essays are repetitions of the same item. This distribution is reflected to a smaller degree in the high essays, where 52% of the total lexical ties fall into the *same item* subcategory. Writers of high-rated essays, however, form many more lexical collocations. Lexical collocations appear 94 times per 100 T-units in the high-rated essays in contrast to 28.8 times per 100 T-units in the low-rated essays.

Cohesion and Invention

These cohesion profiles suggest to us an important difference between the invention skills of the two groups of writers. The better writers seem to have a better command of invention skills that allows them to elaborate and extend the concepts they introduce. The poorer writers, in contrast, appear deficient in these skills. Their essays display a much higher degree of lexical and conceptual redundancy. The high percentage of lexical redundancy and the low frequency of lexical collocation in the low-rated essays are indications of this difference. The text-span categories also point to this difference. In the low-rated essays two-thirds of the cohesive ties are interrupted ties—*mediated-remote* or *remote* ties—which reach back across one or more T-units, indicating that the writers of the low-rated essays generally fail to elaborate and extend concepts through successive T-units.

The larger proportion of interrupted ties in the low-rated papers strongly suggests that substantially less new information or semantic content is introduced during the course of a low-rated essay than during the course of a high-rated essay. If more new information had been introduced in the low-rated essays, the writers would have had to rely more heavily than they did on *immediate* and *mediated* cohesive ties in order to integrate, to weave, the new information into the text. The writers of the low-rated papers tend more toward reiteration of previously introduced information than do the writers of the high-rated papers. Indeed, in reading the low-rated essays one can not help noting a good deal of what might be called conceptual and lexical redundancy. The following example illustrates this characteristic:

> Some people have to change their behavior around different acquaintances. One reason is that they want to make a good impression on others. You have to act different in front of a person who is giving you a job interview because you want to make a good impression. You, most of the time, act differently to fit in a crowd. You will change your behavior to get people to like you. You change your behavior to agree with peoples [sic] in the crowd.

This paragraph from a low-rated paper has a fairly strong beginning: it states a topic in the first sentence, modifies that topic in the second sentence, illustrates the topic in the third sentence, and gives another example in the fourth sentence. The next two sentences, however, simply reiterate what is said in the fourth sentence. The principal lexical items in the last two sentences—*change, behavior, people,* and *crowd*—are repetitions of items introduced earlier in the paragraph and offer little new information. Although for purposes of attaining cohesion in a text some redundancy is a virtue, the redundancy in the low-rated essays seems to be a flaw because these writers failed to supply additional information at the point where it would be expected to appear. Had this additional information been supplied, the writers would have had to use *immediate* and *mediated* ties in order to connect it to the rest of the text.

Compare the previous example paragraph from a low-rated paper with the following paragraph from a high-rated paper.

It is a job that really changes our behavior. Among other changes, we change the way we dress. In many jobs college graduates want to look responsible and mature, projecting an image of competence. The college student who wore faded blue jeans is now in three-piece suits. He feels the need to be approved of and accepted by his boss and associates. While he talked of socialism in college, he now reaps the profits of capitalism. While in college he demanded honesty in the words and actions of others, on the job he is willing to "kiss ass" to make friends or get a promotion. Indeed, working can change behavior.

Notice that in the paragraph from the high-rated paper, *behavior* is repeated only one time. Yet the reader never questions that the paragraph is about changes in behavior. The writer repeatedly supplies examples of types of behavior, which are linked to the topic by a series of lexical collocations (e.g., *behavior, dress, look, responsible, blue jeans, three-piece suits*). Clearly, the paragraph from the high-rated paper extends the semantic domain of the concept *behavior* to include a number of differentiated lexical items. Low-rated papers rarely show such extended series of collocations.

Analyses of cohesion thus measure some aspects of invention skills. The low-rated essays stall frequently, repeating ideas instead of elaborating them. Our analyses also suggest that the writers of the low-rated papers do not have working vocabularies capable of extending, in ways prerequisite for good writing, the concepts and ideas they introduce in their essays. Indeed, skill in invention, in discovering what to say about a particular topic, may depend in ways yet unexplored on the prior development of adequate working vocabularies. If students do not have in their working vocabularies the lexical items required to extend, explore, or elaborate the concepts they introduce, practice in invention can have only a limited effect on overall writing quality.

Our analyses further point to the underdevelopment of certain cognitive skills among the writers of the low-rated papers. The low-rated papers not only exhibit a great deal of redundancy, but (as noted earlier) also include relatively fewer *conjunctive* and *reference* ties and *immediate* and *mediated* ties. Besides lacking adequate vocabularies, writers of the low-rated essays seem to lack in part the ability to perceive and articulate abstract concepts with reference to particular instances, to perceive relationships among ideas, and to reach beyond the worlds of their immediate experience.

All this is to suggest that analyses of cohesion may be potentially useful in distinguishing between stages of writing development. Clearly, cohesion analyses measure more sophisticated aspects of language development than do error analyses and syntactic analyses. Cohesion analyses also give us some concrete ways of addressing some of the differences between good and poor writing, differences which heretofore could not be explained either to ourselves or to our students in any but the most abstract ways. We thus anticipate that Halliday and Hasan's taxonomies can be usefully applied in developmental studies as well as in studies such as the present one.

Cohesion, Coherence and Writing Quality

However promising cohesion analysis appears as a research tool and however encouraging the results of the present study seem, we feel that a number of important questions cannot be answered by analyzing cohesion. The first of these questions concerns writing quality. The quality or "success" of a text, we would argue, depends a great deal on factors outside the text itself, factors which lie beyond the scope of cohesion analyses. Recall that Halliday and Hasan exclude *exophoric*, or outside-text, references from their taxonomy of explicit cohesive ties. We think that writing quality is in part defined as the "fit" of a particular text to its context, which includes such factors as the writer's purpose, the discourse medium, and the audience's knowledge of and interest in the subject—the factors which are the cornerstones of discourse theory and *mutatis mutandis*, should be the cornerstones of research in written composition.[10] We are not alone in this view. Several students of written discourse—among them Joseph Grimes,[11] Teun van Dijk,[12] Nils Enkvist,[13] and Robert de Beaugrande[14]—distinguish *cohesion* and *coherence*. They limit cohesion to explicit mechanisms in the text, both the types of cohesive ties that Halliday and Hasan describe and other elements that bind texts such as parallelism, consistency of verb tense, and what literary scholars have called "point of view."[15] Coherence conditions, on the other hand, allow a text to be understood in a real-world setting. Halliday and Hasan's theory does not accommodate real-world settings for written discourse or, consequently, the conditions through which texts become coherent. We agree with Charles Fillmore's contention that

> the scenes . . . [audiences] construct for texts are partly justified by the lexical and grammatical materials in the text and partly by the interpreter's own contributions, the latter being based on what he knows about the current context, what he knows about the world in general, and what he assumes the speaker's intentions might be.[16]

Hence lexical collocations within a text are understood through cues which the writer provides and through the reader's knowledge of general discourse characteristics and of the world to which the discourse refers.

Thus lexical collocation is in all likelihood the subcategory of cohesion that best indicates overall writing ability, as well as disclosing distinctions among written texts that represent different discourse modes and purposes. An examination of lexical cohesive ties shows how writers build ideas, how they are able to take advantage of associations to weave together a text. But a fundamental problem lies in the analysis of a writer's text. Whose collocations do we analyze—the reader's or the writer's? One simple proof that the two do not always coincide can be found in the unintentional sexual references that students occasionally produce—the kind that get passed around the faculty coffee room.

Consider again the mountaineering guidebook passage in sentences 24, 25, and 26. We have already established that for mountaineers and glaciologists, *bergschrund* probably collocates with *glacier*, but for many other persons the two items do not collocate. Yet a naive reader presented this text probably would not stop to consult a dictionary for the lexical item, *bergschrund*, but would infer from its context that it is some type of obstacle to climbers and continue reading. Herbert Clark theorizes that we comprehend unknown items like *bergschrund* by drawing inferences.[17] We make inferences on the basis of what we can gather from the explicit content and the circumstances surrounding a text, through a tacit contract between the writer and reader that the writer will provide only information relevant to the current topic. In the case of the mountaineering passage, the circumstances of the text greatly affect our understanding of it. The type of text—a guidebook—follows a predictable organization, what has been called a *script* in research on artificial intelligence.[18] The guidebook contains a series of topics with a clear, yet implicit, goal: to inform the reader how to get to the top of a mountain. We expect the author to give us only information relevant to the particular route. Accordingly, readers understand *bergschrund* as an obstacle through a combination of cues—overt signals in the text such as the parallelism of the *bergschrund* sentence with the sentence about crevasses above it and, for those readers familiar with the type of text, implicit signals such as the following of the guidebook "script." Although Halliday and Hasan do not include parallelism in their taxonomy, parallelism often creates a cohesive tie.

Cohesion and coherence interact to a great degree, but a cohesive text may be only minimally coherent. Thus cohesion-based distinctions between texts rated high and low in quality can be misleading. Besides explicit links within a text, a text must conform to a reader's expectations for particular types of texts and the reader's knowledge of the world. A simple example will illustrate this point:

38. The quarterback threw the ball toward the tight end.
39. Balls are used in many sports.
40. Most balls are spheres, but a football is an ellipsoid.
41. The tight end leaped to catch the ball.

Sentences 39 and 40, while cohesive, violate a coherence condition that the writer provide only information relevant to the topic. The major problem with this short text is that a reader cannot construct what Fillmore calls a real-world scene for it; that is, the text neither seems to have a clear purpose nor appears to meet the needs of any given audience. Because it has no clear purpose, it lacks coherence, in spite of the cohesive ties which bind it together. In addition to a cohesive unity, written texts must have a pragmatic unity, a unity of a text and the world of the reader. A description of the fit of a text to its context, as well as descriptions of what composition teachers call writing quality, must specify a variety of coherence conditions, many of them outside the text itself.

Implications for the Teaching of Composition

One implication of the present study is that if cohesion is better understood, it can be better taught. At present, in most college writing classes, cohesion is taught, explicitly or implicitly, either through exercises, classroom instruction, or comments on student papers. Many exercises not explicitly designed to teach cohesion do in fact demand that students form cohesive ties. Open sentence-combining exercises, for example, offer as much practice in forming cohesive ties as they do in manipulating syntactic structures, a fact which may explain the success of certain sentence-combining experiments as well as the failure of research to link syntactic measures such as T-unit and clause length to writing quality.[19] An open sentence-combining exercise about Charlie Chaplin might contain a series of sentences beginning with the name *Charlie Chaplin*. Such an exercise would, at the very least, demand that students change most of the occurrences of *Charlie Chaplin* to *be* in order to produce an acceptable text. Students working either from contextual cues or from their knowledge of Chaplin might also use phrases like *the comic genius* or *the little tramp* to substitute for the proper name *Chaplin*.

If cohesion is often implicitly incorporated in writing curricula, coherence is often ignored. A great portion of the advice in composition textbooks stops at sentence boundaries. Numerous exercises teach clause and sentence structure in isolation, ignoring the textual, and the situational, considerations for using that structure. The passive is a classic example:

42. The police apprehended the suspect as he left the bank.
43. He is being held in the county jail.
43a. The police are holding the suspect in the county jail.

A student following her teacher's advice to avoid the passive construction might revise sentence 43 to 43a. If she did so, she would violate the usual sequence of information in English, where the topic or "old" information is presented first.[20] In active sentences, such as 43a, where the object expresses the topic, a revision to the passive is often preferable. Avoiding the passive with 43a would also require the unnecessary and uneconomical repetition of *police* and *suspect*. Consequently, maxims such as "Avoid passives" ignore the coherence conditions that govern the information structure of a text.

Other discourse considerations are similarly ignored in traditional advice on how to achieve coherence. As E. K. Lybert and D. W. Cummings have observed, the handbook injunction "Repeat key words and phrases" often *reduces* coherence.[21] Our analysis of cohesive ties in high- and low-rated essays substantiates Lybert and Cummings' point. While the low-rated papers we examined contain fewer cohesive ties than the high-rated papers in equivalent spans of text, the low-rated papers rely more heavily on lexical repetition. Also contrary to a popular notion, frequent repetition of lexical items does not necessarily increase readability. Roger Shuy and Donald Larkin's recent study shows lexical redundancy to be a principal reason why insurance policy language is difficult to read.[22]

Our analysis of cohesion suggests that cohesion is an important property of writing quality. To some extent the types and frequencies of cohesive ties seem to reflect the invention skills of student writers and to influence the stylistic and organizational properties of the texts they write. However, our analysis also suggests that while cohesive relationships may ultimately affect writing quality in some ways, there is no evidence to suggest that a large number (or a small number) of cohesive ties of a particular type will positively affect writing qualtiy. All discourse is context bound—to the demands of the subject matter, occasion, medium, and audience of the text. Cohesion defines those mechanisms that hold a text together while coherence defines those underlying semantic relations that allow a text to be understood and used. Consequently, coherence conditions—conditions governed by the writer's purpose, the audience's knowledge and expectations, and the information to be conveyed—militate against prescriptive approaches to the teaching of writing. Indeed, our exploration of what cohesion analyses can and cannot measure in student writing points to the necessity of placing writing exercises in the context of complete written texts. Just as exclusive focus on syntax and other formal features in writing instruction probably will not better the overall quality of college students' writing, neither will a narrow emphasis on cohesion probably produce significantly improved writing.[23]

Notes

[1] Most notably, Mina Shaughnessy, *Errors and Expectations*, (New York: Oxford University Press, 1977).

[2] See Ann O. Gebhard, "Writing Quality and Syntax: A Transformational Analysis of Three Prose Samples," *Research in the Teaching of English*, 12 (October 1978), 211-231.

[3] Composition theorists, however, have not stopped at sentence boundaries. Several of the early efforts to describe the relationships across sentences are summarized in Richard L. Larson, "Structure and Form in Non-Fiction Prose," in *Teaching Composition: Ten Bibliographical Essays*, ed. Gary Tate (Fort Worth, TX: Texas Christian University Press, 1976), pp. 45-71. The reader will note certain similarities between Halliday and Hasan's taxonomy of cohesive ties set out later in the present essay and the work of previous composition theorists.

[4] "Measuring Syntactic Growth: Errors and Expectations in Sentence-Combining Practice with College Freshmen," *Research in the Teaching of English,* 12 (October 1978), 233-244.

[5] No comprehensive overview of work in discourse in all of these fields exists at present. Extensive bibliographies, however, can be found in *Current Trends in Textlinguistics*, ed. Wolfgang U. Dressler (Berlin: de Gruyter, 1978) and Robert de Beaugrande, *Text, Discourse, and Process* (Norwood, NJ: Ablex, 1980).

[6] (London: Longman, 1976).

[7] The term *T-unit*, of course, comes from Kellogg Hunt's *Grammatical Structures Written at Three Grade Levels*, NCTE Research Report No. 3 (Champaign, IL: National Council of Teachers of English, 1965). Hunt defined a *T-unit* as an independent clause and all subordinate elements attached to it, whether clausal or phrasal. Halliday and Hasan do not use the term *T-unit*, but they do define their four "text-span" classes according to the

number of simple and complex sentences that the presupposing element of a cohesive tie must reach across for the presupposed element (see pp. 340-355). There is good reason to define the four "text-span" classes in terms of T-units. To examine only cohesive ties that span the boundaries of orthographic sentences would ignore the large number of conjunctive relationships, such as addition and causality, between independent clauses.

[8] Max Morenberg, Donald Daiker, and Andrew Kerek, "Sentence Combining at the College Level: An Experimental Study," *Research in the Teaching of English*, 12 (October 1978), 245-256. This topic asks students to write about why we act differently in different situations, using specific illustrations from personal experience.

[9] Detailed analyses for data summarized in this section are reported in Stephen P. Witte and Lester Faigley, *A Comparison of Analytic and Synthetic Approaches to the Teaching of College Writing*. Unpublished manuscript. The high-rated essays are, on the average, more than twice as long as the low-rated essays (647 words/270 words). Errors in three major categories were counted—punctuation, spelling, and grammar. Grammatical errors include errors in verb tenses, subject-verb agreement, pronoun reference, pronoun number agreement, and dangling or misplaced modifiers. The low-rated essays exhibit an error of some type nearly three times as often as the high-rated essays—one every 29 words as opposed to one every 87 words. For example, errors in end-stop punctuation, resulting in either a comma splice or a fragment, occur nearly eight times as often in the low-rated essays as in the high-rated essays. Misspelled words are over four times as frequent in the low-rated essays, and grammatical errors appear over twice as often.

Syntactic comparisons were made according to the number of words per T-unit and clause, and according to the frequency and placement of nonrestrictive or "free" modifiers. The low-rated essays contain T-units and clauses considerably shorter than the high-rated essays (High: 15.3 words per T-unit, 9.3 words per clause/Low: 13.7 words per T-unit, 7.5 words per clause). Nonrestrictive modifiers in all positions—initial, medial, and final—appear in the T-units of the high-rated essays nearly three times as frequently as in the low-rated essays (High: 28.5% of all T-units contain nonrestrictive modifiers/Low: 10.1% contain nonrestrictive modifiers). The high-rated essays also have twice the percentage of total words in nonrestrictive modifiers that the low-rated essays have.

[10] Stephen P. Witte, "Toward a Model for Research in Written Composition," *Research in the Teaching of English*, 14 (February 1980), 73-81.

[11] *The Thread of Discourse* (The Hague: Mouton, 1975).

[12] *Text and Context* (London: Longman, 1977).

[13] "Coherence, Pseudo-Coherence, and Non-Coherence," in *Reports on Text Linguistics: Semantics and Cohesion*, ed. Jan-Ola Ostman (Abo, Finland: Research Institute of the Abo Akademi Foundation, 1978), pp. 109-128.

[14] "The Pragmatics of Discourse Planning," *Journal of Pragmatics*, 4 (February 1980), 15-42.

[15] Susumo Kuno describes some linguistic features controlled by point of view, which he calls "empathy." See "Subject, Theme and the Speaker's Empathy—A Reexamination of Relativization Phenomena," in *Subject and Topic*, ed. Charles N. Li (New York: Academic Press, 1976), pp. 417-444.

[16] "Topics in Lexical Semantics," in *Current Issues in Linguistic Theory*, ed. Roger W. Cole (Bloomington: Indiana University Press, 1977), p. 92.

[17] "Inferences in Comprehension," in *Basic Processes in Reading: Perception and Comprehension*, ed. David LaBerge and S. Jay Samuels (Hillsdale, NJ: Erlbaum, 1977), pp. 243-263.

[18] R. C. Schank and R. P. Abelson, *Scripts, Plans, Goals, and Understanding: An Inquiry into Human Knowledge Structures* (Hillsdale, NJ: Erlbaum, 1977).

[19] See Lester Faigley, "Names in Search of a Concept: Maturity, Fluency, Complexity, and

Growth in Written Syntax," *College Composition and Communication,* 31 (October 1980), 291-300.

20 The theme-rheme distinction is the product of the Prague school of linguistics. Other researchers use the terms "topic-comment" or "given-new" information to refer to essentially the same concept. See Vilem Mathesius, *A Functional Analysis of Present Day English on a General Linguistic Basis,* ed. Josef Vachek (Prague: Academia, 1975). Also relevant are Wallace L. Chafe, *Meaning and the Structure of Language* (Chicago: University of Chicago Press, 1970): M. A. K. Halliday, "Notes on Transitivity and Theme in English: II," *Journal of Linguistics,* 3 (October 1967), 199-244; Herbert Clark and Susan Haviland, "Comprehension and the Given-New Contract," in *Discourse Production and Comprehension,* ed. Roy Freedle (Norwood, NJ: Ablex, 1977), pp. 1-40; and Liisa Lautamatti, "Observations on the Development of Topic in Simplified Discourse," in *Text Linguistics, Cognitive Learning, and Language Teaching,* ed. Viljo Kohonen and Nils Erik Enkvist (Turku, Finland: University of Turku, 1978), pp. 71-104.

21 "On Repetition and Coherence," *College Composition and Communication,* 20 (February 1969), 35-38.

22 "Linguistic Consideration in the Simplification/Clarification of Insurance Policy Language," *Discourse Processes,* 1 (October-December 1978), 305-321.

23 John Mellon and James Kinneavy both make the point that while the Miami University sentence-combining students improved significantly in writing quality, they may not have done so because they learned to manipulate syntactic structures better, but because they were taught to put together complete texts. See "Issues in the Theory and Practice of Sentence Combining: A Twenty-Year Perspective," in *Sentence Combining and the Teaching of Writing,* ed. Donald Daiker, Andrew Kerek, and Max Morenberg (Akron, OH: University of Akron, 1979), p. 10; and "Sentence Combining in a Comprehensive Language Framework" in the same volume, p. 66.

Paradigms as Structural Counterparts of *Topoi*

FRANK J. D'ANGELO

The few histories of invention that we have available seem to suggest that the art of invention declined and subsequently disappeared in the late 19th century, except for the purposes of formal debate.[1] Several reasons have been given for the demise of classical invention: the influence of Coleridge and the Romantic emphasis on intuition; the rise of science with its stress on empirical research; and the advent of a large middle class whose main concern was with literacy and practical discourse.[2]

My contention, however, is that rhetorical invention did not disappear in the late 19th century, but that it took a different form and thus went unnoticed. It is there, buried in the four forms of discourse (exposition, argumentation, description, and narration), under the guise of the "methods of development" (analysis, classification, definition, comparison and contrast, cause and effect, and so forth).[3] In the 20th century, the methods of development split off from the forms of discourse and reappeared in textbooks as patterns of organization.

I would like to suggest that this shift from thinking of invention as the search for ideas *before one begins to write* to thinking of it as *an ongoing process* that continues throughout the arrangement of those ideas makes good historical sense. In classical antiquity and perhaps up to the invention of printing, the art of invention had to be concerned primarily with the retrieval of information, since there were no books, and manuscripts were not readily available for the masses; thus the art of invention was closely allied with the art of memory. But in an age when knowledge is easily accessible, when writing and electronic media make available modes of thought not possible in antiquity,[4] then a new view of the composing process is necessary.

Such a view is implicit in the 19th century methods of development and the 20th century patterns of organization, and explicit in the work of more recent rhetorical theorists.[5] Theorists following this view of the composing process argue that composition is a sequence of connected activities that result in a unified piece of writing. They maintain that invention, arrangement, and style are parts of an organic whole. Patterns of organiza-tion appear in writing because a mental process puts them there, because a conceptual structure supports them, and underlying these larger organiza-tional patterns are paradigms which are the structural counterparts of *topoi.* These paradigms guide thought in the act of composing. The assumption is that the modern writer has access to a wealth of ideas, but that he or she needs a heuristic procedure for developing those ideas.

To illustrate the foregoing ideas more concretely, in the remainder of this paper I would like to examine the paradigmatic structure of an essay which exemplifies this new view of the composing process and then discuss some pedagogical implications. But before I begin this examination, I would like to make a few comments about paradigms.

Paradigms are patterns, or models, or algorithms. As algorithms, they are not only procedures for solving problems, but they are also recursive. Thus they can be repeated indefinitely, or at least until a particular goal is met. . . . The kind of paradigms I have in mind are structural counterparts of the topics of invention. These paradigms are not simply static conventional forms, but they represent *dynamic, organizational processes* and *patterns of thought.* A paradigm is a *principle of forward motion* that enables a writer to move his or her thinking in an orderly manner from the beginning of an essay to its conclusion.

In their most abstract form, paradigms look like this:

Classification Paradigm
Introduction (states the thesis)
Type 1
Type 2
Type 3
Types 4, 5, 6 . . .
Conclusion (restates the thesis, summarizes, and so forth)

Exemplification Paradigm
Introduction (states the thesis)
Example 1
Example 2
Example 3
Example 4, 5, 6 . . .
Conclusion (restates the thesis, summarizes, and so forth)

Cause-to-Effect Paradigm
Introduction (states the thesis)
Cause 1
Cause 2
Cause 3
Causes 4, 5, 6 . . .
Effect
Conclusion (restates the thesis, summarizes, and so forth)

Obviously, these are just a few examples of some characteristic patterns. Not only are there many more patterns, but there can be infinite variations on these patterns.

In their sentence form, paradigms consist of a thesis sentence, supporting sentences, and a clincher or summary sentence. Naturally the sentences of a paradigm must take a certain linguistic form. The linguistic form supports the conceptual form, and both provide some of the functions of explicit methods of invention. Clearly, not every essay has a thesis sentence or a clincher sentence. The pattern I have described is an idealized version of a paradigm. This version represents the linguistic and rhetorical competence of the writer. The writer's performance is the actual pattern embedded in the discourse, with all of its imperfections. Thus paradigms at their most abstract and in their most ideal form constitute a kind of deep structure of the essay.

The model I have chosen for analysis is taken from Bertrand Russell's *Autobiography*.[6] It is a good example of the kind of paradigmatic form we have been discussing. I have indented the sentence levels so that the logical divisions stand out more clearly.

What I Have Lived For

Bertrand Russell

1

1　Three passions, simple but overwhelmingly strong, have governed my life: the longing for love, the search for knowledge, and unbearable pity for the suffering of mankind.
　2　These passions, like great winds, have blown me hither and thither, in a wayward course, over a deep ocean of anguish, reaching to the very verge of despair.

2

　　3　I have sought love, first, because it brings ecstasy—ecstasy so great that I would often have sacrificed all the rest of life for a few hours of this joy.
　　3　I have sought it, next, because it relieves loneliness—that terrible loneliness in which one shivering consciousness looks over the rim of the world into the cold unfathomable lifeless abyss.
　　3　I have sought it, finally, because in the union of love I have seen, in a mystic miniature, the prefiguring vision of the heaven that saints and poets have imagined.
　　　4　This is what I sought, and though it might seem too good for human life, this is what—at last—I have found.

3

　3　With equal passion I have sought knowledge.
　　4　I have wished to understand the hearts of men.
　　4　I have wished to know why the stars shine.
　　4　And I have tried to apprehend the Pythagorean power by which number holds sway above the flux.
　　　5　A little of this, but not much, I have achieved.

4

3 Love and knowledge, so far as they were possible, led upward toward the heavens.
3 But always pity brought me back to earth.
   4 Echoes of cries of pain reverberate in my heart.
     5 Children in famine, victims tortured by oppressors, helpless old people a hated burden to their sons, and the whole world of loneliness, poverty, and pain make a mockery of what human life should be.
     6 I long to alleviate the evil, but I cannot, and I too suffer.

5

1 This has been my life.
2 I have found it worth living, and would gladly live it again if the chance were offered me.

Because paradigms are based on the principle of repetition (syntactic or semantic), in getting at these paradigms, we must look for key words and phrases that recur with enough frequency that the pattern will be unmistakeable. Since there is always the possibility of an essay having several interrelated forms, we would want to abstract only those sentences that relate to the specific topic of invention under consideration: analysis, classification, comparison, and so forth. In the beginning stages, we might abstract the appropriate sentences exactly as they appear in the text and put them into a paradigm. However, if it appears necessary, we would *regularize* the text to reveal the underlying pattern more clearly. We can do this by using a sentence paraphrase, recasting the sentences in simpler form. The resultant paradigm represents the core structure of the essay.

The thesis sentence of the paradigm marks the *origination* of a pattern that is transmitted through space and time. The supporting sentences represent *stages in thinking*. And the clincher sentence exemplifies *closure*. When we isolate the abstract paradigm, the organic unit seems to fade into the background. The pattern seems static. Yet the enduring pattern is wholly derived from aspects of the various temporal sections of the essay. The pattern endures in isolation, but it also exhibits itself in the whole. Thus a paradigm constitutes a patterned *value* with permanence inherent throughout the parts.

In beginning our analysis of the Bertrand Russell essay, notice that the opening sentence is not only the *thesis* sentence, but also the sentence that indicates the plan of development. The word *three* suggests that a pattern of enumeration will follow. The word *passions* indicates a complementary pattern of classification. The sentence, in the outline form, looks something like this:

1 Three passions . . . have governed my life:
  2 the longing for love,
  2 the search for knowledge, and
  2 unbearable pity for the suffering of mankind.

This thesis gives us a clue, a hint for what is to follow.

The second sentence in this paragraph qualifies and expands the idea of passions in the first sentence. The explicit tie-in is the repetition of the word *passions*:

> These passions, like great winds, have blown me hither and thither, in a wayward course, over a deep ocean of anguish, reaching to the very verge of despair.

You will note that in paragraph 2 no one sentence advances the pattern. There is, for example, no topic sentence. Instead, the first three sentences advance the pattern by giving the reasons why the author sought love. So we provide a sentence that can serve as the top sentence of the paradigm and add to it those sentences or phrases that constitute its support. The result is the following pattern:

> [I have sought love . . .]
> I have sought love, first, because it brings ecstasy . . .
> I have sought it, next, because it relieves loneliness . . .
> I have sought it, finally, because . . . I have seen . . . the prefiguring vision of the heaven that saints and poets have imagined.

The first sentence of the next paragraph enumerates the second of Bertrand Russell's passions, knowledge:

> With equal passion I have sought knowledge.

And the subsequent sentences in that paragraph form the support structure:

> With equal passion I have sought knowledge . . .
> I have wished to understand the hearts of men . . .
> I have wished to know why the stars shine . . . And
> I have tried to apprehend the Pythagorean power by which number holds sway above the flux . . .

The first sentence of the fourth paragraph repeats the words *love* and *knowledge* of the two previous paragraphs and continues the main idea. It is a transitional sentence. The second sentence of that paragraph advances the overall pattern by enumerating the third passion that has governed Bertrand Russell's life. So we use this sentence and add to it the supporting details, but this time regularize the support pattern to make it parallel the structure of the support patterns of the previous paragraphs:

> But always pity brought me back to earth . . .
> [I have pitied] children in famine . . .
> [I have pitied] victims tortured by oppressors . . .
> [I have pitied] helpless old people a hated burden to their sons . . .
> [I have pitied] the whole world of loneliness, poverty, and pain . . .

Finally, the first sentence of the last paragraph completes the pattern and coupled with the first sentence of the essay acts as a *frame device* for the entire paradigm:

> This has been my life.

If we put the various stages of the paradigm together, we get this overall pattern:

1

Three passions, simple but overwhelmingly strong, have governed my
life: the longing for love, the search for knowledge, and unbearable pity
for the suffering of mankind.

    These passions, like great winds, have blown me hither and thither,
in a wayward course, over a deep ocean of anguish, reaching to the
very verge of despair.

2

[I have sought love . . .]
    I have sought love, first, because it brings ectasy . . .
    I have sought it, next, because it relieves loneliness . . .
    I have sought it, finally, because . . . I have seen the prefiguring vision
of the heaven that saints and poets have imagined . . .

3

With equal passion I have sought knowledge . . .
    I have wished to understand the hearts of men . . .
    I have wished to know why the stars shine . . .
    I have tried to apprehend the Pythagorean power by which number
holds sway above the flux . . .

4

Love and knowledge . . . led upward toward the heavens.
But always pity brought me back to earth.
    [I have pitied] children in famine . . .
    [I have pitied] victims tortured by oppressors . . .
    [I have pitied] helpless old people a hated burden to their sons . . .
    [I have pitied] the whole world of loneliness, poverty, and pain . . .

5

This has been my life.
    I have found it worth living, and would gladly live it again if the
chance were offered me.

If we "normalize" the pattern, taking a few more liberties with the
phrasing, we get the following paradigm:
1 Three passions . . . have governed my life: the longing for love, the
   search for knowledge, and unbearable pity for the suffering of mankind.
2 I have sought love.
    I have sought love because it brings ecstasy.
    I have sought it because it relieves loneliness.
    I have sought it because it contains a vision of the heavens that saints
    and poets have imagined.

3 I have sought knowledge.
  I have wished to understand the hearts of men.
  I have wished to know why the stars shine.
  I have tried to apprehend the Pythagorean power by which number holds sway above the flux.
4 I have sought pity.
  I have pitied children in famine.
  I have pitied victims tortured by oppressors.
  I have pitied the whole world of loneliness, poverty, and pain.
5 This has been my life.

This pattern represents the organizational structure of the entire essay. The first unit states the main idea. Russell is going to talk about the three passions that have governed his life. The next unit enumerates the first passion, *love*, then supports it with the reasons why the author sought love. The next unit enumerates the second passion, *knowledge,* and supports it with an explanation of the kinds of knowledge Russell sought. The fourth unit names the last passion, *pity*, and the supporting details tell who it is the author pities. The last unit concludes the pattern and returns to the beginning.

It is obvious that although the overall organizational pattern is *classification* (what is being classified is "kinds" or "types" of passions) reinforced by *enumeration*, the structure of the supporting paragraphs could have differed. For example, paragraph 3 could just as easily have been supported by reasons as by an explanation and enumeration of the kinds of knowledge that Bertrand Russell sought. This leads us to conclude that the main plan of the essay is carried by the underlying patterns of classification and enumeration. This is the pattern that represents the working-idea of the essay and the principle of forward motion. If we normalize the text again, reducing it to its essential structure, we get a pattern that is more workable for compositional purposes:

1 Three passions have governed my life.
2 The first passion is the longing for love.
3 The second passion is the search for knowledge.
4 The third passion is pity for the suffering of mankind.
5 These are the passions that have governed my life.

For compositional purposes, we can abstract even more from the original pattern. We can then take the resultant pattern and put our own subject matter into it.

1 Three passions have governed my life.
2 The first passion is . . .
3 The second passion is . . .
4 The third passion is . . .
5 These are the passions that have governed my life.

We can also vary the pattern by substitution:

1 Three (four, five) things (passions, emotions, events) have governed my life.
2 The first thing is . . .
3 The second thing is . . .
4 The third thing is . . .
5 The fourth thing is . . .
6 The last thing is . . .
7 These are the things that have governed my life.

Or we can abstract even more, reducing the underlying pattern (or patterns) to a single abstract pattern:

1 Introduction (states the *thesis*)
2 Type 1 (or Characteristic 1)
3 Type 2 (or Characteristic 2)
4 Type 3 (or Characteristic 3)
5 Type 4 (or Characteristic 4)
6 Types 5, 6, 7 . . . (or Characteristics 5, 6, 7 . . .)
7 Conclusion (restates the thesis, summarizes, and so forth).

Not every essay is as regular as Bertrand Russell's essay. Not every essay will have the paragraphs arranged in such a convenient order. Some essays may have several introductory paragraphs. The thesis, rather than being the first sentence of the essay, may be embedded in the second or third paragraph. In addition to containing the support paragraphs for the thesis, some essays may contain numerous transitional paragraphs or even paragraphs that digress from the main idea. Nevertheless, with enough practice and skill in analyzing, we should be able to abstract the underlying paradigm and make it generative in our own writing.

The parts of the abstracted pattern do not necessarily bear a one to one relationship to corresponding paragraphs. The divisions represent "sections" of the essay. These sections could be paragraph divisions, or they could be larger thought units as the following scheme indicates:

Paragraph 1 (introduction)
Paragraph 2 (statement of the *thesis*)
Paragraph 3 (type 1)
Paragraph 4 (qualification of paragraph 3)
Paragraph 5 (type 2)
Paragraph 6 (digression)
Paragraph 7 (transitional paragraph)
Paragraph 8 (type 3)
Paragraph 9 (conclusion)

Thus far I have related the paradigmatic structure of the essay to the topics of invention, but I have said little about style. If my assumptions about the organic nature of the composing process are correct, then style is not something tacked on to an essay. It is not ornament, nor is it mere embellishment. It is a function of the whole. In this view, the style of the essay is partially determined by the paradigmatic structure. For example, in the Bertrand Russell essay, the thesis sentence necessarily determines what certain features of the style will be like. Since the thesis combines enumeration with classification, we would naturally expect the sentences to exhibit a great deal of syntactic repetition. And this is exactly what we find. In paragraph 2, the first three sentences exhibit features of anaphoric repetition and parallelism, with the fourth sentence exhibiting a kind of epanalepsis:

I have sought love, first, because . . .
I have sought it, next, because . . .
I have sought it, finally, because . . .
This is what I sought . . .
this is what . . . I have found.

Paragraph 3 picks up the pattern of anaphoric repetition again:
. . . I have sought knowledge
I have wished to . . .
I have wished to . . .
And I have tried to . . .
. . . I have achieved

In addition to the anaphoric repetition, there are numerous instances of other kinds of sentence and phrasal parallelism and of antithesis. . . . In the Bertrand Russell essay, then, the paradigmatic structure seems to mediate between invention, on the one hand, and style, on the other. In this essay, invention, arrangement, and style are all parts of an organic whole.

What are the implications for the teaching of composition in this new view of the composing process?

The first implication is that in teaching rhetorical invention, we might more profitably begin with paradigms of various kinds, in their abstract form as well as in their actual shape in a discourse, and then go back and relate them to the topics of invention. Since one of the biggest failings of students is an inability to follow a logical plan of development in their writing, it makes sense to start with form and structure first. But because these paradigms can also serve as explicit models of invention, students will be learning discovery procedures at the same time that they are learning something about form.

The second implication is that a paradigmatic approach to the essay can provide the student with a stock of flexible forms. These forms (or paradigms) are analogous to the transformational linguists's phrase structures. They represent the writer's rhetorical competence. The flexibility of these patterns is a result of the possibility of an infinite number of transformations upon the basic design. Paradigms, then, are conventional enough to give writers some control over their material, yet flexible enough to allow for imagination and invention. . . .

The third implication is that no longer should we tell students that the best plan in writing an essay is to first discover ideas, then put these ideas into a traditional outline, and then select an appropriate style. The mind does not follow one set of mental processes in getting ideas, another in arranging these ideas, and a third in selecting an appropriate style.

A fourth implication is that a paradigmatic approach to the essay may help students grasp the structure of the main ideas in materials that they read. Following the processes of thought in the writing of others is analogous to recreating the process of composition in their own minds. For in analyzing an essay, students must assimilate the formal characteristics of the writing into their own mental structures.

The final implication is that a paradigmatic view of the composing process is *developmental*. This means that no longer should teachers of composition conceive of themselves too narrowly as purveyors of superficial skills. Rather they should think of their roles more properly as that of facilitators in the important task of helping students to develop mental abilities that will govern much of what they do in later life. Acquiring, understanding, and using paradigms can help them to ascend to higher levels of linguistic and conceptual development.

Notes

[1] See, for example: Edward P. J. Corbett, "A Survey of Rhetoric," in *Classical Rhetoric for the Modern Student* (New York: Oxford University Press, 1965), pp. 535-568; Richard C. Jebb, "Rhetoric" in *Encyclopaedia Britannica*, 11th ed., XXIII, 233-37; Thomas O. Sloan, "Rhetoric," in *Encyclopaedia Britannica*, 15 (1974), 798-805; and Lester Thonssen, A. Craig Baird, and Waldo W. Braden, *Speech Criticism*, 2nd ed. (New York: Ronald Press, 1970), pp. 33-156.

[2] Richard E. Young, Alton L. Becker, and Kenneth L. Pike, *Rhetoric: Discovery and Change* (New York: Harcourt, Brace & World, Inc., 1970), p. 5.

[3] Most prominent of the 19th century theorists who attempted to broaden the range of discourse from persuasion to include other modes were: Alexander Bain, *English Composition and Rhetoric*, American Edition, Revised (New York: D. Appleton and Co., 1890); William B. Cairns, *The Forms of Discourse* (Boston: Ginn and Co., 1896); for a bibliographical survey of the forms of discourse, see: Frank J. D'Angelo, "Modes of Discourse," in *Teaching Composition: 10 Bibliographical Essays*, ed. Gary Tate (Fort Worth: Texas Christian University Press, 1976), pp. 111-135.

[4] See, for example, Walter J. Ong's comments on the relationships that exist among writing, rhetoric, and consciousness in *Rhetoric, Romance, and Technology* (Ithaca and London: Cornell University Press, 1971), pp. 2, 4, 9-24.

[5] Frank J. D'Angelo, *A Conceptual Theory of Rhetoric* (Cambridge, MA: Winthrop Publishers, Inc., 1975); *Process and Thought in Composition* (Cambridge, MA: Winthrop Publishers, Inc., 1977); Richard L. Larson, "Invention Once More: A Role for Rhetorical Analysis," *College English*, 32 (March 1971), 668-672; "Toward a Linear Rhetoric of the Essay," *College Composition and Communication*, 22 (May 1971), 140-146; W. Ross Winterowd, "The Grammar of Coherence," *College English*, 31 (May 1970), 828-35.

[6] Bertrand Russell, "Prologue, 'What I Have Lived For'," *The Autobiography of Bertrand Russell* (Boston: Little, Brown and Co., 1951), pp. 3, 4. I have used this model in a different context for a different purpose in *Process and Thought in Composition* (Cambridge, MA: Winthrop Publishers, Inc., 1977), pp. 72-79.

Intentionality in the Writing Process:
A Case Study

C. H. KNOBLAUCH

Everyone agrees that a writer's sense of purpose usefully directs choices about what to say and where and how to say it. Typically, the writer strives to coordinate that sense with an estimate of the needs and expectations of some intended reader in order to convey effective assertions in a coherent sequence. The coordination is most evident in writing that Britton would locate in the "transactional" range, where communication is an explicit goal.[1] But even in "poetic" or "literary" discourse, the writer does not forsake all audience awareness (recall Robert Lowell's remark that he wrote poems for himself and a few friends). Literary writing usually assumes, and either honors or strategically violates, formal expectations in readers which partly condition their responses.[2] It may be that only the most private and idiosyncratic writing remains truly unconscious of the public dimension which ordinarily helps to shape a writer's behavior.

Some researchers consider the sense of purpose, or more exactly, its interaction with an estimate of reader-response, as the cornerstone of any comprehensive theory of discourse. James Kinneavy, most notably, insists that "purpose . . . is all important. The aim of a discourse determines everything else in the process of discourse." He adds that "both a theory of language and a theory of discourse . . . should be crowned with a viable framework of the uses of language."[3] Several such frameworks have recently been advanced. Britton, for instance, ranges purposes along transactional, expressive, and poetic spectra, differentiating texts according to their perceived functions, whether as means to ends or as ends in themselves. Kinneavy orders intentions within four discrete categories: expressive, literary, persuasive, and referential.[4] Richard Lloyd-Jones, in connection with the theory of primary trait scoring, has suggested a model comprised of explanatory, persuasive, and expressive modes.[5] There are still others, with similarly overlapping categories and terminology. All proceed from the same controlling assumption, which James Moffett has stated precisely: "Beneath the content of every message is intent. And form embodies that intent. Intuitively or not, an author chooses his techniques according to his meaning."[6]

College Composition and Communication, 31 (May 1980), pp. 153-159. Copyright © 1980 by the National Council of Teachers of English. Reprinted by permission of the publisher and the author.

The effort to taxonomize discourse according to purpose and reader-expectation has, of course, ancient origins. Aristotle distinguished logical, rhetorical, and poetic statements on the basis of subject, intention, and the requirements of a situation. His categorizing of speeches as deliberative, forensic, and epideictic may differ in scope from the work of Britton or Kinneavy or I. A. Richards, but it does not differ in aspiration or methodological focus. The value of the approach is evident: it seeks to emphasize the motives that animate discourse, not merely its formal constraints, the context of writing as a human behavior rather than merely text-in-itself as a structure of technical features. But these taxonomizing efforts, from Aristotle to the present, share a deficiency as well. As Lee Odell has recently pointed out, their perceptions of discourse derive from retrospective analysis, from surveys of the products of composing rather than the processes.[7] As a consequence, they encourage a static, monolithic view of such concepts as "purpose" and "reader," oversimplifying them after the fact in a way that fails to preserve the vitality of their function in actual composing.

This needs explaining. Certainly, it would be naive to insist triumphantly on what everyone already takes for granted, that a writer may be responding to many purposes, some broad and open to analysis, others deeply personal and unpredictable. It is also naive to assume that the reduction of these purposes to certain general types in Kinneavy or Britton implies an ignorance of that complexity. Britton, for one, concedes the potential diversity of motives for writing, but points out that methodological necessity limits concern "to what is *typical* within the conventions that govern discourse."[8] The inadequacy lies, not in oversimplification as such, which is inevitable, but in the blurring of an important distinction between the kinds of purposes that actually initiate discourse and those that merely define categories in which completed discourse may be located. Kinneavy's range, for example, does not derive from the observation of how writers behave but from the analysis of a sample of texts. His approach is that of traditional literary criticism, adequate for describing and labelling textual features but inadequate for explaining the rhetorical decisions that account for them. The discrimination of "persuasive" and "referential" intentions is merely generic, yielding broad categories in which to group statements that share similiar characteristics. Writers do not look to such lofty purposes as functional support for their choice-making; that is, they do not set out to "be referential" except in an unhelpfully general way.

The sense of purpose that actually shapes strategy is something more concrete, more immediate, and less encompassing: it is not generic but operational. Generic purposes are ideal and therefore simple: most taxonomies include only three or four. Operational purposes are specific to real situations and often quite complex. Indeed, composing typically entails responding to multiple purposes, the interaction of which motivates and shapes performance. James McCrimmon has suggested the difference: "By 'purpose' we mean the controlling decisions a writer makes when he determines what he wants to do and how he wants to do it. We do *not* mean anything so general as deciding to 'inform,' 'persuade,' or 'amuse,' since these terms can mean so many different things that they give almost no help."[9]

Kinneavy explicitly rejects the notion of operational purpose by invoking the intentional and affective fallacies, in which the "actual" intent of a discourse is mistakenly assumed to be equivalent to the intent of its author or its impact on some intended reader. He argues that neither encoder nor decoder can reliably characterize actual intent, so that "it seems better to find the aim which is embodied in the text itself."[10] Possibly, if "text itself" were as important in composition theory and teaching as it is in literary criticism, Kinneavy would have a point. And, to be sure, as long as mere taxonomizing is the goal, the features of completed discourses are more dependably accessible to analysis than their creators' complex motives. But in composition theory, writers' behaviors and what stimulates them are at least as valuable as generated texts. Indeed, in writing courses those behaviors are primary, since one concern is to reduce disparities between what writers set out to do and what their completed discourses actually achieve. The composer's own sense of purpose, however tentatively conceived or even misapprehended, is a crucial reference for measuring writing effectiveness. Kinneavy's objections notwithstanding, therefore, a comprehensive theory of discourse must account for operational purposes if it is to achieve more than a static cataloguing of documents.

A recent practical experience underlies my argument. For the past 14 months I have served as a communications advisor with a large, New York-based consulting agency specializing in business management, systems planning, and computer software. The firm's success depends significantly on the effectiveness of its writing, which can be readily defined as transactional or referential-persuasive. Executives write proposals within competitive-bidding situations and win or lose contracts from businesses and corporations depending on the pertinence and persuasiveness of their recommendations. I have interviewed some 250 executives on three levels within the firm, partner, manager, and staff, and have evaluated as many proposals. The results make an interesting case study supporting my distinction of generic and operational perceptions of intentionality.

These writers set out to achieve conflicting purposes simultaneously while responding to the needs of several, quite different, intended readers, each with different expectations of the writing. One evident purpose, for example, is to sell a service, to put the company's expertise in the best possible light. In order to accomplish this objective, proposal-writers must impress prospective clients with the firm's understanding of their business problems. The writer's knowledge and credentials must be expressed in the engaging, informal language of persuasive discourse. It would be inadequate to browbeat a client with the technical jargon of computer science, although the writer's skill lies chiefly in this area and although the client's problems will be approached through systems analysis. The experienced writer knows that accuracy is futile in the absence of comprehension, that intricately reasoned arguments do not in themselves guarantee successful communication and the winning of a contract. One measure of the firm's commitment to translating their expertise into an unintimidating, client-focused language is their enthusiastic advocacy, rightly or wrongly, of Robert Gunning's "Fog Index,"[11] which they apply quite rigorously in their internal evaluation of documents going out to customers.

If this process of translation were the proposal-writer's only concern, the task would be complicated enough. But it is not. Another purpose, as important as the first, is to define a contractual obligation between firm and client, one which is sufficiently detailed to withstand a court test if the work is not done to the client's satisfaction. If this purpose is to be served, the language of the proposal must have an appropriate technical accuracy so that the firm's diagnosis of business problems and its recommended solutions are coherent to professional systems analyst and client alike, with none of the ambiguities that a looser language might encourage, for all its persuasive advantages. A rather complex rhetorical situation results: the writer seeks to mediate between two opposed communicative purposes, making choices about what to say and where and how to say it according to the dominant pressure of one motive or the other at different times. Usually, a proposal begins with a paragraph that establishes contact with the client and an agreeable atmosphere for the more technical discussion to follow: "Thank you for inviting us to submit this proposal to assist you in developing a General Ledger functional design . . . "; or "We very much enjoyed our recent meetings with you to discuss the development of auditor-oriented documentation for your XYZ system . . . " The writing will grow more neutral in tone and complex in language, but will never entirely lose sight of the needs of the non-specialist client.

It is accurate, then, but not very helpful, to describe proposals as transactional in aim. The fact is, operational purposes, such as the two mentioned above, dictate rhetorical choices, while the generic purpose that Britton or Kinneavy might describe is plainly irrelevant as a motivating agency in the writing. Identifying operational purposes is, therefore, a valid, indeed essential, goal in company writing seminars, but not the static designation of referential versus persuasive modes. I might add that the analysis of this kind of rhetorical problem, the conflict between selling a service and making a contract within the same statement, is a more fruitful activity in business and technical writing courses than the arid discrimination of superficial constraints such as the form of a business letter.

But to continue: the flux of authorial intentions in this writing is not exhausted in the two communicative motives just described. Other, more "expressive" concerns are also at stake and have a determinable impact on strategy. For example, since staff-level writers' promotions depend partly on managers' judgments of their effectiveness, and managers' promotions depend similarly on partners' judgments, they will wish to impress superiors through the skill of their verbal performances—typically measured in terms of the amount of praise or criticism the writing attracts. Extensive review goes on at each level, staff through partner, before a proposal is passed to a client, and this review becomes intolerably costly and time-consuming if a document is so poorly prepared at the start that it requires major rewriting at each later stage. Hence, writers know that a favorable internal reception is at least as important as communicating to a client: they are revealing themselves as bright, capable, promotable people. In fact, the pressure to create a beneficial self-portrait will sometimes override the concern for effective communication, depending on how writers perceive the expectations of their superiors. Despite the firm's effort to recommend simplicity and directness, it has not yet managed to convince junior staff members that insinuating their technical expertise (through inflated style and trade jargon) is really less important than addressing a client's needs. These writers sometimes equate simple language with naive thinking, regarding it as inadequate to their professional self-image and potentially damaging to their hopes for promotion. The impact of an "expressive" purpose on choice-making is substantial in this instance, though it is also, from a stylistic point of view, unfortunate.

Just as these compound purposes interact to direct the writer's choices, so the needs of diverse readers affect strategy as well. Two readers have already been mentioned, the client and the writer's own superior. But these are over-simplified. In fact, more than one client-reader will react to the proposal and more than one internal reader will review it. The writer knows that the senior executive who decides whether or not to approve the engagement (and its costs) will ordinarily not be the same person, for instance, a computerized-records specialist, who will actually cooperate on the project. Often, therefore, a proposal will contain a cover letter pertinent to the concerns of the chairman of the board, followed by appendices with detailed information appropriate for the specialist employee. Other times, though it is a more problematic alternative, different sections of a single document will emphasize the concerns of one reader or the other. Meanwhile, the writer is also aware that several internal reviews can be expected and that different readers will concern themselves with different features of the text. A manager may be more interested in its technical accuracy, while a partner will concentrate on its legal implications or its selling effectiveness. Obviously, the writer cannot accommodate all the quirks of these anticipated readers, but an awareness of their presence and their different needs nonetheless affects rhetorical choices. In my seminars with these executives, we have frequently crawled word-by-word through a document in order to evaluate its impact on one or another client or internal reader. For example, in a case where the client has not yet accepted an engagement, the question often arises whether the proposal should be written conditionally: "We *would* perform the following tasks . . . " or in the future: "We *will* perform . . . " The future is presumptuous but more energetic; the conditional is more accurate but sounds indecisive. How will one reader or another respond?

Some special complexities of intention and response can also arise: for instance, when the client is persuaded that, say, zero-based budgeting is the answer to a problem while the consultants have determined that management auditing would be preferable. To what extent should the client be accommodated and to what extent (and in what manner) disabused? Another case is the client who is determined to purchase a computer system that is more elaborate and expensive than the company requires, while the consulting firm's own, much cheaper software package is more appropriate. The writer must steer a hazardous course between potential accusations of self-interest in one direction and dishonesty in another. In such circumstances, ethical as well as legal considerations complicate the rhetorical environment and the writer's sense of purpose.

It may be that the fascinating difficulties these business writers face exaggerate the conditions that an "ordinary" writer experiences. But I would argue that they are not idiosyncratic, that the process of mediating among conflicting purposes and the anticipated needs of more than one reader is a typical feature of composing, the recognition of which can have valuable research and pedagogical implications. Odell has suggested that we must further investigate the reasons writers give for the choices they make, noting that students, sometimes, "seem to be working toward contradictory purposes or establishing different speaker-audience relationships within what would appear to be a single writing task."[12] It seems to me that this rhetorical adjustment to competing purposes is normal. But Odell is surely right to imply that we teachers often set up presumably simple exercises that are actually loaded with hidden problems of intentionality and reader-focus that we neither control in advance nor consider during evaluation. Probably, several purposes intrude with sufficient intensity in classroom writing to deserve notice, among them these: (1) solving a problem or performing a task according to the instructor's directions and anticipating that instructor's expectations; (2) impressing (or refusing to impress) the instructor; (3) receiving an acceptable grade (that is, acceptable to the student, not necessarily a high grade); (4) revealing or concealing real attitudes, opinions, and beliefs; (5) creating or sustaining an acceptable self-image; (6) receiving peer approval or avoiding peer disapproval. The point is, even a classroom exercise is a writing situation, however contrived, and activates the writer's entire range of expressive behaviors, not merely the ones a teacher has specified in the assignment or has decided to emphasize in the evaluation.

Perhaps we deceive ourselves if we suppose that the generic purposes which may be theoretically adequate for a taxonomy of discourses are also pedagogically useful to initiate writing or to assess its effectiveness. A theory of discourse that presumes to offer adequate conceptual bases for teaching and scholarship alike must be able to accommodate an operational perception of intentionality as well as the generic; that is, its focus ought to be behavioral as well as textual. The elementary case study I have offered suggests the complexity, but also the definability, of operational purposes, and I believe that this line of inquiry deserves extension. Odell has submitted some procedures that can guide additional research, including, in the case of academic writing, a set of questions designed to probe the motives that students bring to composing. The same questions could be adapted to many different writers and situations: What reasons do the writers offer for their choices? Do they justify those choices with reference to some "basic purpose"? What other justifications do they give? Does current theory adequately anticipate their explanations? Do the explanations vary with the kind of task involved or according to the competence of a particular writer?[13] The accumulation and analysis of answers to such questions may eventually lead to significant advances in both theory and pedagogy: a deeper awareness of how and why writers behave as they do, and a better understanding of how to develop those behaviors advantageously in the classroom.

Notes

[1] See James Britton, *Language and Learning* (London: Penguin Books, 1970), p. 174.

[2] For an interesting account of the role that readers' formal expectations played in conditioning one writer's behavior, see Paul Fussell, *Samuel Johnson and the Life of Writing* (New York: Harcourt Brace Jovanovich, 1971).

[3] James L. Kinneavy, *A Theory of Discourse* (Englewood Cliffs, NJ: Prentice-Hall, 1971), p. 48, p. 38.

[4] See Richard Lloyd-Jones, "Primary Trait Scoring," in Charles R. Cooper and Lee Odell, eds., *Evaluating Writing: Describing, Measuring, Judging* (Urbana, IL: NCTE, 1978), p. 39.

[5] See Kinneavy, *passim*.

[6] James Moffett, *Teaching the Universe of Discourse* (Boston: Houghton Mifflin, 1968), p. 145.

[7] See Lee Odell, "Teachers of Composition and Needed Research in Discourse Theory," *CCC*, 30 (February 1979), 39-45.

[8] James Britton, "The Composing Processes and the Functions of Writing," in Charles R. Cooper and Lee Odell, eds., *Research on Composing: Points of Departure* (Urbana, IL: NCTE, 1978), p. 16.

[9] James McCrimmon, *Writing with a Purpose* (Boston: Houghton Mifflin, 1973) p. 8.

[10] Kinneavy, p. 49.

[11] See Robert Gunning, *The Technique of Clear Writing* (New York: McGraw-Hill, 1952).

[12] Odell, p. 41.

[13] Odell, pp. 40-41.

PART FIVE

The Pedagogy of Composition:
From Classical Rhetoric to Current Practice

"By and large, we who preside over the composition courses have refused to solve the problem of teaching, or have failed to solve it and some even to see that there is a problem."

Francis Christensen

For a long time the composition curriculum has operated on the assumption that young people already "know" how to write, and that the teacher's primary job is to make assignments. This idea, which has been called "the vitalist assumption" by Richard E. Young, for many years prevented genuine progress in our understanding of how to teach and learn the skill of writing. Here is the way Young describes it in his essay on invention in Gary Tate's *Teaching Composition: 10 Bibliographical Essays*:

> For some time the composition teacher has struggled with a dilemma, a false one but nevertheless capable of impeding the development of more adequate theories and pedagogies. Vitalist assumptions, which have dominated our thinking about the composing process since Coleridge, appear to be inconsistent with the rational processes and formal procedures required by an art of invention. Vitalism leads to a view of writing ability as a knack and to a repudiation of the possibility of teaching the composing process; composition tends to dwindle into an art of editing. [pp. 20-21]

Now that the vitalist assumption has been widely discredited, the value of pedagogy in the composition curriculum has become apparent. There is an unstated but widespread belief in the profession that teachers can make a difference in the writing of their students, providing those teachers understand the nature of the composing process and have at their disposal a variety of teaching techniques and strategies. The purpose of this section is to provide an overview of some of those techniques and strategies. Obviously, all the essays ever written about composition imply a pedagogy of some kind. What makes this section distinct is that each essay here illustrates a specific approach or technique.

One of the findings growing out of the National Writing Project summer institutes is that teaching techniques are not as grade-level specific as we previously thought. Elementary, secondary, and college teachers, returning home after the summer institutes, found that techniques used by a colleague could be successfully adapted at a different grade level. For example, the technique of using models is well-known at the college level, but with a slight change in the model itself the same technique can also be used in the elementary grades. For this reason, the essays in this section are not grouped according to grade level. Almost all the techniques and approaches described here are useful across the curriculum; it is left to the ingenuity of the individual teacher to make the application to his or her classroom.

The first three essays are rooted in the fertile tradition of classical rhetoric, a field of inquiry which provides the theoretical origins for the teaching of composition. Drawing from a lifetime of experience as teacher and writer, Marcus Fabius Quintilian uses the general technique of *advice* to describe the road to eloquence. Those readers who have never encountered Quintilian will be astonished at the freshness and wisdom of this splendid teacher's insight into the composing process. Quintilian wrote the work about 93 A.D., after he had retired from a successful career as teacher of rhetoric in Rome. Even though rhetoric at that time included public speaking and training for the practice of law, and even though the mechanical means of writing were primitive compared to our own, Quintilian nevertheless has the highest praise for the written word: "It is the pen which at once brings the most labor and most profit. [It is] the best producer and teacher of eloquence." Even though nineteen centuries separate us, his advice still rings true today. For centuries his grand perspective of rhetoric and education, his thorough scholarship, and his dedication to the highest ideals of teaching have inspired teachers throughout the world.

In "The Theory and Practice of Imitation in Classical Rhetoric," Edward P. J. Corbett convincingly demonstrates the effectiveness of using *models* in the learning process. The author traces the history of this time-honored technique and, most important, shows how it can be related to the creative urge. Some of the most powerful personal writing I have seen has been inspired by this technique. Again, drawing from the resources of classical rhetoric, Gayle B. Price traces the history and practice of keeping a *journal*. A variety of entries can be placed in the commonplace book—observations, impressions, favorite quotations, all of which can be used in the writing process.

The rationale for teaching a lesson in *style* appears in "Mending the Fragmented Free Modifier" by Muriel Harris. Drawing on the work of Kline and Memering and of Christensen, Harris argues that the minor sentence (in contrast to the broken sentence) often is a mispunctuated final free modifier. Rather than critically mark such constructions as fragments, English teachers should see them as opportunities for teaching about style; they should "let the natural growth of late blooming structures occur and not stamp out every budding shoot which doesn't instantly appear in full flower."

In describing the training of peer tutors, Leonard Podis speaks of the role of the *writing lab* in the composition curriculum. Teachers/tutors are learners too, argues Podis. As our students learn to write, we too become involved in a process of growth, not just in coming to know our subject but in deepening our awareness of the dynamics of the pupil-teacher relationship. The idea of growth is also implicit in *a developmental approach* described by Barry Kroll. Kroll looks to the philosophy of John Dewey and the research of Jean Piaget for the theoretical bases of his approach. And whereas Kroll emphasizes social interaction in a group setting, Donald M. Murray sees a one-to-one student-teacher *conference* as one way of teaching composition. Murray describes himself as a "counter puncher . . . , circling my students, waiting, trying to shut up—it isn't easy—trying not to interfere with their learning, waiting until they're learned something so I can show them what they've learned." From between the lines of Murray's work emerges a picture of someone who is both tough and compassionate, someone who, like Podis and Kroll, understands that growth is the central idea in the teaching of writing.

In the concluding piece in this section, Flower and Hayes argue that learning to write should be seen as a *problem-solving* activity; "as a thinking problem, rather than an arrangement problem," as they put it. Several original insights appear here which both teachers and writers will find valuable. For example, the authors have coined terms which faithfully reflect the realities of the composing process: "nutshell your ideas and teach them," they suggest, "tree your ideas," "find a rich bit" (key word or key concept). The tree diagrams included here provide a dynamic, working picture of the process of arrangement—*and* invention.

The sampling in this section is representative of current thinking about the teaching of composition. Above all, it represents the dynamisim and diversity occurring in the discipline at the present time.

from *Institutio Oratoria*

MARCUS FABIUS QUINTILIAN
(Book X, iii-iv)

Such are the aids which we may derive from external sources; as regards those which we must supply for ourselves, it is the pen which brings at once the most labour and the most profit. Cicero is fully justified in describing it as the best producer and teacher of eloquence, and it may be noted that in the *de Oratore* he supports his own judgment by the authority of Lucius Crassus, in whose mouth he places this remark. We must therefore write as much as possible and with the utmost care. For as deep ploughing makes the soil more fertile for the production and support of crops, so, if we improve our minds by something more than mere superficial study, we shall produce a richer growth of knowledge and shall retain it with greater accuracy. For without the consciousness of such preliminary study our powers of speaking extempore will give us nothing but an empty flow of words, springing from the lips and not from the brain. It is in writing that eloquence has its roots and foundations, it is writing that provides that holy of holies where the wealth of oratory is stored and whence it is produced to meet the demands of sudden emergencies. It is of the first importance that we should develop such strength as will not faint under the toil of forensic strife nor be exhausted by continual use. For it is an ordinance of nature that nothing great can be achieved in a moment, and that all the fairest tasks are attended with difficulty, while on births as well she has imposed this law, that the larger the animal, the longer should be the period of gestation.

There are, however, two questions which present themselves in this connexion, namely, what should be our method and what the subjects on which we write, and I propose to treat them in this order. At first, our pen must be slow yet sure: we must search for what is best and refuse to give a joyful welcome to every thought the moment that it presents itself; we must first criticise the fruits of our imagination, and then, once approved, arrange them with care. For we must select both thoughts and words and weigh them one by one. This done, we must consider the order in which they should be placed, and must examine all the possible varieties of rhythm, refusing neces-

Reprinted by permission of the publishers and the Loeb Classical Library from Quintilian, *Institutio Oratoria*, Vol. 4, translated by H. E. Butler, Cambridge, MA: Harvard University Press, 1922.

sarily to place each word in the order in which it occurs to us. In order to do this with the utmost care, we must frequently revise what we have just written. For beside the fact that thus we secure a better connexion between what follows and what precedes, the warmth of thought which has cooled down while we were writing is revived anew, and gathers fresh impetus from going over the ground again. We may compare this process with what occurs in jumping matches. The competitors take a longer run and go at full speed to clear the distance which they aim at covering; similarly, in throwing the javelin, we draw back our arms, and in archery pull back the bow-string to propel the shaft. At times, however, we may spread our sails before the favouring breeze, but we must beware that this indulgence does not lead us into error. For we love all the offspring of our thought at the moment of their birth; were that not so, we should never commit them to writing. But we must give them a critical revision, and go carefully over any passage where we have reason to regard our fluency with suspicion. It is thus, we are told, that Sallust wrote, and certainly his works give clear evidence of the labour which he expended on them. Again, we learn from Varius that Virgil composed but a very small number of verses every day. It is true that with orators the case is somewhat different, and it is for this reason that I enjoin such lowness of speed and such anxious care at the outset. For the first aim which we must fix in our minds and insist on carrying into execution is to write as well as possible; speed will come with practice. Gradually thoughts will suggest themselves with increasing readiness, the words will answer to our call and rhythmical arrangement will follow, till everything will be found fulfilling its proper function as in a well-ordered household. The sum of the whole matter is this: write quickly and you will never write well, write well and you will soon write quickly. But it is just when we have acquired this facility that we must pause awhile to look ahead and, if I may use the metaphor, curb the horses that would run away with us. This will not delay our progress so much as lend us fresh vigor. For I do not think that those who have acquired a certain power in writing should be condemned to the barren pains of false self-criticism. How can anyone fulfil his duties as an advocate if he wastes his time putting unnecessary finish on each portion of his pleadings? There are some who are never satisfied. They wish to change everything they have written and to put it in other words. They are a diffident folk, and deserve but ill of their own talents, who think it a mark of precision to cast obstacles in the way of their own writing. Nor is it easy to say which are the most serious offenders, those who are satisfied with everything or those who are satisfied with nothing that they write. For it is of common occurrence with young men, however talented they may be, to waste their gifts by superfluous elaboration, and to sink into silence through an excessive desire to speak well. I remember in this connexion a story that Julius Secundus, my contemporary, and, as is well known, my very dear friend, a man with remarkable powers of eloquence, but with an infinite passion for precision, told me of the words once used to him by his uncle, Julius Florus, the leading orator of Gaul, for it was there that he practised, a man eloquent as but few have ever been, and worthy of his nephew. He once noticed that Secundus, who was still a student, was looking depressed, and asked him the meaning of his frowns. The youth made no concealment of the reason: he had been working for three days, and had been unable, in spite of all his efforts, to devise an exordium for the theme which he had been given to write, with the result that he was not only vexed over his immediate difficulty, but had lost all hope of future success. Florus smiled and said, "Do you really want to speak better than you can?" There lies the truth of the whole matter. We must aim at speaking as well as we can, but must not try to speak better than our nature will permit. For to make any real advance we need study, not self-accusation. And it is not merely practice that will enable us to write at greater length and with increased fluency, although doubtless practice is most important. We need judgement as well. So long as we do not lie back with eyes turned up to the ceiling, trying to fire our imagination by muttering to ourselves, in the hope that something will present itself, but turn our thoughts to consider what the circumstances of the case demand, what suits the characters involved, what is the nature of the occasion and the temper of the judge, we shall acquire the power of writing by rational means. It is thus that nature herself bids us begin and pursue our studies once well begun. For most points are of a definite character and, if we keep our eyes open, will spontaneously present themselves. That is the reason why peasants and uneducated persons do not beat about the bush to discover with what they should begin, and our hesitation is all the more shameful if it is simply the result of education. We must not, therefore, persist in thinking that what is hard to find is necessarily best; for, if it seems to us that there is nothing to be said except that which we are unable to find, we must say nothing at all. On the other hand, there is a fault which is precisely the opposite of this, into which those fall who insist on first making a rapid draft of their subject with the utmost speed of which their pen is capable, and write in the heat and impulse of the moment. They call this their rough copy. They then revise what they have written, and arrange their hasty outpourings. But while the words and the rhythm may be corrected, the matter is still marked by the superficiality resulting from the speed with which it was thrown together. The more correct method is, therefore, to exercise care from the very beginning, and to form the work from the outset in such a manner that it merely requires to be chiselled into shape, not fashioned anew. Sometimes, however, we must follow the stream of our emotions, since their warmth will give us more than any diligence can secure.

The condemnation which I have passed on such carelessness in writing will make it pretty clear what my views are on the luxury of dictation which is now so fashionable. For, when we write, however great our speed, the fact that the hand cannot follow the rapidity of our thoughts gives us time to think, whereas the presence of our amanuensis hurries us on, and at times we feel ashamed to hesitate or pause, or make some alteration, as though we were afraid to display such weakness before a witness. As a result our language tends not merely to be haphazard and formless, but in our desire to produce a continuous flow we let slip positive improprieties of diction, which show neither the precision of the writer nor the impetuosity of the speaker. Again, if the amanuensis is a slow writer, or lacking in intelligence, he becomes a stumbling-block, our speed is checked, and the thread of our ideas is interrupted by the delay or even perhaps by the loss of temper to which it gives rise. Moreover, the gestures which accompany strong feeling, and sometimes even serve to stimulate the mind, the waving of the hand, the contraction of the brow, the occasional striking of forehead or side, and those which Persius notes when he describes a trivial style as one that

"Thumps not the desk nor smacks of bitten nails,"

all these become ridiculous, unless we are alone. Finally, we come to the most important consideration of all, that the advantages of privacy are lost when we dictate. Everyone, however, will agree that the absence of company and deep silence are most conducive to writing, though I would not go so far as to concur in the opinion of those who think woods and groves make the most suitable localities for the purpose, on the ground that the freedom of the sky and the charm of the surroundings produce sublimity of thought and wealth of inspiration. Personally I regard such an environment as a pleasant luxury rather than a stimulus to study. For whatever causes us delight, must necessarily distract us from the concentration due to our work. The mind cannot devote its undivided and sincere attention to a number of things at the same time, and wherever it turns its gaze it must cease to contemplate its appointed task. Therefore, the charm of the woods, the gliding of the stream, the breeze that murmurs in the branches, the song of birds, and the very freedom with which our eyes may range, are mere distractions, and in my opinion the pleasure which they excite is more likely to relax than to concentrate our attention. Demosthenes took a wiser view; for he would retire to a place[1] where no voice was to be heard, and no prospect greeted the sight, for fear that his eyes might force his mind to neglect its duty. Therefore, let the burner of the midnight oil seclude himself in the silence of the night, within closed doors, with but a solitary lamp to light his labours. But for every kind of study, and more especially for night work, good health and its chief source, simple living, are essential; for we have fallen into the habit of devoting to relentless labour the hour which nature has appointed for rest and relaxation. From those hours we must take only such time as is superfluous for sleep, and will not be missed. For fatigue will make us careless in writing, and the hours of daylight are amply sufficient for one who has no other distractions. It is only the busy man who is driven to encroach on the hours of darkness. Nevertheless, night work, so long as we come to it fresh and untired, provides by far the best form of privacy.

But although silence and seclusion and absolute freedom of mind are devoutly to be desired, they are not always within our power to attain. Consequently we must not fling aside our book at once, if disturbed by some noise, and lament that we have lost a day: on the contrary, we must make a firm stand against such inconveniences, and train ourselves to concentrate our thoughts as to rise superior to all impediments to study. If only you direct all your attention to the work which you have in hand, no sight or sound will ever penetrate to your mind. If even casual thoughts often occupy us to such an extent that we do not see passers-by, or even stray from our path, surely we can obtain the same result by the exercise of our will. We must not give way to pretexts for sloth. For unless we make up our mind that we must be fresh, cheerful and free from all other care when we approach our studies, we shall always find some excuse for idleness. Therefore, whether we be in a crowd, on a journey, or even at some festive gathering, our thoughts should always have some inner sanctuary of their own to which they may retire. Otherwise what shall we do when we are suddenly called upon to deliver a set speech in the midst of the forum, with lawsuits in progress on every side, and with the sound of quarrels and even casual outcries in our ears, if we need absolute privacy to discover the thoughts which we jot down upon our tablets? It was for this reason that Demosthenes, the passionate lover of seclusion, used to study on the seashore amid the roar of the breakers that they might teach him not to be unnerved by the uproar of the public assembly.

There are also certain minor details which deserve our attention, for there is nothing too minute for the student It is best to write on wax owing to the facility which it offers for erasure, though weak sight may make it desirable to employ parchment by preference. The latter, however, although of assistance to the eye, delays the hand and interrupts the stream of thought owing to the frequency with which the pen has to be supplied with ink. But whichever we employ, we must leave blank pages that we may be free to make additions when we will. For lack of space at times gives rise to a reluctance to make corrections, or, at any rate, is liable to cause confusion when new matter is inserted. The wax tablets should not be unduly wide; for I have known a young and over-zealous student write his compositions at undue length, because he measured them by the number of lines, a fault which persisted, in spite of frequent admonition, until his tablets were changed, when it disappeared. Space must also be left for jotting down the thoughts which occur to the writer out of due order, that is to say, which refer to subjects other than those in hand. For sometimes the most admirable thoughts break in upon us which cannot be inserted in what we are writing, but which, on the other hand, it is unsafe to put by, since they are at times forgotten, and at times cling to the memory so persistently as to divert us from some other line of thought. They are, therefore, best kept in store.

The next point which we have to consider is the correction of our work, which is by far the most useful portion of our study: for there is good reason for the view that erasure is quite as important a function of the pen as actual writing. Correction takes the form of addition, excision and alteration. But it is a comparatively simple and easy task to decide what is to be added or excised. On the other hand, to prune what is turgid, to elevate what is mean, to repress exuberance, arrange what is disorderly, introduce rhythm where it is lacking, and modify it where it is too emphatic, involves a two-fold labour. For we have to condemn what had previously satisfied us and discover what had escaped our notice. There can be no doubt that the best method of correction is to put aside what we have written for a certain time, so that when we return to it after an interval it will have the air of novelty and of being another's handiwork; for thus we may prevent ourselves from regarding our writings with all the affection that we lavish on a newborn child. But this is not always possible, especially in the case of an orator who most frequently has to write for immediate use, while some limit, after all, must be set to correction. For there are some who return to everything they write with the presumption that it is full of faults and, assuming that a first draft must necessarily be incorrect, think every change an improvement and make some alteration as often as they have the manuscript in their hands: they are, in fact, like doctors who use the knife even where the flesh is perfectly healthy. The result of their critical activities is that the finished work is full of scars, bloodless, and all the worse for their anxious care. No! let there be something in all our writing which, if it does not actually please us, at least passes muster, so that the file may only polish our work, not wear it away. There must also be a limit to the time which we spend on its revision. For the fact that Cinna[2] took nine years to write his Smyrna, and that Isocrates required ten years, at the lowest estimate, to complete his Panegyric does not concern the orator, whose assistance will be of no use, if it is so long delayed.

Notes

[1] An underground room.
[2] C. Helvius Cinna, the friend of Catullus. The Smyrna was a short but exceptionally obscure and learned epic.

The Theory and Practice of Imitation in Classical Rhetoric

EDWARD P. J. CORBETT

The first point that needs to be made in a paper about the theory and practice of imitation in classical rhetoric is that the term *imitation* had a variety of meanings in antiquity. In his article "Literary Criticism and the Concept of Imitation in Antiquity,"[1] Richard McKeon has carefully and elaborately discriminated five distinct meanings of *imitation* in classical theory. The three meanings of *mimesis* most familiar to teachers of English are (1) the Platonic notion of an image-making faculty which produces extensions of ideal truth in the phenomenal world, (2) the Aristotelian notion of the representation of human actions, and (3) the rhetorical notion of copying, aping, simulating, emulating models. Fascinating as it would be to trace out the evolutions and the interrelationships of these concepts of imitation, I will confine myself in this paper to exploring the theory and practice of imitation in the rhetorician's sense of emulating models.

Curiously enough, Aristotle, who wrote a major work in rhetoric, did not treat of imitation in the sense of emulating successful practitioners of an art. In Chapter 4 of his *Poetics*, he did mention that man is the most imitative of all creatures, that he learns at first by imitation, and that he takes a natural delight in the contemplation of works of imitation. Moreover, as McKeon has reminded us,[2] Aristotle frequently made the distinction in his other works between sciences, which are acquired by learning; virtues, which are acquired by habit; and arts, which are acquired by practice. It was Isocrates who in his *Against the Sophists*[3] first propagated the suggestion about the value of imitating accomplished orators. All of the subsequent major classical rhetoricians—Dionysius of Halicarnassus, Longinus, Cicero, and Quintilian—recommended the practice of imitation. And there is ample evidence that imitation was fervently recommended and diligently practiced in the medieval and Renaissance schools.

The ancient rhetoricians taught that oratorical skills are acquired by three means—theory, imitation, and practice. These three means are succintly defined in the *Ad Herennium*:

By theory (*ars*) is meant a set of rules that provide a definite method

College Composition and Communication, 22 (October 1971), pp. 243-250. Copyright © 1971 by the National Council of Teachers of English. Reprinted by permission of the publisher and the author.

and system of speaking. Imitation (*imitatio*) stimulates us to attain, in accordance with a studied method, the effectiveness of certain models in speaking. Practice (*exercitatio*) is assiduous exercises and experience (*usus* and *consuetudo*) in speaking.[4]

A recollection of our own experience is enough to confirm this doctrine that the acquisition of any skill, whether it be a manual skill like knitting or an athletic skill like playing tennis or an intellectual skill like speaking or writing, is effected by one or other or a combination of these three means. There are countless examples of people who learned how to play a musical instrument simply by trial-and-error practice. What usually happens, however, once a person has acquired the rudiments of a skill, is that he yearns to improve that skill. So he observes other practitioners and tries to assimilate their techniques. Eventually, he may feel the urge to study the theory of his art. The most universal instance, of course, of acquiring a skill by these three means is the sequence a child usually follows in learning how to speak his language: first imitation, then practice, ultimately theory or the grammar of the language.

The ancient rhetoricians were not making a very original or profound observation about the learning process when they formulated this triad of theory, imitation, and practice. Anyone who had the faculty to observe and the patience to reflect could have come up with that formula. But it is remarkable how that simple triadic formula provided a structure and a direction for the teaching of the language arts in the schools for over two thousand years. And the roster of famous men who made a contribution to the theoretical and pedagogical development of that triadic orientation constitutes a Who Was Who of the great minds of the Western World. By concentrating in this paper on just one member of that trinity of disciplines, I hope I do not give a distorted picture of how the rhetoricians and the teachers of the past tried to bring their pupils to a functional level of proficiency in the arts of discourse.

One of the words that keeps recurring in all Latin discussions of imitation is *similis*. Apparently, one of the objectives of imitation was to make someone *similar* to someone else, presumably to someone superior. Quintilian put it this way:

> In fact, we may note that the elementary study of every branch of learning is directed by reference to some definite standard that is placed before the learner. We must, in fact, be either like or unlike (*aut similes aut dissimiles*) those who have proved their excellence. It is rare for nature to produce such resemblance, which is more often the result of imitation.[5]

But in order not to contribute to the unsavory connotation that *imitation* has for many people—namely that imitation succeeds only in producing carbon-copies—I hasten to remind you that *similar* did not mean for Quintilian and the other classical rhetoricians *identical*. Perhaps it was unfortunate that the rhetoricians used the verb *imitate* to designate this activity, because the Latin verb *imitari* does denote "to produce an image of," a meaning which suggests a reproducing of copies of an original. The verb *aemulari*, which is the source of our verb *emulate* and which in Latin has remotely the same roots as *imitari* and *imago*, would have been a more precise word to designate what the rhetoricians hoped to accomplish by imitation, since *aemulari* meant "to try to rival or equal or surpass." The motto of imitation was "Observe and do likewise." Imitation asked the student to observe the manner or pattern or form or means used by a model and then attempt to emulate the model. A friend of mine who coached Little League baseball teams both before and after television sets became a common appliance in the home told me that the big difference he noted in the boys he worked with over the years is that he rarely had to spend any time showing the TV-conditioned youngsters how to assume a stance in the batter's box or how to hold and swing a bat; imitating the major-league heroes that they had seen on the television screen, they readily assumed classic stances in the box and held a bat as though they had been born with it in their hands. It was that kind of "striving to be like" that the rhetors tried to instill in their pupils. They did not want to reproduce facsimiles of Demosthenes; they wanted to produce orators who could speak *as effectively as* Demosthenes. The ultimate objective of all rhetorical training, imitation included, was well stated by Quintilian: "For what object have we in teaching them but that they may not always require to be taught" (*Institutio Oratoria*, II,v,13).

Since many records of imitative practices in Greek and Roman schools are extant, we must turn to the written accounts of imitative exercises in the English schools of the sixteenth and seventeenth centuries for information about specific practices.[6] Imitative exercises involved two steps—Analysis and Genesis. Analysis was the stage in which students, under the guidance of the teacher, made a close study of the model to observe how its excellences followed the precepts of art. Genesis was the stage in which students attempted to produce something or to do something similar to the model that had been analyzed. Donald Lemen Clark has pointed out that Analysis took two forms: "(1) where a literary principle is announced and then illustrated by examples from an author or authors; (2) where the text of an author is given intact and accompanied by an explanation or commentary."[7] Genesis too might be said to have taken two forms: (1) where the schoolboy wrote something closely patterned on the author he had just been studying; (2) where the schoolboy was cut loose from his models and was asked to write something on his own. But when the schoolboy is asked to produce an original composition (like the themes we assign our students to write), he is moving out of the stage of imitation into the stage of *exercitatio* or practice. It is sometimes difficult to tell whether a particular exercise in the Tudor schools should be classified as part of the *genesis* stage of imitation or as part of the *practice* stage of original composition. The criterion for distinguishing imitation from practice should be the length of the tether with the model, but since the length of the tether is a relative matter, it will not always be possible to firmly categorize the exercise as imitation or practice.

A discussion of the *prelection* is a good way to summarize the analysis stage of imitation. *Prelection* is merely the Latinate term for the kind of close analysis of a text that teachers today conduct in the classroom, sometimes with the aid of invited or preferred comments from their students. The elaborate commentary, which sometimes proceeds sentence by sentence and occasionally focuses on units as small as the word, is designed to expose the strengths (and sometimes the weaknesses) in selection, structure, and style to be found in the composed text. Doubting that his students will detect these strengths and weaknesses from a mere exposure to the text, the teacher explicitly points out the excellences, explains how and why they are functioning, and relates them to the rhetorical principles his students have been studying in the abstract. What the prelection is comparable to is the Brooks-and-Warren method of explicating a poem that many of us learned in graduate school right after World War II.

Some of those Renaissance prelections must have been brilliantly illuminating, but because those rhetorical analyses were delivered orally and extemporaneously, very few of these classroom performances have been preserved for inspection. Quintilian, however, has elaborately described the classroom procedure in his *Institutio Oratoria* (II,v,6-16), and we have an excellent example of the practice in Plato's *Phaedrus*, where Socrates indulges in an impromptu analysis of a speech by Lysias that has just been read to him from a manuscript.

The prelection was not intended to be a mere display of the teacher's virtuosity in reading a text. It was designed to prepare the student for some imitative exercise that he was subsequently to be assigned to perform. In the lower grades at least, the prelection was not an exhaustive *explication de texte*; instead, it often concentrated on a single rhetorical feature, such as the organization of the discourse or the use of figures of speech—a feature which the student was then expected to imitate in a written assignment. Teachers today who discuss only the ideas in a prose text and neglect to point out the strategies of form are not giving their students the kind of help with their writing problems that the prelection provided. And until teachers are given the kind of training in rhetorical reading that Mortimer Adler is talking about in his book *How to Read a Book*, they are not likely to be able to provide this kind of help for their students.

The three most common species of imitative exercises in the Renaissance schools were *memorizing, translating* and *paraphrasing*. Let me say something about each of these practices.

Roger Ascham in his *The Scholemaster* and John Brinsley in his *Ludus Literarius* both testify that memorizing textbook principles and select passages from esteemed authors was the prevailing method of learning in the Tudor grammar schools.[8] Memorization was one of the five canons of classical rhetoric, along with invention, arrangement, style, and delivery, but after the invention of printing in the fifteenth century, there was less attention paid in the classroom to the memorizing and the oral delivery of a composed discourse, mainly of course because messages could now be transmitted by written or printed copy. Although occasionally English schoolboys were required to memorize their themes and declamations for delivery before a classroom audience, most of the energy of memorizing was expended on the precepts and passages available to everyone in cheaply printed texts. A good deal of this effort of course was just rote memory, which the schoolboys spouted back at the teacher on command and often without really understanding what they were saying. But even at its most mechanical, memorizing paid some dividends to the schoolboys. Quintilian had long ago suggested what some of those dividends might be:

> [The boys] will form an intimate acquaintance with the best writings, will carry their models with them and unconsciously reproduce the style of the speech which has been impressed upon their memory. They will have a plentiful and choice vocabulary and a command of artistic structure and a supply of figures which will not have to be hunted for, but will offer themselves spontaneously from the treasure-house, if I may so call it, in which they are stored. (*Institutio Oratoria*, II, vii, 3-4)

I call attention especially to the words *unconsciously* and *spontaneously* in the above quotation, because they suggest the chief benefit of saturating one's memory with select passages from admired authors. It is a commonplace that the book which has the profoundest effect on the styles of English and American authors is the King James version of the Bible. Passages of that magnificent prose were so deeply ingrained in the memory of earlier English and American readers that when they came to write they unconsciously and spontaneously reproduced much of the rhythm, the phraseology, and the structures of the Biblical passages. The practice of memorizing passages of poetry and prose seems to have disappeared from American classrooms at about the time that the elocution contest disappeared, and the only thing that young people memorize today is the lyrics of their favorite songs. But anyone who has had the experience while writing of having a phrase or a structure come back to him unbidden from the deep well of the subconscious might be willing to concede that the restoration of the practice of memorizing might be a good thing.

An imitative exercise that can serve as a substitute for memorizing and that can pay much the same dividends is the practice of copying verbatim select passages from accomplished writers. A variation of this practice is the daily stint of taking down a dictated passage, a discipline that Rollo Walter Brown, in his book *How the French Boy Learns to Write*, tells us was once widely practiced in French schools. And recently we learned from Chapter XI of his Autobiography that Malcolm X acquired his command of language by laboriously copying out the entire dictionary.

The second most common imitative exercise in the Tudor schools was the practice of double translation. Until well into the seventeenth century the English schoolboy had to be at least bilingual to survive in school. Latin was the language of most of his textbooks and the language in which he did most of his reading and writing. Many of the schoolboys also had a smatter-

ing of Greek, and a few of them, like John Milton at St. Paul's School, were
even introduced to Hebrew. The schoolboy then was language-oriented to a
degree that he has never been since. Accordingly, he was expected to be able
to turn a Latin passage into idiomatic if not elegant English, and then perhaps to turn his English version back into a semblance of classical Latin.
Sometimes the translations went through three versions: from Greek to
Latin to English. The themes he composed in English often had to be later
rendered into Ciceronian Latin.

Since Latin and Greek are inflected languages, it may be difficult for us
to imagine what benefit there could be in this practice of double translation
for the schoolboy when he wrote in English, which is essentially a word-
order language. Perhaps the chief benefit was that this incessant activity
made the Tudor schoolboy extremely language-conscious. But I dare say that
the English schoolboy also realized some of the benefits that Cicero and
Quintilian confessed they had reaped from translating Greek into their native
language. Cicero said that in rendering into Latin what he had read in Greek
he "not only used the best words, and yet such as were of common occurrence, but also formed some words by imitation, which would be new to our
countrymen, taking care, however, that they were appropriate."[9] Quintilian
recognized something of the same value in this practice but also pointed out
some others:

> The purpose of this form of exercise is obvious. For Greek authors are
> conspicuous for the variety of their matter, and there is much art in all
> their eloquence, while, when we translate them, we are at liberty to use
> the best words available, since all that we use are our very own. As re-
> gards figures, too, which are the chief ornament of oratory, it is neces-
> sary to think out a great number and variety for ourselves, since in this
> respect the Roman idiom differs largely from the Greek. (*Institutio
> Oratoria*, X, v, 2-3)

Since most of our students are functionally monolingual and since we
rarely have available in any one class a group of students who are in command of another common modern language—except perhaps in certain
Puerto Rican sections of large cities like Chicago and New York or in certain
Mexican-American communities in the Southwest—we cannot make use in
our classrooms of the imitative exercise of translation. But we can make use
of the third kind of imitative exercise widely practiced in the English Renaissance schools—the practice of paraphrasing. The precedent for teaching paraphrase was established by Erasmus, when he recommended for the curriculum of St. Paul's School the practice of turning poetry into prose and of
turning prose into poetry. Those Renaissance humanists who believed in the
inviolable relationship between matter and form objected vehemently to this
practice. Roger Ascham stated the reason for the objection in these words:
" . . . because the author, either orator or poet, had chosen out before, the
fittest words and aptest composition for the matter, and so he, in seeking
other, was driven to use the worse" (*The Scholemaster*, ed. Arber, p. 93).

But the schoolmaster who persisted in the practice had the authority of Quintilian behind him. Quintilian defended the practice in these terms:

> For if there were only one way in which anything could be satisfactorily expressed, we should be justified in thinking the path to success had been sealed to us by our predecessors. But, as a matter of fact, the methods of expression still left us are innumerable, and many roads lead us to the same goal. Brevity and copiousness each have their own peculiar grace, the merits of metaphor are one thing and of literalness another, and, while direct expression is most effective in one case, in another the best result is gained by a use of figures. (*Institutio Oratoria*, X, v, 7-8)

Those who view style as a matter of choices made from the available lexical and syntactical resources of a language can easily salve their consciences about subjecting their students to the discipline of the paraphrase. And, indeed, of all the Renaissance imitative exercises, the paraphrase, in a variety of forms, is the one most often practiced in our schools today. Some teachers give their students a sentence and ask them to phrase the same idea in two or three different ways. Those teachers are probably not aware that Erasmus also set the precedent for that practice, when in his *De copia verborum ac rerum* he turned the simple sentence "Your letter pleased me greatly" into 150 different versions—in some instances substituting different words, in other instances by altering the word-order, and in still other instances by rendering the literal statement into figurative language. Students who have some acquaintance with transformational grammar are especially amenable to this kind of exercise. Another variation on paraphrase is what is now called "pattern practice." The teacher presents a sentence to the students, analyzes the structure of the sentence with them, and then asks them to write a sentence of their own on the pattern of the model. A recently published book called *Copy and Compose* (Englewood Cliffs, N.J.: Prentice-Hall, 1969) by Winston Weathers and Otis Winchester exposes students to a series of progressively more sophisticated sentence patterns. I have heard of some teachers who engage their students in a periphrastic exercise that Benjamin Franklin confessed he had practiced as a young man and that Hugh Blair recommended to the students in his rhetoric class at the University of Edinburg in the eighteenth century. The student takes a passage of prose that he especially admires, reads it over and over again in order to absorb the sense and structure of it, then puts the passage aside and tries to render the thought of the passage in his own words. Précis-writing is another form of paraphrase, but I have not seen much evidence lately that this kind of reductive writing is much practiced now in the schools. Another periphrastic exercise that some of us may have inflicted on our students is the assignment to render the "thought" of a poem into prose, but we may have been persuaded to abandon that practice by Cleanth Brooks' cry about the "heresy of paraphrase."

I could go on to talk about the Renaissance practice of keeping commonplace books and of exercising students in the writing of the graded series of fourteen elementary theme-forms set forth in Aphthonius's widely used textbook *Progymnasmata*. But the commonplace book was less an aid for the learning of form than a resource for the finding of subject-matter, and the formulary exercises in Aphthonius's textbook very soon moved the student from close observance of theme-forms into the writing of original themes, and thus moved him out of the realm of Imitation into the realm of Practice. But I hope I have said enough to give you some idea of the rationale of imitation as a learning device and of specific imitative exercises.

Although there is no question that students still learn their writing skill, as well as other skills, largely through imitation, I seriously doubt that formal exercises in imitation will make much of a comeback in our schools during the coming decade. For one thing, the present mood of education theorists is against such structured, fettered training. The emphasis now is on creativity, self-expression, individuality. Then too there is the suspicion among us that imitation stultifies and inhibits the writer rather than empowers and liberates him. The nineteenth-century Samuel Butler expressed that attitude when he said, "I never knew a writer yet who took the smallest pain with his style and was at the same time readable. . . . I cannot conceive how any man can take thought for his style without loss to himself and his readers."[10]

But the number of creative and expository writers who would testify to the value of imitation to them during their apprenticeship years is legion. We can let Robert Louis Stevenson, the classic example of the "sedulous ape," speak for this group of grateful writers:

> But enough has been said to show by what arts of impersonation and in what purely ventriloquial efforts, I first saw my words on paper. That, like it or not, is the way to learn to write; whether I have profited or not, that is the way. It was so Keats learned, and there was never a finer temperament for literature than Keats's; it was so, if we could trace it out, that all men have learned; and that is why a revival of letters is always accompanied or heralded by a cast back to earlier and fresher models.[11]

More recently, in an article in the *Quarterly Journal of Speech*, W. Ross Winterowd went right to the heart of the value of imitative exercises:

> In this sense, stylistic exercises enable. That is, "mere" exercises in style allow the student to internalize structures that make his own grammar a more flexible instrument for combining and hence enable the student to take experience apart and put it together again in new ways, which is, after all, the generative function of language. . . . Such imitation is not slavish, for it brings about a mix that equals individuality: the resources of the language per se and the individual sensibility that will use them.[12]

The phrase "to internalize structures" hits the nail right on the old bong. For it is that internalization of structures that unlocks our powers and sets us free to be creative, original, and ultimately effective. *Imitate that you may be different.*

Notes

[1] Reprinted in *Critics and Criticism*, ed. Ronald S. Crane (Chicago: University of Chicago Press, 1952), pp. 147-175. See also Donald L. Clark, "Imitation: Theory and Practice in Roman Rhetoric," *Quarterly Journal of Speech*, 37 (1951), pp. 11-22.

[2] McKeon, p. 168.

[3] *Isocrates*, trans. George Norlin, Loeb Classical Library (Cambridge, MA: Harvard University Press, 1962), II, 175.

[4] *Ad Herennium*, II, ii, 3, trans. Harry Caplan, Loeb Classical Library (Cambridge, MA: Harvard University Press, 1954).

[5] *Institutio Oratoria*, X, ii, 2-3, trans. H. E. Butler, 4 vols., Loeb Classical Library (Cambridge, MA: Harvard University Press, 1922).

[6] The best primary sources for information about imitative practices in Tudor grammar schools are John Brinsley, *Judus Literarius: or The Grammar Schoole*, ed. E. T. Campagnac (Liverpool: University of Liverpool Press, 1917); Charles Hoole, *A New Discovery of the Old Art of Teaching Schoole*, ed. E. T. Campagnac (Liverpool: University of Liverpool Press, 1913); Roger Ascham, *The Scholemaster*, ed. Edward Arber, English Reprints (Boston: D.C. Heath, 1898). The secondary work that I have relied on heavily for this paper is Donald L. Clark's *John Milton at St. Paul's School: A Study of Ancient Rhetoric in English Renaissance Education* (New York: Columbia University Press, 1948).

[7] *John Milton at St. Paul's School*, p. 158.

[8] *The Scholemaster*, ed. Arber, p. 88; *Ludus Literarius*, ed. Campagnac, pp. 175, 177.

[9] Cicero, *De Oratore*, I, xxxix, 155, trans. E. W. Sutton, Loeb Classical Library (Cambridge, MA: Harvard University Press, 1959).

[10] Samuel Butler, *Notebooks*, ed. Geoffrey Keynes and Brian Hill (London: Jonathan Cape, 1951), pp. 290-1.

[11] "A College Magazine," *The Works of Robert Louis Stevenson* (New York: Charles Scribner's Sons, 1902), XIII, pp. 213-214.

[12] "Style: A Matter of Manner," *QJS*, 56 (1970), pp. 164, 167.

A Case for a Modern Commonplace Book

I am of this opinion, that young children might muche more to their profecte and benefite bee exercised in the grammar schooles with themes, or arguments to write on . . . so that the schoolemaister dooe open and declare the rewlis and waies how that which is briefly spoken maye bee dilated and sette out more at large, and how that that is fondly spoken . . . maye bee turned or applyed to a serious use and purpose.[1]

Erasmus, 1531

What I need is a way to help students come up with ideas to write about. It does no good to drill them in rules and techniques of writing without dealing with the initial problem—helping them find something to say.

Everyteacher, 1979

Helping students get ideas to write about—certainly the basic issue in the above quotation from the Renaissance educator Erasmus and that from our hypothetical colleague Everyteacher—is an essential part of showing them how to write. And it is obviously no more a new issue than it is a dead or a resolved one in the modern pedagogy of composition. As even those with only a smattering of knowledge about classical rhetoric know, the problem of discovering themes and arguments—of *inventio* as the ancients termed it— was discussed as an essential part of discourse some eighteen centuries before Erasmus made his pertinent comments on the matter. And as even those with only a smattering of experience in the composition classroom know, the problem of "getting started" is one of the most consistently observed and frequently lamented hindrances to writing among students on all levels of education and achievement. Most teachers would, in fact, likely agree with Mina Shaughnessy that this is "the most difficult of all the writing problems."[2]

Perhaps then it is again in antiquity that some comfort may be found for those of us who are daily struggling to find ways to help students dredge

College Composition and Communication, 31 (May 1980), pp. 175-182. Copyright © 1980 by the National Council of Teachers of English. Reprinted by permission of the publisher and the author.

up not merely *something* to write about, but something meaningful, interesting, or even inspiring, *and* to do it somewhat systematically and efficiently. For as the new rhetoric's many adaptations and expansions of the old rhetoric persistently are reminding us, when the problem existed in the past, so often did a practice or theory which might be revived and revised as at least a partial solution. I am referring to a practice which has been mentioned but not elaborated upon by no less esteemed a contingent of the new rhetoricians than Corbett, D'Angelo, and Shaughnessy.[3] It is the commonplace book.

According to Donald L. Clark,[4] a commonplace was originally an oration that amplified, dilated, and colored acknowledged truths about the good or evil which is *common* to everyone. And two types of commonplace books were widely used in the Latin grammar schools of Tudor England to help students learn to enlarge upon common truths in their discourse. The earlier type consisted of collections of quotations from classical literature and history compiled by scholars to provide schoolboys with themes and information to develop for their rhetorical exercises. One of the most ancient examples was *Valerius Maximus,* and three of the most famous Renaissance versions were Eramus' *Adagia* (1500), *Parabolae, sine Similia* (1513), and *Apophthegmatum* (1531). This type of commonplace book eventually fell out of vogue, however, because of a tendency which developed to substitute use of these "literary digests" for actual reading of the primary works. Thus developed a second type, compiled by the individual student for personal use, which was simply a notebook in which the student could enter select quotations that he encountered in his reading and deemed worthy of later development in his school essays. Frequently such a notebook would have divisions where entries could be organized under appropriate headings such as education, marriage, and government.

It is an expansion of this latter type of the Tudor schoolboy's commonplace book—and of the term "commonplace"—which I am suggesting for modern students of composition. My version of the modern commonplace book is also a sectional notebook in which students record ideas under appropriate headings for later development into essays. Yet it is more than that, too. It is a central part of the composition course. But, further, it has the potential to be a part of *all* the academic activity of students, thus contributing to fulfillment of the writing teacher's fondest but probably most seldom realized dream—improving students' performance not only in the composition class but in *all* their writing. The particular kinds of entries which individual teachers would have students make in their commonplace books would, of course, best be left to personal preference and perception of needs. I wish simply to suggest several possibilities, most of which have been discussed in various forms by other writers on composition, and all of which I believe can help to solve students' problems with *inventio*, particularly if they are collected in a "common place" to which students have quick access.

Of great value in the book are two sections (I like students to have them first) which consist as much of information provided by the teacher as of material independently obtained by students. Both are concerned with places to get ideas. First is a section on the Aristotelian common topics.[5] In *A Conceptual Theory of Rhetoric* (p. 38), D'Angelo discusses two perceptions of the topics: (1) as actual subject matter or arguments to be used, or (2) as abstract, analytical guidelines for thought. The second view, which is D'Angelo's and which he develops thoroughly in the remainder of the chapter, seems to originate in Aristotle's work and to have been extended by Cicero, D'Angelo says. According to this conception, such topics as definitions, division, comparison, cause, effect, genus, species, etc., are "symbols of abstract, underlying mental processes which take place in the brain" (p. 41). Since we cannot directly observe mental processes, we must construct models to represent them (which D'Angelo does in the form of branching tree diagrams of categories of the topics). The categories of the topics, whose hierarchical relationships are shown by the diagrams, can then serve as heuristic techniques for developing ideas on any subject.

I have found, of course, that the topics must be presented in varying degrees of detail, depending on students' abilities. It is probably always a good idea to work through the development of some themes using the topics with the class as a whole until students thoroughly understand how they work. And some students need considerable guidance to understand that just as we use different mental processes to arrive at different types of knowledge, so we must use appropriate topics to work out different ideas. But once they arrive at that realization, it seems to be a real breakthrough in helping them to organize their thinking.

An extremely practical method for teaching students how to use the topics to generate ideas is that suggested by Richard L. Larson:[6] giving them the topics posed as questions. Teachers can provide students with either Larson's list of questions or a similar one they develop themselves. The commonplace book is simply a convenient location for keeping the questions for easy reference at those times when students need a catalyst for generating ideas on their own. Instructing them to keep blank paper in the commonplace book along with the topics and questions and to work out ideas for essays there will soon give them a self-produced store of examples at their fingertips, also. This working out of ideas can be done individually or sometimes in pairs or small groups. Students simply write at the top of a blank sheet of paper one subject they might be interested in writing about. If they are using questions like Larson's to generate thought, they find the category of questions that fits their subject and go through that list, quickly jotting down answers in regard to their subject. If this exercise—which seems to be much less threatening than actually writing an essay—is repeated with several different ideas, students learn to select the subject that showed the most promise when they thought it through to develop later into a full essay. Without this commonplace book activity, however, very seldom would they take the time to think through ideas and discard insubstantial ones before sitting down to write a complete piece.

Another practical format for presenting at least some of the topics is through simple charts such as that Mina Shaughnessy developed for introducing the comparison to basic writing students.[7] As illustration, here is my chart for using the topic *Division* or *Partition* to develop an argument by elimination:

State organizing principle:

List all *divisions* you can think of	All Possible Opposition	All Possible Defense

---

An "organizing principle" is simply a label for a subject which has several parts or divisions. For example, if students wanted to write about what direction the government should take in freeing the United States from dependence on foreign oil, their organizing principle might be *alternate sources of energy.* On the left-hand side of the chart they would then list all the alternate energy sources they had read about or heard of (*coal, the sun, shale oil,* etc.). Taking the divisions one at a time, students would jot down all the oppositions (*coal - harmful to environment*) or defenses (*coal - cheap, plentiful*) they could think of for each. The result would be not only a base of specifics on which to build the argument but also an outline of sorts to help the writer stick to a factual line of development of the original idea. Along with illustration for utilizing such a chart, the teacher can provide students with a supply of blank charts to keep in the commonplace book for later use on different subjects. Similar schemata can be devised for most of the topics.

Another section of the book which must be developed with extensive teacher input is information on what Corbett calls the "external aids to invention,"[8] the standard reference works. As he points out, many college students are aware of the existence of few references beyond encyclopedias. Corbett provides a thorough discussion of the most widely used works in *Classical Rhetoric for the Modern Student* (pp. 168-199), but teachers might help students develop lists of references to keep in their commonplace books based on what is actually available in their libraries. I have found that giving students exercises in using the various works and encouraging them to make notes, in the process of doing the exercises, on the particular merits and concerns of certain works increases the utility of this section as well as helps them to become more comfortable with using the library to get information to use in compositions.

The bulk of my version of the modern commonplace book is, as I stated earlier, topically organized and student-generated. One section of this portion of the book is somewhat analogous to artists' sketch pads. It is devoted to recording personal observations of the students' own world. Only two things are required for such ideas to become valuable parts of the commonplace book: (1) that students be given some instruction and considerable practice in making detailed observations, and (2) that they develop the habit of keeping their commonplace books with them so that they can record observations when good opportunities arise. Observing techniques for generating writing are certainly not original with me; they have been taught by scores of teachers for years. But I think that they are more effective when approached in an organized manner.

Ken Macrorie was possibly first to suggest that teachers acquaint students with the value of recording observations in *journals* for the purpose of saving them for later development into pieces of writing.[9] He recommended that students keep such journals for several weeks in order to record anything striking which they see or think of. I feel that the commonplace book has an advantage over journals for such a purpose. So many teachers have used journals as a device simply to keep students writing on *anything* that often students fail to see real value in them. The commonplace book can be shown to have very practical, immediate value. I also recommend leaving matters a little less to chance— at least at first—than does Macrorie by sending students actively to *seek* observations, *after* giving them a little instruction in methods. For example, I might assign students the task of recording some observations about people under topics of their choice in their commonplace books. To prepare them for their search we might look at a brief example of expert "people watching" such as the Prologue to *The Canterbury Tales* and determine just what sorts of things Chaucer recorded that made his observations memorable. Then students might set about making a specified number of detailed observations of people and recording them for use in later assignments of descriptive writing.

An obvious value of using these fairly common techniques with the commonplace book is that students are likely to have access to their observations for future development if they are taught to keep them in a "common place." Furthermore, I have had students whose previous writing had been totally uninspired who produced incisive, sensitive, and often tremendously entertaining character sketches after regular practice at watching people and recording exactly what they saw where they could find their observations later. Having a collection of previously recorded observations from which to choose for later development in writing seems to have this additional benefit: the lapse of time since recording observations helps students to see how much of the flavor of what they originally saw was captured in their notes. If what they recorded does not call forth the memory of the character as vividly as it should, students have an opportunity to learn through their own experience some things about specificity in descriptive writing.

Another type of entry in the topically organized, student-generated portion of the books is those ideas produced through such in-class activities as "pre-writing,"[10] "free writing,"[11] or "five to ten minute write-ins."[12] The shared characteristic of all these popular activities (which might be thought of as a sort of private brainstorming) is that they press students' pens into service in the hope that their minds will follow, as in fact they frequently do. Again, any meaningful ideas that are produced can be maintained in the commonplace book (under appropriate headings attached after the idea takes shape) so that students can find them later to serve as inspiration and basis for more extended and formal writing.

An alternate form of such private brainstorming activities is real brainstorming—the working out of a given topic by the class as a whole or by small groups in the class.[13] As McCrimmon suggests, the frequent result is more material than one student could develop into an essay, so having students record information from this source in their commonplace books could also serve future writing.

A final kind of entry I would suggest for the modern commonplace book is that which is probably most like the entries those Tudor schoolboys made nearly half a millennium ago, and it is also that which is most likely to fulfill the claim I made earlier for the books' wide-ranging potential. That is, having students make entries—under appropriate headings—of particularly important and/or interesting ideas and quotations which they encounter during all their reading and learning. Ideas from science, history, and mathematics courses (or from extracurricular reading on serious topics) are included along with quotations from literature, as are items from newspapers, popular and news magazines, and books read solely for pleasure. And in our electronic culture, certainly we cannot overlook radio and television as sources of information worth writing about, either.

The key to the effectiveness of this important aspect of the commonplace book is that students learn to tune into what they read and hear to the extent that they will notice things worth writing down, and that they will remember to record them. Every teacher will likely have favorite methods for encouraging development of the latter skill—perhaps simply checking for certain numbers of entries per week as part of the course requirements. Many methods can and should be used for helping students acquire the skill of noticing things worth writing about. In *Errors and Expectations* (pp. 87-88), Mina Shaughnessy suggested asking teachers across the curriculum to encourage or even require students to write down information and ideas. In high school teaching I have devoted class days on a regular basis to having students read magazines and newspapers for the sole purpose of locating and recording potential essay topics. The activity included noting not only facts but personal reactions to them. Thus reading about current events in order to be more informed writers not only helped students' writing but their reading also, which sometimes became more thoughtful and critical. Then, once students begin to acquire a really usable collection of ideas and information and to discover that their writing is indeed made easier by having this resource, success itself can lead to increased observations and recording.

I have noticed many other benefits with many of my students from the practices I have described. Acquiring the habit of recording facts and ideas from other courses and reading for development into English essays not only has sometimes improved the quality of their writing by making it more substantial, it has increased their interest in and improved their attitude toward what they write, and it also has increased their knowledge about certain topics in which they already had an interest but which they had never taken the time to explore in depth. Thus they learned the value of "writing as a way of knowing," of coming truly to understand a concept or a subject by forcing it into the shape of words, reexamining it, and often trying different words. And then there have been those incorrigible student-writers—so prevalent in all our classrooms—who withstand all determined efforts to teach them the need for revision and rewriting. Through some of the commonplace book exercises where they actually "worked out" the germs of ideas —such as the various techniques for using the Aristotelian topics, the character observations activity, free writing and brainstorming, recording information and reactions from reading in current literature—I won a victory so subtle that I don't think they were ever aware of it. The initial assignment was a rough draft of sorts for the fuller writing assignment which followed sometimes weeks later. Yet it was so purposeful and specific and far enough removed from the labor of getting a complete essay onto paper that it did not seem as distasteful as sitting down and toiling through several versions of a composition in relatively quick succession. Also, it encouraged students to begin to utilize a principle which I consider basic to good writing and characteristic of the way professionals go about it—that it often takes days, weeks, months, maybe years of mulling over an idea before it is brought to fruition on the printed page. Certainly the victory was not complete with these students (there was still the matter of editing that fleshed out version of the initially jotted down ideas), but at least they were brought temporarily out of the habit of submitting to readers the first thing they wrote down.

My favorite success story with the commonplace book concept, however, culminated quite recently. I have regularly had a few students tell me that they intend to keep up their books after they finish my course. Recently I received a letter and a manila envelope of fiction and non-fiction writing from a very good writer I taught three years ago in an honors class of high school seniors. She had continued her writing in college as an English major as well as contributor to and editor of the campus literary magazine. She had sent me a number of pieces she had written over the past two years in college for the magazine, a writing class, and her own enjoyment, and was soliciting my comments. Among the pieces were several which were developments of ideas she had initially recorded and begun to work out as commonplace book assignments in my class. Obviously her book was still very much in use.

Certainly the process of getting started, of invention, of discovering ideas will always remain one of the hardest parts of the composition process. But I am convinced that our educational ancestors had a sound idea when they encouraged in their students—through the commonplace book—the habit of having a "common place" for recording and "exercising" embryo "themes and arguments" so that, when needed, they could be "sette out more at large, and . . . applyed to a serious use and purpose."

Notes

[1] Desiderius Erasmus, *Apophthegmes*, trans. by Nicolas Udall (1542; rpt. Amsterdam: Da Capo Press, 1969), pp. xxvi-xxvii.

[2] Mina Shaughnessy, *Errors and Expectations* (New York: Oxford University Press, 1977), p. 82.

[3] Edward P. J. Corbett, "The Theory and Practice of Imitation in Classical Rhetoric," *College Composition and Communication*, 22 (October 1971), 243-250; Shaughnessy, p. 88; Frank J. D'Angelo, *A Conceptual Theory of Rhetoric* (Cambridge, MA: Winthrop Publishers, Inc., 1975), p. 39.

[4] Donald L. Clark, *John Milton at St. Paul's School: A Study of Ancient Rhetoric in English Renaissance Education* (1948; rpt. New York: Archon Books, 1964), pp. 217-226, 238-239.

[5] See Edward P. J. Corbett, *Classical Rhetoric for the Modern Student*, 2nd ed. (New York: Oxford University Press, 1971), pp. 110-145 for a thorough discussion.

[6] Richard L. Larson, "Discovery Through Questioning: A Plan for Teaching Rhetorical Invention," *College English*, 30 (November 1968), 126-34. Conveniently reprinted in *Classical Rhetoric for the Modern Student*, pp. 163-167.

[7] See Shaughnessy, p. 262, for diagram and discussion.

[8] *Classical Rhetoric for the Modern Student*, p. 167.

[9] Ken Macrorie, "To Be Read," *English Journal*, 57 (May 1968), 686-692.

[10] See James M. McCrimmon, "Writing as a Way of Knowing," in *The Promise of English: NCTE 1970 Distinguished Lectures* (Urbana, IL: National Council of Teachers of English, 1970), pp. 115-130, for a detailed discussion of three types.

[11] See Macrorie, p. 53, for examples.

[12] See Jean Pumphrey, "Teaching English Composition as a Creative Art," *College English*, 34 (February 1973), 666-673, for explanation.

[13] McCrimmon describes a particular method of the former as a type of pre-writing on p. 9; Shaughnessy of the latter on p. 83.

Mending the Fragmented Free Modifier

MURIEL HARRIS

When the subject of fragments crops up in the composition classroom, teachers often follow a standard instructional route offered in many textbooks. That is, they begin by explaining the basic requirements of a complete sentence, the subject and predicate. Then, perhaps, they assign exercises which help students to distinguish between sentences and fragments, those sentence-level errors which, as most students know, can incur inordinately heavy penalties. Fragments are indeed costly mistakes in freshman themes, and some instructors can even quantify the cost. "No paper can get a passing grade if it has more than three fragments," or "each fragment lowers the grade one letter," and so on.

However, as I intend to demonstrate, lumping all varieties of fragments together in this manner is both an overly harsh and also a potentially destructive reaction. Moreover, the usual instructional sequence for remedying fragments, as suggested above, is a particularly ineffective way to proceed because the "fragment" label is at best a blanket term for several kinds of sentence errors that ought *not* to be equated. Further, if we don't make distinctions among the various kinds of incomplete sentences and don't offer appropriately different instruction, we may well be inhibiting the development of a late-blooming syntactic structure in student writing, a structure regarded by Francis Christensen and others as characteristic of mature writing.

However, before we can proceed, it is necessary first to differentiate among the varieties of fragments that exist. Although a great deal of work remains to be done, particularly in analyzing the types of fragments produced by student writers at various stages of their development, Charles R. Kline, Jr., and W. Dean Memering have already identified several kinds which appear in published prose, in their study, "Formal Fragments: The English Minor Sentence," *Research in the Teaching of English*, 11 (Fall, 1977), 97-110. One variety not found in formal writing is the broken sentence, described by Kline and Memering as "fragmented, discontinuous, and/or noncontinuous *thought* . . . " which does not "express a complete idea or com-

College Composition and Communication, 32 (May 1981). Copyright © 1981 by the National Council of Teachers of English. Reprinted by permission of the publisher and the author.

plete a previously stated idea" (p. 108). In these constructions, then, communication is incomplete and confusing, as in a typical student example I
saw recently:

> In a little nightclub in Louisville, a couple of my friends, Rick and Lon,
> the duo who were providing the entertainment that night for the club.
> Rick plays an organ with three synthesizers included.

If we join the broken sentence, the first one, to the second sentence, the
thought is not completed and the broken sentence does not become any
clearer. Kline and Memering, having found no examples of such broken sentences in formal writing, conclude that this type of construction is always an
error, a judgment with which teachers of writing can easily concur.

In contrast to the broken sentence, however, Kline and Memering offer
the minor sentence, a category which includes sentences that do express a
complete idea or that complete a previously stated idea (though these constructions may lack one or more of the items typically present in an English
sentence). Included here, for example, are the comparative (e.g., She invited
everyone. The more, the merrier.) and the short answer to a rhetorical question (e.g., Is plagiarism excusable? Never.). Kline and Memering describe
other types of minor sentences, but my particular interest here is a kind of
fragment which appears frequently in students' writing and which can be
considered as a variety of minor sentence, though it does not neatly fit in to
Kline and Memering's classifications. This type, caused by a misplaced
period, is a phrase or clause that has become separated from the main or base
clause which either precedes or follows it, as in these student examples:

> She had a very funny look on her face. As if she was scared and just
> wanted to be left alone.

or

> With my brother standing by my side, I reached for the pot handle.
> Stretching way too much.

These kinds of sentences should look fairly familiar because my sampling of
student fragments indicates that, by a huge majority, they are the most frequent type found in the themes of college freshmen.

Viewed in light of Kline and Memering's study, these cases of the misplaced period are not errors, because such constructions are found in formal
writing and are, in fact, "a stylistic feature of many writers" (p. 109). In response, some teachers will argue that students still ought to know the rules
of the complete—or major sentence—before breaking them. True enough,
and we ought to help students distinguish between major and minor sentences. But my point is that we also ought to be particularly gentle in react-
ing to cases of misplaced periods because many of them are likely to be early
appearances of a late blooming syntactic structure, a structure described in
Christensen's system as the final free modifier. Moreover, to nurture the
development of such budding structures, we also need to offer some appropriate instruction which is not merely an avoidance tactic.

In Christensen's system of sentence construction, these final free modifiers include all non-essential phrases and clauses set off by commas (or other punctuation) at the end of the sentence, after the bound predicate. The varieties of final free modifiers specified in Christensen's work are non-essential prepositional phrases; relative and subordinate clauses; nominative absolutes; and noun, verb, adjectival, and adverbial phrases.[1] A typical sentence containing a final free modifier is the following one by John Steinbeck, a sentence Christensen uses in an exercise in *The New Rhetoric*:

> His hands were hard, with broad fingers and nails as thick and ridged as little clam shells. (p. 51)

A few student examples of final free modifiers, though fragmented because of misplaced periods, are as follows:

> Her arms were long and small, but there was strength in them. Hands rough and calloused from long hard hours of work.

> or

> The story hinged on growing up and only wandered off twice. Once in the beginning when he told about where he lived and then again when they constructed a dam.

As yet, we cannot state with absolute certainty that final free modifiers are late blooming structures, but what evidence we have does point firmly in that direction. In "Early Blooming and Late Blooming Syntactic Structures," Kellogg Hunt has isolated one particular type of free modifier, the verb phrase, as a structure which was produced by "9 out of 10 university students studied . . . , whereas only 1 out of 10 twelfth graders had done so." Some examples of this construction in the sentences of university students included in Hunt's article are as follows:

> He caught the chicken, *planning* to eat it the next morning, and placed it in a pen located below his window.

> and

> The old man caught the chicken and put her in a pen under his window *planning* to the eat the chicken for breakfast the next morning.[2]

As Hunt's T-unit analysis does not depend on the position of the structure in the sentence, we do not know how many were in the final position and how many were in the initial or medial position. However, Christensen did sort out the position of free modifiers when he analyzed the prose of six published authors, and he concluded that "a mature style will have a relatively high frequency of free modifiers, especially in the final position" ("The Problem of Defining a Mature Style," p. 579).

Several subsequent studies have confirmed the corollary to Christensen's conclusion, that college students do not use free modifiers as frequently as professional writers do, and use final free modifiers hardly at all. In one of these studies, conducted by Anthony Wolk,[3] college composition students counted the frequency and location of free modifiers both in current professional expository writing and in their own prose. The data they collected support Christensen's findings rather closely (see Table 1), as do the results of Wolk's own analysis of twelve current essays of professional writers. Like Christensen, Wolk concluded that "the free modifier separates student from professional and the final free modifier more so" (p. 67). In another study, an extensive and detailed analysis of the syntax of student and professional writers, Ann Gebhard offered further confirmation of this particular characteristic of the sentences of skilled or mature writers; and lest there be any doubters still among us, Lester Faigley compared sentences of freshman essays to those of some writers included in a popular anthology of readings for college composition classes.[4] Again, as we see in Table 1, student sentences were noticeably deficient in the use of free or loose modification, particularly as additional structures after the bound modifiers.

TABLE 1

Percent of Total Words Used in Free Modification

	Student			Advanced/ Professional		
	% of Total Words Free Modifiers	% Initial Free Modifiers	% Final Free Modifiers	% of Total Words in Free Modifiers	% in Initial Position	% in Final Position
Christensen				32	9	17.8
Wolk's students	20.9	8.7	8.4	31.0	9.7	13.7
Wolk				32.5	9.8	16.8
Gebhard:						
poor freshmen	38.1	20.7	7.3			
good freshmen	38.6	19.5	10.1	55.9	22.5	16.3
Faigley	16.1	11.8	3.5	30.3	8.8	17.3

Searching for reasons why student writers tend not to put loose modification at the end of the sentence, Christensen concluded that English teachers contribute to the tendency because they stress the use of initial free modification as the road to instant sentence maturity. Having noted the composition teacher's infatuation with sentence openers, Christensen also pointed out that a prolific use of such structures at the beginning of the sentence did not match the reality he found in the sentences of professional writers.[5] The point is reiterated in a prefatory note to his text, *A New Rhetoric*, for we are told that "modern writers have given us teachers of composition the slip. . . . While we urge variety in sentence beginnings (and get dangling modifiers), they put sentence modification at the end" (p. xvi). This English teacher's preference for initial modification is apparently still with us, as Faigley reports on having heard a speaker at a national conference of English teachers expound on the merits of using "frequent introductory subordinate ideas" (p.20). And as we see from the numbers in Table 1, students do attempt to please their teachers, because the overwhelming tendency in the student writing analyzed was to put free modification before the main clause. Interestingly enough, Gebhard's comment in her study was that it was the poorer students who were most prone to following their teachers' suggestion to employ more phrases and clauses before the subject as sentence beginnings (p. 230). Similarly, as Hunt concluded when he noted that adverb clauses in the initial position were preferred more strongly by fourth-graders than by eighth- or twelfth-graders, a preference for such clauses at the beginning of the sentence can hardly be a mark of maturity.[6]

While an English teacher's preference for sentence openers can cause students to shift modification to the initial position, the other probable cause of the noticeable lack of final free modifiers in student writing is, as suggested above, that such modifiers are late blooming structures. Yet, inadvertently, we trample on the faltering attempts of students to try out these structures before they are completely under control. Rather than risk a blow to their grade point averages, many students in composition classes probably opt not to experiment. For example, at the end of his study, Wolk reported the comment of a graduate student instructor who "had made such a negative point about run-on sentences that his students had taken the safest way out and avoided most modification after the base clause—and so, fewer F[inal] F[ree] M[odifiers] s" (p. 68).

An equally important reason for students' hesitation, however, may be that incorrect punctuation of these loose modifiers can also lead the student to the equally deadly error, the fragment. That mispunctuated final free modifiers are indeed a frequent cause of student fragments is not a hypothesis I set out to verify, but was instead a somewhat surprising finding from an analysis of fragments that I undertook as preparation for materials development work in our writing lab. Like most labs, we have gone from the initial stage of writing instructional materials based on text book advice to a more advanced stage of realizing that such text book advice frequently does not match the reality we deal with in tutorials. Thus, after discarding the materials on fragments developed during the first few semesters of our existence, we were faced with the need to analyze the real fragments students write, fragments too often unlike anything in the text book examples. To do so, we collected one hundred fragments from a random assortment of papers that, over a period of several years, had accompanied students to the lab from freshman composition courses. Table 2 summarizes the types of fragments we found.

As Table 2 indicates, the first major division was the separation of broken sentences from "misplaced periods," those pieces of sentences which got detached from their base clauses by inappropriate insertions of periods. The overwhelming majority of the fragments we collected turned out to be cases of the misplaced period. Of these seven (7%) were phrases of clauses that should have preceded the base clause of the sentence (e.g., "And when I turned and looked at her. There were tears in her eyes, when she said that he had died."). This meant that 83% of the fragments were modifying phrases and clauses which should have been included after the base clause. Of this

TABLE 2

Analysis of Student Fragments

	N=100
A. Broken Sentences	10
B. Misplaced periods:	
1. Initial	7
2. Final:	
a. Bound	26
b. Free	57

group, 26% were in Christensen's terms "bound modifiers," primarily subordinate clauses at the ends of the sentences (e.g., "*Playboy* has a reputation for getting a sophisticated and elite group of readers. Although this is a value judgment and in some circumstances, not a true premise."). The most interesting result, in light of the research studies mentioned earlier, is that of 100 randomly collected fragments, 57 would, if properly joined to the base clause with a comma or dash instead of a period, be considered final free modifiers. Of these, 24 were noun phrases (e.g., "I believe that the author is trying to convey the meaning of life to the reader. A sense of purpose and fulfillment to life."), 12 were nominative absolutes (e.g., "The story appealed to your sense of nostalgia and proved a point. The point being that at maturity we have to fit into a style and become responsible."), and 9 were verb phrases (e.g., "She opened the door and let us into her home. Not realizing at the time that we would never enter that door in her home again."). A recurring aspect of these final free modifier fragments, though I am not able to explain how or why it contributes to the problem, was that in 24 of the 57 cases, some element of the final free modifier was compounded. For example, the head noun of the noun phrase was frequently compounded:

The less pleasant things in the room are against the east wall. The books from my classes and the alarm that awakes me early in the morning.

The verbid from the verb phrase was also likely to be compounded:

She was a constant aggravation to the men. Leaving her door slightly ajar and standing naked to be seen.

Given this likelihood that students will try some loose modification at the ends of their sentences, though without complete control over the structures, what ought we do or not do? If we accept Christensen's description of mature writing, we ought not to push students into overusing sentence openers. We also ought not to treat fragmented free modifiers as serious errors, particularly in view of recent reminders that it may possibly be dysfunctional or an "arbitrary constraint upon the writer" not to allow him or her some freedom to make errors while learning.[7] To assist students in acquiring a firmer control of final free modifiers, we can of course turn to sentence combining techniques or to Christensen's program. But even if we decide not to use these approaches to sentence building, we can also help students use final free modifiers more confidently by explaining the punctuation needed. Some teachers, like Lester Faigley, grow irritable when told (especially by colleagues in other departments) that our job as teachers of writing is to teach freshmen "how to spell and where to put their commas" (p. 18). Since Faigley's interest is to help his students achieve syntactic maturity by increased use of final free modifiers, the correct use of the comma does turn out to be necessary if students are to avoid fragments and/or rid themselves of the fear of writing fragments. Or, we can work with such punctuation problems in terms of why and how they create difficulties for the reader. As Linda Flower has pointed out, in her work on Writer-Based vs. Reader-Based prose, the problem with such fragments is that they can cause the reader difficulty when they violate both the reader's intonation pattern and strong structural expectations as he or she attempts to read such a fragment as an introductory clause for the next sentence.[8] Seen from this perspective, such fragments are but one more characteristic of Writer-Based prose which does not take the needs of the reader into consideration, and could then be dealt with when examining ways to turn Writer-Based prose into Reader-Based prose. . . .

Notes

[1] See, for example, Christensen's "The Problem of Defining a Mature Style," *English Journal*, 57 (April 1968), 572-79, or *A New Rhetoric* (New York: Harper and Row, 1976).

[2] In *Evaluating Writing*, ed. Charles R. Cooper and Lee Odell (Urbana, IL: National Council of Teachers of English, 1977), p. 100.

[3] Anthony Wolk, "The Relative Importance of the Final Free Modifier: A Quantitative Analysis," *Research in the Teaching of English*, 4 (Spring 1970), 59-68.

[4] Ann Gebhard, "Writing Quality and Syntax: A Transformational Analysis of Three Prose Samples," *Research in the Teaching of English*, 12 (October 1978), 211-31; Lester Faigley, "Another Look at Sentences," *Freshman English News*, 7, No. 3 (Winter 1979), 18-21.

[5] Francis Christensen, "Sentence Openers," *College English*, 25 (October 1963), 7-11.

[6] Kellogg Hunt, *Grammatical Structures Written at Three Grade Levels* (Champaign, IL: National Council of Teachers of English, 1965), p. 82.

[7] Julia S. Falk, "Language Acquisition and the Teaching and Learning of Writing," *College English*, 41 (December 1979), 441; Mike Rose, "Rigid Rules, Inflexible Plans, and the Stifling of Language," in the *UCLA Writing Research Project Working Papers*, Vol. I (Los Angeles: UCLA Office of Undergraduate Affairs, 1979), p. 107; or *CCC*, 31 (December 1980), 389-401.

[8] Linda Flower, "Writer-Based Prose: A Cognitive Basis for Problems in Writing," *College English*, 41 (September 1979), 32.

Training Peer Tutors for the Writing Lab

LEONARD A. PODIS

For the past several years I have taught a course designed to train peer tutors to work in the writing lab at Oberlin College. The guiding philosophy of the course has been that the ideal tutor should strive to be both knowledgeable and helpful. In this regard the course anticipates a problem and is prepared to deal with it: namely, that being knowledgeable and being helpful are not always complementary, and that unless one is conscious of keeping them in balance, the two qualities may even interfere with each other. What the course attempts to do is to train tutors to be knowledgeable about writing and rhetoric while using a personal approach different from that of the traditional college faculty member. In other words, the course seeks to produce tutors who really know their stuff, but who are not the intimidating "little teachers" that Kenneth Bruffee has cautioned against.[1]

All attempts in our tutor training process can be categorized under three basic areas: (1) to give tutors some rigorous knowledge about language, discourse, and composition; (2) to give them insight into, and encourage them to be receptive to, various helping pedagogical styles; and (3) to give them practice in the interpersonal aspect of tutoring through actual practice in the lab. The hoped-for result is a happy blending of the three: a tutor who relates well personally to the tutee, and who has a sharp analytic approach to discourse and composition, but who knows as well how to *hold back* an objective analysis as how to apply it in constructive ways. The tutor is urged to help the tutee by proceeding slowly and building strength upon strength, confronting only one kind of error at a session in order to avoid overwhelming and demoralizing the student with a systematic dismantling of the student's work.

The first step in the process is a selection of the tutor trainees. Shortly before the end of each semester I ask for nominations (*for the coming semester*) from the English faculty and the student majors committee. Most tutors are junior or senior English majors who write well themselves and have good intuitive knowledge of grammar, mechanics, and essay technique; they are usually planning careers in teaching, and in fact the tutor training couse is

College Composition and Communication, 31 (February 1980), pp. 70-75. Copyright © 1980 by the National Council of Teachers of English. Reprinted by permission of the publisher and the author.

approved by the education department as an elective which counts toward the teacher certification requirement in English. At any rate, students who are nominated and who come forth are then interviewed by the lab director (myself) and given two tasks to qualify them. The first task is to correct a sheet of ten sentences containing errors in grammar and mechanics. In this task, potential tutors needn't demonstrate knowledge of formal terminology but they should be able to spot the existence of error and be able to offer a correct alternative for each sentence. The second task is to read a sample student paragraph containing both major and minor problems and to offer two written responses to it: (1) an objective analysis of its strengths and weaknesses and (2) a statement which might be made to the student writer as a first step towards revision and improvement. Again on this task the potential tutors need not show *expertise* as much as *promise*; they should show sensitivity to both good and bad points in the piece as well as some recognition that part two of their response—the statement to the student writer—should not be identical to part one, the objective analysis. The potential tutor's willingness to accept this last premise is essential because the premise governs much of the practice in paper marking which is done in the course.

The course itself is run as a small discussion group which meets once, sometimes twice, a week for an hour, and for which students receive two credit hours. The first half of the semester is spent solely on preparing the tutors while the second half includes actual tutoring in the lab. (During the first half of the semester, established tutors from previous semesters cover the lab.) The main emphases of the course are the practice exercises in paper marking and the tutoring work itself, but there are some secondary emphases which provide a formal and theoretical framework for the tutor. Generally the more theoretical work is handled earlier in the course while practice in paper marking covers most of the semester. A tutor trainee interested in theory, however, may do independent work in rhetoric or linguistics and, for a third credit hour, can write a paper on the subject.

The theoretical part of the course starts off with some reading and discussion of the relative value of languages and dialects, and the arbitrariness of standards of usage. The idea is to orient tutors towards enlightened acceptance of many non-standard errors as being culturally different, not linguistically inferior. The tutor is to see himself/herself as a guide who can help the tutee learn standard practices, not as a guard righteously defending the English language against those who would defile it. I usually have students read the first chapter of W. Nelson Francis's *The Structure of American English* to dispel myths about language. Students are also required to review the central chapters of a standard freshman composition text, McCrimmon's *Writing with a Purpose*, in order to get an understanding of what I call the "party line" approach to teaching writing. We then discuss the strengths and weaknesses of this standard approach—how it reflects or fails to reflect the writing process as we ourselves know it. To balance the standard classroom approach represented by McCrimmon's book, I send the students to a number of articles from composition journals covering such topics as individualized instruction, small group discussion, and mimetic writing exercises, all topics which wouldn't be included in a text.[2] In addition, the tutor trainees read one chapter a week from Gary Tate's *Teaching Composition: Ten Bibliographical Essays.* This is their sourcebook for rhetoric; each chapter provides an overview of an area of rhetoric while supplying extensive bibliography for those who want to follow up on a topic.

Finally, students in the course must review a standard handbook (I usually use *Prentice-Hall Handbook for Writers*). The purpose here is not only to brush up on basic grammar but to learn the formal terminology for various errors in mechanics. Trainees may not wish to use these terms when they tutor, but they should have the option open to them. In fact, I discourage the trainees from much reliance on formal terminology when they are working with tutees. As the trainees begin their first paper-marking exercises, I refer them instead to the following set of guidelines I have developed:

First Reading (React)

1. Underline or circle words or sentences which seem particularly effective or particularly weak.
2. Ask yourself: what is the purpose of the paper? What central point is it trying to make?
3. Consider your reaction to the paper and its subject. Is it positive or negative? Does the paper hold your interest?

Second Reading (Analyze)

1. Again, what is the main idea or purpose of the paper? Is it stated explicitly? If so, underline the sentence(s). If not, formulate a topic or thesis sentence yourself.
2. If there is no main idea, then what are the minor ideas? How many are there and why don't they add up to a main idea?
3. Can you trace the flow of the main idea? If so, how is the idea carried through? Through logical explanation, through illustration (specify examples), through chronological process, through comparison/contrast?
4. If you cannot follow the flow, where does the progression break down? Are there any sentences or groups of sentences which seem irrelevant?
5. Are all sentences clear and grammatical? Go back to the sentences or words you underlined or circled in #1 of the "react" section. Can you describe why these usages are effective or weak?

Although the guidelines do call for attention to mechanics and style, their emphasis is largely holistic. When tutor trainees get their first paper-marking assignment, I urge them to deal with the papers in this spirit.

As I indicated earlier, the practice in paper marking takes up a good deal of the course. The papers which are the subject of these practice exercises are actually student essays which I have collected over the years. Rather than working immediately and directly with current student writing, the trainees spend a good deal of time practicing and sharpening their technique on true-to-life samples. The following is a typical sample paper, except that it is shorter than most:

SCHOOL BUSING

My Educational Experience in Philadelphia was one that I deeply regret. My elementary school experience proved to be the most Enjoyable and profitable; But after that everything went down hill. I can remember the teachers not being able to carry on lessons due to behavior problems. Either the gangsters or the less harmful talkers stood in my way. In high school there was a combination of poor teaching and behavior problems. If school busing could relieve this problem in my community, good! But, until the chances of getting a quality Education will remain slim. Some do manage to get by, for instance both of my sisters went to the same schools as I. And went on to college to become successful. But there were too many of my friends who were Just satisfied to graduate and find a job. I was lucky Enough to get into music, which in turn got me here. Unfortunately my parents didn't know what was going on or weren't able to do anything at all, I didn't talk much about it. It should be brought to everyone's attention.

The tutor trainees are required for the first few weeks to grade their samples twice—first by objectively analyzing the piece and then by providing a comment that they might make if they were talking directly to the student. Thus, if the piece just quoted were given as a practice exercise, a tutor trainee might produce something like the following two responses to it:

(1) *Objective Analysis*

The writer of this paragraph has problems with focusing. First of all, the paragraph has very little to do with its ostensible topic—busing. Second, there are at least three main ideas rather than a single unifying idea: (1) the regrettable educational experience; (2) the success of some students in spite of the circumstances; and (3) the lack of general awareness of the problem. Mechanically, there are numerous difficulties: fragments, comma splices, faulty punctuation and capitalization. Sentence seven indicates that part of the problem with grammar stems from the informal style of the paragraph: the subordinate clause (If school busing . . .) is followed by a single word (good!) rather than a complete main clause. This sentence would work well in speech but not in writing. This informal style also indicates the paragraph's main strength: it is drawn from personal experience and has an energetic and honest feel about it.

(2) *Comment to Student*

You've chosen an important personal experience to write about, but now that you've decided on the general area you want to work with, you should try to narrow the paragraph to one main idea. If you'd rather talk about poor conditions in your school than about busing, that's okay, but try to stick to that subject once you've picked it. Could you write the whole paragraph about types of behavior problems in your high school?

These responses are somewhat condensed, but they capture the essence of both types of comment.

The point of this two-part process is to train the tutors to see on the one hand what it is *possible* to say about a paper and what, on the other hand, it is *practical* or *useful* to comment on. Most trainees readily accept the idea that they will not help their tutees by being hypercritical or by systematically demolishing the tutee's writing. By the same token the tutors understand that they cannot simply be cheerleaders who give false praise to writing which needs work. Thus the goal for the trainees becomes to develop a style which allows them to be as positive and encouraging as they can while still directing the tutee to work in areas needing improvement. Toward this end the tutor trainees often help each other. One thing I like to do is ask them to exchange their marked papers with each other (the samples are identical—only their comments will differ). In this way they can pick up valuable marking techniques from each other and also attempt to resolve differences of opinion about how to mark a paper. Usually one of the biggest challenges discussed in the trainee group at this point is how to recognize and comment upon *strengths,* which are too often taken for granted in the general rush to find critical things to say.

One technique which I've found helpful to the trainees as they mark sample papers is to suggest that they view what they read as a *draft* rather than a *paper.* When one looks at the draft, the natural tendency is to think in terms of strengths which can be expanded. Thinking of a piece as a finished paper, on the other hand, is more likely to lead to a fault finding attitude—a feeling that "this is not good enough," rather than a feeling that "you've got something here you could develop." Thus, the "draft technique" involves more than a superficial change of terms; it serves to remind tutors of the need on their part for a helpful orientation toward their tutees. Eventually (by the fourth or fifth week of the course), the students are instructed to cease marking the papers from a double perspective and to concentrate all their efforts on only what they would say to the tutee. And by the seventh week, most trainees are ready for actual tutoring.

For the first week of their tutoring practice, the trainees are limited to working with one tutee with whom they may meet two or three times. Once they begin to feel more confident, they expand their tutorial contacts. During this part of the course, tutors use the course meetings to exchange their impressions about tutoring and to talk over any problems or successes they have had. One of the points raised most often by the trainees in these sessions is that they are surprised by the extent to which tutees' problems are not strictly writing problems. The tutee may not be able to write the paper because he or she dislikes the course or the teacher, or doesn't understand the assignment, or hasn't been able to budget his or her time to allow for writing. In other words, while the tutors have been trained to analyze writing and to give helpful suggestions for improving writing, they often find themselves discussing with their tutees many things *surrounding* the actual paper.

At any rate, in the four years that I have been staffing the lab in this way our tutors have done very well. Tutees have consistently evaluated the tutors favorably and the tutors themselves have felt good about their work. As future English teachers most of them have also appreciated the chance to learn some theory and get some tutoring experience. The administration has been happy, too, to staff the lab with competent tutors working for the minimum wage (though tutoring is *required* in the training course, the trainees do get paid for their work). And finally, I've found the course an enjoyable alternative to teaching only straight composition courses.

Notes

[1] Paula Beck, Thom Hawkins, and Marcia Silver, "Training and Using Peer Tutors," *CE,* 40 (1978), 446.

[2] For example, Lester Fisher and Donald Murray, "Perhaps the Professor Should Cut Class," *CE,* 35 (1973), 169-73, and Thom Hawkins, "Group Inquiry Techniques for Teaching Writing," *CE,* 37 (1976), 637-46.

Some Developmental Principles for Teaching Composition

BARRY M. KROLL

Of the many theoretical perspectives from which to approach written composition, the one that has come to interest me most is the developmental perspective, with its emphasis on human intellectual growth. Specifically, the "cognitive-developmental" approach, based on the psychology of Jean Piaget and the educational philosophy of John Dewey, provides a particularly appropriate basis for thinking about composing. In his theory of development, Piaget maintains that growth is always a function of the interaction of external environmental forces and internal intellectual structures. In the act of knowing the world, people transform the environment to fit their cognitive structures and in the process have their cognitive structures elaborated and transformed. Thus, intellectual growth takes place through a person's interaction with the environment. Such a theory differs both from "nurture" theories of development, which view the environment as the source of growth, and from "nature" theories of development, which view the person as the source of growth.[1]

This Piagetian view of development has certain implications for research and teaching. In a recent essay, Loren Barritt and I tried to sketch four of the implications for composition research: (1) that speaking and writing may entail somewhat different intellectual processes, (2) that errors can provide insight into students' composing strategies, (3) that an egocentric orientation—in which the writer has difficulty viewing the world from multiple perspectives—affects the writer's audience awareness, and (4) that social-emotional development may be facilitated through expressive writing. We suggested that a "developmental rhetoric," modeled on developmental psychology, might emerge as a new research focus in composition.[2]

But the cognitive-developmental perspective also has implications for teaching, because development is seen as an educational aim. In brief, the specific educational theory, outlined in the work of John Dewey, maintains that the basic conditions for educational development are fulfilled when students become actively and cooperatively engaged in a prolonged, meaningful activity which involves solving some sort of problem through thinking.[3] Like

Piaget, Dewey saw learning as the dynamic interaction of internal and external forces, thus implying that teaching involves a balance between freedom and constraint, and that learning involves a balance between the concerns of the self and the demands of society. If we apply the insights of Piaget and Dewey in a cognitive-developmental approach to college composition, I believe that we discover six core principles which can serve as guides for instruction.

1. Provide Writing Problems

Perhaps the key claim of the cognitive-developmental approach to composition is that students need to engage in holistic writing tasks—tasks with a genuine aim and audience. These tasks should be "problems" in that they require students to work to extend their skills, to stretch their intellectual muscles, to actively discover both the way they think and how to best present this knowledge in writing. Providing such tasks demands sensitivity, because the teacher needs to set problems that challenge the students without discouraging them.

There have been a number of suggestions for composition classes based on a "problem solving" model, but the approach I like best is the "team-learning" approach devised over ten years ago by Leonard Greenbaum and Rudolf Schmerl, and piloted both at the University of Michigan and at Tuskegee Institute of Technology.[4] This course presented students with a topic area for the semester's work (e.g., the impact of the Viet Nam war in Ann Arbor; a Congressional election campaign). Working in groups, the students then broke this area into manageable units, gathered information from many sources, and wrote three papers collaboratively during the semester. Funds were available to have these papers printed in a monograph which was distributed to university and community groups. Three features of this course bear emphasizing: (1) students worked intensively for an extended period of time on a challenging writing problem. (2) The written products had a purpose and a broad, interested audience. (3) The teachers, while providing guidance, allowed students to make independent decisions and did not intervene to prevent "mistakes." Such a course seems to embody the most important of Dewey's conditions for education.

2. Emphasize Writing as a Process

An emphasis on the process of writing is a natural outcome of a cognitive-developmental approach because students are working from the beginning of a course on holistic writing tasks—producing discourse. This necessitates a period of prewriting (discovering ways to approach the task), a period of gathering information, sorting out one's ideas, and writing drafts and a period of reviewing and assessing what one has written. However, the trouble with many discussions of the writing "process" is that they make everything sound neater than it is: three quick and easy steps to good compositions—prewriting, writing, rewriting. Anyone who has reflected on his or her own writing experiences knows that this linear sequence of steps is only a very rough approximation of the process, ignoring recursive activity and the interaction among stages. Thinking and writing are usually so wrapped up together that the influence of each is difficult to separate out. Students need to know that writing is manageable, that there are ways of getting ideas when one runs dry, but they also need a realistic understanding of the complexities of the writing process so that they don't adopt a simplistic model that doesn't work for them—and perhaps doesn't work for anyone.

3. Facilitate Social Interaction

The interactive composition class—a class that involves students in writing for one another, reading and responding to each other's papers, and writing some papers collaboratively—has been getting increased attention, and rightly so.[5] Cooperation and collaboration are valuable social organizations for learning. There are at least three specific benefits of an interactive composition classroom. First, social interaction in the form of talk about paper topics is beneficial in the "prewriting" stage, when students are exploring subjects they may write about later. Talk is vital at this stage. Who knows that better than a college teacher? When I get an idea for a project or article, the first thing I do is corner a colleague and talk about it. As I talk, I discover things: I need to justify a certain point, there are weak spots in my argument, the problem is more interesting than I anticipated at first. My colleague asks questions, suggests objections or alternative approaches, or maybe looks so puzzled that I know I have major work to do. Students should have similar experiences, but often don't—sometimes because we don't value group talk in the classroom, and sometimes because we haven't shown them *how* to conduct profitable small-group work. I hear this complaint frequently from secondary-school English teachers: "I tried that social interaction business. What a chaotic disaster! One day was all that I could stand." Of course. We cannot expect students conditioned by years of exposure to the typical school classroom to make the transition easily or quickly. It takes patient teaching to make an interactive class work, but the results are worth it.

Second, social interaction in the form of peer teaching, when successful, has distinct advantages over the professional-teacher/thirty-students model: both tutor and tutored learn a great deal in such an encounter, and there is an opportunity for effective individualization. Third, social interaction in the form of group readings of student papers provides an audience for writing and can help teach students the importance of writing from the reader's perspective. By alternately taking the roles of reader and writer, students begin to see the complementary relationship of these roles: a piece of "writing" is really a piece of "reading"—that is, we write "reading." Hopefully, through this kind of experience students will internalize the perspective of the reader and bring it to bear when writing.

4. Recognize the Importance of Attitudes

The cognitive-developmentalist takes a "learning" rather than a "teaching" perspective on education. That is, the general goal for a composition course is that students learn to write better—more willingly, more fluently, more correctly. The teacher can set problems, arrange experiences, and give advice—and all of these are important—but the students, ultimately, must become engaged in writing, actively applying and extending what they know and discovering what skills they lack. Thus, it is crucial that students willingly invest energy in writing, that they value the process and products of composing. Therefore, the attitudes that students have about writing are really quite central to the composition class, and the teacher needs to deal effectively with apprehensive or discouraged writers. Diederich characterizes his remedial students this way: "They hate and fear writing more than anything else they have had to do in school. If they see a blank sheet of paper on which they are expected to write something, they look as though they want to scream."[6] Such attitudes interfere with learning to write. While there is no panacea for curing negative attitudes, the most fruitful approach seems to be to work simultaneously both on helping students master some of the basic skills that impede their writing fluency (and are often sources of embarrassment) and also on valuing their language competencies and acknowledging their successes.

5. Extend Language Facility

When cognitive-developmentalists claim that development is the aim of education, they mean that students should be encouraged to extend their composing competencies, moving to more developmentally mature levels of language and communication skills. Thus, one goal of a writing course would be to enhance students' writing fluency, helping them to produce discourse more efficiently. This means a lot of writing practice, particularly use of free writing techniques such as those advocated by Peter Elbow in *Writing Without Teachers.*[7] Another goal would be to extend students' syntactic and rhetorical skills by making use of such techniques as sentence combining or Christensen rhetoric.[8] While these techniques can be misused (as rote drill or as the sole answer to all writing problems), they are, used judiciously, extremely effective means for extending students' language facility.

6. Deal Forthrightly with Errors

Perhaps the wisest statement on the importance of students' errors comes from Mina Shaughnessy: "Errors count but not as much as most English teachers think."[9] The point is that errors do interfere with many students' abilities to express themselves fluently and to communicate *effectively.* But granting that point, how is one to deal with errors? Not simply by marking every violation of standard written conventions, leaving it to the student to interpret the meaning of the red ink. Rather, the cognitive-developmentalist views error as a valuable analytical tool, a way to understand the strategies that a student is using in his or her writing, a way to show the student the logic of an error, and, of course, a way to demonstrate a thinking process which leads to the correct form. The approach is one of "error analysis": identifying and systematically categorizing mistakes, dealing with each student's most salient and consistent writing errors, and refusing either to overwhelm the students by pointing out every deviation from written conventions or to discourage the student by dwelling on the negative aspects of a composition.[10]

In sum, a composition course based on cognitive-developmental theory entails the presentation of challenging—but realistic and interesting—writing tasks which require students to extend their skills of thought and language. To the greatest extent possible, we should create situations in which students produce writing that will mean something to a group of readers—writing that will be read, at least by peers and hopefully by even a broader audience. In the process of fulfilling such composing tasks, students will probably make mistakes, but these should be greeted as promising signs of development, as opportunities to explore the composing strategies the students are trying out. And since the development of competent, self-reliant writers is our aim, we should show students how to extend their language facility and help them to systematically reduce their troublesome writing errors. . . .

Notes

[1] Two excellent texts elaborate the points made briefly in this paragraph: Jonas Langer, *Theories of Development* (New York: Holt, 1969) and Richard M. Lener, *Concepts and Theories of Human Development* (Reading, MA: Addison-Wesley, 1976).

[2] Loren S. Barritt and Barry M. Kroll, "Some Implications of Cognitive-Developmental Psychology for Research on Composing," in *Research on Composing: Points of Departure*, ed. Charles R. Cooper and Lee Odell (Urbana, IL: NCTE, 1978), pp. 49-57.

[3] John Dewey, *Democracy and Education* (New York: Macmillan, 1916). See also William K. Frankena, *Three Historical Philosophies of Education* (Chicago: Scott, Foresman, 1968), pp. 133-91. I deal with these issues more fully in "Developmental Perspectives and the Teaching of Composition," *College English*, 41 (1980), 741-752.

[4] Leonard A. Greenbaum and Rudolf B. Schmerl, "A Team Learning Approach to Freshman English," *College English*, 29 (1967), 135-152; Rudolf B. Schmerl, "Team Learning in the Engineering English Class," *Southern Engineering Intercom*, 1 (October-November 1976), 5-11.

[5] As examples see Kenneth A. Bruffee, "Collaborative Learning: Some Practical Models," *College English*, 34 (1973), 634-43; and Thom Hawkins, *Group Inquiry Techniques for Teaching Writing* (Urbana, IL: ERIC and NCTE, 1976).

[6] Paul B. Diederich, *Measuring Growth in English* (Urbana, IL: NCTE, 1974), p. 21.

[7] Peter Elbow, *Writing Without Teachers* (New York: Oxford University Press, 1973).

[8] For example William Strong, *Sentence Combining: A Composing Book* (New York: Random House, 1973); Francis Christensen and Bonniejean Christensen, *A New Rhetoric* (New York: Harper & Row, 1976).

[9] Mina P. Shaughnessy, *Errors and Expectations: A Guide for the Teacher of Basic Writing* (New York: Oxford University Press, 1977), p. 120.

[10] Barry M. Kroll and John C. Schafer, "Error Analysis and the Teaching of Composition," *College Composition and Communication*, 29 (1978), 242-48.

The Listening Eye:
Reflections on the Writing Conference

DONALD M. MURRAY

It was dark when I arrived at my office this winter morning, and it is dark again as I wait for my last writing student to step out of the shadows in the corridor for my last conference. I am tired, but it is a good tired, for my students have generated energy as well as absorbed it. I've learned something of what it is to be a childhood diabetic, to raise oxen, to work across from your father at 115 degrees in a steeldrum factory, to be a welfare mother with three children, to build a bluebird trail, to cruise the disco scene, to be a teen-age alcoholic, to salvage World War II wreckage under the Atlantic, to teach invented spelling to first graders, to bring your father home to die of cancer. I have been instructed in other lives, heard the voices of my students they had not heard before, shared their satisfaction in solving the problems of writing with clarity and grace. I sit quietly in the late afternoon waiting to hear what Andrea, my next student, will say about what she accomplished on her last draft and what she intends on her next draft.

It is nine weeks into the course and I know Andrea well. She will arrive in a confusion of scarves, sweaters, and canvas bags, and then produce a clipboard from which she will precisely read exactly what she has done and exactly what she will do. I am an observer of her own learning, and I am eager to hear what she will tell me.

I am surprised at this eagerness. I am embedded in tenure, undeniably middle-aged, one of the gray, fading professors I feared I would become, but still have not felt the bitterness I saw in many of my own professors and see in some of my colleagues. I wonder if I've missed something important, if I'm becoming one of those aging juveniles who bound across the campus from concert to lecture, pleasantly silly.

There must be something wrong with a fifty-four-year-old man who is looking forward to his thirty-fifth conference of the day. It is twelve years since I really started teaching by conference. I average seventy-five conferences a week, thirty weeks a year, then there's summer teaching and workshop teaching of teachers. I've probably held far more than 30,000 writing conferences, and I am still fascinated by this strange, exposed kind of teaching, one on one.

College English, 41 (September 1979), pp. 13-18. Copyright ©1979 by the National Council of Teachers of English. Reprinted by permission of the publisher and the author.

It doesn't seem possible to be an English teacher without the anxiety that I will be exposed by my colleagues. They will find out how little I do; my students will expose me to them; the English Department will line up in military formation in front of Hamilton Smith Hall and, after the buttons are cut off my Pendleton shirt, my university library card will be torn once across each way and let flutter to the ground.

The other day I found myself confessing to a friend, "Each year I teach less and less, and my students seem to learn more. I guess what I've learned to do is to stay out of their way and not to interfere with their learning."

I can still remember my shock years ago when I was summoned by a secretary from my classroom during a writing workshop. I had labored hard but provoked little discussion. I was angry at the lack of student involvement and I was angry at the summons to the department office. I stomped back to the classroom and was almost in my chair before I realized the classroom was full of talk about the student papers. My students were not even aware I had returned. I moved back out to the corridor, feeling rejected, and let the class teach itself.

Of course, that doesn't always happen, and you have to establish the climate, the structure, the attitude. I know all that, and yet . . .

I used to mark up every student paper diligently. How much I hoped my colleages would see how carefully I marked my student papers. I alone held the bridge against the pagan hordes. No one escaped the blow of my "awk." And then one Sunday afternoon a devil bounded to the arm of my chair. I started giving purposefully bad counsel on my students' papers to see what would happen. "Do this backward," "add adjectives and adverbs," "be general and abstract," "edit with a purple pencil," "you don't mean black you mean white." Not one student questioned my comments.

I was frightened my students would pay so much attention to me. They took me far more seriously than I took myself. I remembered a friend in advertising told me about a head copywriter who accepted a piece of work from his staff and held it overnight without reading it. The next day he called in the staff and growled, "Is this the best you can do?"

They hurried to explain that if they had more time they could have done better. He gave them more time. And when they met the new deadline, he held their copy again without reading it, and called them together again and said, "Is *this* the best you can do?"

Again they said if only they had more time, they could . . . He gave them a new deadline. Again he held their draft without reading it. Again he gave it back to them. Now they were angry. They said, yes, it was the best they could do and he answered, "I'll read it."

I gave my students back their papers unmarked, and said, make them better. And they did. That isn't exactly the way I teach now, not quite, but I did learn something about teaching writing.

In another two-semester writing course I gave 220 hours of lecture during the year. My teaching evaluations were good: students signed up to take this course in advance. Apparently I was well-prepared, organized, entertaining. No one slept in my class, at least with their eyes shut, and they did well on the final exam. But that devil found me in late August working over my lecture notes and so, on the first day of class, I gave the same final exam I had given at the end of the year. My students did better before the 220 hours of lectures than my students had done afterwards. I began to learn something about teaching a non-content writing course, about under-teaching, about not teaching what my students already know.

The other day a graduate student who wanted to teach writing in a course I supervise indicated, "I have no time for non-directive teaching. I know what my students need to know. I know the problems they will have—and I teach them."

I was startled, for I do not know what my students will be able to do until they write without any instruction from me. But he had a good repu-tation, and I read his teaching evaluations. The students liked him, but there was a minor note of discomfort. "He does a good job of teaching, but I wish he would not just teach me what I already know" and "I wish he would listen better to what we need to know." But they liked him. They could under-stand what he wanted, and they could give it to him. I'm uncomfortable when my students are uncomfortable, but more uncomfortable when they are comfortable.

I teach the student not the paper but this doesn't mean I'm a "like wow" teacher. I am critical and I certainly can be directive but I listen before I speak. Most times my students make tough—sometimes too tough—evaluations of their work. I have to curb their too critical eye and help them see what works and what might work so they know how to read evolv-ing writing so it will evolve into writing worth reading.

I think I've begun to learn the right questions to ask at the beginning of a writing conference.

"What did you learn from this piece of writing?"
"What do you intend to do in the next draft?"
"What surprised you in the draft?"
"Where is the piece of writing taking you?"
"What do you like best in the piece of writing?"
"What questions do you have of me?"

I feel as if I have been searching for years for the right questions, ques-tions which would establish a tone of master and apprentice, no, the voice of a fellow craftsman having a conversation about a piece of work, writer to writer, neither praise nor criticism but questions which imply further drafts, questions which draw helpful comments out of the student writer.

And now that I have my questions, they quickly become unnecessary. My students ask these questions of themselves before they come to me. They have taken my conferences away from me. They come in and tell me what has gone well, what has gone wrong, and what they intend to do about it.

Some of them drive an hour or more for the conference that is over in fifteen minutes. It is pleasant and interesting to me, but don't they feel cheated? I'm embarrassed that they tell me what I would hope I would tell them, but probably not as well. My students assure me it is important for them to prepare themselves for the conference and to hear what I have to say.

"But I don't say anything," I confess. "You say it all."

They smile and nod as if I know better than that, but I don't.

What am I teaching? At first I answered in terms of form: argument, narrative, description. I never said comparison and contrast, but I was almost as bad as that. And then I grew to answering, "the process." "I teach the writing process." "I hope my students have the experience of the writing process." I hear my voice coming back from the empty rooms which have held teacher workshops.

That's true, but there's been a change recently. I'm really teaching my students to react to their own work in such a way that they write increasingly effective drafts. They write; they read what they've written; they talk to to me about what they've read and what the reading has told them they should do. I nod and smile and put my feet up on the desk, or down on the floor, and listen and stand up when the conference runs too long. And I get paid for this?

Of course, what my students are doing, if they've learned how to ask the right questions, is write oral rehearsal drafts in conference. They tell me what they are going to write in the next draft, and they hear their own voices telling me. I listen and they learn.

But I thought a teacher had to talk. I feel guilty when I do nothing but listen. I confess my fear that I'm too easy, that I have too low standards, to a colleague, Don Graves. He assures me I am a demanding teacher, for I see more in my students than they see in themselves. I certainly do. I expect them to write writing worth reading, and they do—to their surprise, not mine.

I hear voices from my students they have never heard from themselves. I find they are authorities on subjects they think ordinary. I find that even my remedial students write like writers, putting down writing that doesn't quite make sense, reading it to see what sense might be in it, trying to make sense of it, and—draft after draft—making sense of it. They follow language to see where it will lead them, and I follow them following language.

It is a matter of faith, faith that my students have something to say and a language in which to say it. Sometimes I lose that faith but if I regain it and do not interfere, my students do write and I begin to hear things that need saying said well.

This year, more than ever before, I realize I'm teaching my students what they've just learned.

They experiment, and when the experiment works I say, "See, look what happened." I put the experiment in the context of the writing process. They brainstorm, and I tell them that they've brainstormed. They write a discovery draft, and I point out that many writers have to do that. They revise, and then I teach them revision.

When I boxed I was a counterpuncher. And I guess that's what I'm doing now, circling my students, waiting, trying to shut up—it isn't easy—

trying not to interfere with their learning, waiting until they've learned something so I can show them what they've learned. There is no text in my course until my students write. I have to study the new text they write each semester.

It isn't always an easy text to read. The student has to decode the writing teacher's text; the writing teacher has to decode the student's writing. The writing teacher has to read what hasn't been written yet. The writing teacher has the excitement of reading unfinished writing.

Those papers without my teacherly comments written on them haunt me. I can't escape the paranoia of my profession. Perhaps I should mark up their pages. There are misspellings, comma splices, sentence fragments (even if they are now sanctified as "English minor sentences.") Worse still, I get papers that have no subject, no focus, no structure, papers that are undeveloped and papers that are voiceless.

I am a professional writer—a hired pen who ghostwrites and edits—yet I do not know how to correct most student papers. How do I change the language when the student writer doesn't yet know what to say? How do I punctuate when it is not clear what the student must emphasize? How do I question the diction when the writer doesn't know the paper's audience?

The greatest compliment I can give a student is to mark up a paper. But I can only mark up the best drafts. You can't go to work on a piece of writing until it is near the end of the process, until the author has found something important to say and a way to say it. Then it may be clarified through a demonstration of professional editing.

The student sits at my right hand and I work over a few paragraphs, suggesting this change, that possibility, always trying to show two, or three, or four alternatives so that the student makes the final choice. It is such satisfying play to mess around with someone else's prose that it is hard for me to stop. My best students snatch their papers away from my too eager pen but too many allow me to mess with their work as if I knew their world, their language, and what they had to say about their world and their language. I stop editing when I see they really appreciate it. It is not my piece of writing; it is not my mind's eye that is looking at the subject: not my language which is telling what the eye has seen. I must be responsible and not do work which belongs to my students, no matter how much fun it is. When I write it must be my own writing, not my students'.

I realize I not only teach the writing process, I follow it in my conferences. In the early conferences, the prewriting conferences, I go to my students; I ask questions about their subject, or if they don't have a subject, about their lives. What do they know that I don't know? What are they authorities on? What would they like to know? What would they like to explore? I probably lean forward in these conferences; I'm friendly, interested in them as individuals, as people who may have something to say.

Then, as their drafts begin to develop and as they find the need for focus, for shape, for form, I'm a bit removed, a fellow writer who shares his own writing problems, his own search for meaning and form.

Finally, as the meaning begins to be found, I lean back, I'm more the

reader, more interested in the language, clarity. I have begun to detach myself from the writer and from the piece of writing which is telling the student
how to write it. We become fascinated by this detachment which is forced
on student and teacher as a piece of writing discovers its own purpose.

After the paper is finished and the student starts on another, we go
back through the process again and I'm amused to feel myself leaning forward, looking for a subject with my student. I'm not coy. If I know something I think will help the student, I share it. But I listen first—and listen
hard (appearing casual)—to hear what my student needs to know.

Now that I've been a teacher this long I'm beginning to learn how to be
a student. My students are teaching me their subjects. Sometimes I feel as if
they are paying for an education and I'm the one getting the education. . . .

I expected to learn of other worlds from my students but I didn't
expect—an experienced (old) professional writer—to learn about the writing
process from my students. But I do. The content is theirs but so is the experience of writing—the process through which they discover their meaning.
My students are writers and they teach me writing most of the time.

I notice my writing bag and a twenty-page paper I have tossed towards
it. Jim has no idea what is right or wrong with the paper—neither do I. I've
listened to him in conference and I'm as confused as he is. Tomorrow morning I will do my writing, putting down my own manuscript pages, then,
when I'm fresh from my own language, I will look at Jim's paper. And when
he comes back I will have at least some new questions for him. I might even
have an answer, but if I do I'll be suspicious. I am too fond of answers, of
lists, of neatness, of precision; I have to fight the tendency to think I know
the subject I teach. I have to wait for each student draft with a learning,
listening eye. Jim will have re-read the paper and thought about it too and I
will have to be sure I listen to him first for it is his paper, not mine.

Andrea bustles in, late, confused, appearing disorganized. Her hair is
totally undecided; she wears a dress skirt, lumberjack boots, a fur coat, a
military cap. She carries no handbag, but a canvas bag bulging with paper as
well as a lawyer's briefcase which probably holds cheese and bread.

Out comes the clipboard when I pass her paper back to her. She tells me
exactly what she attempted to do, precisely where she succeeded and how,
then informs me what she intends to do next. She will not work on this
draft; she is bored with it. She will go back to an earlier piece, the one I liked
and she didn't like. Now she knows what to do with it. She starts to pack up
and leave.

I smile and feel silly; I ought to do something. She's paying her own
way through school. I have to say something.

"I'm sorry you had to come all the way over here this late."

Andrea looks up surprised. "Why?"

"I haven't taught you anything."

"The hell you haven't. I'm learning in this course, really learning."

I start to ask Andrea what she's learning but she's out the door and
gone. I laugh, pack up my papers, and walk home.

Problem-Solving Strategies and the Writing Process

LINDA S. FLOWER and JOHN R. HAYES

In the midst of the composition renaissance, an odd fact stands out: our basic methods of teaching writing are the same ones English academics were using in the seventeenth century.[1] We still undertake to teach people to write primarily by dissecting and describing a completed piece of writing. The student is (a) exposed to the formal descriptive categories of rhetoric (modes of argument—definition, cause and effect, etc.—and modes of discourse—description, persuasion, etc.), (b) offered good examples (usually professional ones) and bad examples (usually his/her own) and (c) encouraged to absorb the features of a socially approved style, with emphasis on grammar and usage. We help our students analyze the product, but we leave the process of writing up to inspiration.[2]

Within the classroom, "writing" appears to be a set of rules and models for the correct arrangement of preexistent ideas. In contrast, outside of school, in private life and professions, writing is a highly goal-oriented, intellectual performance. It is both a strategic action and a thinking problem. But because writing as an act of thinking is messy and mysterious compared to the concrete reality of the product, we tend to leave composing up to the vagaries of chance and god-given talent, to relegate it to independent warm-up exercises designated as "*pre*-writing." The inner, intellectual *process* of composing, the complex and sometimes frustrating experience we all go through as we write, is a virtually unexplored territory.

This gap between the textbook and the experience is a problem composition must face. Because the act of writing is a complex cognitive skill, not a body of knowledge, teaching writers to analyze the product often fails to intervene at a meaningful stage in the writer's performance. Such teaching leaves a gap because it has little to say about the techniques and thinking process of writing as a student (or anyone else) experiences it.

I. Writing as a Form of Problem Solving

In an effort to treat writing as a thinking problem, rather than an arrangement problem, this paper will offer an introduction to some of the underlying problem-solving processes writers use in the act of composing. The research and teaching experiment it is based on started as an attempt to

College English, 39 (December 1977), pp. 449-461. Copyright © 1977 by the National Council of Teachers of English. Reprinted by permission of the publisher and the authors.

understand the mental process of writing as it exists for "normal" writers, and then to apply that knowledge to helping people write. "Problem solving," as a relatively new area in cognitive psychology, is uniquely adapted for this plan because it combines a well-developed experimental method for studying thought processes with a teaching method Aristotle used—teaching the student heuristic procedures for thinking through problems. In studying writing as a problem-solving process we have attempted, first, to describe some of the basic heuristic procedures which underlie writing, and then to translate these heuristics into teachable techniques.

As the study of cognitive or thinking processes, problem solving explores the wide array of mental procedures people use to process information in order to achieve their goals.[3] People use basic problem-solving procedures (such as planning, means/ends analysis, inference making) to solve all kinds of "problems," which range from inventing a mouse trap to designing a course syllabus or writing a sonnet. Articulating our own ideas and intentions to someone else—getting the right words on paper—draws on a staggering array of mental gymnastics, from simply generating language to highly sophisticated concept formation. However, the heuristic procedures which help us do this are often surprisingly simple. Such heuristics can often be brought to consciousness and improved by training.

A heuristic is an alternative to trial and error. It is simply the codification of a useful technique or cognitive skill. It can operate as a discovery procedure or a way of getting to a goal.[4] Many fields have them; for example, the scientific method is itself a heuristic, as is journalism's efficient Who? What? When? Where? Why? formula for collecting information. The important thing about heuristics is that they are not rules, which dictate a right or wrong way, but are alternative methods for doing something—methods which often formalize the efficient procedure a good scientist or journalist would use unconsciously. Because they make an intuitive method explicit, heuristics open complex processes up to the possibility of rational choice.

Strategies for Writing: Inspiration, Prescription, and Writer's Block

In the hope of opening the writing process up to increased self-awareness, we have studied the heuristics and strategies of both good and poor writers, using the methods of "protocol analysis." In order to tap the process itself, not the writer's later version of what he thought he did, protocol analysis uses the taped transcript (or experimental "protocol") of a writer asked to compose out loud. That is, he is asked to verbalize all thoughts that go through his mind, including false starts, stray thoughts, and repetitions.

The first striking fact that emerges from these protocols is that some writers have a very limited repertory of thinking techniques to call on as they write. They may find themselves trapped, for example, in the endless frustration of a "word search" when they really need to be generating an idea structure. This limited repertory is often linked to an inability to change tactics when the current procedure (e.g., trying to perfect a first sentence) has led to a block or dead end. Although the writer has alternative procedures, she/he may not have enough self-conscious awareness of his/her own skills to invoke them when needed.

Many inexperienced writers, whether they are students, businesspeople, or academics, feel they have only three major alternative strategies for writing: prescription (how the textbooks pretend people do it), inspiration (the infinitely mysterious way people really do it), and writer's block (a default behavior if neither of the above work). Our hope is to add a fourth alternative to this repertory: problem-solving techniques for thinking through the process.

Many writers depend heavily on inspiration because it produces their best, most efficient, and most satisfying writing. Many believe inspiration comes from the outside and must simply be waited upon; most have no effective recourse when it fails. Unfortunately, many writing problems are thinking problems which inspiration is ill-adapted to solve. Because inspiration is always dependent on the mental preparation that went before, it often does fail for the passively expectant writer waiting for the magic flow of ideas.

As an alternative to waiting out truant inspiration, a writer may resort to one of the prescriptive methods of writing taught in grade school, endorsed by his textbooks, and prized by those who want a sure-fire formula for required writing. The method is simple: name the topic, generate an outline of the obvious points ("cliches I know about the value of team sports or facts about thermal pollution"), and elaborate to fill in the blanks created by the outline. The result will probably bore the writer even though he may strongly feel it should pass muster: he followed the rules and, anyway, teachers are supposed to like that sort of thing. When inspiration breaks down, it's a grim picture for both the writer who has to grind something out and for the reader (teacher) who has to pretend it resembles serious thought.

A Problem-Solving Strategy for Writing

A problem-solving approach to writing offers an alternative strategy for confronting the thinking process. The remainder of this paper will present an overview of the heuristics we have learned from protocol analysis (the way good writers do it), from psychological studies of creativity, and from the traditions of rhetoric and composition teaching. We have used these heuristics to teach writing not only in composition courses, but as a condensed unit in problem-solving courses and management courses, and in workshops for teachers.

One advantage of these heuristics is that they give the writer a repertory of alternatives and the power of choice even as he is caught up in the struggle with words. Because these heuristics are a kind of shorthand for cognitive operations, they give the writer self-conscious access to some of the thinking techniques that normally constitute "inspiration." A second advantage of these heuristics is that they focus directly on the two major intellectual tasks the writer faces: the need (1) to generate ideas in language and then (2) to construct those ideas into a written structure adapted to the needs of a reader and the goals of the writer.

In formulating our strategy in this two-part way, we have made a fundamental assumption about the composing process: namely, that it can often be divided into two complementary but semi-autonomous processes, which we designate as generating versus constructing on one level and playing versus pushing on another. This division in our model reflects one of the essential dichotomies that pervades the literature on creativity and imagination. In their various ways, artists, critics, and psychologists have long recognized a distinction between what we might call inspiration and work; between romanticism's principle of organic unity and neoclassicism's equal veneration of conscious craft; between that nature-given "grace beyond the reach of art" and the man-made art of the commonplace "n'er so well expressed." Over time the prestige and precise definition of each mode varies, but together they represent two stable, complementary dimensions of the creative process. Although experienced writers fluidly switch from one mode of thinking to the other as they write, there are important practical reasons for writers to be conscious about this distinction and to recognize the multiple cognitive styles writing requires.

II. A Heuristic Strategy for Analytical Writing

The following heuristics, developed primarily for analytical writers, draw in part on established methods (such as brainstorming and synectics); others are our attempt to embody, in a teachable technique, some of the underlying problem-solving strategies good writers use. This shorthand version of the Heuristic Strategy was written for students with a limited to nonexistent background in writing, but an interest in treating it as a problem they could solve.

PART ONE: PLANNING

1. Plan

1. *Set Up a Goal*
Planning toward a goal is one of the most powerful of all problem-solving techniques because it lets you factor large problems down to manageable size.[5] When you write a paper, you are choosing among an immense number of possible things you could say, all of which could be potentially "correct." You can streamline this decision process by shifting from focusing on your topic (what you know) to focusing on your goal (what you want to do with what you know).

In practical terms this means that you start to write by trying to answer the blunt question readers always ask—"so what?" Why is this particular information being written down, why should anyone else read it, and what do you hope to accomplish by writing it? By contrast, some writers start by making elaborate outlines, filling in all the facts and thoughts they happen to have on the topic (say, the psychological effects of noise). But outlines, especially premature ones, are often dominated by the structure of the available information (what all could be said about noise); whereas a plan is governed by the writer (what *you* want or need to say to explain your idea, educate your reader, or perhaps even change his mind).

2. *Find Operators*
As you make your plans keep in mind that some plans have what are

called "operators"; that is, they have built-in directions which tell you how to go about reaching your goal. Compare these two plans, one with operators, one without: (1) I want to be rich and famous, vs. (2) I want to study probability, statistics, and problem solving so I can get rich quick at Las Vegas and become famous writing a bestseller on how I did it. For a writer a plan with operators might be, "I want to forcefully argue both sides of this controversy to show the reader that I have pinpointed the crucial issues, but also to pave the way for my own ideas."

Plans without operators are often highly abstract; for example, "I want to discuss team sports . . . impress my reader . . . get an A in this course." Such goals are so large, vague, and difficult that they are more likely to lead to writer's block than to purposeful thinking. An operator creates a manageable subgoal and gives you a place to start working.

PART TWO: GENERATING IDEAS IN WORDS

These techniques increase your creativity by helping you (1) to break set and get out of conventional patterns of thinking, (2) to foster those important elusive intuitions which might otherwise be censored or slip away, and (3) to discover among your own ideas important connections you may not have seen. However, the real problem you are working on here is not just getting ideas, but *verbalizing* them. Your goal is to get your thinking down in words, phrases, sentences—fragments of writing. Until you can express what's in your mind in words, it can be said you don't really know it yet. These techniques will help you follow out your ideas and turn them into language.

1. Play Your Thoughts

1. *Turn off the Editor and Brainstorm*

Once you have a sense of your goal and the problem before you, brainstorming is a good way to jump in. Brainstorming is a form of creative, *goal-directed play*. It has two rules: keep writing and don't try to censor or perfect as you go.

Start in the middle, at the end, or with any issue that's on your mind; start any place you want, but get started writing. Don't censor ideas—write them down. When you come up with an idea or expression that isn't quite "right," resist the temptation to throw it out and start again. Instead, write it down so you can tease out the good idea or intuition that was hidden inside it. If you don't see how it all fits together now, don't worry; just get your ideas in words. When you've exhausted a topic or feel you can't go much further right now, skip to another topic that is simmering in your mind.

Secondly, don't spend time polishing your prose or making it "flow." Because you are not trying to turn out a finished paper in one pass, you don't need to worry about following an outline or writing introductions and transitions. (In fact, isn't it unreasonable to try to write those *before* you've actually articulated the ideas you want to connect or introduce?)

Brainstorming is like "free writing" in that it encourages you to follow where intuition leads. But it has one important difference: free writing is a form of free association, stream of consciousness expression—one idea leads to another which leads to another, like links in a chain. Brainstorming, on the other hand, is goal-directed thinking. Although your thought is encouraged to go off on fresh and productive tangents, it is always returning, like spokes in a wheel, to focus on the problem at hand.

2. *Stage a Scenario*

People often come up with their best ideas and most powerful arguments when they are caught up in a live discussion. You can give yourself this same advantage by staging your own discussion. All of us have considerable powers of role playing which will let us take on not only certain familiar roles (such as the mature and responsible person we try to project at a job interview) but will also let us play the part of another person. That is, we can also switch parts, take on the attitudes and assumptions of the interviewer, and play that role when we want to.

You can use this ability to help generate better ideas in words by simulating the response of various readers or listeners: make them ask you questions (basic questions and difficult ones), raise objections, or make their own interpretations. For example, imagine what would be your reader's first response, and what would you say back to him? To get extra power out of this technique, give yourself different audiences with distinct expectations: a professor or supervisor listening critically to your logic, an employer looking to see what you can do, an audience of other experts at your lecture, or a friend trying to understand your main idea over a beer.

3. *Play Out An Analogy*

Whether we are conscious of it or not, much of our creative thinking is done by using analogies. When we see a partial resemblance between two things (going through high school is like serving time), we acquire a whole new set of concepts to think with.

In using analogies, you have to both encourage and harness their tendency to overflowing, undirected productivity. Suppose, for example, you are analyzing the operation of a university. It occurs to you that universities have much in common with big businesses. The *potential* connections between the two are numerous: the analogy could suggest that both need professional management, or that both would benefit from healthy competition, or perhaps that both turn out a product but seem to spend most of their advertising budget marketing a self-image, etc. To tap this potential you could simply brainstorm all the possibilities your analogy will yield, though many will be spurious. Or you could take your intuition seriously and try to discover the hidden connection, implicit in your thinking, which initially suggested the analogy. By making the connection explicit, you can also decide if it is valid. You thought of big business in this context for a reason; why? what was the hook for you?

There are a number of other generating techniques which tap the power of analogic thinking.[6] The most elaborate and formal one is synectics, in which you systematically explore four kinds of analogies: Personal, Symbolic, Direct, and Fantasy analogies. The most obvious technique is simply to apply the operator "like" to your idea: "Running a university is like . . . "

If these two techniques seem a little formal or artificial you can take advantage of analogic thinking in a more common way: simply change your vocabulary.

One powerful way to broaden your idea base is to talk about your subject from a different perspective, using a different vocabulary. As a systems engineer you might analyze university life in terms of work flow and productivity. But if that perspective (and its language) only tells half the story, you could try the outlook and special language of a consumer: are a QPA and diploma devalued commodities offered at inflated prices? Or are they real products a university offers? The goal is to change your idea set: the most natural way to do that is to change roles or vocabulary.

Why does this work? One reason is that by changing terms, you tap different pockets of knowledge. Playing out analogies in this way sorts through your stored knowledge for good ideas which aren't yet cross-indexed to each other in your memory. Changing your vocabulary, like changing roles in a scenario, lets you get to new, independent pockets of ideas and words.

4. Rest and Incubate

This can be an important part of the creative process if you do it well. When you need to stop work, do so only after you have formulated the next unsolved problem before you. Let your unfinished business simmer *actively* in the back of your mind and return to it from time to time. The corollary to using incubation well is that you are prepared, whenever a new idea or connection comes to you, to write it down. Don't expect inspiration to knock twice. The language you lose may be a loaded term that will only reveal its full possibilities later when you push it.

II. Push Your Ideas

1. Find a Cue Word or Rich Bit

Your own private cue words, if you can mine them, are a source of original ideas. Often in the process of brainstorming a writer will find that a single word, expression, or idea seems particularly important or that it keeps returning to her/his mind. For example, when people try to analyze their own writing process, many say that getting things to "flow" is a key concept for them, although they can't say exactly what that means. The expression "flow" is apparently functioning for them as a cue word, or what psycholinguists call a "rich bit": it stands as the center of a network of ideas and associations which are unique to the writer. By a kind of mental shorthand, that single expression brings together a whole body of ideas and experiences which are related to the person's thoughts.

When several writers were asked to push their ideas of "flow," one explained the experience as a process of hammering out rhythm and tight syntactic relations between sentences. For another writer, "flow" represented a radically different experience: getting things to flow meant following out a train of associations until he reached either a catharsis or a dead end. Both had much more information about their intimidating assignment—to analyze the process of writing—than they had realized.

From a semantic perspective, code words are a familiar problem: I say cow, meaning Bossie, and you think Bessie. But from a writer's perspective they are a virtual gold mine—easily accessible sources of original ideas. For many students, especially basic writers who fear they don't have "original ideas," pushing their own code words can be a powerful, even liberating, experience.

We think in rich bits and codes because it's more efficient than processing all the particulars. However, the particulars a rich bit stands for may only be related in some vague or as yet undefined way. If you have not yet pushed those relationships into language, it would not be accurate to call them an idea. Rich bits are like any intuition; they need to be pushed and examined if they are going to yield solid ideas. This is the heart of the writer's job—pushing potential ideas into communicable ones; that is, into language.

2. Nutshell Your Ideas and Teach Them

Find a listener/fellow-student/long-suffering friend to whom you can condense and explain the essentials of your thinking. In two or three sentences—in a nutshell—lay out the whole substance of your paper. Nutshelling practically forces you to make the relationship between your major ideas explicit. (In doing so you generate an issue tree which will be more useful to you than an ordinary outline.) Nutshells put noisy supporting information in its place and help you focus on the essentials of what you have to say.

Teaching also helps focus ideas because it taps our intuitive strategies for dealing with an audience. Like nutshelling, it forces you to conceptualize your information and make sure your listener gets *the point*, not just the data. When a writer begins to feel agog with an accumulation of ideas and information, teaching in a nutshell can help generate the new concepts and categories that can put all those ideas in order.

3. Tree Your Ideas

Most of the generation techniques described so far require you to think and write without the crutch or the straightjacket of a tidy outline. However, one of your major goals is to produce a paper with a clear and tight structure. Experienced writers resolve this apparent dilemma in the following way: they try to *pull* an outline *out* of the material they generate, rather than write to fill an outline in. Building an issue tree is a technique for structuring your ideas *after* you've begun to generate. It has two major advantages over starting with an outline: (1) It offers a more graphic representation of how ideas are related; (2) it shows you what you haven't yet said and where you need to do more thinking. A simple issue tree starts by trying to put the fragments of brainstorming into a hierarchical order:

Fragments   *Tree*

a. Speech habits have social aspects.
b. Speech is related to class.   Speech Habits   1.
c. Speech is affected by education.
d. Speech is determined by regional
   background.
x. Breathiness is considered a sexy
   trait in women.   class   education   region   2.

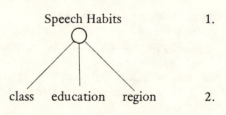

y. Throatiness is "unfeminine" in women, "mature" in men.

z. A wide pitch range is heard as "effeminate" in men or women.

A preliminary tree shows two things: (1) fragments b, c, and d are at equal levels of abstraction and belong on the second level of the tree. They give the writer a focus for further idea generation. (2) Fragments x, y, and z, by contrast, are related to speech habits but they won't fit on level 2 along with b, c, d, nor will they fit under them as sub-categories. However, added together, x, y, and z could produce a fourth level-2 category.

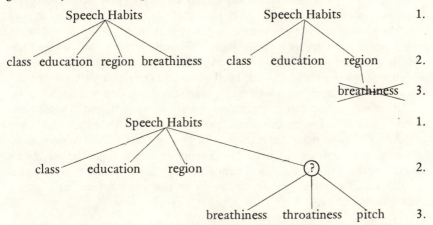

Trying to build an issue tree shows the writer that his/her next problem is to generate a new concept—an idea which will tie these three fragments together. The chief advantage of an issue tree is precisely this: it is a working tool which helps the writer see the structure of his/her thought as it develops and see where s/he needs to do more thinking.

In this example the issue tree goes on working. Once the writer has generated a new concept, s/he can see that while b, c, d, and e, all "relate" to a, they do so in different ways. A more developed tree, such as the one below, might not only clarify the writer's thinking, but suggest areas in which to generate ideas.

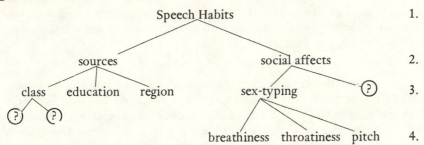

An outline, by contrast, can encourage a writer to paint by numbers—to simply fill in the blanks. An early outline, unlike an issue tree with empty slots, assumes that a writer *starts* writing with a clear knowledge of his/her high level concepts. Writing is reduced to a process of filling in the details. The truth of the matter, unfortunately, is that a writer's normal task is a thinking task. S/he must transform information into ideas and forge new, more adequate structures for those ideas than the ones s/he started out with.

4. *Test Your Writing Against Your Own Editor*

Try reading what you have written as if you were a first-time reader by going straight through your draft and locating any places that leave you somewhat confused. The sharpest analyst is the one who can pinpoint what he doesn't yet know or where he needs to go to work.

There are two techniques which will help you play the role of an objective reader who sees only what is written—not what you *meant* to say. The first is to read your prose carefully, word for word, as if you had never seen it before, and let its logic, syntax, and vocabulary lead you where they actually go. Read only what is on the page and cut out the well-inflected oral performance that goes on in your head when you *skim* over your own prose. If you let it, the inner voice will create emphasis, jump over the unclear bits, and fill in extra meanings from memory, while it lets you nod in agreement at familiar ideas and enjoy the pleasure of your own confirmed anticipations.

An even more powerful technique, if you can find a place to do it, is to read your own writing out loud. Don't whisper or you'll just be talking to yourself again. Read it in a good firm voice and listen to find out what you actually said. Better yet, create a scenario by positing your audience sitting there listening to you.

PART THREE: CONSTRUCTING FOR AN AUDIENCE

A first draft often satisfies a writer; it seems to say just what s/he meant. But when s/he comes back a day, a week, or a year later, many of the supporting assumptions and loaded meanings s/he brought to the first reading have vanished. The gaps, which s/he once filled in unconsciously, now stand out in the writing and demand explanation.

This week-after experience is often the plight of our readers. The goal of constructing heuristics is to help you figure out ahead of time how to structure your private version of a paper so it fills the gaps and fits the needs of another mind, namely, your audience.

In essence, what these heuristics ask you to do is perform a means/ends analysis on your own writing. That is, they ask you to decide what *ends* you hope to achieve by writing and then to consider some of the specific *means* that might help you do it.

I. Ends

What, exactly, are you trying to achieve in this paper or this paragraph, and what effect do you intend to have on your reader? Working from even a simple plan with operators lets you break out of the haphazard momentum writing sometimes imposes ("I'll just write a version and see how it turns out") and work as a goal-directed problem-solver. Good plans themselves are flexible and will probably keep changing as you go along. What separates a problem-solving writer from a simply intuitive writer is not the plan itself, but the fact that s/he is planning. You can use the four questions which follow to generate plans not only for an entire paper, when necessary, but for individual paragraphs and even sentences that are giving you trouble.

1. *Identify a Mutual End You and the Reader Share*

This is the "so what" question again, with the emphasis on your reader this time. What common goal do the two of you share? The desire to know your opinions on a subject is rarely enough to motivate most readers. Presuppose a reader with six papers on her/his desk and the time to read one. This statement, which you may even use later in your introduction, says why yours is the one s/he wants to read now.

2. *Decide on Your Own Specific Ends*

a. What do you want the reader to *know* at the end of your paper? What is the central information you want him/her to remember? When you know this, you can focus the rest of your writing around it.

b. What do you want your reader to *think* about that information? What *conclusions* would an ideal reader, one who really understood you, draw from your discussion? Generally speaking, this is the most difficult part of your paper to articulate, but the most important part for your reader. Assume you have a normal reader who will go away with two or three main ideas. What do *you* want those to be? If you can't explicitly state these summary concepts, the Nutshelling or Teaching heuristics are good techniques for forming such concepts.

c. What do you want your reader to *do*? Given what your reader will know and possibly think at the end of your paper, do you want him/her to apply it, and if so, how? Tell him/her.

II. Roadblocks

Once you have planned what you want your writing to accomplish, consider possible roadblocks. Is your reader likely to have any expectations or assumptions, negative attitudes, or crucial gaps in knowledge that would block your Mutual Ends? If so, you will have to decide what you are going to do: confront them, detour, or ignore?

III. Means

1. *Develop a Rhetorical Strategy*

Developing a rhetorical strategy necessarily involves a wide range of skills and methods, from the sophisticated ones of Aristotle to simplistic formulas for packing three examples beneath every point. Rather than review some of these familiar methods we will focus here on a new heuristic based on the cognitive needs of the reader. The goal of this heuristic is to transform Writer-Based prose and its typical structures into Reader-Based prose. This rhetorical strategy is designed to help the reader comprehend more of what the wrtier has to say.

Writer-Based Prose. Writing is inevitably a somewhat egocentric enterprise. It is always easiest to talk to ourselves, and we naturally tend to express ideas in the same patterns in which we store them in our mind. But if our goal is to communicate to someone else, those patterns in our own head may not be particularly clear or effective for a reader. The writer's job is to translate his/her own train of thought into a rhetorical structure. That is, s/he must translate his/her own egocentric or writer-based organization of information into a reader-based structure that meets the practical and cognitive needs of a reader.

Writer-Based prose is often the natural result of generating ideas; it borrows its structure from either the writer's own discovery process or from a structure inherent in the material the writers examined. For example, papers which start, "Shakespeare wrote three kinds of plays . . . " or "In the economy a business cycle is defined as . . . " often let the writer "print out" his stored knowledge about the subject instead of reshaping that information to a purpose. Writing which depends on a textbook or list structure often buries its point in a mass of related information. Because the writer failed to restructure information to support a conclusion, the job is left to the reader, who may be unwilling or unable to undertake the task.

A second, even more compelling, way to organize a paper is to simply follow the pattern of your own discovery process. ("In studying the stress patterns in this design, the first thing to consider is . . . " or "If income level, then, is a strong indicator of energy consumption, we can start to develop a predictive model which will . . . ") This pattern has the virtue of any form of drama: it keeps interest by withholding closure, if, that is, the audience is willing to wait that long for the point. Unfortunately, most academic and professional readers are impatient and tend to interpret such narrative, step-by-step structures as either wandering and confused (does he have a point?) or as a form of hedging.

Both of these examples of Writer-Based prose have advantages—for the writer. They are an easy and natural way to express one's thought. Furthermore, it is often most efficient to generate ideas in this form. The point is that in constructing a paper, a writer must recognize his/her own use of code words and writer-based structures and try to transform them to meet the needs of his/her reader.

Reader-Based Prose. There are many ways to write with a reader in mind. We will offer two heuristics well suited for analytical papers. The first is to set up a paper around the problem it is intended to solve and the conclusion you intend to argue for. Papers organized around problems not only focus a reader's attention, they help the writer subordinate his information to his goals and draw conclusions.

A second technique is to organize ideas in a clear hierarchy or tree. In composing, writers often work from the bottom of the tree up to more inclusive concepts. But readers understand best when they have an overview, when they can see an idea structure from the top down.[7]

2. Test Your Rhetorical Strategy

If you are lucky, you can test the effectiveness of your rhetorical structure on a live reader. Ask someone else to read your writing and to tell you in their own words what they thought you were saying. Use this feedback to compare what you intended with what you actually communicated. . . .

III. Teaching and Using Heuristics

The Process as a Whole

What does the entire process of writing look like? Do writers dutifully Plan, Generate, Construct, then turn out the light with the paper done? The answer is an emphatic *no*. Although we have grouped these heuristics together by their function, the process of writing rarely if ever exhibits those autonomous stages textbooks describe as Gather Information, Outline, and Write. Instead, thought in writing moves in a series of non-linear jumps from one problem and procedure to another.

We frequently talk of writing as if it were a series of independent temporarily bounded actions (e.g., pre-writing, writing, rewriting). It is more accurate to see it as a hierarchical set of subproblems arranged under a goal or set of goals. The process then is an iterative one. For each subproblem along the way—whether it is making a logical connection between hazy ideas, or finding a persuasive tone—the writer may draw on a whole repertoire of procedures and heuristic strategies. Having conscious access to some of those heuristics can make a process a lot easier.

Teaching

What are the implications of this unorderly but dynamic process for teaching? We will emphasize three:

1. Heuristics do not offer a step-by-step formula for how to write. They are available, and powerful, but optional techniques for solving problems along the way. Although it makes sense, in general, to plan before you generate and to generate ideas before juggling them for a reader, these processes can often be collapsed together in a writer's thinking. Furthermore, as our subjects show, the entire process of plan, generate, and construct may be reiterated time and again at all levels of the process, from the act of articulating a key phrase to producing a sentence, paragraph, or entire paper. Problem solving asks the writer to trade in his/her set of rules for How to Write (Gather, Outline, and Write), which never worked too well anyway, for a set of Alternative Ways to Reach Your Goal When You Write.

2. A second basic fact about teaching heuristics is that people must experience a new thinking technique to learn it. Brainstorming, for example, is an acquired skill and may go against the grain for writers geared to producing usable prose on a first sitting. Students will not blithely relinquish their habitual composing techniques, no matter how inefficient, at the sight of a new idea. To make a new heuristic an *available* option it must be presented as a classroom experience which ensures that the writer actually learns how to use and apply a new technique. Even the inexperienced writer is never a tabula rasa; he comes equipped with many well-engrained, if counter-productive habits. It is one thing to teach students a new formula, another to actually change behavior. But writing, like problem-solving thinking in general, is a performance art. Unless we deal with writing as a form of thinking, we have simply taught the student the ropes of another classroom genre—the composition paper.

3. Finally, a problem-solving approach to writing works for many writers because it allows for the disorderly dynamics of serious thinking and encourages an analytical and experimental attitude in the writer. Heuristics ask the student to see writing as a communication problem they are setting up to solve with all the strategies they can muster. In practice, perhaps the most remarkable result of using heuristics is that early in the course students develop a conviction that writing is an important skill they can in fact master. Obviously, such a conviction is not always one hundred per cent warranted, but in replacing the mystique of talent and the fear of failing with the possibility of an attainable goal, problem solving helps writers draw more fully on the abilities they do have.

Notes

[1] Wilbur Samuel Howell, *Logic and Rhetoric in England, 1500-1700* (Princeton: Princeton University Press, 1956), pp. 3-11, 64-145.

[2] We would, however, qualify that rather general statement by noting at least three books which, although they do not focus on the process in quite the same way, are taking different roads into the same territory. The most influential book for us has been Richard Young, Alton Becker, and Kenneth Pike, *Rhetoric: Discovery and Change* (New York: Harcourt, Brace and World, 1970). As rewarding and intellectually significant for teachers as for students it combines analytical, historical, and psychological approaches to writing. Peter Elbow's *Writing Without Teachers* (Oxford: Oxford University Press, 1973) is a wonderfully teachable book which shares our interest in the experience of the writer, although we would take issue with him on some aspects of the process as he describes it. Finally, William Coles's *Composing: Writing as a Self-Creating Process* (Rochelle Park, NJ: Hayden Book Co., 1974) represents a radically different teaching approach than the one here, but a shared body of assumptions about the importance of cognition and creative perception in writing.

[3] The ground-breaking work in this field is Allen Newell and Herbert Simon's, *Human Problem Solving* (Englewood Cliffs: Prentice-Hall, Inc., 1972). For a more basic textbook introduction see Peter Lindsay and Donald Norman, *Human Information Processing: An Introduction to Psychology* (San Diego: Academic Press, 1972); or Wayne Wickelgren, *How to Solve Problems* (San Francisco: W. H. Freeman, 1974). Finally, for a direct application of problem solving to problems in creativity, see John R. Hayes, *Thinking and Creating: An Introduction to Cognitive Psychology* (Homewood, IL: Dorsey Press, forthcoming).

[4] Heuristics are, in fact, a psychological necessity since most problems allow far more alternatives than we could ever evaluate. For example, in a chess game you have 10^{120} different paths to chose from, but less than 10^{16} microseconds in a century to explore them. So heuristics, or rules of thumb such as "try to control the center with your pawns," cut down the field of choices and offer the high probability of a good solution.

[5] For a highly readable and important study on the nature of planning see George Miller, Eugene Galanter and Karl Pribram's *Plans and the Structure of Behavior* (New York: Holt Rinehart and Winston, 1960).

[6] Two very useful books in this area are James L. Adams, *Conceptual Blockbusting: A Guide to Better Ideas* (San Francisco: W. H. Freeman and Co., 1974) and William Gordon's *Synectics: The Development of Creative Capacity* (New York: Harper and Row, 1961).

[7] An extended analysis of writer-based prose and its transformation is available in Linda Flower, "Writer-Based Prose: A Cognitive Basis for Problems in Writing," in preparation.

PART SIX

New Perspectives, New Horizons

"Within the new paradigm, old terms, concepts, and experiments fall into new relationships one with the other."

Thomas S. Kuhn

Perhaps the most prominent characteristic of our discipline at the present time is the enormous amount of energy being generated within it. New journals, newsletters, and professional societies are being formed. Sessions at professional conferences are often animated and lively, sometimes even electric. From all reports, space in the established journals and on national programs is growing more and more difficult to obtain. This section presents a picture of a growing, restless discipline. It is a sampling of the research, the terminology, the metaphors and ideas which show promise of shaping the future.

The first two essays bring into question certain long-held beliefs about the teaching of writing. In "Teacher Commentary on Student Writing: The State of the Art," Knoblauch and Brannon explore a question that English teachers have been asking privately for years: Do comments on student papers really make a difference? Their carefully thought-out answer is a depressing "No." If Knoblauch and Brannon are right, then the traditional pattern of assign-grade-return papers is suspect. Those readers who would like to see the kind of curriculum these writers propose should look at their article, "On Students' Rights to Their Own Texts: A Model of Teacher Response" in the May 1982 issue of *College Composition and Communication.* In the same spirit of critical inquiry, Martha Kolln examines the established view of the role of grammar in the composition curriculum. The author carefully analyzes two important statements on the subject—one the influential passage by Braddock *et al.*, the other a lesser-known work by Henry Meckel. After carefully reviewing years of research, Kolln concludes that the research does not support the "strong and unqualified" rejection of grammar as Braddock suggests. "The alchemists have been in charge long enough," she writes. The role of grammar in learning to write is still a live issue.

Drawing on the work of Eugene Gendlin, a University of Chicago philosopher, Sondra Perl shows how writers can discover resources in the wellspring of their own personal experience, from their "felt sense." This powerful heuristic, which combines elements from both Eastern and Western thought, "is always there within us." I have found that the approaches described by Perl are extremely effective with writers of all ages. David Bartholomae's award winning essay, "The Study of Error," classifies errors by three types: "errors that are evidence of an intermediate system; errors that could truly be said to be accidents . . . ; and, finally, errors of language transfer, or, more commonly, dialect interference. . . . " Bartholomae's analysis is rich with implications for teaching, and for different reasons the same is true of Nancy Sommers' research, which is described in "Revision Strategies of Student Writers and Experienced Adult Writers."The composing process is recursive, not linear, argues Sommers. Revision strategies are not simply the last stages of writing but rather "a part of the process of *discovering meaning altogether.*"

As interest in writing spreads to other academic areas, teachers of composition will increasingly find themselves in the position of teaching their colleagues. "Very touchy business," writes Toby Fulwiler in "Showing, Not Telling, in a Writing Workshop." Fulwiler provides five field-tested models for across-the-curriculum writing workshops. The reader might note that the techniques Fulwiler describes are similar to the ones employed in the National Writing Project summer institutes. Dixie Goswami views the role of composition teacher from a different perspective. In "Teachers as Researchers" she draws a picture of the teacher as a learner, someone who *learns* from students—from asking questions, from conducting informal surveys, from observing, from maintaining a questioning mind and a posture of inquiry.

"All of us, including senior faculty and advisors, must learn far more about biology and physiology than we have previously been asked to learn," writes Janet Emig. The act of writing is a complex mental and physical process; it involves not only the use of language, but perception, consciousness, the nervous system, and basic muscular coordination as well. Consequently, it is important for the teacher of writing to appreciate and understand these important psycho-physiological functions. "Eye, Hand, and Brain: Some 'Basics' in the Writing Process" is both an invitation to deepen our understanding in these and an introduction to what such study involves.

The final selection is taken from a work that continues to inspire and challenge composition teachers—Lev Vygotsky's *Thought and Language.* Although the subjects he describes are small children, his focus is on learning itself, and his work has implications for learners of all ages. Vygotsky reflects on questions which continue to intrigue us: At what age should we first begin to teach writing and how? Why is writing difficult when speaking seems so easy? Does the study of grammar aid in learning to write? How? Should instruction come before or after "the development of the corresponding psychological functions"? What kind of instruction transfers into functional writing ability? What is the role of cooperation in problem solving? What is the function of imitation? The questions he asks as well as the solutions he proposes are fascinating.

Vygotsky's lively discussion will bring to mind much current work on the composing process. There is a small touch of irony in that the thinking of a Russian psychologist should, almost a half century after his death, figure so prominently in influencing the direction of our discipline.

Teacher Commentary on Student Writing:
The State of the Art

C. H. KNOBLAUCH and LIL BRANNON

Arguably, nothing we do as writing teachers is more valuable than our commenting on individual student texts in order to facilitate improvement. We know that successful writers achieve their communicative purposes by correctly anticipating the needs and expectations of intended readers. We also know that inexperienced writers find it especially difficult to imagine audience responses in advance or to use them as a guide to composing. Accordingly, we comment on student essays to dramatize the presence of a reader who depends on the writer's choices in order to perceive the intent of a discourse. Thoughtful commentary describes when communication has occurred and when it has not, raising questions that the writer may never have considered from a reader's point of view. The aim of repeated cycles of writing, teacher response (perhaps peer response as well), and more writing is to enable students gradually to internalize this Questioning Reader so that they can better realize their intentions. Presumably, the more facilitative voices people hear in response to their writing, and the more often they hear them, the more quickly they will achieve that internal control of choices which our teaching strives to nurture.

At any rate, so the theory goes. The depressing trouble is, we have scarcely a shred of empirical evidence to show that students typically even comprehend our responses to their writing, let alone use them purposefully to modify their practice. This is not to say that we have never sought empirical support. Over the past 25 years, from J. H. Warmsbacker in 1955 to Searle and Dillon in 1980,[1] better than two dozen studies have looked at diverse modes of teacher intervention, and compared their effects, within student populations ranging from grade school to college age. Nina Ziv's recent study of the relevant literature[2] shows the diversity, but also the futility, of this completed work. Some research has contrasted responses offering praise with others offering criticism, for instance, Taylor and Hoedt in 1966[3] or Earl Seidman in 1967.[4] Not surprisingly, this research concluded that students who are praised tend to write longer essays and to have better attitudes about writing. But it also found no necessary connection between higher motivation and a higher quality of performance. Other researchers

Freshman English News, 10 (Fall 1981), pp. 1-4. Reprinted by permission of the editor and the authors.

have contrasted oral and written comments, including McGrew in 1969, Coleman in 1973, and Miller in 1978.[5] Again, attitudes seemed better among students who received taped oral responses than among those who received only comments written on their essays. But neither group wrote demonstrably better essays because of the commentary they received. In 1972 Evelyn Bata contrasted marginal and end comments but found no important differences in their impact.[6] Marzano and Arthur, in 1978, wrote varying types of comment to students in three different groups, one group receiving abbreviated grammatical responses ("awk," "sp"), one receiving actual corrections of mechanical errors, and the third receiving substantive commentary "designed to foster thinking." Once again, no significant differences in the quality of student writing could be discerned.[7] The morose conclusion of their study could well summarize a dominant impression to be gained from all the research cited here: "different types of teacher comments on student themes have equally small influences on student writing. For all practical purposes, commenting on student essays might just be an exercise in futility. Either students do not read the comments or they read them and do not attempt to implement suggestions and correct errors."

Actually, Marzano and Arthur overlooked the drearier possibility that students simply fail to appreciate what teachers are trying to tell them. Jean King approaches this conclusion in a 1979 study of types of grammatical intervention.[8] King discriminated three varieties of comment, one an outright correction of errors, a second only naming kinds of error (e.g., "lacks subject-verb agreement"), and a third offering rules (e.g., "singular subjects take singular verbs"). She found that students rarely understood directly corrective commentary and that, even when they did understand comments in the other two categories, they were not necessarily aided by either, or by one more than the other, in making corrections on their own. The implications of her research, to the extent that they can be generalized, are as plain as they are troubling: (1) students often do not comprehend teacher responses to their writing; (2) even when they do, they do not always use those responses and may not know how to use them; (3) when they use them, they do not necessarily write more effectively as a result. In light of these findings, the question whether one type of comment might be more or less helpful than another is conspicuously irrelevant.

Is there reason to persevere in the time-honored practice of commenting on student essays in the face of all these unpromising empirical studies of its relevance to writing improvement? Seemingly, either that practice is deficient and the available research has proven it so, or the research is somehow deficient and has failed to reveal the true promise in teacher commentary. We would argue that responding supportively to student writing is indeed central to enlightened instruction, despite the apparent weight of evidence to the contrary. But we would also implicate both previous research assumptions and certain traditional commenting practices in the repeated failure of studies endeavoring to show its value. One problem is methodological: it concerns the habitual focus of these studies on types or modes of commentary, which has led researchers to expect too much from isolated marginal remarks on essays and to reflect too little on the larger conversation between teacher and student to which they only contribute. A second, more important problem concerns the actual practice of commenting, its peripheral and largely judgmental role in conventional teaching. If research efforts have failed to show the use of teacher commentary, one reason may be the larger ineffectiveness of the instructional format within which it has been evaluated. In other words, those efforts may say more about the limitations of a widespread and traditional teaching method than about the potential value of our intervention in student composing.

Consider, first, the matter of research focus. Nearly every study has distinguished types of comment and then tried to evaluate the impact of one against another. We have already noted the implausibility of attempting to determine degrees of effectiveness amidst such gross uncertainty about the value of *any* kind of commenting. But the problem of focus goes beyond its present impracticality: even when we can finally show the positive effect of intervention under certain conditions, we will not necessarily be able to prove a qualitative difference in types. For the implicit assumptions of such an undertaking are, first, that the process of commenting can be isolated from the whole environment of oral and written communication between teacher and student, and, second, that categories of response can be further isolated according to the intrinsic merits of their superficial features (such as, statement versus question, or marginal comment versus end comment, or abbreviated reference versus extended reference) and thereby ordered as a hierarchy. It is hard to imagine that any experienced writing teacher would find intuitive validity in either of these assumptions. The first one in particular seems demonstrably false.

The flaw in both assumptions lies in their reductive view of the dialogue between teachers and their students. A single comment on a single essay is too local and contingent a phenomenon to yield general conclusions about the quality of the conversation of which it is a part. Any remark on a student essay, whatever its form, finally owes its meaning and impact to the governing dialogue that influences some student's reaction to it. Remarks taken out of this context can appear more restrictive or open-ended, more facilitative or judgmental, than they really are in light of a teacher's overall communicative habits. Potentially facilitative questions ("Is this really the best word to use here?"; "Can't you be more specific?") may be implicitly judgmental if an instructor's posture in the classroom tends to be judgmental. Grammatical references ("See Harbrace, p. 53"; "Comma splice") can be facilitative, not merely evaluative, if the teacher has previously shown ways to respond to them. Therefore, the difference that Kelley introduces in her 1973 study of "clarifying" versus "directive" responses,[9] or that Ziv offers between "explicit" and "implicit" revision cues, or that Seidman describes between praise and blame comments, is probably illusory, since individual teachers can make superficially similar comments bearing vastly different connotations. Other surface features such as the location of comments or their oral versus written forms are certainly distinguishable, but their difference seems largely irrelevant to the issue of communicative effect. We suspect that, if it ever becomes possible to separate modes of teacher response, the starting point will be, not the superficial features of comments, but the attitudes, postures, and motives that teachers communicate both through and apart from their reactions to particular texts. Perhaps we will discover commenting styles, such as the Harsh Grammatical Critic, the Kindly Question-Raiser, or the Old-Fashioned Nitpicker, rather than commenting "types."

In any case, the problem of research focus is secondary to a larger difficulty concerning our typical practice as responders to student writing, a practice that has conditioned the persistently negative findings accumulated over the past quarter century. Most studies have accepted, as a "given" of the research setting, the view that commenting is essentially a product-centered, evaluative activity resembling literary criticism. Convention-ally, students write essays and teachers describe their strengths and weak-nesses, grading them accordingly. The essays are then retired and new ones are composed, presumably under the influence of recollected judgments of the previous ones. Our assumption has been that evaluating the product of composing is equivalent to intervening in the process. Teachers concentrate on retrospective appraisals of "finished" discourses, so that students seldom rewrite in direct response to comments. Rather, they only notice the critical reception of earlier work and strive to do better next time. The recent *RTE* study by Searle and Dillon shows how pervasive this procedure is: they categorized 59% of the responses to student writing in their survey as "didactic/correction form," that is, summatively judgmental in their intent. By contrast, they found pratically no responses in the category "moving outside the writing," that is, anticipating eventual revision (p. 239).

We suspect that intervening in the composing process, by allowing stu-dents to write successive drafts immediately responding to facilitative com-mentary, can measurably improve student writing, provided that a teacher adequately supports revising efforts. Certain studies already bear out parts of this surmise. The earliest of them dates, in fact, from 1936, when John Fellows showed that students receiving mechanics corrections with the chance to revise improved in grammar and punctuation[10] —not a startling conclusion but perhaps a suggestive one. A more contemporary, and more broadly conceived, study is Ziv's, in which students rewrote essays in re-sponse to both technical and rhetorical "revision cues" ranging from "ex-plicit" directives to "implicit" suggestions for development. Her results show that intervention can affect writing improvement in multiple-draft assign-ments. Apparently, students found explicit technical and rhetorical advice more helpful than merely suggestive comments, as we might expect. But even her implicit cues stimulated rewriting, although the expanded state-ments often featured new grammatical and organizational problems. Ziv suggests, ingeniously, that teachers gradually adjust their emphasis from explicit to implicit cues as students grow more comfortable with their ex-pectations and more adept at anticipating them. In any case, her research supports the potential of teacher intervention as a central activity of workshop instruction concerned with stimulating and directing revision. It successfully argues the advantage of making our commentary facilitative rather than merely evaluative.

However, an important limitation in this positive research is that it fails to consider the natural impediments to revising that we can assume in most inexperienced writers, a resistance that grows more acute as more radical rewriting is suggested. As a result, few of the studies that have included direct student response to teacher comments have shown the happy results that Ziv achieved. In a 1963 study, for example, Lois Arnold asked one group of students to revise with reference to teacher comments while a second group did not. After a year, she could find no difference in the performance of the two groups, suggesting that the chance to rewrite did not affect growth.[11] Kelley reached a similar conclusion in 1973, finding no difference in writers' maturation as a result of opportunities to revise in light of "clarifying" or "directive" commentary. But the deficiency in these studies, we believe, is their assumption that revising is a spontaneous, self-initiating activity for unskilled writers, requiring no explicit support from teachers beyond simply focusing attention on errors or development possibilities. The experience of countless writing teachers argues the inadequacy of this expectation.

Our own experiences in workshop classrooms, where students revise through several drafts, has been that unsophisticated writers ordinarily limit their revising to changes that minimally affect the plan and order of ideas with which they began, readily making only those adjustments that place least pressure on them to reconceive or significantly extend the writing they have already done. Often, their revised statements are actually poorer than the first drafts because of their reticence to change anything that has not attracted specific attention, even when a recommended change in one place implicitly necessitates changes elsewhere. The motive for this resistance seems more complicated than laziness. We think the resistance is natural, rising out of the anxiety that even experienced writers feel at having to reduce an achieved coherence, however inadequate, to the chaos of fragments and undeveloped insights from which they started. Practiced writers overcome their anxiety through habitual success in rewriting, but no such comforting pattern of successes exists to steady the resolve of the apprentice. Hence, we should not be surprised that revision, which entails repudiating what we may have struggled mightily to say in the mere hope of saying it better, represents a more sophisticated compositional habit than the young writer may yet have developed.

Nor is this natural psychological resistance the only barrier to self-initiated revising. Even assuming that our commenting language is clear (and obviously it is not always), another barrier is the ordinary student's inability to perceive alternatives to the choices that have already been made, choices that lie reified as a document. The temptation is strong, even among experienced writers, to forget the arbitrariness of so many initial decisions about what to say and where or how to say it, imagining in retrospect an inevitability about the patterns and connections that make up the existing discourse. Seeing through that apparent inevitability in order to recover additional options requires an intellectual discipline and a rhetorical awareness that beginning writers frequently lack, even when their writing suggests a fairly mature verbal competence. Writers with underdeveloped verbal skills will have all the more difficulty conceiving what else might be said when herculean effort may already have been required to say anything at all. We must concede the fact that commenting on drafts will not, by itself, inevitably assure effective follow-through in revision efforts. Additional support must attend the stages of rewriting.

Minimally, that support would include helping students to understand the comments they receive, both by defining our commenting vocabularies in advance and by discussing plans for revision before students actually attempt to rewrite. Once rewriting has occurred, we might also wish to review the new choices, emphasizing the positive value of changes, deletions, and additions in revised essays. But a different kind of assistance may be the most valuable of all: it involves preparing students to appreciate the potential for development implicit in their writing and to tolerate the pressures that accompany extensive revision in the effort to realize that potential. This is, of course, no easy matter. Frequent efforts to rewrite paragraphs or short paragraph sequences, which can be done rather painlessly, and then discussing the changes, might help to create a receptive attitude about the advantages of rewriting. But however we undertake to stimulate the habit of revising, we should bear in mind that it entails learned skills requiring some conscious nurturing and guidance before it is likely to assume a substantial role in the typical student's composing process.

We have found only one study that includes, at least embryonically, all the features of effective instruction that might enable researchers to show the real value of teacher intervention. In 1958 Earl Buxton asked one group of students to revise essays in response to extensive commentary while another group, which also received comments, did no revising. The "revision group" rewrote their essays in class as raters went from student to student answering questions and giving advice. A statistical analysis of pre- and post-test scores suggested that writers who revised their work improved demonstrably compared to those who did not revise.[12] One study hardly makes the case for requiring guided rewriting following teacher commentary. But it may offer a prototype for additional, more restrictively designed research based on the teaching model that Buxton implicitly recommends and that we have been describing. The model includes these features: (1) an emphasis on writers' performance rather than exclusively on their finished products; (2) a facilitative rather than judgmental view of our commenting practices; (3) a preference for multiple-draft assignments so that teachers can intervene directly in their students' composing and so that students can respond directly through revision; (4) a concern for actively educating students, perhaps through short, acclimating exercises, about what rewriting involves (and how it is different from editing), what it can accomplish, and how it can be done; (5) a concern for supporting revision by insuring that students understand what comments mean, by discussing possible changes and additions before rewriting begins, and by reviewing completed revisions, perhaps in conference, to see what they have achieved. Assuming this teaching environment, new research might profitably seek, not to discriminate comment types by their presumed intrinsic merits or deficiencies, but rather to study the full teacher-student dialogue accompanying efforts to shape writers' performance. . . .

Notes

[1] J. H. Warmsbacker, "A Comparative Study of Three Methods of Grading Compositions," Unpublished Master's Thesis, University of British Columbia, 1955; Dennis Searle and David Dillon, "The Message of Marking: Teacher Written Responses to Student Writing at Intermediate Grade Levels," *Research in the Teaching of English,* 14 (October 1980), 233-42. The fact that most of the empirical work on teacher commentary is in the form of graduate, usually doctoral level studies suggests a critical need for additional research by more experienced professional investigators.

[2] Nina Ziv, "The Effect of Teacher and Peer Comments on the Writing of Four College Freshmen," Unpublished Ph.D. Dissertation, New York University, 1981.

[3] Winnifred F. Taylor and Kenneth C. Hoedt, "The Effect of Praise Upon the Quality of Creative Writing," *Journal of Education Research*, 60 (1966), 80-83.

[4] Earl Seidman, "Marking Students' Compositions: Implications for Achievement Motivation Theory," Unpublished Ph.D. Dissertation, Stanford University, 1967.

[5] Jean B. McGrew, "An Experiment to Assess the Effectiveness of the Dictation Machine as an Aid to Teachers in Evaluation and Improvement of Student Compositions," Report to Lincoln Public Schools, Lincoln, Nebraska, 1969 (ERIC 034776); V. B. Coleman, "A Comparison between the Relative Effectiveness of Marginal-Interlinear-Terminal Commentary and of Audio Tape Commentary in Responding to Student Compositions," Unpublished Ph.D. Dissertation, University of Pittsburgh, 1973; T. E. Miller, "A Comparison of the Effects of Oral and Written Teacher Feedback Only on Specific Writing Behaviors of Fourth Grade Children," Unpublished Ed.D. Dissertation, Ball State University.

[6] Evelyn J. Bata, "A Study of the Relative Effectiveness of Marking Techniques on Junior College Freshmen English Composition," Unpublished Ph.D. Dissertation, University of Maryland, 1972.

[7] R. J. Marzano and S. Arthur, "Teacher Comments on Student Essays: It Doesn't Matter What You Say," Study at University of Colorado, Denver, 1977 (ERIC, ED 147864).

[8] Jean Anne King, "Teachers' Comments on Students' Writing: A Conceptual Analysis and Empirical Study," Unpublished Ph.D. Dissertation, Cornell University, 1979.

[9] Marie E. Kelley, "Effects of Two Types of Teacher Response to Essays," Unpublished Ph.D. Dissertation, Michigan State University, 1974.

[10] John E. Fellows, "The Influence of Theme Readings and Theme Correction on Eliminating Technical Errors in the Written Composition of Ninth Grade Pupils," Unpublished Ph.D. Dissertation, University of Iowa, 1936.

[11] Lois V. Arnold, "Effects of Frequency of Writing and Intensity of Teacher Evaluation Upon Performance in Written Composition of Tenth-Grade Students," Unpublished Ph.D. Dissertation, Florida State Univeristy, 1963.

[12] Earl W. Buxton, "An Experiment to Test the Effects of Writing Frequency and Guided Practice upon Students' Skills in Written Expression," Unpublished Ph.D. Dissertation, Stanford University, 1958.

Closing the Books on Alchemy

MARTHA KOLLN

In 1963 two publications appeared, one from NCTE, the other from the NEA, both summarizing the state of the art, or science, of composition research. One of them created a wave so big that even after seventeen years its ripples continue to wash the shores of the English curriculum; the other, unfortunately, sank without a trace.

The authors of the NCTE report, *Research in Written Composition*—Richard Braddock, Richard Lloyd-Jones, and Lowell Schoer—recognized that such research was not highly developed; in fact, they compared research in composition "to chemical research as it emerged from the period of alchemy" (p. 5). We've come a long way since then. Recent work in such areas as invention, error analysis, the process of writing, holistic scoring, and sentence combining testifies to the progress we have made as researchers; the variety of program topics at CCCC demonstrates how far we have come and how much we have learned since 1963. That NCTE report, in fact, with its detailed accounts of empirical studies and scientific research methods, probably had a great deal to do with bringing us out of the dark ages.

Yet the biggest wave that report made had just the opposite effect: it encouraged the alchemists. The most quotable statement in all of its pages effectively turned back the clock on grammar research; it is still causing ripples:

> In view of the widespread agreement of research studies based upon many types of students and teachers, the conclusion can be stated in strong and unqualified terms: the teaching of formal grammar has a negligible or, because it usually displaces some instruction and practice in actual composition, even a harmful effect on the improvement of writing. (pp. 37-38)

I suspect that the authors were surprised at the press coverage that statement received. Perhaps if they had anticipated such attention, they would have been more careful in applying their criteria for good research to themselves; they might have defined their terms. What do they mean by

College Composition and Communication, 32 (May 1981), pp. 139-151. Copyright © 1981 by The National Council of Teachers of English. Reprinted by permission of the publisher and the author.

"formal grammar"? Do they mean memorizing rules and definitions? Diagramming and parsing sentences? Or does "formal grammar" simply refer to an organized subject in the curriculum? And certainly they would have asked another, related question: If formal grammar has a negative effect, is there an alternative that might have a positive one?

That's one of my criticisms of that quotable line: its undefined terms. The other is its "strong and unqualified" language. The authors' conclusions in every other area of composition, without exception, are couched in tentative language, as well they should be: "with these cautions" (p. 30); "some of his procedures . . . seem very questionable, and some of his conclusions seem to leap beyond the reasonable distance" (p. 31); "it is not clear yet" (p. 35); "certainly it has not been proved" (p. 36). Such qualifications concern the methodology as well as the interpretation of data in every area except the teaching of grammar. The authors do admit that much of the research on instruction in grammar is based on objective tests rather than actual writing; and they concede that "carefully conducted research which studies the effect of formal grammar on actual composition over an extended period of time" is uncommon (p. 37). Yet they still summarize the research on the teaching of grammar with that "harmful effects" statement in "strong and unqualified terms"—clearly, the last word in grammar research.

The highly-quotable, 56-word statement has appeared over and over again these seventeen years, in books and articles and convention papers and classrooms and casual conversations. As recently as December, 1979, in fact, it turned up yet again in the pages of *College English*.[1] Alchemy persists.

But what of the other 1963 report? In "Research on Teaching Composition and Literature," his contribution to the 1200-page *Handbook of Research on Teaching* (N. L. Gage, Editor [Chicago: Rand McNally and Company]), Henry C. Meckel describes many of the same research studies that Braddock et al. looked at, but he reaches far different conclusions. (I quote his summary in full):

1. There is no research evidence that grammar as traditionally taught in the schools has any appreciable effect on the improvement of writing skills.

2. The training periods involved in transfer studies have been comparatively short, and the amount of grammar instruction has frequently been small.

3. There is no conclusive research evidence, however, that grammar has *no* transfer value in developing composition skill.

4. More research is needed on the kind of grammatical knowledge that may reasonably be expected to transfer to writing. For example, commonly accepted principles of transfer of training would not lead an experimenter to expect much transfer value from knowledge of grammar which has not included the knowledge and ability to apply grammatical principles to the construction of the pupil's own sentences. [See J. M. Stephens, "Transfer of Learning," in C. W. Harris, ed., *Encyclopedia of Educational Research* (3rd Edition. New York: Macmillan Company,

1960), pp. 1535-1543.]

5. Research does not justify the conclusion that grammar should not be taught systematically. In some appraisals of research there has been a confusion between the term *formal grammar* as used to denote systematic study and mastery and the term as used to mean grammar taught without application to writing and speaking. Systematic study does not preclude application.

6. There are more efficient methods of securing *immediate* improvement in the writing of pupils, both in sentence structure and usage, than systematic grammatical instruction.

7. Improvement of usage appears to be more effectively achieved through practice of desirable forms than through memorization of rules.

8. The items of usage selected for inclusion in the curriculum should be determined not only by "errors" made in students' papers but also by descriptive studies of national usage by linguistic experts.

9. In determining what grammar is functional and what is not, teachers cannot safely rely on textbooks used in schools but must depend on the expert opinion of linguists based on modern studies of the usage and structure of the language. (pp. 981-982)

Meckel also suggests that "much of the earlier research on teaching grammar must be regarded as no longer of significance outside the period in educational history which it represents" (p. 982).

Unfortunately, Meckel's advice was lost in the wake of the strong and unqualified language of the Braddock report. As a result, no one heard his call for a definition of "formal grammar" or his conclusion, in paragraph five, that the "systematic study [of formal grammar] does not preclude application." Not only can we teach grammar—the internalized system of rules that the speakers of a language share—we can do so in a functional way, in connection with composition. When we teach our students to understand and label the various structures of the system, when we bring to conscious awareness those subconscious rules, we are, in fact, teaching grammar.

But Meckel's advice went unheard. As a result, instead of determining what grammar is functional, instead of discovering what aspects of grammar study would be the most helpful for our students, we continue to cite those early studies, which Meckel judged "no longer of significance," to justify excluding grammar study of any kind from the curriculum.

To mention only one example of the alchemist's continuing influence, Dean Memering has recently asserted that "the evidence is incontestable that grammar teaching achieves nothing useful in composition":

There is no way to teach students grammatical terminology and a set of rules for describing the language that will have any effect on writing. No amount of practice in analyzing, dissecting, or diagramming sentences will change student performance in composition. It makes no difference whether we teach Latin, structural, transformational, stratification, tagmemic, or any other brand of grammar: endless efforts to show that grammar does too affect writing have repeatedly come up with the same weary findings—no significant difference. This finding has been advertised since 1906 when Hoyt concluded that there was "an absence of relationship between a knowledge of technical grammar and the ability to use and interpret language." The same results or worse have been noted more or less consistently by researchers since that time: Rapeer, 1913; Asker, 1923; Segal and Barr, 1926; Symonds, 1931; Frogner, 1939; Harris, 1926. If we know anything at all about composition, we know that students can't be "grammared" into better writers.[2]

With seven reports to back him up, we're not surprised that Memering states his opinions in such strong and unqualified terms. But perhaps we should give those reports a closer look to see if they justify his conclusions.

In 1906 Hoyt questioned the place that formal grammar study occupied in the elementary school curriculum, mainly because of what we know about children's psychological development.[3] He described grammar study, from the child's point of view, as consisting, "very largely of generalizations to be memorized and applied to the classification and parsing of words and combinations of words by a kind of mental assortment of them into given groups . . . tagged with technical names, usually meaningless to the child" (p. 475). Influenced by Thorndike's research into learning, Hoyt considered this kind of mental exercise "ill-adapted to immature pupils." However, he did believe that for students beyond elementary school, "the study of formal grammar may be pursued entirely in accordance with psychological principles" (p. 476).

With his research Hoyt hoped to disprove two of the arguments commonly advanced for teaching grammar to young children: "that a knowledge of grammar leads to the use of better English in oral and written expression," and "that a knowledge of grammar is a considerable aid in the interpretation of language" (p. 478). For the experiment, ninth-graders in Indianapolis wrote 40-minute essays, restated in prose four stanzas of Gray's "Elegy Written in a Country Churchyard," and answered ten grammar questions about four other stanzas of the same poem. He found the correlations between scores on the three sub-tests—composition, interpretation, and grammar—low, but nonetheless positive, ranging from .30 between grammar and composition to .41 between interpretation and composition. But on the basis of these results Hoyt concluded, as Memering quotes, that there was no relationship between grammar and the other skills. He also concluded, after correlating grammar scores and marks in other subjects, such as arithmetic and geography, that the mental processes involved in grammar study contribute little to general mental training.

In light of Hoyt's concerns about the content of the elementary school grammar curriculum and its appropriateness for children, we can understand his eagerness to present conclusive findings. But certainly questions remain. First, the tests were scored subjectively by two raters, who, as far as we know, were given no specific training. Hoyt briefly mentions inter-rater reliabilities, giving them as percentages rather than correlations: 86 percent on the grammar test, 83 percent on interpretation, and, not surprisingly, only 58 percent on composition. Perhaps even more questionable are the tests themselves. For instance, had the essay topic been tested? We know from our own experiences, as well as from the reports of ETS, what a difference the topic itself makes both to the writer and the reader. And what exactly was he measuring? Were the tests valid? Was the level of difficulty on the grammar and interpretation tests appropriate for first-term ninth graders? One grammar question asked students to identify the part of speech of the first word in stanzas like this one:

Save that, from yonder ivy-mantled tower,
The moping owl does to the moon complain
Of such as, wandering near her secret bower,
Molest her ancient solitary reign.

Other questions asked them to name the adjectives in this stanza, explaining their use in the sentence, and to give the voice, mode, tense, and number of the verbs, telling whether they are transitive or intransitive and why.

But questions of reliability and validity aside, let's look at Hoyt's own conclusions. He clearly does not advocate the banishment of grammar, as Memering would have us to believe. His criticisms were directed at the place it occupied in the elementary curriculum. He suggested two possible solutions to the problem of grammar study: either postpone it until high school or change the character of instruction "so that its study may be more fruitful." He urged that grammar study in elementary school be taught "in connection with the language work . . . to become an effective tool in the work in composition and interpretation" (p. 490).

Rapeer (1913), in a replication of Hoyt's study, concurs with these conclusions, suggesting that only those grammatical terms that are actually necessary be taught in the elementary grades and that formal grammar instruction be postponed to the last half of the eighth year.[4] Both Hoyt and Rapeer emphasized the need to evaluate the amount of time devoted to formal grammar study in an overcrowded curriculum when the schools had to provide "the whole range of vocational, hygenic, and socializing training needed by our 'nation of sixth graders' " (p. 131). We should also emphasize that in these sudies Hoyt and Rapeer did not compare students who studied grammar with others who did not, nor did they compare methods of teaching grammar; they simply correlated scores on a three-part test.

In comparison with the next three studies on the Memering list, even Hoyt's research design looks meticulous. None of the other early studies include actual composition. Asker (1923) did nothing but compare scores on grammar tests with grades in college freshman composition courses.[5] The erroneous assumption that writing ability alone determines course grades is a problem that Braddock et al. cite in their discussion of research design, and they list eight other factors that commonly raise or lower composition grades (p. 22). Yet on the basis of such a comparison, Asker jumps to the conclusion that "time spent on formal grammar in the elementary school is wasted as far as the majority of students is concerned" (p. 111).

The Segal and Barr report (1926) makes no such unsupported claims, but Memering errs in thinking that it supports his bias against grammar study.[6] On the contrary, in comparing results of a "formal-grammar test" with an "applied-grammar test," Segal and Barr conclude that "there may be a decided transfer value" for "specialists in English speech in particular and college students in general" (p. 402). They base this conclusion on the finding that even though "formal grammar" scores of juniors were lower than those of sophomores, the "applied grammar" scores were higher. "Evidently," they report, "formal grammar is forgotten but language usage improved" (p. 402). Segal and Barr's only negative finding was based on the correlation of .48 between the two grammar tests, which was no higher than the correlation between marks in any two subjects in high school. On that evidence they conclude that formal grammar has no immediate transfer value to applied English grammar. This experiment included no actual writing, however; what they refer to as "practice" or "applied grammar" is nothing more than a series of workbook exercises on usage ("I [can't, can] hardly see it"; James [done, did] his work yesterday"). So whatever the outcome, we can certainly draw no valid conclusions about the students' writing ability.

The other two studies from the 1930's that Memering cites compare teaching methods by means of objective tests. The purpose of the Symonds experiment (1931) was to discover what influence learning grammar has on usage.[7] In what he calls a test-teach-test experiment, Symonds administered a pre-test to six groups of sixth graders in New York City, using a 40-item usage test in which students rewrote sentences containing errors, such as these:

Are you most ready to go?
He said that I was most there.

He then subjected each group to one of six different experimental procedures—methods of teaching that were suspect even while he was using them. Some were the very methods of teaching grammar that twenty-five years earlier Hoyt had recommended be abandoned. And Symonds himself reports in his summary that "time and again during the course of the work reported in this article, principals and teachers would complain that the methods . . . were too formal and dry to be practically used" (p. 95).

But Symonds persevered. For example, one group did nothing but memorize definitions, rules, and principles, with teachers being explicitly cautioned about letting the students stray from the method being tested:

Do *not* ask the pupils to make up examples of their own illustrating the rules.
Do *not* give the pupils additional examples of the rules.
Do *not* ask pupils to analyze the rules.
Do *not* give the pupils practice in applying any of the rules. (p. 84)

Then there were the repetition groups who studied no rules or definitions; they simply read aloud, in unison, one or three or five or ten times a list of forty correct sentences like these:

The boy was almost killed by an automobile.
My baby brother is almost two years old. (p. 83)

Still another recitation group chanted both right and wrong sentences aloud, in unison:

'The boy was most killed by an automobile' is wrong;
'The boy was almost killed by an automobile' is right.
'My baby brother is most two years old' is wrong;
'My baby brother is almost two years old' is right. (p. 84)

Another group practiced correct constructions by filling in blanks; two others used combinations of all of the above. To evaluate these so-called "teaching methods," Symonds administered the same forty-item test at the end of the experiment. We surely aren't surprised at his conclusion:

In the writer's opinion it is relatively unprofitable for the average child either to study grammar as a means for learning correct usage (because there are more direct, simpler, and easier means for learning usage) or as a means of summarizing the correct usage which one has learned (because there are other things more worthwhile in the curriculum). (p. 94)

What does surprise us is that Memering and others can seriously consider such research as proof that grammar study has no positive effect on composition.

Some of the studies designed to demonstrate that traditional grammar study is ineffective have shown that other methods of teaching grammar do, in fact, work. Frogner (1939) compared two teaching methods, the "grammar" approach and the "thought" approach, neither of which included the obvious weaknesses of Symonds' methods.[8] Frogner describes her grammar group as going somewhat beyond what she considered "typical of grammar teaching today." For example, in studying the subordination of ideas in phrases, the grammar group did more than simply learn to recognize prepositional, appositive, participle, gerund, and infinitive phrases and to differentiate their kind and use in the sentence; they applied the principles they learned by effectively combining short, choppy sentences and then "proceeded to the discussion and correction of errors in the use of phrases, such as the misplaced prepositional phrase or the dangling participle" (p. 521). The thought group, on the other hand, began their study of phrases not by learning to identify types and labeling them but "by noticing the various ways of subordinating ideas" (p. 521). They discussed examples written on the board and combined ideas in as many ways as possible. Here is Frogner's illustration of one such lesson:

'Mr White is our class advisor. He grasped the seriousness of the situation. He immediately called a meeting of the officers.' How could the ideas be combined to avoid the monotonous childish sentences? Several possibilities were suggested, one of which was: 'Having grasped the seriousness of the situation, Mr. White, our class advisor, immediately called a meeting of the officers.' Pupils improved the expression of thought by means of subordinating ideas in a participial and an appositive phrase; yet they were not drilled in the recognition of the grammatical construction. (pp. 521-522)

It is clear even from her brief description of this and other lessons that what the "thought" group thought about was, of course, grammar. They thought about and discussed coordination and subordination of ideas, parallel structure, and the relationship of punctuation to meaning. Apparently what they did not do was the drilling and memorizing of labels and definitions that in 1939 was synonymous with the study of grammar.

Unfortunately, Frogner's conclusions were based on objective tests rather than actual writing, and although she claims significant differences in favor of the thought group, she fails to report either the nature of the tests or the exact levels of confidence of her findings. But the more important issue in Frogner's study has been ignored: What is the "thought" approach, the one that worked? Both Frogner and, two decades later, Harris set out to prove that writing can be taught without teaching grammar. But what both studies actually bring to light are alternative methods that seem to work. Frogner's thought approach, in fact, looks very much like sentence combining. But unfortunately, only the negative results of the study have received any attention.

In the case of the Harris study, too, only the negative aspects have been reported.[9] In fact, it is this study, which Braddock et al. considered the "most soundly based" of all the research on the teaching of grammar they examined, that supplied them with the phrase "harmful effects." Working with junior-high level classes in five London schools in 1960, Harris "investigated the relative teaching usefulness of what might be loosely referred to in the United States as 'formal grammar' and a 'direct method' of instruction" (Braddock et al., p. 70).

All of the classes in the experiment met five times a week; four of the five periods were the same. The difference between the two methods

. . . came in the fifth period, when one group emphasized formal grammar and the other focused on direct methods of instruction . . . Some of the time released by omitting study of the terminology of formal grammar could be devoted to writing activity projects and to drawing illustrative sentences, points of usage, and paragraphs from the stories to teach the improvement of writing. A piece of continuous writing was also attempted in the Formal Grammar classes, but not much time was available for the project inasmuch as these classes were carefully following the integrated grammar and composition lessons in their textbooks. (p. 78)*

A sample lesson included in the Braddock report shows the direct method teacher leading the students to an understanding of subject-verb

---

*The textbooks were published in 1939.

agreement through inductive reasoning, by plumbing their own linguistic resources, using examples from their own compositions ("Me and Jim was
going into the cave"):

> Would you say 'We was going into the cave'? [negative reply]
> What would you say? ['We were . . . ']
> How many is 'we'? [More than one . . . ']
> Well, 'Jim and me' is more than one. (p. 71)

The formal grammar students tackled such errors using traditional terminology. To do so, as Harris points out, they had already learned such concepts
as agreement and case.

At the end of two years, Harris analyzed compositions written at the
beginning and at the end of the experiment, using eleven different measures,
including sentence length, frequency of subordinate clauses and compound
sentences, sentence variety, and the like. All of the results that were statisti-
cally significant (the majority of the measures, incidentally, were not) favored the direct method group. However, for each of the eleven measures, the
grammar group came out on top in at least one of the five schools; for two
of the measures, results in three of the five schools favored the grammar
group. Nevertheless Harris claims to have discovered what he set out to discover: the "functions and value of formal traditional grammar in the teaching of English"—or, as it turned out, the lack thereof.

Harris concludes his study in these words: "It seems safe to infer that
the study of English grammatical terminology had a negligible or even a relatively harmful effect upon the correctness of children's writing in the early
part of the five Secondary schools" (p. 83). And while the Braddock report
does put this conclusion in some sort of perspective with the qualification
"because it usually displaces practice in actual composition," it remains a
misleading and simplistic conclusion. A positive—and more accurate—version
of that conclusion might read like this: "The student who spends an extra
period every week for two years on actual composition will show more improvement in certain aspects of writing than the student who does not."
Harris, after all, did not simply test the effect of studying formal grammar
on writing ability; rather, he tested the effect of replacing writing practice
with something else—in this case with formal grammar study and, we assume,
the traditional memorizing and drilling associated with it. The only surprise
in his outcome is that no significant difference showed up after the first year.

In all fairness I must add that Braddock et al. conclude their summary
of the Harris study with a parenthetical disclaimer: "Based as it was on the
use of traditional grammar, the Harris study does not necessarily prove, of
course, the ineffectiveness of instruction based on structural or generative
grammar" (p. 83). Unfortunately that qualification appears forty pages away
from their well-known "harmful effects" quotation with its "strong and unqualified" finality.

That famous statement has probably had a more harmful effect on our
students these past seventeen years than all the time spent memorizing rules
and diagramming sentences ever had. The babies born in 1963 are babies no
longer, they are juniors and seniors in high school. That 1963 report has prob-

ably affected the education of every one of them. Shortly after its appearance, textbooks on teaching methods began quoting its memorable line. And before long our elementary and secondary English classes were staffed by eager young teachers who believed that teaching grammar was a waste of time—even worse, it was downright harmful. In her 1965 text, for example. Fowler quotes that sentence along with other findings and then summarizes: "Despite the overwhelming and incontrovertible evidence, large amounts of class time are still being spent on the study of grammar to the neglect of practice in writing and reading."[10] In 1969 Loban, Ryan and Squire follow the "harmful effects" statement with the concession that knowledge of grammar is valuable for its own sake.[11] Then they explain that while the study of usage has a place in the curriculum, it must be taught without recourse to grammar terminology. Stephen Judy offers a chapter entitled "Twenty Alternatives to the Study of Grammar."[12]

While these authors do offer sensible instruction on teaching composition, such strong and unqualified positions on grammar are hard for impressionable students to dispute—and to forget. No doubt countless English Education majors have left their methods courses convinced that they needn't concern themselves with grammar, that no one teaches grammar anymore. Often, in fact, their own experiences as high school and junior high students confirm these beliefs. Their college curriculum may confirm them as well, with perhaps only one required course in grammar or linguistics to prepare them as teachers. For years my students, in describing their own secondary school experience, have told me they studied no grammar at all, often because their English teachers didn't like it; they stuck to literature. The Braddock report certainly justifies this position. So instead of trying to discover what does work—for example, what is Frogner's "thought" approach? what is Harris's "direct method"?—instead of seeking ways to use what the linguists have pointed out about the rules we have within us, to help our students better understand their own linguistic resources, we have quoted over and over again that unqualified and misleading statement about the harmful effects of teaching formal grammar. And we have bent over backwards to avoid spending classroom time on anything that smacks of grammar, old or new.

Is there room in the language arts curriculum or in the freshman composition class for grammar study? Certainly. In some classrooms it never left; many teachers have never stopped believing that the teaching of composition and literature can be more effective when they are able to discuss the details of syntax with their students. In other classrooms grammar actually slipped in quite some time ago under the guise of sentence combining. Frank O'Hare, who introduced many of us to sentence combining some years ago, might disagree with such a notion; after all, he introduced his well-known study, *Sentence Combining: Improving Student Writing without Formal Grammar Instruction*,[13] by quoting the "harmful effects" statement on page one. In fact, he explicitly denies any connection between sentence combining and grammar:

The greatest attraction for both teacher and pupils of the system of sentence-combining practice described here is, of course, that it does not necessitate the study of a grammar, traditional or transformational. The English teacher who simply "doesn't like grammar" can use this system. (p. 30)

But even though O'Hare perpetuates the myth, his experimental students, like Frogner's "thought" group back in 1939 and Harris's "direct method" group, actually did study grammar. They didn't memorize Mellon's transformational formulas, it's true, but they did study the system underlying their own language ability; they learned to manipulate sentences in a conscious way.[14] That they labeled clause modifiers as "who statements" rather than "relative clauses" doesn't mean they didn't study grammar. Among the recent versions of sentence combining at least one that includes traditional terminology with apology. Students using *The Writer's Options: College Sentence Combining* by Daiker, Kerek, and Morenberg learn all about—and learn to control—relative clauses in Chapter One, participles in Chapter Two, appositives in Chapter Three, and absolutes in Chapter Four.[15] If sentence combining does indeed have transfer value—that is, if it improves the writing that students do beyond the sentence combining lesson—then surely a conscious understanding of such structures, along with the labels that help them think about the structures and remember them, can only add to that value.

Perhaps Hoyt was right in 1906 to believe as he did that young children did not profit from studying abstract concepts of grammar; perhaps grammar classes of old were too prescriptive, too bound up with drilling and memorizing, too non-functional in their methods. But even very young writers can come to understand consciously the structures they use in their writing and can profit by that understanding. "Sesame Street" watchers, including preschoolers, easily learn the ways of words, from principles underlying the "silent e" to the meaning of prepositions and the importance of word order. Elementary language arts teachers can capitalize on that beginning, not by routinely drilling year after year the traditional sequence of topics that begins with the parts of speech and ends with complex sentences, but by helping the students discover and understand and appreciate their innate language abilities.

"Grammar" need not be synonymous with diagramming or drillwork or memorizing rules; studying grammar can also mean thoughtful discussion of choices in generating and combining and manipulating sentences—at every level of the curriculum. O'Hare asserts that "most teachers of writing either ignore or neglect the importance of syntactic manipulative ability" (p. 75). Surely he is wrong. We do understand its importance. But we have been misled into thinking we should somehow be able to teach such skills without giving our students a conscious understanding of grammar, the system of syntax, in any systematic way. We have been warned so often against teaching grammar for its own sake, we are even wary about asking our students to learn basic terminology. We haven't learned, as Jim W. Corder puts it, "to use grammar as a sprightly instrument in composition."[16] Nor have we been encouraged to do so.

Is there room in the composition class for that "sprightly instrument"? Of course, Grammar is there whether we like it or not. The question is, do we acknowledge its presence and its importance in our teaching? The alchemists have been in charge long enough. Nothing is more important to our students than an understanding of language, the mark of their humanity, which they use every hour of every day—if not in reading and writing, then in speaking and listening and thinking. Our goal should be to help them understand consciously the system they know subconsciously as native speakers, to teach them the necessary categories and labels that will enable them to think about and talk about their language, so that when they use it consciously, as they do in writing, they will do so with control and grace and enthusiasm.

Notes

[1] Julia S. Falk, "Language Acquisition and the Teaching and Learning of Writing," *College English*, 41 (December 1979), 446.

[2] Dean Memering, "Forward to the Basics," *College English*, 39 (January 1978), 559. Most of what Memering has to say about going forward, not backwards, to the basics makes good sense. He believes in the sentence as the basic unit of composition; he extols the merits of sentence combining and sentence generating; he urges us "to go *forward* to a literary and rhetorical appreciation of the sentence" (p. 561).

[3] Franklyn S. Hoyt, "Grammar in the Elementary Curriculum," *Teachers College Record*, 7 (November 1906), 473-494.

[4] Louis W. Rapeer, "The Problem of Formal Grammar in Elementary Education," *The Journal of Educational Psychology*, 4 (March 1913), 124-317.

[5] William Asker, "Does Knowledge of Formal Grammar Function?" *School and Society*, (January 27, 1923), pp. 109-111.

[6] D. Segal and N. R. Barr, "Relation of Achievement in Formal Grammar to Achievement in Applied Grammar," *Journal of Educational Research*, 12 (December 1926), 401-402.

[7] Percival M. Symonds, "Practice Versus Grammar in Learning to Correct English Usage," *Journal of Educational Psychology*, 22 (February 1931), 81-95.

[8] Ellen Frogner, "Grammar Approach Versus Thought Approach in Teaching Sentence Structure," *English Journal*, 28 (September 1939), 518-526.

[9] Roland J. Harris, "An Experimental Inquiry into the Functions and Value of Formal Grammar in the Teaching of Written English to Children Aged Twelve to Fourteen." Unpublished Ph.D. dissertation, University of London, 1962. (Summarized in Richard Braddock, Richard Lloyd-Jones, and Lowell Schoer, *Research in Written Composition* [Champaign, IL: National Council of Teachers of English, 1963], pp. 70-83.)

[10] Mary Elizabeth Fowler, *Teaching Language Composition, and Literature* (New York: McGraw-Hill Book Company, 1965), p. 131.

[11] Walter Loban, Margaret Ryan, and James R. Squire, *Teaching Language and Literature, Grades Seven-Twelve*, 2nd Edition (New York: Harcourt Brace and World, 1969).

[12] Stephen N. Judy, *Explorations in the Teaching of Secondary English* (New York: Dodd, Mead & Company, 1974).

[13] Urbana, IL: National Council of Teachers of English, 1973.

[14] Donald A. Daiker, Andrew Kerek, Max Morenberg, *The Writer's Options* (New York: Harper & Row, 1979).

[15] The O'Hare experiment was a replication of an earlier sentence combining study by John Mellon that required students to learn certain transformational formulas. O'Hare's version eliminated that aspect of the experiment.

[16] Jim W. Corder, "Outhouses, Weather Changes, and the Return to Basics in English Education," *College English*, 38 (January 1977), 480.

Understanding Composing

SONDRA PERL

> Any psychological process, whether the development of thought or voluntary behavior, is a process undergoing changes right before one's eyes. . . . Under certain conditions it becomes possible to trace this development.[1]
>
> L.S. Vygotsky

It's hard to begin this case study of myself as a writer because even as I'm searching for a beginning, a pattern of organization, I'm watching myself, trying to understand my behavior. As I sit here in silence, I can see lots of things happening that never made it onto my tapes. My mind leaps from the task at hand to what I need at the vegetable stand for tonight's soup to the threatening rain outside to ideas voiced in my writing group this morning, but in between "distractions" I hear myself trying out words I might use. It's as if the extraneous thoughts are a counterpoint to the more steady attention I'm giving to composing. This is all to point out that the process is more complex than I'm aware of, but I think my tapes reveal certain basic patterns that I tend to follow.

> Anne
> New York City Teacher

Anne is a teacher of writing. In 1979, she was among a group of twenty teachers who were taking a course in research and basic writing at New York University.[2] One of the assignments in the course was for the teachers to tape their thoughts while composing aloud on the topic, "My Most Anxious Moment as a Writer." Everyone in the group was given the topic in the morning during class and told to compose later on that day in a place where they would be comfortable and relatively free from distractions. The result was a tape of composing aloud and a written product that formed the basis for class discussion over the next few days.

One of the purposes of this assignment was to provide teachers with an opportunity to see their own composing processes at work. From the start

College Composition and Communication, 31 (December 1980), pp. 363-369.

of the course, we recognized that we were controlling the situation by assigning a topic and that we might be altering the process by asking writers to compose aloud. Nonetheless we viewed the task as a way of capturing some of the flow of composing and, as Anne later observed in her analysis of her tape, she was able to detect certain basic patterns. This observation, made not only by Anne, then leads me to ask "What basic patterns seem to occur during composing?" and "What does this type of research have to tell us about the nature of the composing process?"

Perhaps the most challenging part of the answer is the recognition of recursiveness in writing. In recent years, many researchers including myself have questioned the traditional notion that writing is a linear process with a strict plan-write-revise sequence.[3] In its stead, we have advocated the idea that writing is a recursive process, that throughout the process of writing, writers return to substrands of the overall process, or subroutines (short successions of steps that yield results on which the writer draws in taking the next set of steps); writers use these to keep the process moving forward. In other words, recursiveness in writing implies that there is a forward-moving action that exists by virtue of a backward-moving action. The questions that then need to be answered are, "To what do writers move back?" "What exactly is being repeated?" "What recurs?"

To answer these questions, it is important to look at what writers do while writing and what an analysis of their processes reveals. The descriptions that follow are based on my own observations of the composing processes of many types of writers including college students, graduate students, and English teachers like Anne.

Writing does appear to be recursive, yet the parts that recur seem to vary from writer to writer and from topic to topic. Furthermore, some recursive elements are easy to spot while others are not.

1. The most visible recurring feature or backward movement involves re-reading little bits of discourse. Few writers I have seen write for long periods of time without returning briefly to what is already down on the page.

For some, like Anne, rereading occurs after every few phrases; for others, it occurs after every sentence; more frequently, it occurs after a "chunk" of information has been written. Thus, the unit that is reread is not necessarily a syntactic one, but rather a semantic one as defined by the writer.

2. The second recurring feature is some key word or item called up by the topic. Writers consistently return to their notion of the topic throughout the process of writing. Particularly when they are stuck, writers seem to use the topic or a key word in it as a way to get going again. Thus many times it is possible to see writers "going back," rereading the topic they were given, changing it to suit what they have been writing or changing what they have written to suit their notion of the topic.

3. There is also a third backward movement in writing, one that is not so easy to document. It is not easy because the move, itself, cannot immedi-

ately be identified with words. In fact, the move is not to any words on the page nor to the topic but to feelings or non-verbalized perceptions that *surround* the words, or to what the words already present *evoke* in the writer. The move draws on sense experience, and it can be observed if one pays close attention to what happens when writers pause and seem to listen or otherwise react to what is inside of them. The move occurs inside the writer, to what is physically felt. The term used to describe this focus of writers' attention is *felt sense*. The term "felt sense" has been coined and described by Eugene Gendlin, a philosopher at the University of Chicago. In his words, felt sense is

> the soft underbelly of thought . . . a kind of bodily awareness that . . . can be used as a tool . . . a bodily awareness that . . . encompasses everything you feel and know about a given subject at a given time. . . . It is felt in the body, yet it has meaning. It is body *and* mind before they are split apart.[4]

This felt sense is always there, within us. It is unifying, and yet, when we bring words to it, it can break apart, shift, unravel, and become something else. Gendlin has spent many years showing people how to work with their felt sense. Here I am making connections between what he has done and what I have seen happen as people write.

When writers are given a topic, the topic itself evokes a felt sense in them. This topic calls forth images, words, ideas, and vague fuzzy feelings that are anchored in the writer's body. What is elicited, then, is not solely the product of a mind but of a mind alive in a living, sensing body.

When writers pause, when they go back and repeat key words, what they seem to be doing is waiting, paying attention to what is still vague and unclear. They are looking to their felt experience, and waiting for an image, a word, or a phrase to emerge that captures the sense they embody.

Usually, when they make the decision to write, it is after they have a dawning awareness that something has clicked, that they have enough of a sense that if they begin with a few words heading in a certain direction, words will continue to come which will allow them to flesh out the sense they have.

The process of using what is sensed directly about a topic is a natural one. Many writers do it without any conscious awareness that that is what they are doing. For example, Anne repeats the words "anxious moments," using these key words as a way of allowing her sense of the topic to deepen. She asks herself, "Why are exams so anxiety provoking?" and waits until she has enough of a sense within her that she can go in a certain direction. She does not yet have the words, only the sense that she is able to begin. Once she writes, she stops to see what is there. She maintains a highly recursive composing style throughout and she seems unable to go forward without first going back to see and to listen to what she has already created. In her own words, she says:

My disjointed style of composing is very striking to me. I almost never move from the writing of one sentence directly to the next. After each sentence I pause to read what I've written, assess, sometimes edit and think about what will come next. I often have to read the several preceding sentences a few times as if to gain momentum to carry me to the next sentence. I seem to depend a lot on the sound of my words and . . . while I'm hanging in the middle of this uncompleted thought, I may also start editing a previous sentence or get an inspiration for something which I want to include later in the paper.

What tells Anne that she is ready to write? What is the feeling of "momentum" like for her? What is she hearing as she listens to the "sound" of her words? When she experiences "inspiration," how does she recognize it?

In the approach I am presenting, the ability to recognize what one needs to do or where one needs to go is informed by calling on felt sense. This is the internal criterion writers seem to use to guide them when they are planning, drafting, and revising.

The recursive move, then, that is hardest to document but is probably the most important to be aware of is the move to felt sense, to what is not yet *in words* but out of which images, words, and concepts emerge.

The continuing presence of this felt sense, waiting for us to discover it and see where it leads, raises a number of questions.

Is "felt sense" another term for what professional writers call their "inner voice" or their feeling of "inspiration"?

Do skilled writers call on their capacity to sense more readily than unskilled writers?

Rather than merely reducing the complex act of writing to a neat formulation, can the term "felt sense" point us to an area of our experience from which we can evolve even richer and more accurate descriptions of composing?

Can learning how to work with felt sense teach us about creativity and release us from stultifying repetitive patterns?

My observations lead me to answer "yes" to all four questions. There seems to be a basic step in the process of composing that skilled writers rely on even when they are unaware of it and that less skilled writers can be taught. This process seems to rely on very careful attention to one's inner reflections and is often accompanied with bodily sensations.

When it's working, this process allows us to say or write what we've never said before, to create something new and fresh, and occasionally it provides us with the experience of "newness" or "freshness," even when "old words" or images are used.

The basic process begins with paying attention. If we are given a topic, it begins with taking the topic in and attending to what it evokes in us. There is less "figuring out" an answer and more "waiting" to see what forms. Even without a predetermined topic, the process remains the same. We can ask ourselves, "What's on my mind?" or "Of all the things I know about, what would I most like to write about now?" and wait to see what comes. What we pay attention to is the part of our bodies where we experience ourselves directly. For many people, it's the area of their stomachs; for others, there is a more generalized response and they maintain a hovering attention to what they experience throughout their bodies.

Once a felt sense forms, we match words to it. As we begin to describe it, we get to see what is there for us. We get to see what we think, what we know. If we are writing about something that truly interests us, the felt sense deepens. We know that we are writing out of a "centered" place.

If the process is working, we begin to move along, sometimes quickly. Other times, we need to return to the beginning, to reread, to see if we captured what we meant to say. Sometimes after rereading we move on again, picking up speed. Other times by rereading we realize we've gone off the track, that what we've written doesn't quite "say it," and we need to reassess. Sometimes the words are wrong and we need to change them. Other times we need to go back to the topic, to call up the sense it initially evoked to see where and how our words led us astray. Sometimes in rereading we discover that the topic is "wrong," that the direction we discovered in writing is where we really want to go. It is important here to clarify that the terms "right" and "wrong" are not necessarily meant to refer to grammatical structures or to correctness.

What is "right" or "wrong" corresponds to our sense of our intention. We intend to write something, words come, and now we assess if those words adequately capture our intended meaning. Thus, the first question we ask ouselves is "Are these words right for me?" "Do they capture what I'm trying to say?" "If not, what's missing?"

It seems as though a felt sense has within it many possible structures or forms. As we shape what we intend to say, we are further structuring our sense while correspondingly shaping our piece of writing.

It is also important to note that what is there implicitly, without words, is not equivalent to what finally emerges. In the process of writing, we begin with what is inchoate and end with something that is tangible. In order to do so, we both discover and construct what we mean. Yet the term "discovery" ought not lead us to think that meaning exists fully formed inside of us and that all we need do is dig deep enough to release it. In writing, meaning cannot be discovered the way we discover an object on an archeological dig. In writing, meaning is crafted and constructed. It involves us in a process of coming-into-being. Once we have worked at shaping, through language, what is there inchoately, we can look at what we have written to see if it adequately captures what we intended. Often at this moment discovery occurs. We see something new in our writing that comes upon us as a surprise. We see in our words a further structuring of the sense we began with and we recognize that in those words we have discovered something new about ourselves and our topic. Thus when we are successful at this process, we end up with a product that teaches us something, that clarifies what we know (or what we knew at one point only implicitly), and that lifts out or explicates or enlarges our experience. In this way, writing leads to discovery.

All the writers I have observed, skilled and unskilled alike, use the process of retrospective structuring while writing. Yet the degree to which they do so varies and seems, in fact, to depend upon the model of the writing process that they seem to have internalized. Those who realize that writing can be a recursive process have an easier time with waiting, looking, and discovering. Those who subscribe to the linear model find themselves easily frustrated when what they write does not immediately correspond to what they planned or when what they produce leaves them with little sense of accomplishment. Since they have relied on a formulaic approach, they often produce writing that is formulaic as well, thereby cutting themselves off from the possibility of discovering something new.

Such a result seems linked to another feature of the composing process, to what I call *projective structuring,* or the ability to craft what one intends to say so that it is intelligible to others.

A number of concerns arise in regard to projective structuring; I will mention only a few that have been raised for me as I have watched different writers at work.

1. Although projective structuring is only one important part of the composing process, many writers act as if it is the whole process. These writers focus on what they think others want them to write rather than looking to see what it is they want to write. As a result, they often ignore their felt sense and they do not establish a living connection between themselves and their topic.

2. Many writers reduce projective structuring to series of rules or criteria for evaluating finished discourse. These writers ask, "Is what I'm writing correct?" and "Does it conform to the rules I've been taught?" While these concerns are important, they often overshadow all others and lock the writer in the position of writing solely or primarily for the approval of readers.

Projective structuring, as I see it, involves much more than imagining a strict audience and maintaining a strict focus on correctness. It is true that to handle this part of the process well, writers need to know certain grammatical rules and evaluative criteria, but they also need to know how to call up a sense of their reader's needs and expectations.

For projective structuring to function fully, writers need to draw on their capacity to move away from their own words, to decenter from the page, and to project themselves into the role of the reader. In other words, projective structuring asks writers to attempt to become readers and to imagine what someone other than themselves will need before the writer's particular piece of writing can become intelligible and compelling. To do so, writers must have the experience of being readers. They cannot call up a felt sense of a reader unless they themselves have experienced what it means to be lost in a piece of writing or to be excited by it. When writers do not have such experiences, it is easy for them to accept that readers merely require correctness.

In closing, I would like to suggest that retrospective and projective structuring are two parts of the same basic process. Together they form the alternating mental postures writers assume as they move through the act of composing. The former relies on the ability to go inside, to attend to what is there, from that attending to place words upon a page, and then to assess if those words adequately capture one's meaning. The latter relies on the ability to assess how the words on that page will affect someone other than the writer, the reader. We rarely do one without the other entering in; in fact, again in these postures we can see the shuttling back-and-forth movements of the composing process, the move from sense to words and from words to sense, from inner experience to outer judgment and from judgment back to experience. As we move through this cycle, we are continually composing and recomposing our meanings and what we mean. And in doing so, we display some of the basic recursive patterns that writers who observe themselves closely seem to see in their own work. After observing the process for a long time we may, like Anne, conclude that at any given moment the process is more complex than anything we are aware of; yet such insights, I believe, are important. They show us the fallacy of reducing the composing process to a simple linear scheme and they leave us with the potential for creating even more powerful ways of understanding composing.

Notes

[1] L. S. Vygotsky, *Mind in Society,* trans. M. Cole, V. John-Steiner, S. Scribner, and E. Souberman (Cambridge, MA: Harvard University Press, 1978), p. 61.

[2] This course was team-taught by myself and Gordon Pradl, Associate Professor of English Education at New York University.

[3] See Janet Emig, *The Composing Processes of Twelfth-Graders.* NCTE Research Report No. 13 (Urbana, IL: National Council of Teachers of English, 1971); Linda Flower and J. R. Hayes, "The Cognition of Discovery," *CCC,* 31 (February 1980), 21-32; Nancy Sommers, "The Need for Theory in Composition Research," *CCC,* 31 (February 1979), 46-49.

[4] Eugene Gendlin, *Focusing* (New York: Everest House, 1978), pp. 35, 165.

The Study of Error

DAVID BARTHOLOMAE

It is curious, I think, that with all the current interest in "Basic Writing," little attention has been paid to the most basic question: What is it? What is "basic writing," that is, if the term is to refer to a phenomenon, an activity, something a writer does or has done, rather than to a course of instruction? We know that across the country students take tests of one sort or another and are placed in courses that bear the title, "Basic Writing." But all we know is that there are students taking courses. We know little about their performance as writers, beyond the bald fact that they fail to do what other, conventionally successful, writers do. We don't, then, have an adequate description of the variety of writing we call "basic."

On the other hand, we have considerable knowledge of what Basic Writing courses are like around the country, the texts that are used, the approaches taken. For some time now, "specialists" have been devising and refining the technology of basic or developmental instruction. But these technicians are tinkering with pedagogies based on what? At best on models of how successful writers write. At worst, on old text-book models that disregard what writers actually do or how they could be said to learn, and break writing conveniently into constituent skills like "word power," "sentence power," and "paragraph power." Neither pedagogy is built on the results of any systematic inquiry into what basic writers do when they write or into the way writing skills develop for beginning adult writers. Such basic research has barely begun. Mina Shaughnessy argued the case this way:

> Those pedagogies that served the profession for years seem no longer appropriate to large numbers of students, and their inappropriateness lies largely in the fact that many of our students . . . are adult beginners and depend as students did not depend in the past upon the classroom and the teacher for the acquisition of the skill of writing.

If the profession is going to accept responsibility for teaching this kind of student, she concludes, "We are committed to research of a very ambitious sort."[1]

Where might such research begin, and how might it proceed? We must begin by studying basic writing itself—the phenomenon, not the course of instruction. If we begin here, we will recognize at once that "basic" does not mean simple or childlike. These are beginning writers, to be sure, but they are not writers who need to learn to use language. They are writers who need to learn to command a particular variety of language—the language of a written, academic discourse—and a particular variety of language use—writing itself. The writing of a basic writer can be shown to be an approximation of conventional written discourse; it is a peculiar and idiosyncratic version of a highly conventional type, but the relation between the approximate and the conventional forms is not the same as the relation between the writing, say, of a 7th grader and the writing of a college freshman.

Basic writing, I want to argue, is a variety of writing, not writing with fewer parts or more rudimentary constituents. It is not evidence of arrested cognitive development, or unruly or unpredictable language use. The writer of this sentence, for example, could not be said to be writing an "immature" sentence, in any sense of the term, if we grant her credit for the sentence she intended to write:

The time of my life when I learned something, and which resulted in a change in which I look upon life things. This would be the period of my life when I graduated from Elementary school to High school.

When we have used conventional T-unit analysis, and included in our tabulations figures on words/clause, words/T-unit and clauses/T-unit that were drawn from "intended T-units" as well as actual T-units, we have found that basic writers do not, in general, write "immature" sentences. They are not, that is, 13th graders writing 7th grade sentences. In fact, they often attempt syntax whose surface is more complex than that of more successful freshman writers. They get into trouble by getting in over their heads, not only attempting to do more than they can, but imagining as their target a syntax that is *more* complex than convention requires. The failed sentences, then, could be taken as stages of learning rather than the failure to learn, but also as evidence that these writers are using writing as an occasion to learn.

It is possible to extend the concept of "intentional structures" to the analysis of complete essays in order to determine the "grammar" that governs the idiosyncratic discourse of writers imagining the language and conventions of academic discourse in unconventional ways. This method of analysis is certainly available to English teachers, since it requires a form of close reading, paying attention to the language of a text in order to determine not only what a writer says, but how he locates and articulates meaning. When a basic writer violates our expectations, however, there is a tendency to dismiss the text as non-writing, as meaningless or imperfect writing. We have not read as we have been trained to read, with a particular interest in the way an individual style confronts and violates convention. We have read, rather, as policemen, examiners, gate-keepers. The teacher who is unable to make sense out of a seemingly bizarre piece of student writing is often the same teacher who can give an elaborate explanation of the "meaning" of a story by Donald Barthelme or a poem by e. e. cummings. If we learn to treat the language of basic writing *as* language and assume, as we do when writers violate our expectations in more conventional ways, that the unconventional features in the writing are evidence of intention and that they are, therefore, meaningful, then we can chart systematic choices, individual strategies, and characteristic processes of thought. One can read Mina Shaughnessy's *Errors and Expectations* as the record of just such a close reading.[2]

There is a style, then, to the apparently bizarre and incoherent writing of a basic writer because it is, finally, evidence of an individual using language to make and transcribe meaning. This is one of the axioms of error analysis, whether it be applied to reading (as in "miscue analysis"), writing, or second-language learning. An error (and I would include errors beyond those in the decoding or encoding of sentences) can only be understood as evidence of intention. They are the only evidence we have of an individual's idiosyncratic way of using the language and articulating meaning, of imposing a style on common material. A writer's activity is linguistic and rhetorical activity; it can be different but never random. The task for both teacher and researcher, then, is to discover the grammar of *that* coherence, of the "idiosyncratic dialect" that belongs to a particular writer at a particular moment in the history of his attempts to imagine and reproduce the standard idiom of academic discourse.[3]

All writing, of course, could be said to only approximate conventional discourse; our writing is never either completely predictable or completely idiosyncratic. We speak our own language as well as the language of the tribe and, in doing so, make concessions to both ourselves and our culture. The distance between text and conventional expectation may be a sign of failure and it may be a sign of genius, depending on the level of control and intent we are willing to assign to the writer, and depending on the insight we acquire from seeing convention so transformed. For a basic writer the distance between text and convention is greater than it is for the run-of-the-mill freshman writer. It may be, however, that the more talented the freshman writer becomes, the more able she is to increase again the distance between text and convention. We are drawn to conclude that basic writers lack control, although it may be more precise to say that they lack choice and option, the power to make decisions about the idiosyncrasy of their writing. Their writing is not, however, truly uncontrolled. About the actual distance from text to convention for the basic writer, we know very little. We know that it will take a long time to traverse—generally the greater the distance the greater the time and energy required to close the gap. We know almost nothing about the actual sequence of development—the natural sequence of learning—that moves a writer from basic writing to competent writing to good writing. The point, however, is that "basic writing" is something our students *do* or *produce*; it is not a kind of writing we teach to backward or unprepared students. We should not spend our time imagining simple or "basic" writing tasks, but studying the errors that emerge when beginning writers are faced with complex tasks.

The mode of analysis that seems most promising for the research we need on the writer's sequence of learning is error analysis. Error analysis provides the basic writing teacher with both a technique for analyzing errors in the production of discourse, a technique developed by linguists to study second langauge learning, and a theory of error, or, perhaps more properly, a perspective on error, where errors are seen as (1) necessary stages of individual development and (2) data that provide insight into the idiosyncratic strategies of a particular language user at a particular point in his acquisition of a target language. Enough has been written lately about error analysis that I'll only give a brief summary of its perspective on second language or second dialect acquisition.[4] I want to go on to look closely at error analysis as a method, in order to point out its strengths and limits as a procedure for textual analysis.

George Steiner has argued that all acts of interpretation are acts of translation and are, therefore, subject to the constraints governing the passage from one language to another.[5] All our utterances are approximations, attempts to use the language of, say, Frank Kermode or the language, perhaps, of our other, smarter, wittier self. In this sense, the analogy that links developmental composition instruction with second language learning can be a useful one—useful that is, if the mode of learning (whatever the "second" language) is writing rather than speaking. (This distinction, I might add, is not generally made in the literature on error analysis, where writing and speech are taken as equivalent phenomena.) Error analysis begins with the recognition that errors, or the points where the actual text varies from a hypothetical "standard" text, will be either random or systematic. If they are systematic in the writing of an individual writer, then they are evidence of some idiosyncratic rule system—an idiosyncratic grammar or rhetoric, an "interlanguage" or "approximate system."[6] If the errors are systematic across all basic writers, then they would be evidence of generalized stages in the acquisition of fluent writing for beginning adult writers. This distinction between individual and general systems is an important one for both teaching and research. It is not one that Shaughnessy makes. We don't know whether the categories of error in *Errors and Expectations* hold across a group, and, if so, with what frequency and across a group of what size.

Shaughnessy did find, however, predictable patterns in the errors in the essays she studied. She demonstrated that even the most apparently incoherent writing, if we are sensitive to its intentional structure, is evidence of systematic, coherent, rule-governed behavior. Basic writers, she demonstrated, are not performing mechanically or randomly but making choices and forming strategies as they struggle to deal with the varied demands of a task, a language, and a rhetoric. The "systems" such writing exhibits provide evidence that basic writers *are* competent, mature language users. Their attempts at producing written language are not hit and miss, nor are they evidence of simple translation of speech into print. The approximate systems they produce are evidence that they can conceive of and manipulate written language as a structured, systematic code. They are "intermediate" systems in that they mark stages en route to mastery, (or, more properly, en route to conventional fluency) of written, academic discourse.

This also, however, requires some qualification. They *may* be evidence of some transitional stage. They may also, to use Selinker's term, be evidence of "stabilized variability," where a writer is stuck or searching rather than moving on toward more complete approximation of the target language.[7] A writer will stick with some intermediate system if he is convinced that the language he uses "works," or if he is unable to see errors *as* errors and form alternate hypotheses in response.

Error analysis begins with a theory of writing, a theory of language production and language development, that allows us to see errors as evidence of choice or strategy among a range of possible choices or strategies. They provide evidence of an individual style of using the language and making it work; they are not a simple record of what a writer failed to do because of incompetence or indifference. Errors, then, are stylistic features, information about *this* writer and *this* language; they are not necessarily "noise" in the system, accidents of composing, or malfunctions in the language process. Consequently, we cannot identify errors without identifying them in context, and the context is not the text, but the activity of composing that presented the erroneous form as a possible solution to the problem of making a meaningful statement. Shaughnessy's taxonomy of error, for example, identifies errors according to their source, not their type. A single type of error could be attributed to a variety of causes. Donald Freeman's research, for example, has shown that, "subject-verb agreement . . . is a host of errors, not one." One of his students analyzed a "large sample of real world sentences and concluded that there are at least eight different kinds, most of which have very little to do with one another."[8]

Error analysis allows us to place error in the context of composing and to interpret and classify systematic errors. The key concept is the concept of an "interlanguage" or an "intermediate system," an idiosyncratic grammar and rhetoric that is a writer's approximation of the standard idiom. Errors, while they can be given more precise classification, fall into three main categories: errors that are evidence of an intermediate system; errors that could truly be said to be accidents, or slips of the pen as a writer's mind rushes ahead faster than his hand; and finally, errors of language transfer, or, more commonly, dialect interference, where in the attempt to produce the target language, the writer intrudes forms from the "first" or "native" language rather than inventing some intermediate form. For writers, this intrusion most often comes from a spoken dialect. The error analyst is primarily concerned, however, with errors that are evidence of some intermediate system. This kind of error occurs because the writer *is* an active, competent language user who uses his knowledge that language is rule-governed, and who uses his ability to predict and form analogies, to construct hypotheses that can make an irregular or unfamiliar language more manageable. The problem comes when the rule is incorrect or, more properly, when it is idiosyncratic, belonging only to the language of the writer. There is evidence of an idiosyncratic system, for example, when a student adds inflectional endings to infinitives, as in this sentence, "There was plenty the boy had to *learned* about birds." It also seems to be evident in a sentence like this: "This assignment calls on *chosing* one of my papers and making a last draft out of it." These errors can be further sub-divided into those that are in flux and mark a fully transitional stage, and those that, for one reason or another, become frozen and recur across time.

Kroll and Schafer, in a recent *CCC* article, argue that the value of error analysis for the composition teacher is the perspective it offers on the learner, since it allows us to see errors "as clues to inner processes, as windows into the mind."[9] If we investigate the pattern of error in the performance of an individual writer, we can better understand the nature of those errors and the way they "fit" in an individual writer's program for writing. As a consequence, rather than impose an inappropriate or even misleading syllabus on a learner, we can plan instruction to assist a writer's internal syllabus. If, for example, a writer puts standard inflections on irregular verbs or on verbs that are used in verbals (as in "I used to runned"), drill on verb endings will only reinforce the rule that, because the writer is overgeneralizing, is the source of the error in the first place. By charting and analyzing a writer's errors, we can begin in our instruction with what a writer *does* rather than with what he fails to do. It makes no sense to teach spelling to an individual who has trouble principally with words that contain vowel clusters. Error analysis, then, is a method of diagnosis.

Error analysis can assist instruction at another level. By having students share in the process of investigating and interpreting the patterns of error in their writing, we can help them begin to see those errors as evidence of hypotheses or strategies they have formed and, as a consequence, put them in a position to change, experiment, imagine other strategies. Studying their own writing puts students in a position to see themselves as language users, rather than as victims of a language that uses them.

This, then, is the perspective and the technique of error analysis. To interpret a student paper without this frame of reference is to misread, as for example when a teacher sees an incorrect verb form and concludes that the student does't understand the rules for indicating tense or number. I want, now, to examine error analysis as a procedure for the study of errors in written composition. It presents two problems. The first can be traced to the fact that error analysis was developed for studying errors in spoken performance.[10] It can be transferred to writing only to the degree that writing is like speech, and there are significant points of difference. It is generally acknowledged, for example, that written discourse is not just speech written down on paper. Adult written discourse has a grammar and rhetoric that is different from speech. And clearly the activity of producing language is different for a writer than it is for a speaker.

The "second language" a basic writer must learn to master is formal, written discourse, a discourse whose lexicon, grammar, and rhetoric are learned not through speaking and listening but through reading and writing. The process of acquisition is visual not aural. Furthermore, basic writers do not necessarily produce writing by translating speech into print (the way children learning to write would); that is, they must draw on a memory for graphemes rather than phonemes. This is a different order of memory and production from that used in speech and gives rise to errors unique to writing.

Writing also, however, presents "interference" of a type never found in speech. Errors in writing may be caused by interference from the act of writing itself, from the difficulty of moving a pen across the page quickly enough to keep up with the words in the writer's mind, or from the difficulty of recalling and producing the conventions that are necessary for producing print rather than speech, conventions of spelling, orthography, punctuation, capitalization and so on. This is not, however, just a way of saying that writers make spelling errors and speakers do not. As Shaughnessy pointed out, errors of syntax can be traced to the gyrations of a writer trying to avoid a word that her sentence has led her to, but that she knows she cannot spell.

The second problem in applying error analysis to the composition classroom arises from special properties in the taxonomy of errors we chart in student writing. Listing varieties of errors is not like listing varieties of rocks or butterflies. What a reader finds depends to a large degree on her assumptions about the writer's intention. Any systematic attempt to chart a learner's errors is clouded by the difficulty of assigning intention through textual analysis. The analyst begins, then, by interpreting a text, not by describing features on a page. And interpretation is less than a precise science.

Let me turn to an example. This is part of a paper that a student, John, wrote in repsonse to an assignment that asked him to go back to some papers he had written on significant moments in his life in order to write a paper that considered the general questions of the way people change:

This assignment call on chosing one of my incident making a last draft out of it. I found this very differcult because I like them all but you said I had to pick one so the Second incident was decide. Because this one had the most important insight to my life that I indeed learn from. This insight explain why adulthood mean that much as it dose to me because I think it alway influence me to change and my outlook on certain thing like my point-of-view I have one day and it might change the next week on the same issue. So in these frew words I going to write about the incident now. My exprience took place in my high school and the reason was out side of school but I will show you the connection. The situation took place cause of the type of school I went too. Let me tell you about the situation first of all what happen was that I got suspense from school. For thing that I fell was out of my control sometime, but it taught me alot about respondability of a growing man. The school suspense me for being late ten time. I had accummate ten dementic and had to bring my mother to school to talk to a conselor

and Prinpicable of the school what when on at the meet took me out
mentally period.

One could imagine a variety of responses to this. The first would be to
form the wholesale conclusion that John can't write and to send him off to a
workbook. Once he had learned how to write correct sentences, then he
could go on to the business of actually writing. Let me call this the "old
style" response to error. A second response, which I call the "investigative
approach," would be to chart the patterns of error in this particular text. Of
the approximately 40 errors in the first 200 words, the majority fall under
four fairly specific categories: verb endings, nouns plurals, syntax, and spelling. The value to pedagogy is obvious. One is no longer teaching a student to
"write" but to deal with a limited number of very specific kinds of errors,
each of which would suggest its own appropriate response. Furthermore, it
is possible to refine the categories and to speculate on and organize them
according to cause. The verb errors almost all involve "s" or "ed" endings,
which could indicate dialect interference or a failure to learn the rules for
indicating tense and number. It is possible to be even more precise. The
passage contains 41 verbs; only 17 of them are used incorrectly. With the
exception of four spelling errors, the errors are all errors of inflection and,
furthermore, these errors come only with regular verbs. There are no errors
with irregular verbs. This would suggest, then, that when John draws on
memory for a verb form, he gets it right; but when John applies a rule to
determine the ending, he gets it wrong.

The errors of syntax could be divided into those that might be called
punctuation errors (or errors that indicate a difficulty perceiving boundaries
of the sentence), such as

Let me tell you about the sitution first of all what happen was that I
got suspense from school. For thing that I fell was out of my control
sometime, but it taught me alot about respondability of a growing man.

and errors of syntax that would fall under Shaughnessy's category of consolidation errors,

This insight explain why adulthood mean that much as it dose to me
because I think it alway influence me to change and my outlook on
certain thing like my point-of-view I have one day and it might change
the next week on the same issue.

One would also want to note the difference between consistent errors, the
substitution of "situation" for "situation" or "suspense" for "suspended,"
and unstable ones, as, for example, when John writes "cause" in one place
and "because" in another. In one case John could be said to have fixed on
a rule; in the other he is searching for one. One would also want to distinguish between what might seem to be "accidental" errors, like substituting
"frew" for "few" or "when" for "went," errors that might best be addressed
by teaching a student to edit, and those whose causes are deeper and require
time and experience, or some specific instructional strategy.

I'm not sure, however, that this analysis provides an accurate representation of John's writing. Consider what happens when John reads this paper out loud. I've been taping students reading their own papers, and I've developed a system of notation, like that used in miscue analysis,[11] that will allow me to record the points of variation between the writing that is on the page and the writing that is spoken, or, to use the terminology of miscue analysis, between the expected response (ER) and the observed response (OR). What I've found is that students will often, or in predictable instances, substitute correct forms for the incorrect forms on the page, even though they are generally unaware that such a substitution was made. This observation suggests the limits of conventional error analysis for the study of error in written composition.

I asked John to read his paper out loud, and to stop and correct or note any mistakes he found. Let me try to reproduce the transcript of that reading. I will italicize any substitution or correction and offer some comments in parentheses. The reader might first go back and review the original. Here is what John read:

This assignment calls on *choosing* one of my incident making a last draft out of it. I found this very diff*i*cult because I like them all but you said I *had* to pick one so the Second incident was decided on. Because (John goes back and rereads, connecting up the subordinate clause.) So the second incident was decided on because this one had the most important insight to my life that I indeed learn*ed* from. This insight explains why adulthood *meant* that much as it dose to me because I think it always influence*s* me to change and my outlook on certain things like my point-of-view I have one day and it might change the next week on the same issue. (John goes back and rereads, beginning with "like my point of view," and he is puzzled but he makes no additional changes.) So in these *few* words *I'm* going to write about the incident now. My exp*e*rience took place *be*cause of the type of school I went to (John had written "too.") Let me tell you about the situation (John comes to a full stop.) first of all what happen*ed* was that I got *suspended* from school (no full stop) for things that I *felt* was out of my control sometime, but it taught me a lot about *responsibility* of a growing man. The school *suspended* me for being late ten times. I had *accumulated* (for "accumate") ten *demerits* (for "dementic") and had to bring my mother to school to talk to a counselor and *the Principal* of the school (full stop) what *went* on at the meeting took me out mentally (full stop) period (with brio).

I have chosen an extreme case to make my point, but what one sees here is the writer correcting almost every error as he reads the paper, even though he is not able to recognize that there *are* errors or that he has corrected them. The only errors John spotted (where he stopped, noted an error and corrected it) were the misspellings of "situation" and "Principal," and the substitution of "chosing" for "choosing." Even when he was asked to reread sentences to see if he could notice any difference between what he was saying and the words on the page, he could not. He could not, for example, see the error in "frew" or "dementic" or any of the other verb errors, and yet he spoke the correct form of every verb (with the exception of "was" after he had changed "thing" to "things" in "for things that I *felt* was out of my control") and he corrected every plural. His phrasing as he read produced correct syntax, except in the case of the consolidation error, which he puzzled over but did not correct. It's important to note, however, that John did not read that confused syntax as if no confusion were there. He sensed the difference between the phrasing called for by the meaning of the sentence and that which existed on the page. He did not read as though meaning didn't matter or as though the "meaning" coded on the page was complete. His problem cannot be simply a syntax problem, since the jumble is bound up with his struggle to articulate this particular meaning. And it is not simply a "thinking" problem—John doesn't write this way because he thinks this way—since he perceives that the statement as it is written is other than that which he intended.

When I asked John why the paper (which went on for two more pages) was written all as one paragraph, he replied, "It was all one idea. I didn't want to have to start all over again. I had a good idea and I didn't want to give it up." John doesn't need to be "taught" the paragraph, at least not as the paragraph is traditionally taught. His prose is orderly and proceeds through blocks of discourse. He tells the story of his experience at the school and concludes that through his experience he realized that he must accept responsibility for his tardiness, even though the tardiness was not his fault but the fault of the Philadelphia subway system. He concludes that with this realization he learned "the responsibility of a growing man." Furthermore John knows that the print code carries certain conventions for ordering and presenting discourse. His translation of the notion that "a paragraph develops a single idea" is peculiar but not illogical.

It could also be argued that John does not need to be "taught" to produce correct verb forms, or, again, at least not as such things are conventionally taught. Fifteen weeks of drill on verb endings might raise his test scores but they would not change the way he writes. He *knows* how to produce correct endings. He demonstrated that when he read, since he was reading in terms of his grammatical competence. His problem is a problem of performance, or fluency, not of competence. There is certainly no evidence that the verb errors are due to interference from his spoken language. And if the errors could be traced to some intermediate system, the system exists only in John's performance as a writer. It does not operate when he reads or, for that matter, when he speaks, if his oral reconstruction of his own text can be taken as a record of John "speaking" the idiom of academic discourse.[12]

John's case also highlights the tremendous difficulty such a student has with editing, where a failure to correct a paper is not evidence of laziness or inattention or a failure to know correct forms, but evidence of the tremendous difficulty such a student has objectifying language and seeing it as black and white marks on the page, where things can be wrong even though the meaning seems right.[13] One of the hardest errors for John to spot, after all my coaching, was the substitution of "frew" for "few," certainly not an error that calls into question John's competence as a writer. I can call this a "performance" error, but that term doesn't suggest the constraints on performance in writing. This is an important area for further study. Surely one constraint is the difficulty of moving the hand fast enough to translate meaning into print. The burden imposed on their patience and short term memory by the slow, awkward handwriting of many inexperienced writers is a very real one. But I think the constraints extend beyond the difficulty of forming words quickly with pen or pencil.

One of the most interesting results of the comparison of the spoken and written versions of John's text is his inability to *see* the difference between "frew" and "few" or "dementic" and "demerit." What this suggests is that John reads and writes from the "top down" rather than the "bottom up," to use a distinction made by cognitive psychologists in their study of reading.[14] John is not operating through the lower level process of translating orthographic information into sounds and sounds into meaning when he reads. And conversely, he is not working from meaning to sound to word when he is writing. He is, rather, retrieving lexical items directly, through a "higher level" process that by-passes the "lower level" operation of phonetic translation. When I put *frew* and *few* on the blackboard, John read them both as "few." The lexical item "few" is represented for John by either orthographic array. He is not, then, reading or writing phonetically, which is a sign, from one perspective, of a high level of fluency, since the activity is automatic and not mediated by the more primitive operation of translating speech into print or print into speech. When John was writing, he did not produce "frew" or "dementic" by searching for sound/letter correspondences. He drew directly upon his memory for the look and shape of those words; he was working from the top down rather than the bottom up. He went to stored print forms and did not take the slower route of translating speech into writing.

John, then, has reached a stage of fluency in writing where he directly and consistently retrieves print forms, like "dementic," that are meaningful to him, even though they are idiosyncratic. I'm not sure what all the implications of this might be, but we surely must see John's problem in a new light, since his problem can, in a sense, be attributed to his skill. To ask John to slow down his writing and sound out words would be disastrous. Perhaps the most we can do is to teach John the slowed down form of reading he will need in order to edit.

John's paper also calls into question our ability to identify accidental errors. I suspect that when John substitutes a word like "when" for "went," this is an accidental error, a slip of the pen. Since John spoke "went" when he read, I cannot conclude that he substitutes "when" for "went" because he pronounces both as "wen." This, then, is not an error of dialect interference but an accidental error, the same order of error as the omission of "the" before "Principal." Both were errors John corrected while reading (even though he didn't identify them as errors).

What is surprising is that, with all the difficulty John had identifying errors, he immediately saw that he had written "chosing" rather than "choosing." While textual analysis would have led to the conclusion that he was applying a tense rule to a participial construction, or overgeneralizing from a known rule, the ease with which it was identified would lead one to conclude that it was, in fact, a mistake, and not evidence of an approximate system. What would have been diagnosed as a deep error now appears to be only an accidental error, a "mistake" (or perhaps a spelling error).

In summary, this analysis of John's reading produces a healthy respect for the tremendous complexity of transcription, for the process of recording meaning in print as opposed to the process of generating meaning. It also points out the difficulty of charting a learner's "interlanguage" or "intermediate system," since we are working not only with a writer moving between a first and a second language, but a writer whose performance is subject to the interference of transcription, of producing meaning through the print code. We need, in general, to refine our understanding of performance-based errors, and we need to refine our teaching to take into account the high percentage of error in written composition that is rooted in the difficulty of performance rather than in problems of general linguistic competence.

Let me pause for a moment to put what I've said in the context of work in error analysis. Such analysis is textual analysis. It requires the reader to make assumptions about intention on the basis of information in the text. The writer's errors provide the most important information since they provide insight into the idiosyncratic systems the writer has developed. The regular but unconventional features in the writing will reveal the rules and strategies operating for the basic writer.

The basic procedure for such analysis could be outlined this way. First the reader must identify the idiosyncratic construction; he must determine what is an error. This is often difficult, as in the case of fragments, which are conventionally used for effect. Here is an example of a sentence whose syntax could clearly be said to be idiosyncratic:

In high school you learn alot for example Kindergarten which I took in high school.[15]

The reader, then, must reconstruct that sentence based upon the most reasonable interpretation of the intention in the original, and this must be done *before* the error can be classified, since it will be classified according to its cause.[16] Here is Shaughnessy's reconstruction of the example given above: "In high school you learn a lot. For example, I took up the study of Kindergarten in high school." For any idiosyncratic sentence, however, there are often a variety of possible reconstructions, depending on the reader's sense of the larger meaning of which this individual sentence is only a part, but also depending upon the reader's ability to predict how this writer puts sentences together, that is, on an understanding of this individual style. The text is being interpreted, not described. I've had graduate students who have reconstructed the following sentence, for example, in a variety of ways:

Why do we have womens liberation and their fighting f⸰r Equal Rights ect. to be recognized not as a lady but as an Individual.

It could read, "Why do we have women's liberation and why are they fighting for Equal Rights? In order that women may be recognized not as ladies but as individuals." And, "Why do we have women's liberation and their fight for equal rights, to be recognized not as a lady but as an individual?" There is an extensive literature on the question of interpretation and intention in prose, too extensive for the easy assumption that all a reader has to do is identify what the writer would have written if he wanted to "get it right the first time." The great genius of Shaughnessy's study, in fact, is the remarkable wisdom and sympathy of her interpretations of student texts.

Error analysis, then, involves more than just making lists of the errors in a student essay and looking for patterns to emerge. It begins with the double perspective of text and reconstructed text and seeks to explain the difference between the two on the basis of whatever can be inferred about the meaning of the text and the process of creating it. The reader/researcher brings to bear his general knowledge of how basic writers write, but also whatever is known about the linguistic and rhetorical constraints that govern an individual act of writing. In Shaughnessy's analysis of the "kindergarten" sentence, this discussion is contained in the section on "consolidation errors" in the chapter on "Syntax."[17] The key point, however, is that any such analysis must draw upon extra-textual information as well as close, stylistic analysis.

This paper has illustrated two methods for gathering information about how a text was created. A teacher can interview the student and ask him to explain his error. John wrote this sentence in another paper for my course:

I would to write about my experience helping 1600 childrens have a happy Christmas.

The missing word (I would *like* to write about . . .) he supplied when reading the sentence aloud. It is an accidental error and can be addressed by teaching editing. It is the same kind of error as his earlier substitution of "when" for "went." John used the phrase, "1600 childrens," throughout his paper, however. The conventional interpretation would have it that this is evidence of dialect interference. And yet, when John read the paper out loud, he consistently read "1600 children," even though he said he did not see any difference between the word he spoke and the word that was on the page. When I asked him to explain why he put an "s" on the end of "children," he replied, "Because there were 1600 of them." John had a rule for forming plurals that he used when he wrote but not when he spoke. Writing, as he rightly recognized, has its own peculiar rules and constraints. It is different from speech. The error is not due to interference from his spoken language but to his conception of the "code" of written discourse.

The other method for gathering information is having students read aloud their own writing, and having them provide an oral reconstruction of their written text. What I've presented in my analysis of John's essay is a method for recording the discrepancies between the written and spoken versions of a single text. The record of a writer reading provides a version of the "intended" text that can supplement the teacher's or researcher's own reconstruction and aid in the interpretation of errors, whether they be accidental, interlingual, or due to dialect interference. I had to read John's paper very differently once I had heard him read it.

More importantly, however, this method of analysis can provide access to an additional type of error. This is the error that can be attributed to the physical and conceptual demands of writing rather than speaking; it can be traced to the requirements of manipulating a pen and the requirements of manipulating the print code.[18]

In general, when writers read, and read in order to spot and correct errors, their responses will fall among the following categories:

1. overt corrections—errors a reader sees, acknowledges, and corrects;
2. spoken corrections—errors the writer does not acknowledge but corrects in reading,
3. no recognition—errors that are read as written;
4. overcorrection—correct forms made incorrect, or incorrect forms substituted for incorrect forms;
5. acknowledged error—errors a reader senses but cannot correct;
6. reader miscue—a conventional miscue, not linked to error in the text;
7. nonsense—In this case, the reader reads a non-sentence or a nonsense sentence as though it were correct and meaningful. No error or confusion is acknowledged. This applies to errors of syntax only.

Corrections, whether acknowledged or unacknowledged, would indicate performance-based errors. The other responses (with the exception of "reader miscues") would indicate deeper errors, errors that, when charted, would provide evidence of some idiosyncratic grammar or rhetoric.

John "miscues" by completing or correcting the text that he has written. When reading researchers have readers read out loud, they have them read someone else's writing of course, and they are primarily concerned with the "quality" of the miscues.[19] All fluent readers will miscue; that is, they will not repeat verbatim the words on the page. Since fluent readers are reading for meaning, they are actively predicting what will come and processing large chunks of graphic information at a time. They do not read individual words, and they miscue because they speak what they expect to see rather than what is actually on the page. One indication of a readers proficiency, then, is that the miscues don't destroy the "sense" of the passage. Poor readers will produce miscues that jumble the meaning of a passage, as in

Text: Her wings were folded quietly at her sides.
Reader: Her wings were floated quickly at her sides.

or they will correct miscues that do not affect meaning in any significant way.[20]

The situation is different when a reader reads his own text, since this reader already knows what the passage means and the attention is drawn, then, to the representation of that meaning. Reading also frees a writer from the constraints of transcription, which for many basic writers is an awkward, laborious process, putting excessive demands on both patience and short-term memory. John, like any reader, read what he expected to see, but with a low percentage of meaning-related miscues, since the meaning, for him, was set, and with a high percentage of code-related miscues, where a correct form was substituted for an incorrect form.

The value of studying students' oral reconstruction of their written texts is threefold. The first is a diagnostic tool. I've illustrated in my analysis of John's paper how such a diagnosis might take place.

It is also a means of instruction. By having John read aloud and, at the same time, look for discrepancies between what he spoke and what was on the page, I was teaching him a form of reading. The most dramatic change in John's performance over the term was in the number of errors he could spot and correct while re-reading. This far exceeded the number of errors he was able to eliminate from his first drafts. I could teach John an editing procedure better than I could teach him to be correct at the point of transcription.

The third consequence of this form of analysis, or of conventional error analysis, has yet to be demonstrated, but the suggestions for research are clear. It seems evident that we can chart stages of growth in individual basic writers. The pressing question is whether we can chart a sequence of "natural" development for the class of writers we call basic writers. If all non-fluent adult writers proceed through some large, longitudinal study, then we will begin to understand what a basic writing course or text or syllabus might look like. There are studies of adult second language learners that suggest that there is a general, natural sequence of acquisition for adults learning a second language, one that is determined by the psychology of language production and language acquisition.[21] Before we can adapt these methods to a study of basic writers, however, we need to better understand the additional constraints of learning to transcribe and manipulate the "code" of written discourse. John's case illustrates where we might begin and what we must know.[22]

Notes

[1] Mina Shaughnessy, "Some Needed Research on Writing," *CCC*, 28 (December 1977), 317, 388.

[2] Mina Shaughnessy, *Errors and Expectations: A Guide for the Teacher of Basic Writing* (New York: Oxford University Press, 1977).

[3] The term "idiosyncratic dialect" is taken from S. P. Corder, "Idiosyncratic Dialects and Error Analysis," in Jack C. Richards, ed., *Error Analysis: Perspectives on Second Language Acquisition* (London: Longman, 1974), pp. 158–171.

[4] Barry M. Kroll and John C. Schafer, "Error Analysis and the Teaching of Composition," *CCC*, 29 (October 1978), 243-248. See also my review of *Errors and Expectations* in Donald McQuade, ed., *Linguistics, Stylistics and the Teaching of Composition* (Akron, Ohio: L & S Books, 1979), pp. 209-220.

[5] George Steiner, *After Babel: Aspects of Language and Tranlsation* (New York: Oxford University Press, 1975).

[6] For the term "interlanguage," see L. Selinker, "Interlanguage," in Richards, ed., *Error Analysis*, pp. 31-55. For "approximate system," see William Nemser, "Approximate Systems of Foreign Language Learners," in Richards, ed., *Error Analysis*, pp. 55-64. These are more appropriate terms than "idiosyncratic dialect" for the study of error in written composition.

[7] The term "stabilized variability" is quoted in Andrew D. Cohen and Margaret Robbins, "Toward Assessing Interlanguage Performance: The Relationship Between Selected Errors, Learner's Characteristics and Learner's Explanations," *Language Learning*, 26 (June 1976), 59. Selinker uses the term "fossilization" to refer to single errors that recur across time, so that the interlanguage form is not evidence of a transitional stage. (See Selinker, "Interlanguage.") M. P. Jain distinguishes between "systematic," "asystematic" and "nonsystematic" errors. (See "Error Analysis: Source, Cause and Significance" in Richards, ed., *Error Analysis*, pp. 189-215.) Unsystematic errors are mistakes, "slips of the tongue." Systematic errors "seem to establish that in certain areas of language use the learner poses construction rules." Asystematic errors lead one to the "inescapable conclusion" that "the learner's capacity to generalize must improve, for progress in learning a language is made by adopting generalizations and stretching them to match the facts of the language."

[8] Donald C. Freeman, "Linguistics and Error Analysis: On Agency," in Donald McQuade, ed., *Linguistics, Stylistics and the Teaching of Composition* (Akron, Ohio: L & S Books, 1979), pp. 143-44.

[9] Kroll and Schafer, "Error Analysis and the Teaching of Composition."

[10] In the late 60s and early 70s, linguists began to study second language acquisition by systematically studying the actual performance of individual learners. What they studied, however, was the language a learner would speak. In the literature of error analysis, the reception and production of language is generally defined as the learner's ability to hear, learn, imitate, and independently produce *sounds*. Errors, then, are phonological substitutions, alterations, additions, and subtractions. Similarly, errors diagnosed as rooted in the mode of production (rather than, for example, in an idiosyncratic grammar or interference from the first language) are errors caused by the difficulty a learner has hearing or making foreign sounds. When we are studying written composition, we are studying a different mode of production, where a learner must see, remember, and produce marks on a page. There may be some similarity between the grammar-based errors in the two modes, speech and writing (it would be interesting to know to what degree this is true), but there should be marked differences in the nature and frequency of performance-based errors.

[11] See Y. M. Goodman and C. L. Burke, *Reading Miscue Inventory: Procedure for Diagnosis and Evaluation* (New York: Macmillan, 1972).

[12] Bruder and Hayden noticed a similar phenomenon. They assisgned a group of students exercises in writing formal and informal dialogues. One student's informal dialogue contained the following:

> What going on?
> It been a long time . . .
> I about through . . .
> I be glad . . .

When the student read the dialogue aloud, however, these were spoken as
>What's going on?
>It's been a long time . . .
>I'm about through . . .
>I'll be glad . . .

See Mary Newton Bruder and Luddy Hayden, "Teaching Composition: A Report on a Bidialectal Approach," *Language Learning,* 23 (June 1973), 1-15.

13 See Patricia Laurence, "Error's Endless Train: Why Students Don't Perceive Errors," *Journal of Basic Writing,* 1 (Spring, 1975), 23-43, for a different explanation of this phenomenon.

14 See, for example, J. R. Frederiksen, "Component Skills in Reading" in R. R. Snow, P. A. Federico, and W. E. Montague, eds., *Aptitude, Learning, and Instruction* (Hillsdale, N.J.: Erlbaum, 1979); D. E. Rumelhart, "Toward an Interactive Model of Reading," in S. Dornic, ed., *Attention and Performance VI* (Hillsdale, N.J.: Erlbaum, 1977); and Joseph H. Denks and Gregory O. Hill, "Interactive Models of Lexical Assessment during Oral Reading," paper presented at Conference on Interactive Processes in Reading, Learning Research and Development Center, University of Pittsburgh, September 1979.

Patrick Hartwell argued that "apparent dialect interference in writing reveals partial or imperfect mastery of a neural coding system that underlies both reading and writing" in a paper, " 'Dialect Interference' in Writing: A Critical View," presented at CCCC, April 1979. This paper is available through ERIC. He predicts, in this paper, that "basic writing students, when asked to read their writing in a formal situation, . . . will make fewer errors in their reading than in their writing." I read Professor Hartwell's paper after this essay was completed, so I was unable to acknowledge his study as completely as I would have desired.

15 This example is taken from Shaugnessy, *Errors and Expectations,* p. 52.

16 Corder refers to "reconstructed sentences" in "Idiosyncratic Dialects and Error Analysis."

17 Shaughnessy, *Errors and Expectations,* pp. 51-72.

18 For a discussion of the role of the "print code" in writer's errors, see Patrick Hartwell, " 'Dialect Interference' in Writing: A Critical View."

19 See Kenneth S. Goodman, "Miscues: Windows on the Reading Process," in Kenneth S. Goodman, ed., *Miscue Analysis: Applications to Reading Instruction* (Urbana, Illinois: ERIC, 1977), pp. 3-14.

20 This example was taken from Yetta M. Goodman, "Miscue Analysis for In-Service Reading Teachers," in K. S. Goodman, ed., *Miscue Analysis,* p. 55.

21 Nathalie Bailey, Carolyn Madden, and Stephen D. Krashen, "Is There a 'Natural Sequence' in Adult Second Language Learning?" *Language Learning,* 24 (June 1974), 235-243.

22 This paper was originally presented at CCCC, April 1979. The research for this study was funded by a research grant from the National Council of Teachers of English.

Revision Strategies of Student Writers and Experienced Adult Writers

NANCY SOMMERS

Although various aspects of the writing process have been studied extensively of late, research on revision has been notably absent. The reason for this, I suspect, is that current models of the writing process have directed attention away from revision. With few exceptions, these models are linear; they separate the writing process into discrete stages. Two representative models are Gordon Rohman's suggestion that the composing process moves from prewriting to writing to rewriting and James Britton's model of the writing process as a series of stages described in metaphors of linear growth, conception—incubation—production.[1] What is striking about these theories of writing is that they model themselves on speech: Rohman defines the writer in a way that cannot distinguish him from a speaker ("A writer is a man who . . . puts [his] experience into words in his own mind"—p.15); and Britton bases his theory of writing on what he calls (following Jakobson) the "expressiveness" of speech.[2] Moreover, Britton's study itself follows the "linear model" of the relation of thought and language in speech proposed by Vygotsky, a relationship embodied in the linear movement "from the motive which engenders a thought to the shaping of the thought, *first* in inner speech, *then* in meanings of words, and *finally* in words" (quoted in Britton, p. 40). What this movement fails to take into account in its linear structure—"first . . . then . . . finally"—is the recursive shaping of thought by language; what it fails to take into account is *revision*. In these linear conceptions of the writing process revision is understood as a separate stage at the end of the process—a stage that comes after the completion of a first or a second draft and one that is temporally distinct from the prewriting and writing stages of the process.[3]

The linear model bases itself on speech in two specific ways. First of all, it is based on traditional rhetorical models, models that were created to serve the spoken art of oratory. In whatever ways the parts of classical rhetoric are described, they offer "stages" of composition that are repeated in contemporary models of the writing process. Edward Corbett, for instance, describes the "five parts of a discourse"—*inventio, elocutio, memoria, pronuntiatio*—and, disregarding the last two parts since "after rhetoric came to

College Compositon and Communication, 31 (December 1980), pp. 378-388. Copyright © 1980 by The National Council of Teachers of English. Reprinted by permission of the publisher and the author.

be concerned mainly with written discourse, there was no further need to deal with them,"[4] he produces a model very close to Britton's conception [*inventio*], incubation [*dispositio*], production [*elocutio*]. Other rhetorics also follow this procedure, and they do so not simply because of historical accident. Rather, the process represented in the linear model is based on the irreversibility of speech. Speech, Roland Barthes says, "is irreversible":

> "A word cannot be retracted, except precisely by saying that one re-
> tracts it. To cross out here is to add: if I want to erase what I have just
> said, I cannot do it without showing the eraser itself (I must say: '*or
> rather . . .* ' '*I expressed myself badly . . .* '); paradoxically, it is ephem-
> eral speech which is indelible, not monumental writing. All that one can
> do in the case of a spoken utterance is to tack on another utterance."[5]

What is impossible in speech is *revision*: like the example Barthes gives, revision in speech is an afterthought. In the same way, each stage of the linear model must be exclusive (distinct from the other stages) or else it becomes trivial and counterproductive to refer to these junctures as "stages."

By staging revision after enunciation, the linear models reduce revision in writing, as in speech, to no more than an afterthought. In this way such models make the study of revision impossible. Revision, in Rohman's model, is simply the repetition of writing; or to pursue Britton's organic metaphor, revision is simply the further growth of what is already there, the "precon-ceived" product. The absence of research on revision, then, is a function of a theory of writing which does not distinguish between writing and speech.

What the linear models do produce is a paraody of writing. Isolating revision and then disregarding it plays havoc with the experiences composi-tion teachers have of the actual writing and rewriting of experienced writers. Why should the linear model be preferred? Why should revision be forgot-ten, superfluous? Why do teachers offer the linear model and students accept it? One reason, Barthes suggests, is that "there is a fundamental tie between teaching and speech," while "writing begins at the point where speech be-comes *impossible*."[6] The spoken word cannot be revised. The possibility of revision distinguishes the written text from speech. In fact according to Barthes, this is the essential difference between writing and speaking. When we must revise, when the very idea is subject to recursive shaping by lan-guage, then speech becomes inadequate. This is a matter to which I will re-turn, but first we should examine, theoretically, a detailed exploration of what student writers as distinguished from experienced adult writers *do* when they write and rewrite their work. Dissatisfied with both the linear model of writing and the lack of attention to the process of revision, I con-ducted a series of studies over the past three years which examined the revi-sion processes of student writers and experienced writers to see what role revision played in their writing processes. In the course of my work the revi-sion process was redefined as *a sequence of changes in a composition— changes which are initiated by cues and occur continually throughout the writing of a work.*

Methodology

I used a case study approach. The student writers were twenty freshmen at Boston University and the University of Oklahoma with SAT verbal scores ranging from 450-600 in their first semester of composition. The twenty experienced adult writers from Boston and Oklahoma City included journalists, editors, and academics. To refer to the two groups, I use the terms *student writers* and *experienced writers* because the principal difference between these two groups is the amount of experience they have had in writing.

Each writer wrote three essays, expressive, explanatory, and persuasive, and rewrote each essay twice, producing nine written products in draft and final form. Each writer was interviewed three times after the final revision of each essay. And each writer suggested revisions for a composition written by an anonymous author. Thus extensive written and spoken documents were obtained from each writer.

The essays were analyzed by counting and categorizing the changes made. Four revision operations were identified: deletion, substitution, addition, and reordering. And four levels of changes were identified: word, phrase, sentence, theme (the extended statement of one idea). A coding system was developed for identifying the frequency of revision by level and operation. In addition, transcripts of the interviews in which the writers interpreted their revisions were used to develop what was called a *scale of concerns* for each writer. This scale enabled me to codify what were the writer's primary concerns, secondary concerns, tertiary concerns, and whether the writers used the same scale of concerns when revising the second or third drafts as they used in revising the first draft.

Revision Strategies of Student Writers

Most of the students I studied did not use the terms *revision* or *rewriting*. In fact, they did not seem comfortable using the word *revision* and explained that revision was not a word they used, but the word their teachers used. Instead, most of the students had developed various functional terms to describe the type of changes they made. The following are samples of these definitions:

Scratch Out and Do Over Again: "I say scratch out and do over, and that means what it says. Scratching out and cutting out. I read what I have written and I cross out a word and put another word in; a more decent word or a better word. Then if there is somewhere to use a sentence that I have crossed out, I will put it there."

Reviewing: "Reviewing means just using better words and eliminating words that are not needed. I go over and change words around."

Reviewing: "I just review every word and make sure that everything is worded right. I see if I am rambling; I see if I can put a better word in or leave one out. Usually when I read what I have written, I say to myself, 'that word is so bland or so trite,' and then I go and get my thesaurus."

Redoing: "Redoing means cleaning up the paper and crossing out. It is looking at something and saying, no that has to go, or no, that is not right."

Marking Out: "I don't use the word rewriting because I only write one draft and the changes that I make are made on top of the draft. The changes that I make are usually just marking out words and putting different ones in."

Slashing and Throwing Out: "I throw things out and say they are not good. I like to write like Fitzgerald did by inspiration, and if I feel inspired then I don't need to slash and throw much out."

The predominant concern in these definitions is vocabulary. The students understand the revision process as a rewording activity. They do so because they perceive words as the unit of written discourse. That is, they concentrate on particular words apart from their role in the text. Thus one student quoted above thinks in terms of dictionaries, and, following the eighteenth century theory of words parodied in *Gulliver's Travels*, he imagines a load of things carried about to be exchanged. Lexical changes are the major revision activities of the students because economy is their goal. They are governed, like the linear model itself, by the Law of Occam's razor that prohibits logically needless repetition: redundancy and superfluity. Nothing governs speech more than such superfluities; speech constantly repeats itself precisely because spoken words, as Barthes writes, are expendable in the cause of communication. The aim of revision according to the students' own description is therefore to clean up the speech; the redundancy of speech is unnecessary in writing, their logic suggests, because writing, unlike speech, can be reread. Thus one student said, "Redoing means cleaning up the paper and crossing out." The remarkable contradiction of cleaning by marking might, indeed, stand for student revision as I have encountered it.

The students place a symbolic importance on their selection and rejection of words as the determiners of success or failure for their compositions. When revising, they primarily ask themselves: can I find a better word or phrase? A more impressive, not so cliched, or less hum-drum word? Am I repeating the same word or phrase too often? They approach the revision process with what could be labeled as a "thesaurus philosophy of writing"; the students consider the thesaurus a harvest of lexical substitutions and believe that most problems in their essays can be solved by rewording. What is revealed in the students' use of the thesaurus is a governing attitude toward their writing: that the meaning to be communicated is already there, already finished, already produced, ready to be communicated, and all that is necessary is a better word "rightly worded." One student defined revision as "redoing"; "redoing" meant "just using better words and eliminating words that are not needed." For the students, writing is translating: the thought to the page, the language of speech to the more formal language of prose, the word to its synonym. Whatever is translated, an original text already exists for students, one which need not be discovered or acted upon, but simply communicated.[7]

The students list repetitions as one of the elements they most worry about. This cue signals to them that they need to eliminate the repetition either by substituting or deleting words or phrases. Repetition occurs, in large part, because student writing imitates—transcribes—speech: attention to repetitious words is a manner of cleaning speech. Without a sense of the developmental possibilities of revision (and writing in general) students seek, on the authority of many textbooks, simply to clean up their language and prepare to type. What is curious, however, is that students are aware of lexical repetition, but not conceptual repetition. They only notice the repetition if they can "hear" it; they do not diagnose lexical repetition as symptomatic of problems on a deeper level. By rewording their sentences to avoid the lexical repetition, the students solve the immediate problem, but blind themselves to problems on a textual level; although they are using different words, they are sometimes merely restating the same idea with different words. Such blindness, as I discovered with student writers, is the inability to "see" revision as a process: the inability to "re-view" their work again, as it were, with different eyes, and to start over.

The revision strategies described above are consistent with the students' understanding of the revision process as requiring lexical changes but not semantic changes. For the students, the extent to which they revise is a function of their level of inspiration. In fact, they use the word *inspiration* to describe the ease or difficulty with which their essay is written, and the extent to which the essay needs to be revised. If students feel inspired, if the writing comes easily, and if they don't get stuck on individual words or phrases, then they say that they cannot see any reason to revise. Because students do not see revision as an activity in which they modify and develop perspectives and ideas, they feel that if they know what they want to say, then there is little reason for making revisions.

The only modification of ideas in the students' essays occurred when they tried out two or three introductory paragraphs. This results, in part, because the students have been taught in another version of the linear model of composing to use a thesis statement as a controlling device in their introductory paragraphs. Since they write their introductions and their thesis statements even before they have really discovered what they want to say, their early close attention to the thesis statement, and more generally the linear model, function to restrict and circumscribe not only the development of their ideas, but also their ability to change the direction of these ideas.

Too often as composition teachers we conclude that students do not willingly revise. The evidence from my research suggests that it is not that students are unwilling to revise, but rather that they do what they have been taught to do in a consistently narrow and predictable way. On every occasion when I asked students why they hadn't made any more changes, they essentially replied, "I knew something larger was wrong, but I didn't think it would help to move words around." The students have strategies for handling word and phrases and their strategies helped them on a word or sentence level. What they lack, however, is a set of strategies to help them identify the "something larger" that they sensed was wrong and work from there. The students do not have strategies for handling the whole essay. They lack procedures or heuristics to help them reorder lines of reasoning or ask questions about their purposes and readers. The students view their compositions in a linear way as a series of parts. Even such potentially useful concepts as "unity" or "form" are reduced to the rule that a composition, if it is to have form, must have an introduction, a body, and a conclusion, or the sum total of the necessary parts.

The students decide to stop revising when they decide that they have not violated any of the rules for revising. These rules, such as "Never begin a sentence with a conjunction" or "Never end a sentence with a preposition," are lexically cued and rigidly applied. In general, students will subordinate the demands of the specific problems of their text to the demands of the rules. Changes are made in compliance with abstract rules about the product, rules that quite often do not apply to the specific problems in the text. These revision strategies are teacher-based, directed towards a teacher-reader who expects compliance with rules—with pre-existing "conceptions"—and who will examine parts of the composition (writing comments about those parts in the margins of their essays) and will cite any violations of rules in those parts. At best the students see their writing altogether passively through the eyes of former teachers or their surrogates, the textbooks, and are bound to the rules which they have been taught.

Revision Strategies of Experienced Writers

One aim of my research has been to contrast how student writers define revision with how a group of experienced writers define their revision processes. Here is a sampling of the definitions from the experienced writers:

Rewriting: "It is a matter of looking at the kernel of what I have written, the content, and then thinking about it, responding to it, making decisions, and actually restructuring it."

Rewriting: "I rewrite as I write. It is hard to tell what is a first draft because it is not determined by time. In one draft, I might cross out three pages, write two, cross out a fourth, rewrite it, and call it a draft. I am constantly writing and rewriting. I can only conceptualize so much in my first draft—only so much information can be held in my head at one time; my rewriting efforts are a reflection of how much information I can encompass at one time. There are levels and agenda which I have to attend to in each draft."

Rewriting: "Rewriting means on one level, finding the argument, and on another level, language changes to make the argument more effective. Most of the time I feel as if I can go on rewriting forever. There is always one part of a piece that I could keep working on. It is always difficult to know at what point to abandon a piece of writing. I like this idea that a piece of writing is never finished, just abandoned."

Rewriting: "My first draft is usually very scattered. In rewriting, I find the line of argument. After the argument is resolved, I am much more interested in word choice and phrasing."

Revising: "My cardinal rule in revising is never to fall in love with what I have written in a first or second draft. An idea, sentence, or even a phrase that looks catchy, I don't trust. Part of this idea is to wait a while. I am much more in love with something after I have written it than I am a day or two later. It is much easier to change anything with time."

Revising: "It means taking apart what I have written and putting it back together again. I ask major theoretical questions of my ideas, respond to those questions, and think of proportion and structure, and try to find a controlling metaphor. I find out which ideas can be developed and which should be dropped. I am constantly chiseling and changing as I revise."

The experienced writers describe their primary objective when revising as finding the form or shape of their argument. Although the metaphors vary, the experienced writers often use structural expressions such as "finding a framework," "a pattern," or "a design" for their argument. When questioned about this emphasis, the experienced writers responded that since their first drafts are usually scattered attempts to define their territory, their objective in the second draft is to begin observing general patterns of development and deciding what should be included and what excluded. One writer explained, "I have learned from experience that I need to keep writing a first draft until I figure out what I want to say. Then in a second draft, I begin to see the structure of an argument and how all the various sub-arguments which are buried beneath the surface of all those sentences are related." What is described here is a process in which the writer is both agent and vehicle. "Writing," says Barthes, unlike speech, "develops like a seed, not a line,"[8] and like a seed it confuses beginning and end, conception and production. Thus, the experienced writers say their drafts are "not determined by time," that rewriting is a "constant process," that they feel as if (they) "can go on forever." Revising confuses the beginning and end, the agent and vehicle; it confuses, *in order to find*, the line of argument.

After a concern for form, the experienced writers have a second objective: a concern for their readership. In this way, "production" precedes "conception." The experienced writers imagine a reader (reading their product) whose existence and whose expectations influence their revision process. They have abstracted the standards of a reader and this reader seems to be partially a reflection of themselves and functions as a critical and productive collaborator—a collaborator who has yet to love their work. The anticipation of a reader's judgment causes a feeling of dissonance when the writer recognizes incongruities between intention and execution, and requires these writers to make revisions on all levels. Such a reader gives them just what the students lacked: new eyes to "re-view" their work. The experienced writers believe that they have learned the causes and conditions, the product, which will influence their reader, and their revision strategies are geared towards creating these causes and conditions. They demonstrate a complex understanding of which examples, sentences, or phrases should be included or excluded. For example, one experienced writer decided to delete public examples and add private examples when writing about the energy crisis because "private examples would be controversial and thus more persuasive." Another writer revised his transitional sentences because "some kinds of transitions are more easily recognized as transitions than others." These examples represent the type of strategic attempts these experienced writers use to manipulate the conventions of discourse in order to communicate to their reader.

But these revision strategies are a process of more than communication; they are part of the process of *discovering meaning* altogether. Here we can see the importance of dissonance; at the heart of revision is the process by which writers recognize and resolve the dissonance they sense in their writing. Ferdinand de Saussure has argued that meaning is differential or "diacritical," based on differences between terms rather than "essential" or inherent qualities of terms. "Phonemes," he said, "are characterized not, as one might think, by their own positive quality but simply by the fact that they are distinct."[9] In fact, Saussure bases his entire *Course in General Linguistics* on these differences, and such differences are dissonant; like musical dissonances which gain their significance from their relationship to the "key" of the composition which itself is determined by the whole language, specific language (parole) gains its meaning from the system of language (langue) of which it is a manifestation and part. The musical composition— a "composition" of parts—creates its "key" as in an over-all structure which determines the value (meaning) of its parts. The analogy with music is readily seen in the compositions of experienced writers: both sorts of composition are based precisely on those structures experienced writers seek in their writing. It is this complicated relationship between the parts and the whole in the work of experienced writers which destroys the linear model; writing cannot develop "like a line" because each addition or deletion is a reordering of the whole. Explicating Saussure, Jonathan Culler asserts that "meaning depends on difference of meaning."[10] But student writers constantly struggle to bring their essays into congruence with a predefined meaning. The experienced writers do the opposite: they seek to discover (to create) meaning in the engagement with their writing, in revision. They seek to emphasize and exploit the lack of clarity, the differences of meaning, the dissonance, that writing as opposed to speech allows in the possibility of revision. Writing has spatial and temporal features not apparent in speech—words are recorded in space and fixed in time—which is why writing is susceptible to reordering and later addition. Such features make possible the dissonance that both provokes revision and promises, from itself, new meaning.

For the experienced writers the heaviest concentration of changes is on the sentence level, and the changes are predominantly by addition and deletion. But, unlike the students, experienced writers make changes on all levels and use all revision operations. Moreover, the operations the students fail to use—reordering and addition—seem to require a theory of the revision process as a totality—a theory which, in fact, encompasses the *whole* of the composition. Unlike the students, the experienced writers possess a non-linear theory in which a sense of the whole writing both precedes and grows out of an examination of the parts. As we saw, one writer said he needed "a first draft to figure out what to say," and "a second draft to see the structure of an argument buried beneath the surface." Such a "theory" is both theoretical and strategical; once again, strategy and theory are conflated in ways that are literally impossible for the linear model. Writing appears to be more like a seed than a line.

Two elements of the experienced writers' theory of the revision process are the adoption of a holistic perspective and the perception that revision is a recursive process. The writers ask: what does my essay as a *whole* need for form, balance, rhythm, or communication? Details are added, dropped, substituted, or reordered according to their sense of what the essay needs for emphasis and proportion. This sense, however, is constantly in flux as ideas are developed and modified; it is constantly "re-viewed" in relation to the parts. As their ideas change, revision becomes an attempt to make their writing consonant with that changing vision.

The experienced writers see their revision process as a recursive process—a process with significant recurring activities—with different levels of attention and different agenda for each cycle. During the first revision cycle their attention is primarily directed towards narrowing the topic and delimiting their ideas. At this point, they are not as concerned as they are later about vocabulary and style. The experienced writers explained that they get closer to their meaning by not limiting themselves too early to lexical concerns. As one writer commented to explain her revision process, a comment inspired by the summer 1977 New York power failure: "I feel like Con Edison cutting off certain states to keep the generators going. In first and second drafts, I try to cut off as much as I can of my editing generators, and in a third draft, I try to cut off some of my idea generators, so I can make sure that I will actually finish the essay." Although the experienced writers describe their revision process as a series of different levels or cycles, it is inaccurate to assume that they have only one objective for each cycle and that each cycle can be defined by a different objective. The same objectives and sub-processes are present in each cycle, but in different proportions. Even though these experienced writers place the predominant weight upon finding the form of their argument during the first cycle, other concerns exist as well. Conversely, during the later cycles, when the experienced writers' primary attention is focused upon stylistic concerns, they are still attuned, although in a reduced way, to the form of the argument. Since writers are limited in what they can attend to during each cycle (understandings are temporal), revision strategies help balance competing demands on attention. Thus, writers can concentrate on more than one objective at a time by developing strategies to sort out and organize their different concerns in successive cycles of revision.

It is a sense of writing as discovery—a repeated process of beginning over again, starting out new—that the students failed to have. I have used the notion of dissonance because such dissonance, the incongruities between intention and execution, governs both writing and meaning. Students do not see the incongruities. They need to rely on their own internalized sense of good writing and to see their writing with their "own" eyes. Seeing in revision—seeing beyond hearing—is at the root of the word *revision* and the process itself; current dicta on revising blind our students to what is actually involved in revision. In fact, they blind them to what constitutes good writing altogether. Good writing disturbs: it creates dissonance. Students need to seek the dissonance of discovery, utilizing in their writing, as the experienced writers do, the very difference between writing and speech—the possibility of revision.

Notes

[1] D. Gordon Rohman and Albert O. Wlecke, "Pre-writing: The Construction and Application of Models for Concept Formation in Writing," Cooperative Research Project No. 2174, U.S. Office of Education, Department of Health Education, and Welfare; James Britton, Anthony Burgess, Nancy Martin, Alex McLeod, Harold Rosen, *The Development of Writing Abilities (11-18)* (London: Macmillan Education, 1975).

[2] Britton is following Roman Jakobson, "Linguistics and Poetics," in T. A. Sebeok, *Style in Language* (Cambridge, MA: MIT Press, 1960).

[3] For an extended discussion of this issue see Nancy Sommers, "The Need for Theory in Composition Research," *College Composition and Communication*, 30 (February 1979), 44-49.

[4] *Classical Rhetoric for the Modern Student* (New York: Oxford University Press, 1965), p. 27.

[5] Roland Barthes, "Writers, Intellectuals, Teachers," in *Image-Music-Text*, trans. Stephen Heath (New York: Hill and Wang, 1977), pp. 190-191.

[6] "Writers, Intellectuals, Teachers," p. 190.

[7] Nancy Sommers and Ronald Schleifer, "Means and Ends: Some Assumptions of Student Writers," *Composition and Teaching*, II (in press).

[8] *Writing Degree Zero* in *Writing Degree Zero and Elements of Semiology*, trans. Annette Lavers and Colin Smith (New York: Hill and Wang, 1968), p. 20.

[9] *Course in General Linguistics*, trans. Wade Baskin (New York, 1966), p. 119.

[10] Jonathan Culler, *Saussure* (Penguin Modern Masters Series; London: Penguin Books, 1976), p. 70.

Acknowledgment: The author wishes to express her gratitude to Professor William Smith, University of Pittsburgh, for his vital assistance with the research reported in this article and to Patrick Hays, her husband, for extensive discussion and critical editorial help.

Showing, Not Telling,
at a Writing Workshop

TOBY FULWILER

How does a teacher of writing encourage colleagues in other disciplines to pay more attention to student writing? And, once encouraged, what specifically can teachers of history, biology, or business do in their classrooms to foster student writing? One approach, of course, is to tell them what they ought to be doing: "Look! You should require those history students to keep journals." You can mail out broadsides, write editorials, and deliver seminars on the virtues of "writing across the curriculum." If your colleagues have strong self-concepts and are not scared off by your enthusiasm, some will actually try what your suggest. But *telling* teachers how to use writing in their classes is very close to telling them that you know a better way to teach their subjects. Very touchy business.

A more politic way, it seems to me, is to *show* other teachers some writing techniques and exercises that work but allow them to pick and choose among them, making up their own minds about what is useful and what not. Showing, not telling, is a principle often taught in freshman English classes; readers can make up their own minds about the narrative's importance. So too is this idea effective at writing across the curriculum workshops. Most teachers in disciplines other than English understand well that writing, like reading and mathematics, cannot be the sole province of teachers in any one discipline. As Dan Fader and James Britton have argued before me, writing is an interdisciplinary learning activity with a place in every classroom. But not all teachers know how to integrate writing instruction easily into their pedagogy, nor are they comfortable "teaching" it outright. Each teacher is already a professional, practicing writer in his or her own field, yet few have ever been trained to teach writing to others.

There is a wealth of knowledge about writing in the pool of teachers who do not teach writing or who think they do not know how to teach writing. Who knows better than the geographer whether or not first person narration is acceptable in professional geography publications? Who knows better than the physics teacher whether or not to use passive construction in laboratory reports? Furthermore, most teachers have a fairly solid grasp, themselves, of the "elements of style" according to Strunk and White or Turabian; it matters little they cannot label a particular modifier as "free" or "dangling"; it does matter that they can identify writing appropriate to good work in their field.

College English, 43 (January 1981), pp. 55-63. Copyright © 1981 by the National Council of Teachers of English. Reprinted by permission of the publisher and the author.

If you want to encourage all teachers to teach more writing in their classes, then start with the knowledge of writing which they already possess and build from there. The best way that I have found to do this is through an off-campus, overnight, retreat-like writing workshop. A place where teachers are on neutral ground, removed from mailboxes, telephones, students, classes, secretaries, and families. In this setting writing can be explored slowly, thoroughly, and experientially among colleagues who are interested because they are mutually concerned with the quality of student writing.

During the last several years I have helped plan, set up, and staff half a dozen writing workshops for teachers at Michigan Tech, where I teach writing; I have also worked with high school and college instructors from schools other than my own. The principles of good writing workshops are remarkably consistent whether the participants are high school English teachers or university engineering professors. Showing works better than telling; induction better than deduction. By introducing workshop particpants to the complex nature of "the composing process," experientially rather than through lecture, I have been able to draw consistently on knowledge and ideas already present among the participants. I avoid, wherever possible, appearing to be the resident expert among a crew of novices, for these teachers are, in fact, my peers in every important sense. The writing workshops work because all lessons are learned through personal experience or an appeal to common sense.

In the rest of this article I will describe five workshops designed to introduce content-area teachers to the theory and practice of writing across the curriculum. These workshops, with minor variations, have worked with teachers from almost every grade level and academic discipline.

Workshop I, Exploring

Many teachers who attend writing workshops believe, initially at least, that they will learn how to banish forever bad spelling and comma splices from student papers. These teachers are usually disappointed because I teach them no such tricks. Instead, during the first five minutes, I ask people to write about the student writing problems they perceive as most common, serious, or troublesome. According to the teachers, who take turns reading their entries, students have these problems:

1. outlining and organizing
2. spelling correctly
3. being interested in a topic
4. finding information about a topic
5. specifying rather than generalizing
6. writing good sentences
7. practicing good study habits
8. thinking maturely
9. punctuating correctly
10. reading critically
11. using a library

12. developing a college-level vocabulary
13. understanding a writing assignment
14. supporting an argument
15. writing a thesis statement

The list may go on even longer, sometimes extending to twenty-five or thirty items. I ask people to take a few more minutes and see if they can simplify and condense the list into fewer, more general categories. The next list of writing problem categories looks something like this:

1. motivation
2. mechanics
3. style
4. reading
5. critical thinking
6. cognitive maturity
7. assignments

Teachers suggest, in turn, strategies they have found successful in dealing with these problems. One teacher defers grading until a lab report is properly complete, a second teaches outlining, while a third hands out written copies of all assignments to eliminate confusion. A genuine dialogue now begins, with participants addressing writing problems with concrete, practical suggestions—the result of years of classroom experience. The teachers are sharing ideas, contributing to the general pool of knowledge, and talking to each other about an issue of mutual concern.

This first session is "exploratory"; during the first hour of an extended workshop it is not too important what particular solutions are offered. Some suggestions might be less useful than others—such as giving automatic "Fs" to papers with five mechanical errors. The primary purpose of this workshop is to get the participants talking to each other, sharing ideas, and recognizing that writing is a rather complicated activity. No participant who helped shape the preceding list can comfortably hold on to the notion that "spelling or grammar drills" will cure all or most writing problems. The "solution" to a "motivation" problem is far different from (though perhaps related to) an "editing skills" problem. Student "skill" problems (outlining, punctuation) require of the teacher a response different from student "developmental" problems (cognitive maturity, reading background); teacher-centered problems (poor assignments, vague feedback) differ from institutional problems (credit hours, course loads, grades). The whole concept of "writing problems" opens up and teachers begin to understand both the complexity and diversity of the composing process. At the conclusion of this sixty-minute session, the teachers write a short summary of the ideas which have emerged during this workshop, ideas which, in most cases, are broader and more complex than they were an hour earlier.

Workshop II, Journal Writing

Participants at writing workshops keep journals for the duration of the workshop. At the very first session participants are asked to write out their reasons for attending the workshop; later on they are given a variety of writing assignments, such as the listing and summary activities described in Workshop I. The journal is the place for participants to record their thoughts, feelings, impressions, insights, and ideas as they travel through the workshop. By the end of the first day, everyone has written eight or nine assigned journal entries.

Journals prove to be active catalysts for stimulating both personal insights and small-group discussions at a writing worshop just as they are in individual classrooms. In addition to the initial journal writing I ask the teachers to do the following tasks:

1. Summarize a particular session by writing about it, to give verbal shape to the session as well as provide a written record for later perusal.
2. Interrupt a discussion with a five-minute journal write to refocus your thoughts and gain perspective about the topic.
3. Clarify difficult concepts in your own words; for example, "What, exactly, does James Britton mean by the term expressive writing?"
4. "Free write" about a topic in order to use this entry, later, as the basis for a short paper.
5. Brainstorm for ten minutes to see how many assignments you can think of for using "peer critics" or "journals" in your classrooms.
6. Reflect personally and privately on the course of the workshop and record your thoughts about being here.

At some point, usually at the end of the first day, we talk about the importance of this personal writing in a formal academic environment. Participants usually are quick to point out a number of possible uses for the journal, especially to reinforce the learning of subject matter and to aid small-group discussions. In particular, however, the teachers want to know: 1) how to give directions for using journals, 2) how often and when to read the journals, and 3) how to evaluate and "count" them as part of the course requirements. Once the discussion reaches this point, the workshop has already turned a corner; the workshop leader can then provide a handout on journal use, discuss his or her personal means of handling the journal in class, or generate guidelines on the spot by drawing on the participants' own experience with journals that day.

The journal-writing activity at the workshop really serves more than one purpose. The journal is a concrete, practical writing assignment for teachers to take back to their history or biology classes. It is a means of introducing the workshop participants to the importance of writing to oneself in order to invent, clarify, interpret, or reflect. Journal writing usually helps relax group members by giving them time, periodically, to get their bearings and examine their thoughts as they participate in workshop exercises. Finally, journal-writing time is an invaluable aid to the workshop leader to help monitor the course of the workshop—by using those five-minute writing "time-outs" the leader is able to continually and quietly evaluate the mood,

progress, and the problems of the group and make cuts, additions, and revisions where necessary. The journal, then, is the workhorse writing assignment throughout the whole workshop experience; after the workshop is
over, each participant's journal provides a lasting written record of insights
and ideas gained during the experience.

Workshop III, Theory

In *The Development of Writing Abilities, 11-18* (London: The Schools
Council, 1975), James Britton develops the idea that "expressive writing" is
the matrix from which other writing modes evolve. Expressive writing is
close to speech or thought; it is informal, personal, speculative, discovery
writing which one does for oneself, to try out new ideas and see what's on
one's mind. First drafts, diaries, and journals are places where such writing
can be found. Britton's other two function categories of writing are already
familiar to academic audiences: "transactional" writing (communicating
messages to audiences) and "poetic" writing (creative writing, language as an
art). Prior to this workshop, most participants will not have considered expressive writing important.

Britton argues, as the workshlop leader can explain in a brief lecture,
that expressive writing is very close to the thinking process itself—thinking
on paper. Students who learn to use it gain a powerful, dependable "learning
tool" with which to speculate, discover, argue, brainstorm, and invent—by
themselves, independent of teachers or classmates. Expressive writing is also
one of the easiest, quickest means of overcoming writer's block and "the ter-
ror of the blank page." Once teachers are aware of its potential, they can use
expressive writing as a means to stimulate student thought and reduce
anxiety at the same time.

Understanding expressive writing is important for the success of the
writing-across-the-curriculum program as Britton conceives it. This writer-
based prose, as Linda Flower calls it, can be used in any discipline where
thinking is important—whether or not the teacher makes other, more formal
writing assignments. Expressive writing should not be critically judged by the
teachers in any discipline where large classes are common or where paper
work is excessive.

This theoretical discussion about the value of expressive writing works
well at the end of a day in which teachers have been actively writing in their
journals. In other words, the participants have been practicing expressive
writing all day—and most recognize that they have used it often in the past
when rough-writing professional articles or grant proposals at home. Examined by the light of personal experience, this mode of writing—at once familiar
and foreign—sells itself.

Once sold, the nature of the rest of the workshop changes dramatically.
The question ceases to be, "So what can you tell us that we do not already
know?" and becomes, "What are some concrete ways that I can incorporate
expressive writing as a learning activity in my classroom?" The workshop
activities which follow this theoretical session all build on Britton's notion of

expressive writing and its root relationship to more transactional modes.

Workshop IV, Responding to Writing

In this workshop participants are asked to read and respond to a piece of student writing. First (ten minutes) teachers evaluate the writing on their own and jot down initial observations about the paper: 1) where it is strong, 2) where weak, and 3) what specific suggestions might help the student writer to improve the paper. Second (twenty minutes), teachers are asked to form groups of three, share their personal commentaries, and agree on a consensus response which would help the student most in rewriting. Third (thirty minutes), teachers come together as a whole group and share, once again, the consensus responses to those papers. During this third activity the director can stand at the chalkboard and outline briefly each group's response, which might include suggestions about thesis statements, outlines, mechanical errors, grades, oral versus written responses, praise versus criticism. and various suggestions for revision.

Finally (fifteen minutes), teachers compare, visually, the responses of the various groups and note similarities and differences. It is important, at this point, for the workshop director to be as non-directive as possible; there really isn't a "right" answer, after all, but rather more or less helpful suggestions. In my experience, any time a group of these teachers talk about a piece of writing, with the purpose of helping a student do better next time, their eventual response is reasonable and helpful. Most teachers understand well the value of such basic helping strategies as positive reinforcement, rewriting, and individual conferencing, even though many of us do not always take the time to practice what we understand. The final consensus list often looks something like this one, which comes from a workshop for biology teachers:

1. Point out strengths, as well as weaknesses, in each paper handed back.
2. Focus on one or two problems at a time rather than insisting that students learn and correct everything in one draft.
3. Be specific when commenting about what is wrong on a paper; what, exactly, can a student do to make it better?
4. Ask for revision prior to grading if you want the student to keep on learning.
5. Be aware when you make a writing assignment whether you want to a) find out what the student already knows or b) enhance his or her learning experience.
6. Hold conferences with students who have the most difficulty writing your assignments.

The value of this particular workshop, however, goes beyond generating a list of helpful hints for responding to student writing; equally important is the self-confidence teachers gain from sharing perceptions and opinions among colleagues. Teachers in content-areas often feel insecure about responding to and evaluating writing; many remember being penalized by error-conscious English teachers and some retain the view that writing, along with responding to writing, is an arcane craft, the precise practice of which belongs exclusively to teachers of English. This exercise puts that notion nicely to rest. Teachers see common-sense practices used by colleagues and approved by writing teachers and so are more likely to trust their own judgments next time.

A variation of this workshop, used later in a several-day workshop, asks participants to respond from "peer critique sheets," which are simply written-out guidelines for students to critique from. Sometimes these critique sheets are used in stages. Critique I asks questions such as: 1) What is the thesis of the paper? 2) Who is the audience for the paper? 3) Where is the strongest writing? 4) Where is the weakest writing? Critique II, used a draft later, asks more particular questions: 1) Is each point well supported by evidence, fact, or example? 2) Does the paper avoid chichés, generalizations, and stereotypes? 3) Are any phrases awkward, vague, or unclear? 4) Are any words repetitious or unnecessary? 5) Can you find errors in spelling, punctuation, or grammar? Colleagues from scientific and technical fields have modified these sheets to reflect their particular needs, adding, for example, questions about mathematical computation or diagram accuracy. Guidelines such as these can help both teacher and novice writer focus more pointedly on different stages in the writing process.

One final note. I think it is important to solicit and use for workshop exercises papers written in subjects other than English. This can be done easily by asking participants, when they sign up to attend the workshop, to send samples of what they consider to be "good" and "bad" writing. The workshop leader can then choose some representative short writings from science and social sicence areas with which most of the faculty audience can identify; I usually include two different papers and allow groups to choose either one. An obvious extension of this workshop, when time permits, is to do a similar exercise with discipline-specific materials, where social science teachers form one cluster, science teachers another, humanities teachers a third and, perhaps, engineers a fourth. In this way specific types of writing, such as "lab reports" or "term papers," especially appropriate to each area, can be studied in detail.

Workshop V, Composing

Perhaps the most important sessions at a faculty workshop require the teachers themselves to write something. Whether the workshop is one day or five weeks, teachers must generate a piece of writing based on personal experience and share that writing with other participants. They must also listen to critical commentary about their efforts.

An easy way to start participants writing is to follow Peter Elbow's suggestion in *Writing Without Teachers* (New York: Oxford University Press, 1973) and ask everybody to do a ten-minute "freewrite." I ask people to "focus" the freewrite and concentrate on "one experience you had with writing—either good or bad," or "a learning experience your remember well."

Faculty members find these topics easy to write about, coming as they do from school environments; the assignment results in fast, furious narrative writing by all, including me. (For the sake of credibility, workshop directors must do all the assignments along with participants.)

Next, participants spend twenty minutes reshaping and revising this piece of personal writing to make it suitable to share with an audience. I tell them to cut out the fat and dead ends, to amplify, explain, and add detail, to edit the parts which might embarrass. Writers then form response groups of three and share in turn their writing according to these guidelines:*

A. First Reader: Read your paper out loud twice to the two persons in your group.
B. Audience: Listen to the reader carefully. After the second reading, respond orally only in these two ways:
   1. What struck you as interesting?
   2. Where did you want more information?

Immediately this exercise creates a hive of activity in the room. Anxiety levels among participants first soar, then drop, as people become more comfortable with their response group. More than any other workshop exercise, this one places the participant back in the role of the student who is asked to write on demand and then submit that writing for some form of evaluation. In this case, however, the responses are deliberately uncritical: the listener practices giving help without saying what was "good" and "bad," what he or she liked or didn't like. The point, of course, is to set up the anxiety-producing situation (reading your writing out loud) and then defuse it by creating a non-threatening environment (small, nonjudgmental response groups).

Participants regroup and do a short journal write about what they felt at various stages of the exercise. Finally, people share their observations and talk about the possible "lessons" for teachers who make writing assignments to students: 1) the value of writing for idea generation (freewriting); 2) the importance of shaping toward an audience (revision of freewrite); 3) the benefits of the non-judgmental peer response; 4) the difficulty (and excitement) of creating under pressure; and also 5) the stimulation which results from having one's writing well-received.

In workshops of more than a day's duration participants revise their writing overnight, in the privacy of their quarters, and write it on ditto masters for duplication the following day. It is then possible to form larger writing groups, five or six each, and read and respond to a visible piece of writing, which creates a different kind of anxiety, but more precise suggestions for revision. I encourage these groups to meet for about two hours and to set up their own response guidelines. For a four- or five-day workshop this same group can meet several times and discuss the progressive revisions of each paper; for longer workshops, such as the five-week Bay Area Writing Projects, these groups can meet regularly each week and talk about several

*I learned this exercise from Lee Odell of the State University of New York, Albany.

pieces of writing. When the group mix is good, the sharing of writing becomes an important ritual.

In any case, this personal writing activity is often cited by participants as the most memorable workshop experience. One engineering teacher told me that he hadn't "done any personal writing since 1951"—and now he was determined to try more. After sweating through this condensed composing process most teachers admit to having more empathy for student writers. After this exercise few teachers who begin the workshop with hard-line responses still retain that attitude. The process of writing, reading, and responding seems to humanize us all.

At the conclusion of the workshop it is important for participants to return briefly to that list of "writing problems" with which the workshop began. I often ask how many of these have we now addressed through the course of the various workshops—and participants are often surprised to find out that we have, in fact, generated numerous suggestions to handle motivation, organization, stylistic and mechanical problems, and so on. In reviewing their journals, which I ask them to do at the end of the workshop, teachers discover personal insights on how journals, multiple drafts, or peer-editing would work in their particular classes. Some insights are "planted": "Write one way you could use journals in your classroom." Other insights depend strictly on the mind of the writer: "Summarize what you learned in the afternoon sessions." Each teacher takes from the workshop what is useful; for a history teacher it may be "book-review journals"; for a biologist it might be "peer-response groups." One accounting teacher did not think he could use any particular activity in his classes, but said he had learned important things about his own writing process.

How do you influence your colleagues to pay more attention to student writing? Ask them to write, to examine what they do when they write, and to share their insights with each other. After all, that's really what a writing workshop is—a time and a place for sharing among teachers who care.

Teachers as Researchers

DIXIE GOSWAMI

As teachers, we are constantly engaged in informal research: observing, keeping diaries, hypothesizing, using whatever means we can to gather information that may help us make sense of what is going on in our classrooms. In the 1950s, some educators in the United States recognized the potential value of systematic inquiries by classroom teachers and called for "action research," a call unheeded by most of us interested at that time in the teaching and learning of writing.

The notion of teachers as researchers gradually evolved into a "movement" in the United Kingdom, however, with a history, well-defined assumptions, and recognized leaders. John Elliott describes the twelve-year span of this evolution in his Foreword to *A Teachers' Guide to Action Research* (1981).[1] Jon Nixon, who edited *A Teachers' Guide*, is the head of the drama department in a North London school and a classroom researcher himself. The reports he presents are useful models for teachers across the disciplines who are trying to frame questions, clarify and define their own skills, and conduct personal inquiries in their own schools. His book demonstrates clearly that the teacher-as-researcher movement is a radical departure from the traditional view of researchers as outside experts and the teacher as consumer rather than producer of research results.

Over the past few years, a new research tradition seems to have been emerging in this country also, not nearly so well-defined as action research in the United Kingdom, and thus far without landmark books and articles. Increasingly, teachers feel the need to ask research questions for themselves and to verify their intuitions. Instead of being the objects of specialists' observations and evaluations, they want to observe, document, and draw conclusions for themselves—and they want to do so throughout their professional lives. Many teachers of writing feel the need to become less vulnerable to fads and more authoritative in their assessment of current research, curricula, textbooks, and teaching methods.

No single formative influence is responsible for this change in perception. Certainly the change is a response to many factors (including the work being done overseas). One major factor is the remarkable shift over the past decade or so in composition research from tight pre- and post-test experimental studies to context-dependent, non-statistical studies. Another is the

National Writing Project, with its commitment to teacher autonomy and its network for reaching thousands of writing teachers.

As a way of looking at the shape this alternate research tradition is taking and trying to understand some of its implications, I will identify just a few of the individuals in this country who have been clarifying issues about classroom research, guiding and supporting teachers who want to study writing as insiders, and providing rationales for the kind of work that is considered by many academics not to be research at all. I also want to describe briefly one program for secondary school teachers of writing which prepares experienced teachers for action research. Finally, I will review some of the outcomes we may expect from classroom research and present some possibilities for encouraging, training, and supporting teachers who want to study writing in their own schools.

It was Mina Shaughnessy, of course, who gave us in *Errors and Expectations* (1977)[2] the stunning example of herself as teacher-scholar, using her classroom as a laboratory and working with her colleagues and students to explore the logic of error, to search for patterns, and to pose hypotheses. Earlier, in 1976, Shaughnessy had published an explicit call for classroom research: "Diving In: An Introduction to Basic Research."[3] In the 1976 article, she presents striking images to represent the four stages that often occur in the development of writing teachers: GUARDING THE TOWER, CONVERTING THE NATIVES, SOUNDING THE DEPTHS, AND DIVING IN. She says that teachers sound the depths by "turning to careful observations, not only of their own students and their writing but also as writers and teachers, seeking a deeper understanding of the behavior called writing and of the special difficulties their students have in mastering the skill."

Janet Emig took up the theme of developmental stages for teachers of writing in 1980, suggesting that growth begins when teachers work on case studies of themselves as writers and teachers of writing, working carefully and unhurriedly to define their skills and clarify their biases and assumptions:

> To inform themselves about how they at once are like and different from their students, teachers of writing need to take an intensive look at actual students, working through extended and systematic observation; interviews with students, peers, former teachers, and parents—in other words, by the preparation of at least two thorough case studies.[4]

In "Inquiry Paradigms and Writing" (1980),[5] Emig addresses an issue that is centrally important to teachers: how to describe what they do when they study writing in their classrooms: "*Inquiry* rather than *research* is used here because it possesses a more generous and less laden cluster of connotations. The generic term *research* suffers from conceptual synecdoche in that, for many, the part has become mistaken for the whole: the single species of empirical research is treated as the entire genus."

In 1976, Lee Odell's widely read article, "The Classroom Teacher as Researcher"[6] appeared in the *English Journal*. Working from his own experience as a teacher and observer of many teachers as well as from a wide knowledge of experimental methods that he believes to be of practical use to classroom teachers, Odell suggests specific ways teachers can plan and carry out research on composing. In "Teachers of Composition and Needed Research," (1979)[7] Odell outlines two specific ways that single teachers or several colleagues can help shape and test current discourse theory: by asking extensive revisers to explain the reasoning that led them to make changes in successive drafts and by asking their reasons for accepting or rejecting changes. Odell claims that such studies, while not definitive, are useful: "If our studies do not lead us to certainty, they should enable us to fulfill our multiple roles of researchers, theorists, and teachers. Our students and our discipline can only benefit."

In 1979, Ann Berthoff made strong assertions about the nature of educational research in an address to the California Association of Teachers of English. In "The Teacher as REsearcher" she says:

Educational research is nothing to our purpose unless we formulate the questions; if the procedures by which answers are sought are not dialectic and dialogic, that is to say, if the questions and answers are not continually REformulated by those who are working in the classroom, educational research is pointless.[8]

In the Preface to *The Making of Meaning* (1981), where "The Teacher as REsearcher" was later published, Berthoff makes it clear that when teachers begin to consider "language and thought, theory and practice, intending and realizing, writing and thinking, when they think about thinking," they become philosophers and their classrooms become philosophical laboratories. The last thing Berthoff wants is for teachers to become pseudo-scientific researchers: she urges teachers to look and look again at the data they have and at the things they know, "to REflect, REformulate and REconsider." Aside from commenting on large issues, Berthoff offers teachers a useful research tool in the observation notebook she invites them to use in *Forming/Thinking/Writing* (1979).[9]

Many classroom researchers are using Ken Macrorie's book, *Searching Writing* (1980),[10] to help them identify and articulate the problems that are important to them, to ask questions and conduct interviews that inform and explore, and to write clear, honest prose that people can read and use. After studying with Macrorie and using *Searching Writing*, one teacher wrote this:

Ken Macrorie's version of classroom research, the I-Search, invited me to really look for myself. I learned to believe that information I got on my own was good, valuable information and that I did not have to use experts unless I wanted and needed to. The topic I searched is vital to me. The observing and interviewing and writing I did helped me clarify my own biases. Now I value my I-Search for itself and for its potential use in battling the grammar groupies.

In "A New Look at Research on Writing" (1981), Donald Graves discusses the relative usefulness to teachers of experimental studies and "process-observational studies and a broadened context to include the study of child growth." Graves is persuasive and absolutely clear about the role of the teacher in writing research in the Eighties:

> In the past, teachers have been excluded from the process of writing research. If this practice continues, then every recommendation written in this chapter won't make any difference. The base of research involvement must be broadened to include an active role by the public school teacher. When the teacher becomes involved in research, researchers not only gather better data, but the context of research—the public school classroom—is enriched by the study itself. Teachers and researchers ought to know each other better for the sake of research and the children.[11]

Graves, Lucy Calkins, and Susan Sowers, in the course of their work at the Writing Process Laboratory at the University of New Hampshire, have repeatedly demonstrated the richness of real collaboration between teachers and researchers-in-residence. Mary Ellen Giacobbe, an elementary school teacher who participated in Graves' study, later designed and carried out a study of her first grade students' writing practices. Her article, "Who Says That Children Can't Write the First Week of School?" (1980),[12] is one of the first reports of teacher-conducted research. Even now, when a number of reports by teachers are available, Giacobbe's article provides a standard for rigorous thinking and clear, useful reporting.

Jana Staton, a researcher now at the Center for Applied Linguistics in Washington, DC, and Leslee Reed, a sixth grade teacher in Los Angeles, are another teacher-researcher team whose work brilliantly illustrates the possibilities of carefully worked out, long-term collaboration. Staton and Reed studied the writing and thinking that took place in the "dialogue journals" of students who wrote daily on topics of their own choice to Reed, who responded, in writing, every day. The dialogue journals are a customary part of Reed's teaching, not a technique introduced by an outsider for purposes of evaluation. Staton describes the remarkable effects of "self-generated, functional, interactive writing" on the writing and thinking of Reed's sixth grade students in "Literacy: An Interactive Process" (1981).[13] The process by which Staton and Reed's working relationship evolved over the course of their study is especially valuable to teachers who want outside help with research and to researchers who want to work with experienced, successful teachers.

Shirley Brice Heath, an anthropologist and linguist at Stanford University, is helping writing teachers learn to use enthnographic insights and methods to study writing inside and outside of their classrooms. At Bread Loaf School of English (Summer 1981) she showed teachers how to use field journals to record and make sense of their observations of their own classrooms and teaching practices. She noted that in classrooms where teachers are students themselves, trying to learn from their students, different relationships among teachers and students emerge: students become researchers themselves and almost as a matter of course engage in observing, recording, classifying, and talking to each other about their processes and conclusions. In the Prologue to *Ways with Words: Ethnography of Communication in Communities and Classrooms* (in press), Heath describes her audience:

> This book is written for what I call "learning researchers," non-academics and academics alike. At the top of the list of such researchers are those teachers at all levels of the curriculum who constantly search out new ways of learning about themselves and their students."[14]

Marie Clay, who teaches at the University of Auckland, New Zealand, received the 1979 David H. Russell award for "Distinguished Research in the Teaching of English" from NCTE, which cited "her pioneering methods of careful observation of behavior over time in natural school settings." In "Looking and Seeing" (1982) she outlines her methods for observing oral language activities: having children repeat sentences and retell stories. She also comments on classroom studies in general:

> Observant teachers not only discover new behaviors and changes but also think about children's learning in new ways. . . . Teachers who are not good observers could well punish the very behaviors that would make their pupils more accurate. It is helpful to become detached observers of children at work, seeing *how* they go about the tasks we set them. If we keep today's record as baseline data and over several occasions observe children again, we can over a short series of observations record change over time, capturing progress.[15]

The teachers and researchers I have cited in some cases come from different disciplines and/or have conflicting views on the nature of research. They bring their disciplinary assumptions and traditions to their discussions of the strengths and limitations of classroom research. But I think it is fair to say that they agree that learning research is an integral part of good teaching. They agree that teachers must work to discover their own research styles and special skills and that teachers need help, not always in the form of researchers-in-residence, money, or direct instruction, if they are to get on with this enterprise.

Institutions as well as individuals far more numerous than the ones I have mentioned here are beginning to reflect the felt needs of teachers to conduct personal inquiries in their own classrooms. One such place is George Mason University, Fairfax, Virginia. Marian Mohr, co-director of the Writing Research Center at GMU, regularly offers a teacher-researcher seminar. Aside from her own paper, "The Teacher as Researcher" (1980),[16] which describes how classroom practice changes when a teacher keeps a process log/teaching journal, Mohr and Anne Legge, an intern in the program, have prepared a bibliography of resources for teacher-researchers (1982).[17] Don Gallehr, a professor at GMU who directs the Northern Virginia Writing Project and serves on the Advisory Board of the National Writing Project, has found support in the form of released time and other services for a number of teacher-researchers. Reports of their studies are now becoming available.

At Bread Loaf School of English's Program in Writing for secondary school teachers, we began in 1979 to provide teachers who wanted to carry out research in their classrooms with materials and resources. Many of our teachers come from rural areas and small towns from throughout the United States. Having been trained in the humanities, we decided from the outset that we should provide them with some shared experiences as researchers during their first summer's study at Bread Loaf (a six-week session) and that learning research should be both an aim and a process of the Program. We were helped by many of those cited earlier in this paper (and by the work of many others) to determine what those shared experiences should be. What follows is a brief summary of one Bread Loaf teacher-researcher course.

The course has two major requirements: teachers must prepare case studies of themselves as writers and they must prepare informal proposals for studies they plan to carry out at their own schools.

Case studies. Teachers reconstruct their writing histories and describe in some detail their successes and failures as they learned to write. They also collect portfolios of the writing they do over a period of several weeks, working in teams of three. They develop taxonomies, describe audiences, and look at the features of their own and their partners' writing. They try to figure out the effects of certain audiences and purposes and subjects on their own writing and to determine how writing functions for them. They find instances in which they use writing to make meaning, to explore, to speculate, to imagine, to remember, and to learn—and they describe the characteristics of writing done for these different purposes. They think about their thinking, reflect, reformulate, and reconsider. They look for connections between what they are discovering about themselves as writers and what they think they know about their students as writers, about their own composing processes and the way they teach.

This approach allows teachers to try various research methods, from observing to conducting retrospective interviews: anything that *works* for them as they investigate and reflect upon their own practices. They experience first-hand the inherent *messiness* of writing research, as well as the strengths and limitations of various procedures. They learn rather quickly that five taped, half-hour interviews translate into a hundred pages of typed transcript. In the process, teachers begin to define their own special skills as researchers: some are excellent observers; others enjoy and are good at analysis; others are experienced interviewers, adept at asking questions and listening to answers. Perhaps the most helpful outcome of this part of the exercise is that teachers learn that there is no established methodology for learning research, no pre-determined questions. The knowledge that they gain about themselves as writers is, of course, of considerable importance to teachers of writing—and much of it comes as a surprise, a new finding.

To conclude this demanding exercise, teachers write up their case studies, describing their methods, reporting results, and drawing out implications. A few excerpts from 1981 case studies give little of the substance but do convey the flavor of these reports:

1. Mrs. O. was on the right track with me, I think. She came closer to giving me what I needed than any of my other high school teachers did: encouragement and an opportunity to be published. I needed more, though. Rather than just a few minutes at the end of class, I needed fifteen minutes now and then of thoughtful adult response to my writing. I was trying just a few kinds of writing then, and I think that with a bit more direction I would have experimented with many more. I might have extended my views and perspectives beyond what I was achieving alone.

2. Before turning to my second conference with Professor K. and describing the resulting changes in my final paper, I'd like to take a closer look at the first draft itself as an example of purely expressive writing. Written for me and my use only, its appearance is dreadful—inky and messy, with about every fifth word scratched out and whole clauses deleted here and there, beginnings of sentences scratched through and others, written above them, starry asterisks in the body to be used for incorporating phrases that are scrawled at the top or bottom of the page. My draft seems to indicate that much of my composing occurs after the thought has been sketched roughly on paper, that the concepts that emerge are very partially and imperfectly formulated at the moment I write them.

3. I recognize my almost obsessive concern with form, with the desire to fit ideas into tidy patterns, to craft, in Moffett's terms, "forming the language only, without nearly sufficient concern for developing the thoughts." Certainly, too, the items in my third group of transactional pieces, the graded and commented-upon student papers, show an overriding concern with form in the work of the young writers I teach. The comment on Susan Gramble's composition, for instance, suggests not that the topic sentence is weak or thoughtless but that it does not follow the very detailed format I gave for the assignment, asking students to place themselves and the person being described in a particular setting. I wrote: "Your topic sentence, however, does not place you and him in a setting from which you would then make these observations." In making comments like this—and I make many of them—I may be imposing upon my students the same priority given to form and structure that I perceive to be a problem in my own writing.

4. My findings from my analysis of myself as a writer past and writer present are fundamentally these three: 1) encouragement in, approval of, and interest in my writing are extremely important in motivating both writing and rewriting; criticism of the ideas in my work have been in the past a major factor inhibiting my desire to write or even to engage in an active intellectual life; 2) writing in the poetic mode was important to me when I was an adolescent and a young adult as a kind of therapy to which I still return at difficult moments; 3) my thorough grounding in conventions and formats has restricted my ability to write

honestly about things I care about. I don't believe that my students are entirely different from me, as learners and writers. Form finds form, as Berthoff says, and I mean to allow my students to discover the organic structures of thought for themselves, without having always to fit their ideas into pre-established molds, like Cinderellas's sisters determinedly trying to put their feet into a glass slipper that did not fit.

I am convinced that this kind of systematic study of themselves as writers is useful to all teachers of writing, whether they plan to do classroom research or not. Preparing the case study helps teachers form their own learning theories—the assumptions and beliefs that underlie what they practice as teachers and writers. It's one thing to read from discourse theory about schemata and structures of knowledge and patterns of cohesion. It's another to discover those aspects of one's own writing and thinking. It is obvious that teachers don't need to return to school to do this kind of work. With some guidance from a number of sources, the best of which would be case studies written by other teachers, they can develop their own techniques and take their own directions. Further, most of us who teach writing want very much for our students to be able to reflect upon themselves as writers: our chances of achieving that goal are much enhanced if we have gone through the process ourselves.

Informal proposals for class-based studies. Teachers plan the studies they would like to carry out at their own schools. At this point, experienced teachers are also experienced researchers. Most have considered the problem of achieving a nice consistency among their situations and the constraints they operate under, the questions they want to try to answer, and their own skills as researchers. This part of the course gives teachers a chance to talk about important issues, such as the ethics of research that involves human beings; and potential problems, such as training oneself to be an "objective insider" and gaining the cooperation of colleagues and supervisors. What follows is a brief excerpt from a fairly representative proposal:

I teach English and developmental reading. My students are in the 7th, 8th, and 9th grades in a rural school in New England. I've been strongly influenced by what Janet Emig calls the positivist tradition, a tradition which views learning as atomistic, moving from parts to wholes in linear, sequential patterns. My theory of how children learn to read came from years of using the best materials the reading curriculum industry has to offer. For a long time I've been aware that developmental reading—at least as it's defined by the publishing and testing industries—systematically omits the use of writing in any form except "fill-in-the-blank," single word, or single letter responses. The justification for this seems to be that a) reading and writing are different and separate skills, and b) it is easier and faster to correct multiple choice answers than to read what children write.

Next year, I want to study alternative methods of teaching reading comprehension. I plan to teach children a whole repertoire of writing methods they can use to help them read and understand new or difficult material. The six methods, which I will describe later in some detail, are parallel to Moffett's hierarchy of writing: children will, I hope, do everything from copying to "true authoring." I'll try to document whether it's feasible (time) and reliable (test scores) to use writing in a reading course. I want to closely observe at least four children over the course of the school year, to discover if children, given the option, will use writing to help them read and learn: under what circumstances and with what results.

Even if this teacher does only a part of what she sets out to do in one year, the process has begun: she is determining the line of inquiry; she is aware of a whole range of research methods that are available to her as a classroom researcher. It is worth noting that she does not plan an "experiment," in the sense that she will try a method she thinks will work with some students and withhold it from others in order to assess the relative merit of two approaches.

Teachers who leave Bread Loaf with plans for classroom research have the option of returning to Bread Loaf for successive summers (*all* students have this option), bringing the data they have collected: scripts, records, field journals, tapes. They are able to work with other teachers, Bread Loaf faculty, and consultants on analysis and interpretation.

At least twenty teachers who have completed a summer's work (or more) at Bread Loaf are doing classroom research. One teacher, in South Dakota, with no released time and no financial support, has collected over six hundred scripts written by his students who speak the Lakotah language. He is now interviewing many students and analyzing seventy scripts, trying to determine the extent to which features of the Lakotah language might be related to features of their written English. He is finding out, in the process, much about attitudes about writing in English that should enlighten and inform his teaching. He is also documenting changes in his teaching practices and in the ways he is now using outside professional resources. A teacher in Alabama is studying the writing students do when ninth grade basic writers write letters to twelfth graders, regularly, over the course of a semester: What do they learn from each other? How does their writing change, over time? Another teacher, who teaches writing chiefly by the conference method, is documenting just what happens in her meeting with students. She's not evaluating. She *is* recording, asking students and a colleague to observe, and asking a number of questions that are important to her: What kinds of topics does she initiate? What kinds of responses do students make? Will the talk about writing change over time, and in what ways? I am interested in finding ways to document changes in her practice that may be the result of the research she is doing.

All of these studies are important. The teachers who propose them are asking significant questions and bringing to their investigations knowledge and insights that outsiders simply do not have. A few of these learning researchers will publish their findings, and I hope their audiences will range from students, parents, colleagues locally to readers of *Research in the Teaching of English* and other professional journals. Many of these teachers will present their findings themselves, to parents, teachers, students, and to national audiences. But publication and presentation are secondary goals when it comes to learning research. Let me review what others have observed and what I have observed myself to happen when teachers conduct research as a regular part of their roles as teachers of writing:

1. When teachers of writing begin to study their own writing and the writing of their students, their teaching is transformed in important ways: they become theorists, articulating their intentions, testing their assumptions, and finding connections with practice.
2. When teachers of writing do classroom research, their perceptions of themselves as writers and teachers are transformed. They step up their use of resources; they form networks; and they become more active professionally.
3. Learning researchers are rich resources who can provide the profession with information we simply do not have. They can observe closely, over long periods of time, with special insights and knowledge. Teachers know their classrooms and students in ways that ousiders cannot.
4. Learning researchers become critical, responsive readers and users of current research, less apt to believe the theories of others, less vulnerable to fads, and more authoritative in their assessment of curricula, methods, and materials.
5. Classroom teachers can study writing and learning and report their findings without spending large sums of money (althought they must have support and recognition). Their studies, while probably not definitive, taken together should help us develop and assess writing curricula in ways that are outside the scope of specialists and external evaluators.

In "Class-Based Writing Research: Teachers Learn from Students" (1982), Nancie Atwell, director of the Boothbay Writing Project, Boothbay Harbor, Maine, and a teaching fellow at Bread Loaf (1982), asserts that these outcomes have been realized in the experiences of Boothbay teachers. Atwell analyzes the changes in fourteen classroom teachers who became writing researchers in Boothbay, and she notes that six months into their inquiry, teachers dramatically altered their approach to teaching writing:

> Rather than conforming writing instruction to our timing, we adjust teaching to attend to individual students' needs, progress, and stages in the writing process. We stop focusing on presenting a lesson and evaluating its results and start observing our students in the process of learning, listening to what they can tell us, and responding as they need us. As a result, a different relationship between teacher and student emerges. The teacher-centered classroom becomes a community of writers and learners in which teachers and students are partners in inquiry.[18]

Changes such as these are the real basis for arguing that teachers who want to be researchers need support, information, and recognition. Learning research, whatever shape it may take, fosters the movement from practice to research to theory and back again. Let me emphasize that in spite of some postive responses to teacher-researchers, most English education departments and rhetoric and composition programs that prepare teachers of writing have not changed much over the past few years to accommodate this alternative tradition.

"Graduate Education in Rhetoric" (1980)[19] reports a national survey which gathered information about what constitutes an effective curriculum for producing competent writing teachers. So far as I can tell, learning research by classroom teachers is neither an aim nor a process of those surveyed. At least it is not reflected in course titles, influences on teaching, or any other categories named in the survey. The striking but not unexpected results of the survey are that teachers are affected (in terms of attitude and practice) more by their own composing processes and teaching experiences than by courses they have taken, books they have read, or others' theories. Yet we find no suggestion that these programs are insuring that prospective teachers learn to reconstruct and document their own composing processes and those of their students and to prepare case studies based on close observation of themselves and other teachers of writing. My own experience, working with more than a hundred teachers who prepared case studies of themselves as writers, leads me to speculate that systematic inquiry into and documentation of one's own ways of forming, thinking, and writing, transform teaching practice. We need many case studies of classroom teachers so as to document and characterize such changes.

Let me repeat here the suggestions that Atwell offers in "Class-Based Writing Research" for expanding the field of writing research to include inquiries by classroom teachers:

1. Univerisities and state departments of education can begin to foster teacher-conducted research by including teacher-researcher courses in certification programs.
2. Teachers can request their directors of inservice programs to provide workshops and seminars in theories and procedures of writing research.
3. Teachers can establish—perhaps through Bread Loaf's Program in Writing or NCTE—nationwide networks of teachers and researchers who can exchange information and assistance.
4. Funding sources which support educational research, such as the National Institute of Education, can begin to look to and finance classroom teachers as researchers.
5. NCTE can demonstrate its commitment to teacher-conducted, class-based research by seeking funding sources to support teachers' research and by publishing research findings of regular classroom teachers—those working without institutional connections, using naturalistic inquiry procedures which do not result in statistical data toward which journals of education are so heavily biased.

Obviously, the work of Atwell, Giacobbe, Reed, and many others like them is the most potent argument we have for supporting and engaging in learning research at every level of education.

Notes

[1] Jon Nixon, *A Teachers' Guide to Action Research: Evaluation, Enquiry and Development in the Classroom* (London: Grant McIntyre, 1981).

[2] Mina P. Shaughnessy, *Errors and Expectations: A Guide for the Teacher of Basic Writing* (New York: Oxford University Press, 1977).

[3] _____,"Diving In: A Guide to Basic Research," *College Composition and Communication*, 27 (October 1976), 234-239.

[4] Janet Emig, "Non-Magical Thinking: Presenting Writing Developmentally in Schools," presented at Bread Loaf School of English (Summer 1980). To appear in *The Nature, Development, and Teaching of Written Communication*, Vol. II, edited by C. Frederickson, Marcia Whiteman, and Joe Dominic (Hillsdale, NJ: Lawrence Erlbaum, in press).

[5] _____,"Inquiry Paradigms and Writing," unpublished paper.

[6] Lee Odell, "Classroom Teachers as Researchers," *English Journal,* 65 (January 1976), 106-111.

[7] _____,"Teachers of Composition and Needed Research in Discourse Theory," *College Compoisiton and Communication*, 30 (February 1979), 39-45.

[8] Ann E. Berthoff, *The Making of Meaning* (Montclair, NJ: Boynton/Cook, 1981).

[9] _____, *Forming/Thinking/Writing* (Montclair, NJ: Boynton/Cook, 1979).

[10] Ken Macrorie, *Searching Writing* (Rochelle Park, NJ: Hayden, 1980).

[11] Donald Graves, "A New Look at Writing Research," in *Perspectives on Writing in Grades 1-8*, edited by Shirley M. Haley-James (Urbana, IL: NCTE, 1981), 93-116.

[12] Mary Ellen Giacobbe, "Who Says That Children Can't Write the First Week of School?" *Learning*, 1980.

[13] Jana Staton, "Literacy and an Interactive Process," *Linguisitc Reporter,* 24 (October 1981), 1-5.

[14] Shirley Brice Heath, *Ways with Words: Enthnography of Communication in Communities and Classrooms* (New York: Cambridge University Press, 1983).

[15] Marie Clay, "Looking and Seeing in the Classroom," *English Journal*, 71 (February 1982), 90-92.

[16] Marian Mohr, "The Teacher as Researcher," *Virginia English Bulletin*, 30 (1980), 61-64.

[17] Anne Legge and Marian Mohr, "The Writing Research Center Bibliography of Resources for Teacher-Researchers," available from the Writing Research Center, George Mason University, Fairfax, Virginia 22030.

[18] Nancie Atwell, "Class Based Writing Research: Teachers Learn from Students," *English Journal*, 70 (January 1982), 84-87.

[19] William Covino, Nan Johnson, and Michael Feehan, "Graduate Education in Rhetoric: Attitudes and Implications," *College English*, 42 (December 1980), 390-398.

Hand, Eye, Brain:
Some "Basics" in the Writing Process

JANET EMIG

Much of the current talk about the basics of writing is not only confused but, even more ironic, frivolous. Capitalization, spelling, punctuation—these are touted as the basics in writing when they represent, of course, merely conventions, the amenities for recording the outcome of the process. The *process* is what is basic in writing, the process and the organic structures that interact to produce it. What are these structures? And what are their contributions? Although we don't yet know, the hand, the eye, and the brain itself surely seem logical candidates as requisite structures (Emig, 1975, pp. 11-13). The purpose [here] is to speculate about the role or roles each may play in the writing process and to suggest hypotheses, with appropriate methodologies, to assess their contributions, as well as to determine the likely forms orchestration and interplay may take.

Appropriately for early inquiries, experimental research into the writing process has thus far consisted of quite simple and direct modes of data collecting involving the observation—naturalistic and contrived—of usually immature but normally functioning writers. Continuing this line of inquiry will probably prove fruitful if the range of the sample is enlarged to include younger and older subjects and, more importantly, if researchers attempt to conceptualize their findings in original ways. As I have noted elsewhere (1975), what seems called for now are not duplications of such studies as *The Composing Processes of Twelfth Graders* (Emig, 1971), but replications which by definition require establishing fresh category-systems. In their dissertations, Frances Weaver (1973) and Donald Graves (1973) have enlarged our understanding with such characterizations of the process and of writers.

At the same time, new vantages are needed, especially if our ambition is to attempt sketching and then constructing a model or models of the writing process. Establishing the essential components and structures of the process is, of course, requisite to such an effort.

How to ascertain what these essentials might be represents a fascinating and intricate problem in research. The major recommendation here is that we study, through the available literature and through direct observation, persons with specific and generalized disabilities, such as the blind, the deaf, and the brain-damaged. Although there have been many criticisms of the legitimacy of tapping these sources of data (as one instance, see Donald Murray's ["Internal Revision: A Process of Discovery"]) attempting to infer the whole from the fragmented, the normal from the aberrant, the functional from the dysfunctional, is a classic research approach. Witness the research into that other intricate languaging process, reading, particularly during the first third of this century (see Robinson, 1946). Some may immediately protest that such an approach is too clinical or antihumanistic. But these studies can and should be informed with the same humanism that has already distinguished the best inquiries in our field, such as those by Graves (1973) and Louise Rosenblatt (1968).

For clarity of presentation, I will focus in turn upon the hand, the eye, and the brain. Treating each of these discretely may be rhetorically satisfactory, but it is, of course, literally misleading. Research into perception has made it quite clear that, in part, we see and hear, as we move our hands, with our brain. To refer to the hand alone as moving, or the eye alone as seeing, then, has only metaphorical or organizational usefulness.

The Hand

In his introduction to *Writers at Work,* Malcolm Cowley recounts a statement Hemingway made after an automobile accident when he feared he had lost the use of his right arm: Hemingway commented simply that he thought he would probably have to give up writing. For how many others of us is the action of the hand, the literal act of writing, the motoric component, equally crucial? If we check sources of data from introspection to interviews with professional writers, we find there are many among us who, like Hemingway, must write at least first drafts by hand. I am one of this group, as are the two editors of this book. (Others like Henry James, Paul Gallico, and Donald Murray can dictate even novels, that mode of perhaps greatest intricacy, to a secretary). We cannot compose initially with any ease or skill at a typewriter or into a tape recorder. Why? The speculations that follow come from introspection and from conversations with "like-handed" friends.

There seem to be at least four possible reasons for the cruciality of literal writing in the composing process. First, the literal act of writing is activating, mobilizing. It physically thrusts the writer from a state of inaction into engagement with the process and with the task. We have actually, physically begun to do something. In a very interesting paper, Linda Bannister of the University of Southern California suggests that the state of inaction is more properly thought of as resistance—"anti-writing" she calls it.[1]

Second, the literal act of writing may be for some of us an aesthetically necessary part of the process. We may be able to make personal statements initially or steadily only in our own personalized script, with all of its individualities, even idiosyncrasies. To employ the impersonal and uniform font of the typewriter may for some of us belie the personal nature of our formulations. Our own language must first appear in our own script. In any case, the aesthetic pleasure of their own script has been important to well known writers. Arnold Bennett, for example, taught himself a special script of great beauty in which to write his works of fiction (Drabble, 1974). And to examine authors' manuscripts is to be struck by the lucidity of many scripts, from Gerard Manley Hopkins's and Thomas Hardy's to John Berryman's and May Swenson's. In writing, our sense of physically creating an artifact is less than in any other mode except perhaps composing music; thus, the literal act of writing may provide some sense of carving or sculpting our statements, as in wood or stone.

Third, and correlated with the first, the literal act of writing, with its linear organization in most Western systems, may reinforce in some way the work of the left hemisphere of the brain, also linear in nature. The matter could just as well be formulated, however, in an inverse way, since we don't know which is the antecedent and which the consequent variable: because of the innate predisposition of the left hemisphere to proceed linearly, most written language is inevitably linear in form as visible analogue of the brain's workings.

A fourth reason is that writing by hand keeps the process slowed down. In an interview (*Literary Guild News*, 1977), Paul Theroux put one value on this slower pace: it allows for surprise, time for the unexpected to intrude and even take over.

> It's fatal to get ahead of yourself. Typing, you can take a wrong turning. But if you do it slowly, writing a foolscap page or two a day, in a year you are all done. That may sound like a long time but it's not. It's like carving a statue. You can't rush it. (p. ii)

Writing by hand of course has disadvantages as well. Observing a slow pace, one can lose as well as find material since such a pace obviously puts a greater strain on the memory. For the child learning, perhaps at almost the same time, both to handwrite and to compose, the act of literally forming the words may well be, or become, the dominant and absorbing activity (those of us who have observed seven and eight year olds writing can attest to the accuracy of this statement). Such simultaneity of learnings may cause the later (lifelong?) confusion many of us have observed in older writers, the reversal of what Michael Polanyi (1967) calls "from-to attending." The writer attends *from* the message *to* the graphic formulation, rather than the other way around.

In all these speculations there are obviously research questions about the role or roles of the hand in the writing process. Here are a few:

Theoretical

For what kind of writer engaging in what mode or modes of writing is writing initially or steadily by hand a crucial component in the writing process? For what kind of writer does initial or later dictation or use of the typewriter serve?

Applied

Should children be presented with composing and handwriting at the same time, age, or grade level?

How can teachers and administrators be made sophisticated enough not to use writing as a term that can mean equally penmanship and composing?

The Eye

Undoubtedly one of the most dramatic statements about the centrality of the eye to the act of writing comes from Jean-Paul Sartre. In an interview reported in the *New York Review of Books* (Contat, 1975), Sartre announced he was giving up writing due to loss of vision in his left eye through hemorrhages, because this, coupled with almost total vision loss in his right eye dating from childhood, amounted to functional blindness:

> I can still see forms vaguely, I can see lights, colors, but I do not see objects or faces distinctly, and, as a consequence, I can neither read nor write. More exactly, I can write, that is to say, form the words with my hand, and I can do this more or less comfortably now, but I cannot see what I write. And reading is absolutely out of the question. I can see the lines, the spaces between the words, but I can no longer distinguish the words themselves. Without the ability to read or write, I no longer have even the slightest possibility of being actively engaged as a writer: my occupation as a writer is completely destroyed. (p. 10)

How does the eye participate in the process of written composing? If the process can be characterized roughly as having three stages—prewriting, writing, and revising—the eye seems to make at least one major contribution during each stage:

1. Prewriting: the eye is probably the major sense modality for presenting experience to the brain.
2. Writing: the eye coordinates with hand and brain for most of us, as Sartre notes, during the literal, physical act of writing.
3. Revision: the eye is the major instrument by which we rescan and review what we have written.

Prewriting. In a fascinating and unique study, Géza Révész (1950) examined four well-known cases of sculptors who, tradition claimed, achieved great success in their art although they were all purportedly born blind. Through studying accounts of their lives, however, Révész became convinced that none of the four was congenitally blind. Speaking of the sculptor Kleinhans, for example, Révész demonstrates, persuasively to me, that "the really remarkable works attributed to him cannot be the creations of one who has been blind from his early youth" (p. 150). The experiment Révész conducted was to juxtapose Kleinhan's works against the sculpting efforts of blindfolded contemporary sculptors and congenitally blind subjects. Congenitally blind subjects never make, it seems, symbolic transformations of the clay into personally or universally meaningful symbols: the clay stays a description—more accurately, a transcription—only. One thinks here of one of Susanne Langer's (1967) comments on symbolic transformation:

A living process . . . entails the projection of "living form" in a symbolic transformation. The basic transformation in art is from felt activity to perceptible quality. . . . (p. 89)

Révész (1950) himself makes the following comment:

From what sources could a blind person, who has never seen the world with all its wealth of forms and colour, derive those manifold experiences? He can never create new forms of expression, for that presupposes a rich and variable phenomenal world, *free fantasy arising from symbolic comprehension of nature. . . .* [Italics mine] It is only the symbolic and creative conception of given reality—in our case, the visual world—which enables the artist to translate the spiritual content into the supra-natural, nonmaterial sphere of art. (The man born blind apprehends nature in only one manifestation: the strongest ties bind him to the material sphere; no one born blind is able to become aware of the diversity of nature and to apprehend all the rich and various appearances of objects.) (p. 150)

Révész makes the compelling point that without sight we do not possess the modality that permits most of us to become, in Ernst Cassirer's telling phrase, *animal symbolicum*, the animal who comprehends and makes *symbolic* representations of the universe. The symbol-making propensity humans possess may have to be visually activated. Only if we can make such representations of our experiences do we possess what is probably the single most basic resource for engaging in writing or, indeed, in any form of composing: combining and transforming *perceived* elements into coherent and sometimes fresh wholes, aesthetically pleasing to ourselves and to others. Certain questions, of course, immediately arise. Can't other sense modalities provide comparable data that will permit symbolic dealings with actuality? Don't the blind have language? Doesn't the possession of language itself make all of us, blind or sighted, *animal symbolicum*?

What kind of evidence based upon what kind of research would help us answer these questions? Before beginning some speculation, a note: I have just begun looking into the matter, but thus far I have not found a single case of a noted writer in any genre who was, or is, congenitally blind. Neither lyricist-composer Stevie Wonder nor dramatist Harold Krementz, for example, was born blind. And we all know that James Thurber and John Milton did not become blind until mid-life. Helen Keller, perhaps the best-known case of all, did not become blind until eighteen months of age. In a recent international writing contest for the blind, sponsored by the Jewish Braille Institute, not one writer adjudged a winner was born blind. Commenting on this fact, the Indian novelist Santha Rama Rau, one of the judges, said in a television interview that seeing for at least a very short period of time seemed requisite to writing successfully. The writing of the congenitally blind had a perceptually barren quality that was very striking, which tends to confirm the observations of Révész about nonsighted sculptors (see also Fraiberg, 1977).

Interesting questions, then, about prewriting and the blind would seem to include the following: Is seeing the sensory mode in which most prewriting is conducted? Do we literally examine a subject or experience visually? If so, what constitutes prewriting for the blind or partially sighted? What obviously is needed is direct observation of such subjects engaged in the writing process, from perception of stimulus through "contemplation" of product, as well as detailed interviews with skilled and unskilled writers, both those congenitally blind and those who became blind in later life. Interviews with writers already cited, such as Wonder and Krementz, would be of great interest.

Writing. During the actual writing process, the eye coordinates with hand and brain to produce the evolving piece of writing. It is through the eye that most of us gain the sense of producing an icon, the product of writing. Bruner (1969), like Piaget, points out that we learn through three basic modes: (1) the motoric or enactive—"on the muscle"; (2) the iconic—"by the image"; and (3) the representational or symbolic—specifically, "restatement in words." If we are sighted, we make use of all three modes at once since the writing hand (motoric) produces the piece (iconic) that is a verbal symbolization (representational).

Research involving blind writers might help provide insight into the eye's role in the writing stage:

Theoretical

Can an icon like a piece of writing be perceived only visually, or can another sense provide the iconic dimension? Does the physical effort of pressing a metal stylus through paper to produce Braille provide a *greater* sense of making an icon? By one interpretation, the page of Braille, with its configuration of raised dots, quaifies as a more obvious and more sensual artifact than a smooth page with its unraised, and consequently more abstract, product. To the blind, does Braille qualify as a graphic manifestation of verbal symbolization?

Applied

In the initial teaching of writing, should there be greater stress upon writing as the making of an icon with far more sensual manifestations (e.g., collage or self-made book)? M. C. Richards, the author of *Centering*, stresses the centrality of the making of an artifact.

Revision. As noted above, the eye is the major instrument by which we rescan and review what we have written. For Sartre (Contat, (1975), the most crucial need for the eye comes here in the process of revision:

I can no longer correct my work even once, because I cannot read what I have written. Thus, what I write or what I say necessarily remains in the first version. Someone can read back to me what I have written or said, and if worst comes to worst, I can change a few details, but that would have nothing to do with the work of rewriting which I would do myself. (p. 10)

When the interviewer asked Sartre the obvious question about using a tape recorder, Sartre made an important distinction between visual and aural rescanning:

> I think there is an enormous difference between speaking and writing. One rereads what one rewrites. But one can read slowly or quickly: in other words, you do not know how long you will have to take deliberating over a sentence. It's possible that what is not right in the sentence will not be clear to you at the first reading: perhaps there is something inherently wrong with it, perhaps there is a poor connection between it and the preceding sentence or the following sentence or the paragraph as a whole or the chapter, etc.
>
> All this assures that you approach your text somewhat as if it were a magical puzzle, that you change words here and there one by one, and go back over these changes and then modify something farther along. . . . If I listen to a tape recorder, the listening speed is determined by the speed at which the tape turns and not by own needs. Therefore I will always be either lagging behind or running ahead of the machine. (p. 10)

The eye, in other words, permits individual rhythms of review to be established and followed. Such individualism in pace, in contrast to the inexorable speed of the recorder, may be an essential feature for the making of substantive revisions and recastings (a distinction I have made among three levels of reformulating seems important in this context).

To determine the role of sight in the composing process, researchers may need to examine the work of the partially sighted or the medically blind writer. Perhaps such a person or group of persons can help us sort out the roles the eye truly plays in writing. To illustrate this point, I will continue to speculate a moment about how we revise. By the time most of us are adults, we have internalized the process of revision, which can be described as the outcome of a dialogue between ourselves as writers and ourselves as audience, an exchange in which our needs as readers become paramount. The blind, on the other hand, often must keep the process of revising externalized; they must, unless they are exceptionally skilled users of tape recorders, continue an outer dialogue with an actual other as audience. This externalized dialogue may be a rich source of information about the commerce in the rest of us between ourselves as writers and as initial audiences. (This is not to suggest there aren't other avenues to comparable information, such as observing and taping the work of sighted writers of all ages as they work in peer groups when the peers serve as immediate, actual audiences; both James Moffett [1968] and Peter Elbow [1973] recommend this approach. And many classrooms employ it—the entire Cooperative Writing Program at Middlesex Community College in Edison, New Jersey, for example, proceeds from this premise.)

The Brain

In dealing with the brain, the questions for research, like the organ itself, are more complex. The current hypothesis about the brain that seems most generative for studies about the writing process is that the two hemispheres, the left and the right, have specialized, though not wholly unique functions. A useful, if rough, delineation of these functions appears in Robert Ornstein's *The Psychology of Consciousness:*

> The cerebral cortex of the brain is divided into two hemispheres, joined by a large bundle of interconnecting fibers called the "corpus callosum." The left side of the body is mainly controlled by the right side of the cortex, and the right side of the body by the left side of the cortex. When we speak of *left* in ordinary speech, we are referring to that side of the body, and to the *right* hemisphere of the brain. Both the structure and the function of these two "half-brains" in some part underlie the two modes of consciousness which simultaneously coexist within each one of us. Although each hemisphere shares the potential for many functions, and both sides participate in most activities, in the normal person the two hemispheres tend to specialize. The left hemisphere (connected to the right side of the body) is predominantly involved with analytic, logical thinking, especially in verbal and mathematical functions. Its mode of operation is primarily linear. This hemisphere seems to process information sequentially. This mode of operation of necessity must underlie logical thought, since logic depends on sequence and order. Language and mathematics, both left-hemisphere activities, also depend predominantly on linear time.
>
> If the left hemisphere is specialized for analysis, the right hemisphere . . . seems specialized for holistic mentation. Its language ability is quite limited. . . . This hemisphere is primarily responsible for our orientation in space, artistic endeavor, crafts, body image, recognition of faces. It processes information more diffusely than does the left hemisphere, and its responsibilities demand a ready integration of many inputs at once. If the left hemisphere can be termed predominantly analytic and sequential in its operation, then the right hemisphere is more holistic and relational, and more simultaneous in its mode of operation. (p. 294)

Ornstein's description needs to be refined and modified in light of very recent research, particularly studies by Roger Sperry and his colleagues at the California Institute of Technology on split-brained subjects. These are people in whom the *corpus callosum* has been surgically severed to prevent epileptic attacks, for example, from spreading in both hemispheres. Some curious, yet logical, findings emerge in these studies. Two examples: if a split-brained patient picks up an unseen object in his or her left hand, the right hemisphere can recognize its shape, although the patient cannot speak the object's name. If the patient is asked to write the object's name, he or she can write it only with the hand controlled by the hemisphere that has perceived the object. These findings suggest at once the specialization and interdependence of the two hemispheres.

In a study of two split-brained patients, Dr. Eran Zaidel, a research fellow working with Sperry, found that the language ability of the right hemisphere, described by Ornstein and others as quite limited, may be less limited than once thought (Rensberger, 1975). Indeed, using an optical device he invented, Zaidel found through a series of language tests that the two subjects' right hemispheres had the vocabulary development of a fourteen year old and the syntactic ability of a five year old. And we know from the work of Brown, McNeill, and Slobin, for example, that the five year old's syntactic ability is considerable.

In addition, the brain-damaged and, as it were, the brain aberrant are a fascinating and important source of information about the roles of the two hemispheres in intra- and intercommunication. In *The Shattered Mind*, his review of the literature on the aphasic, Howard Gardner points out that all aphasics, "irrespective of the site of the injury,"suffer impairment of their ability to write. Gardner ascribes this impairment to the number of competencies—he names "perceptual, motor, linguistic, cognitive"—that the process of writing entails (p. 294). It is with the aphasic, then, than an organic map of the writing process can begin to be sketched very lightly and very tentatively. For example, there are aphasics who can write but not read what they have written. With a condition even more dramatic and traumatic than Sartre's, can they continue in the act of writing without the ability to rescan and review? There are other aphasics who have only long-term or short-term memory. Does writing require the activation of both? Can an amnesiac write? As part of such an inquiry, Dixie Goswami of Middlesex Community College, a doctoral candidate at Rutgers, is currently collecting data for a dissertation concerning the composing behaviors of a small sample of aphasics with lesions in the same hemisphere.

Writing seems to require the establishment of firm figure-ground relations—of what shall be stressed, perhaps through the deployment of superordinates, and what shall be subordinated, through the literal deployment of subordinate phrases and clauses. Persons with organic, chemical, or psychological impairments (I do not want to commit myself to a single hypothesis) often cannot distinguish between elements that are incorporating and those that are illustrative. By one hypothesis (Arieti, 1974), the schizophrenic, for example, consistently treats genus as species. What kind of psychic wholeness is demanded for writing successfully?

The possible implications for research into the writing process of this and comparable work with the brain are immense. One is the logical assumption that there may be biological bases for composing behaviors. Before speculating about what these might be and how we can learn about them, it is important to cite a caution, well formulated recently by George Steiner (1975):

Over the next years there *may* be a spectacular progress of insight into the biochemistry of the central nervous system. Though it is conceptually and practically extremely difficult to isolate a single type of stimulus from the fact of stimulation as such (environment connects at every point), refinements in microbiology may lead to correlations between specific classes of information and specific changes in protein synthesis and neuronal assembly. At the biochemical level, the idea that we are "shaped" by what we learn could take on a material corollary. On present evidence, however, it is impossible to go beyond rudimentary idealizations. (p. 288)

Let me here suggest one hypothesis logically emanating from current work on the brain and share one method for ascertaining its possible validity. Ever since the beginnings of rhetoric study, as early as the fifth century B. C. in Sicily and Greece, there have been attempts to categorize the different modes of discourse in which we speak and write. Aristotle, of course, supplied the definitive early category system which rhetoricians through the centuries have adapted and transformed. In recent rhetorical study and writing research, Jakobson, Kinneavy, and Britton have attempted relatively fresh category systems. Their categories, like Aristotle's, share loose and almost metaphysical understandings about the differences between such seemingly distinct modes as argument and poetry. Even with the most recent work, one has the impression of being in the presence of an inquiry that Thomas Kuhn (1970) would characterize as being in the preparadigmatic stage.

What if it is the case that classical and contemporary rhetorical terms, such as *argument* and *poetry* or *extensive* and *reflexive*, may represent centuries-old intuitive understandings that the mind deals differentially with different speaking and writing tasks? To put the matter declaratively, if hypothetically: modes of discourse may represent measurably different profiles of brain activity.

The elctroencephalogram measures brain activity through electrodes attached to relevant portions of the skull. In fact, there is now a computer program whereby a given encephalograph can be broken into a profile which differentiates left-hemisphere from right-hemisphere activity. Two of us at Rutgers have begun to ask a small sample of normal adult subjects to compose aloud in two seemingly distinct modes while undergoing an EEG and note whether or not composing behaviors yield differentiated profiles of brain activity. (First thoughts suggest that argument would be predominantly left-hemisphere, poetry or narrative, right.)

Implications for Research Training and Teaching

Changes in the directions of English education research obviously require concomitant changes in the training of the researcher in the doctoral curriculum. All of us, including senior faculty and advisers, must learn far more about biology and physiology than we have previously been asked to learn. Closer ties with departments of biological sciences and with the medical schools affiliated with our universities also seem to be suggested.

At Rutgers we have established two connections with our medical school that will undoubtedly grow firmer and more formal as more of our students elect clinical problems to investigate. One is attendance at open lectures on psychophysiology sponsored by the faculty of the medical school; the other is actual participation in the medical school sequence, such as seminars on anatomy and the brain. A third link currently being contemplated is participation of our students in the teaching rounds involving third- and fourth-year medical students and the medical school faculty.

Possible implications for the learning and teaching of writing are even more formidable and far-reaching. Nelson Goodman once commented that the American educational system is half-brained. The situation may be even more serious: What if the schools require students to be split-brained where the learning of writing and complex arts and sciences are concerned? Perhaps the only base for the curriculum should be what research suggests is literally organic. And for the process of writing, what is truly organic? Let us begin to find out.

Notes

[1] Bannister, L. *Anti-writing: A stage in the composing process.* Unpublished manuscript, University of Southern California, 1975.

References

Arieti, S. *Interpretation of Schizophrenia* (2nd ed.). New York: Basic Books, 1974.

Bruner, J. S. *On Knowing: Essays for the Left Hand.* Cambridge: Harvard University Press, 1969.

Contat, M. "Sartre at Seventy: An Interview." *New York Review of Books,* August 7, 1975, pp. 10-17.

Cowley, M. (Ed.). *Writers at Work: The "Paris Review" Interviews* (1st series). New York: Viking Press, 1958.

Drabble, M. *Arnold Bennett.* New York: Alfred A. Knopf, 1974.

Elbow, P. *Writing Without Teachers.* New York: Oxford University Press, 1973.

Emig, J. "The Biology of Writing: Another View of the Process." In W. T. Petty & P.J. J. Finn (Eds.), *The Writing Processes of Students.* Buffalo: State University of New York, Department of Elementary and Remedial Education, 1975.

Emig, J. *The Composing Processes of Twelfth Graders* (NCTE Research Report No. 13). Urbana IL: National Council of Teachers of English, 1971.

Fraiberg, S. *Insights from the Blind.* New York, Basic Books, 1977.

Gardner, H. *The Shattered Mind: The Person after Brain Damage.* New York: Alfred A. Knopf, 1975.

Graves, D. H. *Children's Writing: Research Directions and Hypotheses Based upon an Examination of the Writing Processes of Seven Year Old Children.* Unpublished doctoral dissertation, State University of New York at Buffalo, 1973.

Kuhn, T. S. *Structure of Scientific Revolutions* (2nd ed.; Foundations of the Unity of Science Series, Vol. 2). Chicago: University of Chicago Press, 1970.

Langer, S. K. *Mind: An Essay on Human Feeling* (Vol. 1). Baltimore: Johns Hopkins University Press, 1967.

Literary Guild News, October 1977, p. ii.

Moffett, J. *Teaching the Universe of Discourse.* Boston: Houghton Mifflin, 1968.

Ornstein, R. *The Psychology of Consciousness.* San Francsico: W. H. Freeman, 1972.

Polanyi, M. *The Tacit Dimension.* Garden City, NY: Anchor Books, Doubleday & Co., 1967.

Rensberger, B. "Language Ability Found in Right Side of Brain." *New York Times,* August 1, 1975, p. 14.

Révész, G. *Phsychology and Art of the Blind.* H. A. Wolff, Trans. London: Longmans-Green, 1950.

Richards, M. C. *Centering: In Pottery, Poetry, and the Person.* Middletown, CT: Wesleyan University Press, 1964.

Robinson, H. M. *Why Pupils Fail in Reading: A Study of Courses and Remedial Treatment.* Chicago: University of Chicago Press, 1946.

Rosenblatt, L. M. *Literature as Exploration.* New York: Noble and Noble, 1968.

Steiner, G. *After Babel: Aspects of Language and Translation.* New York: Oxford University Press, 1975.

Weaver, F. *The Composing Processes of English Teacher Candidates: Responding to Freedom and Constraint.* Unpublished doctoral dissertation, University of Illinois, 1973.

from *Thought and Language*

L. S. VYGOTSKY

On Writing and Learning

In formulating our own tentative theory of the relationship between instruction and development, we take our departure from four series of investigations. Their common purpose was to uncover these complex interrelations in certain definite areas of school instruction: reading and writing, grammar, arithmetic, natural science, and social science. The specific inquiries concerned such topics as the mastering of the decimal system in relation to the development of the concept of number; the child's awareness of his operations in solving mathematical problems; the processes of constructing and solving problems by first-graders. Much interesting material came to light on the development of oral and written language during school age, the consecutive levels of understanding of figurative meaning, the influence of mastering grammatical structures on the course of mental development, the understanding of relationships in the study of social science and natural science. The investigations focused on the level of maturity of psychic functions at the beginning of schooling, and the influence of schooling on their development; on the temporal sequence of instruction and development; on the "formal discipline" function of the various subjects of instruction. We shall discuss these issues in succession.

1. In our first series of studies, we examined the level of development of the psychic functions requisite for learning the basic school subjects—reading and writing, arithmetic, natural science. We found that at the beginning of instruction these functions could not be considered mature, even in the children who proved able to master the curriculum very successfully. Written language is a good illustration. Why does writing come so hard to the schoolchild that at certain periods there is a lag of as much as six or eight years between his "linguistic age" in speaking and in writing? This used to be explained by the novelty of writing: As a new function, it must repeat the developmental stages of speech; therefore the writing of an eight-year-old

Reprinted from *Thought and Language* (pp. 97-105.) by L. S. Vygotsky, edited and translated by Eugenia Hanfmann and Gertrude Vakar, by permission of The MIT Press, Cambridge, MA. Copyright © 1962 by the Massachusetts Institute of Technology.

must resemble the speech of a two-year-old. This explanation is patently insufficient. A two-year-old uses few words and a simple syntax because his vocabulary is small and his knowledge of more complex sentence structures nonexistent; but the schoolchild possesses the vocabulary and grammatical forms for writing, since they are the same as for oral speech. Nor can the difficulties of mastering the mechanics of writing account for the tremendous lag between the schoolchild's oral and written language.

Our investigation has shown that the development of writing does not repeat the developmental history of speaking. Written speech is a separate linguistic function, differing from oral speech in both structure and mode of functioning. Even its minimal development requires a high level of abstraction. It is speech in thought and image only, lacking the musical, expressive, intonational qualities of oral speech. In learning to write, the child must disengage himself from the sensory aspect of speech and replace words by images of words. Speech that is merely imagined and that requires symbolization of the sound image in written signs (i.e., a second degree of symbolization) naturally must be as much harder than oral speech for the child as algebra is harder than arithmetic. Our studies show that it is the abstract quality of written language that is the main stumbling block, not the underdevelopment of small muscles or any other mechanical obstacles.

Writing is also speech without an interlocutor, addressed to an absent or an imaginary person or to no one in particular—a situation new and strange to the child. Our studies show that he has little motivation to learn writing when we begin to teach it. He feels no need for it and has only a vague idea of its usefulness. In conversation, every sentence is prompted by a motive. Desire or need leads to request, question to answer, bewilderment to explanation. The changing motives of the interlocutors determine at every moment the turn oral speech will take. It does not have to be consciously directed— the dynamic situation takes care of that. The motives for writing are more abstract, more intellectualized, further removed from immediate needs. In written speech, we are obliged to create the situation, to represent it to ourselves. This demands detachment from the actual situation.

Writing also requires deliberate analytical action on the part of the child. In speaking, he is hardly conscious of the sounds he pronounces and quite unconscious of the mental operations he performs. In writing, he must take cognizance of the sound structure of each word, dissect it, and reproduce it in alphabetical symbols, which he must have studied and memorized before. In the same deliberate way, he must put words in a certain sequence to form a sentence. Written language demands conscious work because its relationship to inner speech is different from that of oral speech: The latter precedes inner speech in the course of development, while written speech follows inner speech and presupposes its existence (the act of writing implying a translation from inner speech). But the grammar of thought is not the same in the two cases. One might even say that the syntax of inner speech is the exact opposite of the syntax of written speech, with oral speech standing in the middle.

Inner speech is condensed, abbreviated speech. Written speech is deployed to its fullest extent, more complete than oral speech. Inner speech is almost entirely predicative because the situation, the subject of thought, is always known to the thinker. Written speech, on the contrary, must explain the situation fully in order to be intelligible. The change from maximally compact inner speech to maximally detailed written speech requires what might be called deliberate semantics—deliberate structuring of the web of meaning.

All these traits of written speech explain why its development in the schoolchild falls far behind that of oral speech. The discrepancy is caused by the child's proficiency in spontaneous, unconscious activity and his lack of skill in abstract, deliberate activity. As our studies showed, the psychological functions on which written speech is based have not even begun to develop in the proper sense when instruction in writing starts. It must build on barely emerging, rudimentary processes.

Similar results were obtained in the fields of arithmetic, grammar, and natural science. In every case, the requisite functions are immature when instruction begins. We shall briefly discuss the case of grammar, which presents some special features.

Grammar is a subject which seems to be of little practical use. Unlike other school subjects, it does not give the child new skills. He conjugates and declines before he enters school. The opinion has even been voiced that school instruction in grammar could be dispensed with. We can only reply that our analysis clearly showed the study of grammar to be of paramount importance for the mental development of the child.

The child does have a command of the grammar of his native tongue long before he enters school, but it is unconscious, acquired in a purely structural way, like the phonetic composition of words. If you ask a young child to produce a combination of sounds, for example *sk*, you will find that its deliberate articulation is too hard for him, yet within a structure, as in the word *Moscow*, he pronounces the same sounds with ease. The same is true of grammar. The child will use the correct case or tense within a sentence but cannot decline or conjugate a word on request. He may not acquire new grammatical or syntactic forms in school but, thanks to instruction in grammar and writing, he does become aware of what he is doing and learns to use his skills consciously. Just as the child realizes for the first time in learning to write that the word *Moscow* consists of the sounds *m-o-s-k-ow* and learns how to pronounce each one separately, he also learns to construct sentences, to do consciously what he has been doing unconsciously in speaking. Grammar and writing help the child to rise to a higher level of speech development.

Thus our investigation shows that the development of the psychological foundations for instruction in basic subjects does not precede instruction but unfolds in a continuous interaction with the contributions of instruction.

2. Our second series of investigations centered on the temporal relation between the processes of instruction and the development of the correspond-

ing psychological functions. We found that instruction usually precedes development. The child acquires certain habits and skills in a given area before he learns to apply them consciously and deliberately. There is never complete parallelism between the course of instruction and the development of the corresponding functions.

Instruction has its own sequences and organization, it follows a curriculum and a timetable, and its rules cannot be expected to coincide with the inner laws of the developmental processes it calls to life. On the basis of our studies, we tried to plot curves of the progress of instruction and of the participating psychological functions; far from coinciding, these curves showed an exceedingly complex relationship.

For example, the different steps in learning arithmetic may be of unequal value for mental development. It often happens that three or four steps in instruction add little to the child's understanding or arithmetic, and then, with the fifth step, something clicks; the child has grasped a general principle, and his developmental curve rises markedly. For this particular child, the fifth operation was decisive, but this cannot be a general rule. The turning points at which a general principle becomes clear to the child cannot be set in advance by the curriculum. The child is not taught the decimal system as such; he is taught to write figures, to add and to multiply, to solve problems, and out of all this some general concept of the decimal system eventually emerges.

When the child learns some arithmetical operation or some scientific concept, the development of that operation or concept has only begun. Our study shows that the curve of development does not coincide with the curve of school instruction; by and large, instruction precedes development.

3. Our third series of investigations resembles Thorndike's studies of the transfer of training, except that we experimented with subjects of school instruction and with the higher rather than the elementary functions, i.e., with subjects and functions which would be expected to be meaningfully related.

We found that intellectual development, far from following Thorndike's atomistic model, is not compartmentalized according to topics of instruction. Its course is much more unitary, and the different school subjects interact in contributing to it. While the processes of instruction follow their own logical order, they awaken and direct a system of processes in the child's mind which is hidden from direct observation and subject to its own developmental laws. To uncover these developmental processes stimulated by instruction is one of the basic tasks of the psychological study of learning.

Specifically, our experiments brought out the following interrelated facts: The psychological prerequisites for instruction in different school subjects are to a large extent the same; instruction in a given subject influences the development of the higher functions far beyond the confines of that particular subject; the main psychic functions involved in studying various subjects are interdependent—their common bases are consciousness and deliberate mastery, the principal contributions of the school years. It follows from these findings that all the basic school subjects act as formal discipline, each facilitiating the learning of the others; the psychological functions stimulated by them develop in one complex process.

4. In the fourth series of studies, we attacked a problem which has not received sufficient attention in the past but which we consider of focal importance for the study of learning and development.

Most of the psychological investigations concerned with school learning measured the level of mental development of the child by making him solve certain standardized problems. The problems he was able to solve by himself were supposed to indicate the level of his mental development at the particular time. But in this way only the completed part of the child's development can be measured, which is far from the whole story. We tried a different approach. Having found that the mental age of two children was, let us say, eight, we gave each of them harder problems than he could manage on his own and provided some slight assistance: the first step in a solution, a leading question, or some other form of help. We discovered that one child could, in co-operation, solve problems designed for twelve-year-olds, while the other could not go beyond problems intended for nine-year-olds. The discrepancy between a child's actual mental age and the level he reaches in solving problems with assistance indicates the zone of his proximal development; in our example, this zone is four for the first child and one for the second. Can we truly say that their mental development is the same? Experience has shown that the child with the larger zone of proximal development will do much better in school. This measure gives a more helpful clue than mental age does to the dynamics of intellectual progress.

Psychologists today cannot share the layman's belief that imitation is a mechanical activity and that anyone can imitate almost anything if shown how. To imitate, it is necessary to possess the means of stepping from something one knows to something new. With assistance, every child can do more than he can by himself—though only within the limits set by the state of his development. Koehler found that a chimpanzee can imitate only those intelligent acts of other apes that he could have performed on his own. Persistent training, it is true, can induce him to perform much more complicated actions, but these are carried out mechanically and have all the earmarks of meaningless habits rather than of insightful solutions. The cleverest animal is incapable of intellectual development through imitation. It can be drilled to perform specific acts, but the new habits do not result in new general abilities. In this sense, it can be said that animals are unteachable.

In the child's development, on the contrary, imitation and instruction play a major role. They bring out the specifically human qualities of the mind and lead the child to new developmental levels. In learning to speak, as in learning school subjects, imitation is indispensable. What the child can do in coopertation today he can do alone tomorrow. Therefore the only good kind of instruction is that which marches ahead of development and leads it; it must be aimed not so much at the ripe as at the ripening functions. It remains necessary to determine the lowest threshold at which instruction in, say, arithmetic may begin since a certain minimal ripeness of functions is required. But we must consider the upper threshold as well; instruction must be oriented toward the future, not the past.

For a time, our schools favored the "complex" system of instruction, which was believed to be adapted to the child's ways of thinking. In offering the child problems he was able to handle without help, this method failed to utilize the zone of proximal development and to lead the child to what he could not yet do. Instruction was oriented to the child's weakness rather than his strength, thus encouraging him to remain at the preschool stage of development.

For each subject of instruction there is a period when its influence is most fruitful because the child is most receptive to it. It has been called the *sensitive period* by Montessori and other educators. The term is used also in biology, for the periods in ontogenetic development when the organism is particularly responsive to influences of certain kinds. During that period an influence that has little effect earlier or later may radically affect the course of development. But the existence of an optimum time for instruction in a given subject cannot be explained in purely biological terms, at least not for such complex processes as written speech. Our investigation demonstrated the social and cultural nature of the development of the higher functions during these periods, i.e., its dependence on co-operation with adults and on instruction. Montessori's data, however, retain their significance. She found, for instance, that if a child is taught to write early, at four and a half or five years of age, he responds by "explosive writing," an abundant and imaginative use of written speech that is never duplicated by children a few years older. This is a striking example of the strong influence that instruction can have when the corresponding functions have not yet fully matured. The existence of sensitive periods for all subjects of instruction is fully supported by the data of our studies. The school years as a whole are the optimum period for instruction in operations that require awareness and deliberate control; instruction in these operations maximally furthers the development of the higher psychological functions while they are maturing. This applies also to the development of the scientific concepts to which school instruction introduces the child.